Bounding Power

Bounding Power

REPUBLICAN SECURITY THEORY FROM THE
POLIS TO THE GLOBAL VILLAGE

Daniel H. Deudney

PRINCETON UNIVERSITY PRESS

PRINCETON AND OXFORD

Library of Congress Cataloging-in-Publication Data

Deudney, Daniel.
Bounding power : republican security theory from the polis to the
global village / Daniel H. Deudney.
p. cm.
Includes bibliographical references and index.

Contents: Tradition and theory—From the polis to
federal union—Toward the global village.

ISBN-13: 978-0-691-11901-4 (alk. paper)
ISBN-10: 0-691-11901-5 (alk. paper)

1. Security, International—Philosophy. 2. Conservatism. I. Title.

JZ5588.D48 2006

355'.0330001—dc22   2006049376

British Library Cataloging-in-Publication Data is available

This book has been composed in Sabon

Printed on acid-free paper. ∞

pup.princeton.edu

Printed in the United States of America

1 3 5 7 9 10 8 6 4 2

To my teachers

———————————————

CONTENTS

FIGURES

PREFACE AND ACKNOWLEDGMENTS

THIS IS A WORK of theory and historical theoretical interpretation with a practical aim. It seeks to provide a 'usable past' to better meet the challenges of the next half century. It is animated by the fear that our existing conceptual frameworks are inadequate to cope with the intensifying processes of globalization, particularly concerning security, and the severe governance problems they are generating. This volume aims to offer a new view of our inherited political wisdom consonant with libertarian-liberal political values and applicable to our rapidly globalizing world. It does so by rereading the development of Western political thought about security-from-violence as one of simultaneously avoiding the extremes of hierarchy and anarchy in material contexts changing due to technological developments.

To read and write about old books while humanity tumbles along uncharted paths may seem irrelevant, indulgent, or at best another example of 'navigating through the rear-view mirror.' But, for better or worse, there is a deep-seated human tendency to look at the future as an extension of the past. Much of what we do now and think is possible for the future is molded by what we think happened in the past. As such, it is best to get this mirror wiped as clear as possible and pointed at an appropriate past.

As a reading of texts and reconstruction of arguments, this work is shaped and rendered imperfect in several ways by the commitments and limitations of its author. These should be acknowledged from the outset. In this sort of enterprise, there is no objective reader or objective vantage point, and the concerns of the interpreter indelibly stamp the interpretation. Within the crowded marketplace of contemporary political and international thought, the views and commitments of this author are, in simple terms, liberal-democratic and globalist.

The genesis of this project can be dated with some precision to my later undergraduate years, when I precociously dedicated my energies to the construction of a political theory to address science and technology and the global. My head was filled with political theory from the Western canon, but this all seemed terribly out of date. So I went down to Washington for most of a decade to learn about these emergent topics firsthand, as a junior policy analyst and occasional minor activist (mainly on nuclear, outer space, energy, and environmental issues). Immersed in these topics and problems, and further reading and reflecting on existing politi-

cal and international theory, I came slowly and unexpectedly to the realization that the problem was not that the ideas of the canon were obsolete,
but rather that they had not been properly interpreted. I came to think of
the canon, for all its baroque detail, as a succession of reinterpretations
and reapplications of a very simple set of core ideas. And so I set about
distilling these ideas and interpreting and applying them for the contemporary situation.

Closely observing the last several decades of political debates and conflicts over global issues in general and American policy toward them in
particular, I also unexpectedly came to the view that for most problems
there are fairly obvious solutions and that these solutions have been developed and actively promoted. I came to the view that a major barrier to
problem solving was the fact that a great many well-intentioned and serious people seemed to be walking around experiencing reality through a
thick set of filters. What seemed more or less obvious from a pragmatic
liberal globalist perspective seemed to many people to be unthinkable
and utopian. Conversely, practices that seemed patently absurd or baneful
were widely seen as both sound and inevitable.

One of these distorting filters, which this work hopes to alter, is the odd
amalgam of ideas known as 'Realism' in international relations theory
and practice. Part of Realism's appeal is its claim to embody a long line
of the best Western thinking about political order and security-from-violence. But, as many have pointed out, there are major weaknesses in Realism's construction of itself as a 'tradition.' Many have sought to abandon
or overthrow Realism, but it contains far too many important insights for
this to be either feasible or prudent. It is far harder, but more important,
to fashion an alternative to the hegemony of Realism than to eliminate
hegemony.

The other major distorting filter in contemporary thinking, particularly
about international security and political liberty, that this work also hopes
to ameliorate is a gross underappreciation or misappreciation of the importance of material-contextual factors, of nature, geography, ecology,
and technology. Despite all the talk of geopolitics, the rampant materialism of much theory, and ambient breathless excitement about the marvels
and perils of contemporary technologies, the role of material-contextual
factors and arguments in actual international and international political
theory is remarkably truncated and unsystematic. We think and act as if
technologies are just our handy tools and as if nature has somehow been
left behind.

This work is also shaped and limited by the fact that it is significantly
American-centered. Such a focus, at this writing, requires more defense
and justification than it once did, or should. The vision of America as
the last best hope for humanity's universal aspirations for security from
predatory violence and for political liberty may not be as compelling as

it once was. But it remains a historical fact of the first magnitude that throughout the late modern period, the United States of America has done more to advance the cause of human liberty and security from predatory violence than any other regime in history. And it is also a vital fact that the legacies of American-led twentieth-century international institution building are, for all their weaknesses and imperfections, the main basis for actually existing global governance. On these facts rests the justification for the narrative architecture of this reconstruction of republican security theory, in which there are two phases, the first beginning in antiquity and culminating in the American founding, and the second centered on the trajectory of theorizing about the United States writ large in the global-industrial and nuclear eras.

As an American writing about a significantly American topic, I am animated by American anxieties (shared by many non-Americans) about America. Specifically, I am troubled by the discrepancy between the historical American role in the world and the principles of the American political tradition on the one side and the role of American political thought in American international theory and aspects of contemporary American foreign policy on the other. International thought among Americans has become increasingly Europeanized, not to the security worldview of the contemporary new Europe of the Union but rather to the old Europe, which America was founded to escape and which the United States did so much to end. Many of the friends of freedom in America congratulate themselves on their role as the indispensable nation and as the agent chosen by History and Providence to spread political freedom in the world. But few seem much troubled by the massive globe-spanning American national security state and its implications for limited constitutional government, political liberty, and global security. Part of the Republican Party, posing as the keeper of the founders' flame of freedom, expends its formidable energies in an at-times hysterical (but not very seriously pursued) war against domestic public welfare government, but largely ignores (or even embraces) the far more ominous (at least from the founders' standpoint) national security state that necessity and opportunity led the Americans to construct over the last half century. The few who do warn of American empire offer no remedy beyond the unlikely and probably counterproductive strategy of global retrenchment. Meanwhile, American liberal progressives and globalists, while pushing on many worthy fronts, lack a well-articulated overall vision of the situation and appropriate solutions, are burdened with perpetual social scientific paradigm and category shifts, and need an overall narrative that discursively connects to the animating principles of the American political tradition. I believe the real lesson Americans should be drawing from our founding and its animating political tradition is that larger and more substantial unions are not intrinsic threats to liberty, nor merely beneficial for realizing humane values, but rather are vital at times for the preservation of political liberty.

Despite its American-centric character, the argument advanced here undermines American triumphalism. The survival and success of political freedom has been a close run thing, and blind circumstance as well as vision and sacrifice have been part of the winning formula. The advances of the last two centuries are seriously incomplete, and ominous perils lie ahead. There is no guarantee that the Americans, even after all options have been pursued and exhausted, will get it right. Furthermore, to say that Americans have been at the lead in expanding liberty over recent centuries and that the innovations of the American founding mark a watershed development in republican security theory and practice does not mean that either the principles of the founding or republican security theory are primarily, inevitably, or permanently American. Like other inventions and arrangements (whether writing, the steam engine, or double-entry accounting), the insights of republican security theory are a possession of all humankind.

It should also be acknowledged plainly that the argument presented here, while broad in some ways, is quite narrow in at least six other significant ways. First, what I refer to as 'republican security theory' is narrowly focused on arguments about the interplay of material contexts, patterns of political authority, and security-from-violence. In reality, no complete security theory or even exegesis and reconstruction of all republican security theorizing could be complete without more extensive treatment of ideational factors as well as political economy. This narrow treatment seems justified, however, by the centrality of such variables and arguments in contemporary international theory, particularly concerning security, and the sheer difficulty of looking at everything at once. Second, the argument is very limited in its engagement with many contemporary international theory debates, most notably the one between 'rational-choice' and 'constructivism.' I have largely steered away from these battles because they are ongoing and intricate, and in order to better let the past speak to us more in its terms than ours. Third, the argument, while globalist in animation, does not address a wide range of global issues of major importance. This limited coverage is not intended to imply that these issues do not matter much either in practice or for theory.

Fourth, a great many arguments and claims made by earlier thinkers are here assembled and related to each other, but are not systematically assessed, are not systematically tested, and are not systematically evaluated against competitive ideas. Fifth, the number of texts, theorists, and events relevant to the argument of this book is staggeringly large, and so it has been necessary to be selective. Among the many figures deserving more attention are Locke and Morgenthau. Sixth, this is a very Western story, in a time when scholars have finally been giving the rest of human thought and accomplishment long overdue treatment. But to recognize that the West has been a colossal global predator over much of modern history does not obviate the fact that Western (white male) thinkers have produced a powerful and intricate body of thought about political order, security, and liberty with enduring value for all peoples everywhere. Finally, much of this book is, annoyingly, mired in analysis of terms and labels. I have not attempted to provide new definitions for words already overloaded with meanings. When I have located a key concept that has not been clearly enough delineated, I have suggested a few new words and terms of art, thus aping in a limited way the practices of the easier sciences, such as physics and biology, where it does not seem at all odd to fashion a distinct word or term to stand for a distinct phenomenon.

Finally, this work cuts across the contemporary scholarly enterprises of international relations theory, political theory, and intellectual history. For the political theory reader, there are far too many simplifications of complexities, neglected nuances, and elisions of differences. For the international theory reader there is too much political theory and too little specificity about the actual historical events and contemporary issues. For historians of both ideas and events, there are gross violations of differences across time. It is hoped that seeing a new whole and old parts in a new light will make these deficiencies tolerable.

The exegesis, in chapters 3 through 9, covers several very complex historical periods and large literatures and my simple and quasi-revisionist treatments leave much unsaid and unaddressed. It is hoped that I will be able to revisit several of the episodes and periods, particularly the contemporary nuclear chapter at greater length. Similarly, the main theory reconstruction laid out in the first chapter deserves further exposition as a testable social science model.

This work has taken a long time to produce, perhaps longer than its potential contribution warrants. Over its long gestation I have been assisted by invaluable support from many institutions and individuals, without which this project would never have been undertaken or completed. My parents and teachers nurtured my interests in politics and history from the earliest age. I have also been privileged to have been educated, employed, and supported by a series of extraordinary research and educational institutions. I was especially fortunate to be taught by many outstanding and inspiring teachers in political theory and political science as an undergraduate at Yale College. During the 1980s Lester Brown and the Worldwatch Institute provided a stimulating home for thinking globally and publishing the first versions of parts of this argument. During the middle and late 1980s I also greatly benefited from my teachers and colleagues, first at the program in Science, Technology, and Public Policy at the George Washington University, and then at the Department of Politics and Program in Nuclear Policy Alternatives at the Center for Energy and Environmental Studies at Princeton University. Since the early 1990s I have been further stimulated and supported by students and colleagues while a faculty member of the Political Science Departments at the University of Pennsylvania and Johns Hopkins University. Over these many years the argument has been advanced through conversations, some going on for many years, with Hayward Alker, Michael Barnett, Tom Biersteker, Lester Brown, Thomas Boudreau, Mlada Bukovansky, Barry Buzan, Ken Conca, Bill Connolly, Campbell Craig, Steven David, Ron Deibert, James der Derian, Michael Doyle, Richard Falk, Ben Frankel, Robert Gilpin, David Hendrickson, Thomas Homer-Dixon, John Ikenberry, Fritz Kratochwill, Richard Matthew, Ethan Nadelmann, Henry Nau, Nick Onuf, John Pike, Barry Posen, Hendrick Spruyt, Ole Waever, Steve Walt, Paul Wapner, Wesley Warren, Alex Wendt, and Bill Wohlforth. Chapter 8, a condensed version of my dissertation on global geopolitics, benefited greatly from the comments from the members of my committee, Robert Gilpin, Michael Doyle, and Richard Falk. Earlier versions of parts of this volume were presented at the following institutions and benefited from comments received: American University, Brown University, Columbia University, Cornell University, Dartmouth College, George Washington University, Harvard University, Johns Hopkins University, London School of Economics, Princeton University, Yale University, and the Universities of California (Berkeley, San Diego, and Santa Cruz), Chicago, Delaware, Pennsylvania, South California, Toronto, Washington, and Wisconsin, as well as at many annual conventions of the International Studies Association and the American Political Science Association. Ron Deibert, Ruth Deudney, Benjamin Frankel, David Hendrickson, Nicholas Onuf, David Welch, and Mark Zacker read earlier versions of the manuscript and offered valuable comments. Able research assistance in the final phases of the project has been provided by Joshua Horton, Vijay Phulwani, Jon Bateman, and especially Simon Glezos. Bill Brenner skillfully made the electronic versions of the figures. Ben Frankel made a hopeless stab at improving the prose. Early stages of research were supported by the MacArthur Foundation, the Hewlett Foundation, and the Bers Foundation. Invaluable financial support for the final lengthy stages of the project was provided by the Seth Feinstein Memorial Fund of Princeton, New Jersey. The patience and skills of Princeton Press editors Malcolm DeBevoise, Malcolm Litchfield, Chuck Myers, Jill Harris, and Cindy Crumrine are also much appreciated. This project would never have been completed without the support of my friends, neighbors, and family members, particularly Norman Nielson, Holly Pittman, Nadivah Greenberg, Heidi Pinkston, Holly McGarraugh, Horace Deudney, Ruth Deudney, and John Welch.

Bounding Power

INTRODUCTION

Before Realism and Liberalism

I study power so as to understand the enemy.
—Stanley Hoffmann[1]

THE GLOBAL VILLAGE AND THE LIBERAL ASCENT

Globalization is the first, most important fact about the human condition at the threshold of the second millennium. Globalization, the rising levels of interdependence on progressively larger spatial scales, has been the dominant trend in human history during the last five centuries, and it has operated in military, ecological, economic, and cultural dimensions. Over this period, all human political communities, initially isolated or loosely connected, have become more densely and tightly interconnected and subject to various mutual vulnerabilities in a manner previously experienced only on much smaller spatial scales. The creation of this villagelike proximity and density on a global scale has occurred through every means imaginable, from genocidal invasion and enslavement to cooperative exchange and progressive emulation. It has produced massive epidemics, world wars, ecological devastation, and cultural annihilation, as well as large populations of humans more secure, more free, and more prosperous than ever before in history. Looking ahead into the new century, globalization shows every indication of further intensifying as human population burgeons, weapons of mass destruction proliferate, lethal new plagues emerge, ecological destruction accelerates, economies further integrate, and information capacities advance.

In the face of these developments, theorists of international relations and world politics have a decidedly divided posture. On one side, numerous globalist and interdependence theorists have charted these realities for more than a century, and many have pointedly drawn the conclusion that increasingly substantive world governance and government are needed to satisfy basic human interests. On the other side, the still hegemonic tradition of Realist[2] international theory maintains a skeptical stance toward globalist claims about the world and doubts the need or the possibility of establishing robust world governance. Labeling these ambitions utopian or idealistic, Realists emphasize the long historical persistence of the fundamentally anarchic sovereign state system and expect the future to look much like the past. The Realist view also seems to gain authority from a conceptually rich tradition of theorizing supposedly stretching back to the ancient Greeks and seemingly vindicated repeatedly by the historical record.

The second most important fact about the contemporary human situation is the liberal-democratic ascent, the rise to an historically unprecedented preeminence of the 'free world' composed of the United States of America and its democratic allies. Republics (polities based on political liberty, popular sovereignty, and limited government) have been historically precarious and rare, generally poor, and massively compromised. They now constitute a zone of peace, freedom, and prosperity far greater than any other in history. For most of history republics were confined to small city-states where they were insecure and vulnerable to conquest or internal usurpation, but over the last two centuries they have expanded to continental size through federal union and emerged victorious from the violent total world conflicts of the twentieth century. In contrast, their major despotic and imperial adversaries have failed spectacularly. The American-led 'free world' overcame the reversals of the 1930s and early 1940s, expanded with the reconstruction of Western Europe and parts of East Asia as capitalist, liberal, constitutional, and federal democracies, and has built a dense network of international institutions.[3] This "compound of federations, confederations, and international regimes"[4] now constitutes a political order more like the domestic spheres of earlier republics than the prototypical Realist state system of hierarchies in anarchy.

On the Liberal ascent international theorists also have a decidedly divided posture. Realists tend to view the United States as simply another nation-state and as a particularly successful great power. They tend to dismiss its exceptionalist liberal-democratic ideology as either dangerously naive or disingenuously self-serving.[5] Realists also have difficulty accepting and conceptualizing the Western liberal order as a distinct type of state system. They have little hope for its persistence and expend little effort in thinking about how it might be sustained or augmented. Contemporary Liberal international theory, growing in strength and sophistication along with the expansion of the liberal system, does better, but its treatment is also fragmented, off center, and increasingly in disarray. In contrast to the pessimistic Realist emphasis on historical patterns of recurrence, contemporary Liberalism, particularly American 'neoconservativism,' has tended toward overoptimism, verging on triumphalism and complacency, thus forgetting the arduous circumstances and severe problems faced by early republican polities.[6] International Liberalism's numerous practical agendas of arms control, democracy promotion, international law, human rights, peacekeeping, international organization, and functional problem-solving regimes still labor inappropriately under the onus of utopianism. These agendas are not well connected to one another or to a larger conceptualization of Liberal and world governance, and the legacies of progressive internationalism are increasingly under assault. Liberals are also increasingly divided about the appropriateness of establishing international restraints on states, and the liberal democracies of America and Europe are increasingly divided about which parts of the liberal-democratic agenda are most important.[7]

The stakes and divisions over intensifying security globalization and the status of broadly liberal political arrangements are particularly acute concerning nuclear weapons. Marking the effective culmination of five centuries of strategic and military globalization, the discovery of nuclear explosives a half century ago created a material context with unprecedented possibilities for large-scale destruction. In the wake of the attacks of 9/11, the increasing credibility of nonstate actors acquiring and using nuclear or other weapons of mass destruction has further raised both the stakes and the intellectual disarray surrounding security globalization and the fate of free polities.

The response of theorists to these destructive possibilities also has been extremely diverse, ranging from the view that the state system is obsolete and must be replaced by effective world government, through the currently dominant middle view that nuclear deterrence has brought about a revolution in interstate relations, to the still influential view that nuclear weapons are not revolutionary in their implications. Within this diverse matrix of theory and policy, Realist views, while themselves varied, have dominated, displacing into increasing marginality early American and liberal views supporting robust international regulation and vigorous arms control.[8] The attacks of 9/11 and the prospects of nonstate nuclear terrorism have brought new urgency to the old question of the relationship between domestic liberty and international order.

THE ARGUMENT

Given these discrepancies between these two contemporary realities—intensifying globalization (particularly concerning security) and the liberal-democratic ascent—and their treatment in contemporary international theory, the goal of this book is to rethink the basic traditions and concepts of international theory.[9] I do so by offering an alternative reading of Western security theorizing that aims to alter our conception of our theoretical past in ways potentially useful for our present and future needs. I focus on the main line of Western theorizing about the relations among security-from-violence, material contexts, and types of government.[10] This reading recovers and reconstructs a line of thinking centered around republicanism and contextual-materialist geopolitics that emerged in the ancient and modern European Enlightenments. This line of theorizing, which I shall refer to interchangeably as *republican security theory* and *security-restraint republicanism,* has been misunderstood and misappropriated in mainstream, and particularly Realist-centered, accounts of international theory. Central ideas of its main successors—Realism and Liberalism—are incomplete fragments of it. While some parts of this line of argument are central to both contemporary Realism and Liberalism, other parts, some of great importance, have been partially lost and marginalized and the connections between them have nearly vanished. Viewing the original formulations of Western structural-materialist security theory in this way reveals a tradition that was doing in the past precisely what we need to be doing in the present and future, namely, grappling with change in material contexts and the extension of republican government on successively larger scales. The net effect of this argument for contemporary international theory is to diminish Realism as a distinct and intelligible tradition, to expand, deepen, and recenter international Liberalism, and to point the way toward a unified structural-material security theory.

In simple terms, I claim that the main axis of intellectual development in Western structural-materialist security theory is composed of two problematiques which seek to understand the interplay between variations and changes in the material context, security-from-violence, and three arrangements of political authority (anarchical, hierarchical, and republican). The overall republican security project has been to achieve security by simultaneously avoiding the extremes of hierarchy and anarchy over successively larger spaces in response to changes in the material context, particularly changes in violence interdependence. The most essential claim of the first problematique is that anarchy is incompatible with security in situations in which there are high levels of violence interdependence, and that such situations vary across both space and time in intelligible patterns shaped by the interaction of geography and technology. A key claim of the second problematique, largely dropped by more recent Realist formulations, is that the extremes of *both* hierarchy and anarchy are intrinsically incompatible with security owing to the absence of restraint. Republican forms, evolving over time to encompass ever-larger spaces, essentially entail the simultaneous negation of both anarchy and hierarchy through the imposition of mutual restraints. As such, the main axis of Western structural-material security theory is about the interplay between restraints—either material contextual or political structural—and security-from-violence. In short, providing security in a world of bounding power, of leaping violence possibilities, requires changes in the scope and types of bounding power, of socially constructed practices and structures of restraint.

Two often overlooked facts suggest the value of rereading the main historical axis of security theory as essentially that of republicanism and its fragmentary successors. First, the terms 'Realism' and 'Liberalism' first appear *during* the nineteenth century, and six of the main ideas now associated with them (for Realism: the anarchy problematique, balance of power, and society of states; for Liberalism: democratic peace, commercial peace, and international institutions) were first formulated *before* the nineteenth century largely within the conceptual idioms of republicanism. Second, almost all the writings from which Realist and Liberal international theory take their main arguments were *written about* the particular problems of a handful of polities (democratic Athens, republican Rome, Renaissance Venice and Florence, and early modern Holland, Britain, and the United States) and were *written by* citizens, inhabitants, or close observers of these polities.[11] Far from being a random selection of polities across Western (let alone global) historical experience, these polities were highly anomalous due to their precocious possession of political liberty, popular sovereignty, and limited government, and several of them had roles within their state systems vastly disproportionate to their size and population. Given these facts, it is easy to entertain the proposition that international security theory originated within the conceptual idioms of these republican polities and to see its overall project as the simultaneous avoidance of the extremes of anarchy and hierarchy. Like the surprise of Molière's bourgeois gentleman upon learning he had been speaking prose his whole life, international theory is surprised to learn that it has long been unknowingly speaking republicanism.

In the remaining sections of this introduction, I unpack more fully my claim that the main ideas recognized as central to contemporary Realist and Liberal international theory are republican in origin, explore the conceptual parameters of this 'republicanism,' specify the role of material contextual variables in these arguments, outline the nature and limits of interpretative rereadings, and summarize the subsequent chapters.

THE 'REALIST TRADITION' AND REPUBLICANISM

To appreciate the value of recovering and reconstructing the structural-materialist security arguments of ancient and early modern republican theory, it is useful to begin with an examination of the commanding heights in the diverse landscape of contemporary international relations theory. There are far more international theorists than ever before, and the lines between different schools and arguments are often blurred. Despite this expansion and blending, the most widely used way to refer to the major clusters of arguments is as *traditions*, three of which are most established and developed—Realism, Liberalism, and Marxism.[12] There is also wide agreement that Realism, despite continued assaults and criticisms, remains the most compelling, even hegemonic tradition, particularly concerning security.[13] Realism is itself diverse, encompassing social science arguments, policy-relevant analysis, and a canonical body of earlier theorists, and there are many debates among Realists.[14]

The construction of Realism as a tradition of international theory has largely been in the 'American social science' of international relations, fashioned during the second half of the 'American Century.'[15] But the essential conceptual building blocks of this enterprise were derived from earlier European thought and largely brought by European émigrés. Realism's rise and contours have been heavily shaped by its aspiration to guide American foreign policy better than indigenous American 'idealism.'[16] Realism's intellectual hegemony is buttressed by its sense of itself as a tradition of practice and theory stretching back to Thucydides in Greek antiquity and claiming many of the leading figures in Western political thought.[17] Reinforcing this hegemony, non-Realists largely define themselves through their attacks on Realism. Although Realists are not a majority of contemporary international theorists, the field (particularly concerning security) resembles a wheel with Realism at the hub and its competitors situated on spokes radiating out from it.

The first step in seeing beyond the Realist-dominated landscape of international theory, particularly concerning security, is to look more closely at the ways in which Realism constitutes itself as a tradition. Despite the claim of Realist international theory to be of great and distinguished antiquity, it is important to remember that the word 'international' and the labels for the three main contemporary traditions—Realism, Liberalism, and Marxism—were all coined in the nineteenth century.[18] Thus the construction of Realism and Liberalism as international traditions has been largely the projection of the categories, concerns, and divisions of the theoretical landscape of the recent past onto the distant past. This reading creates an odd pattern of incomplete appropriation, misappropriation, and nonappropriation of earlier lines of argument. Earlier theorists certainly made arguments that are similar to contemporary Realist claims, but these arguments were formulated in different conceptual languages and were parts of larger arguments substantially different from contemporary Realist claims. To begin to see how this is so, it is useful to examine three rather odd and unsatisfactory features of the contemporary formulation of Realism as a tradition.

First, consider four of the leading stars in the Realist ancestral firmament: Thucydides, Niccolo Machiavelli, Thomas Hobbes, and Jean-Jacques Rousseau. As many critics have observed, Realist readings do violence to the complexity and uniqueness of each of these writers.[19] Less noticed, however, is a more important political fact: all four theorists, each in different ways, held strong political allegiances to particular republican or protoliberal polities, and the focus of their writings was the security problems faced by such polities. Thucydides was not simply a disinterested chronicler of the Peloponnesian War writing for all time, but was a follower of Pericles and a general of democratic Athens.[20] Machiavelli, despite his ironic legacy of inspiration to modern absolutist monarchical state-builders, was an active citizen and tireless public servant in the turbulent Florentine Republic, and his main work sought to inspire emulation of the Roman Republic.[21] Hobbes, while fearful of the discord he associated with republican politics, was a strong proto liberal in that he based his entire program of political renewal upon a concern for individual security.[22] And Rousseau, the devoted (if errant) son of the republican city-state of Geneva, was first and foremost an advocate and theorist of strong democracy and traditional republican virtue against the oppressions and corruptions of large modern despotic monarchies. Each of these theorists was more pessimistic than contemporary Liberals about the human political prospect, but each wrote with a measure of optimism that their advances in knowledge could lead to at least modest amelioration of human miseries. Thus, to the extent these four theorists are understood as 'founders of Realism,' their 'Realism' emerged from reflections on the security of republican, democratic, and liberal polities.

Second, Realists have been remarkably uninterested in reading and remembering the actual founders of a distinctly Realist tradition, the German theorists of the nineteenth and early-twentieth centuries. Not only did the actual term 'realpolitik' emerge here, but the elaborate and strong power political theories of German national statism, *Machtpolitik*, and *Geopolitik* produced by figures such as Johann Gottfried Herder, Johann Gottlieb Fichte, G.W.F. Hegel, Henreich von Trietschke, Friedrich Meinecke, Friedrich Ratzel, Otto Hintze, Karl Haushofer, Max Weber, and Carl Schmitt—to mention only the most prominent—remain the richest cluster of pure and strong Realist thinking.[23] All advocates, with varying degrees of enthusiasm, of German imperial expansion and strong authoritarian government, their large body of work finds virtually no mention in the contemporary Realist construction of itself as a tradition.[24]

Third, remembering the German theorists of the Second Empire and Third Reich points to another problem in Realism's claim to be a hegemonic theory of international politics, particularly concerning security: the neglect of domestic hierarchy as a security threat. 'Death by government,' political murder by the strong hierarchies of twentieth-century totalitarian despotism (most notably Hitler's Germany, Stalin's Russia, Mao's China, and their many lesser imitators), cumulatively killed as many—if not more—of their own hapless subjects as did their foreign aggressions.[25] Yet the topic of hierarchy as a threat to security is oddly absent from Realist international theory and its subfield of 'security studies.' This exclusion has the effect of expelling from the security story one of the greatest extended accomplishments of republican and Liberal theory and practice—the restraint of domestic hierarchy as a security threat over progressively larger spaces. This omission also renders the republican and Liberal program of simultaneously ameliorating and avoiding both hierarchy and anarchy far more utopian than it has actually been.

The intimate unacknowledged relationship between contemporary Realist and earlier republican thought also emerges from a reflection on the origins of some of the main ideas of contemporary Realism. Despite its diversity, three of the 'high poles' in the Realist tent are *anarchy*, the *balance of power*, and *international society*, which taken together constitute an immensely powerful and well-developed image of international politics.[26] The first polar notion, often referred to as the 'anarchy problematique,' is that interstate politics is an anarchy (in the sense of lacking authoritative government) in which states are forced to secure themselves by their own devices. As an 'ordering principle' of state systems, anarchy is held to evoke a set of behaviors and dynamics (such as the security dilemma, balancing, and alliances) that give international politics a distinctive and often warlike character, in contrast to politics inside states, which is said to be authoritatively and hierarchically ordered. The second polar idea is balance of power, about which Kenneth Waltz, the founder of neorealism, observes that "if there is any distinctively political theory of international politics, balance-of-power is it."[27] For states in anarchy, security and the preservation of the plural political order of the anarchic state system is held to depend upon a favorable distribution or balance of power, and the ability of states to maintain it. The third polar idea, international society, most developed by the 'English School,' maintains that international systems can also possess a distinctive society with system-level institutions, most notably sovereignty, diplomacy, and international law, which operate to moderate interstate relations.[28]

One does not have to dig very deeply to unearth the republican origins of these three polar ideas. The anarchy problematique is straightforwardly derived from the thought of early modern thinkers, most notably Hobbes and Rousseau.[29] The first emergence of the balance of power and international society as arrangements for the preservation of plurality and restraint on power occurs, as we shall see at length (in chapter 5), in the early modern characterization of Europe as a whole as a 'republic.' These features of state systems are first systematically conceptualized by analogy with city-state republics. Looking at the overall contemporary 'Realist tradition' it seems clear that "contemporary realists have invented a past and call it a tradition."[30] And so too have Liberals, albeit in different ways.

The 'Liberal Tradition' and Republicanism

Among the many challenges to Realism, perhaps the most substantial has come from Liberalism. Moving to dispel the dismissive Realist labels of 'idealist' and 'utopian,' Liberal theorists have moved beyond primarily offering schemes to change the world for the better and begun providing a variety of concepts useful for understanding and explaining aspects of the world as it actually is. They have also begun to construct a tradition through the recovery and reinterpretation of earlier theorists and writers. Despite many strengths and accomplishments, contemporary Liberal international theory has fallen short of overthrowing Realism's intellectual hegemony, particularly concerning security. In part this shortfall is attributable to the fact that Realism seems to capture so much of history as well as aspects of contemporary world politics. More fundamentally, however, the Liberal challenge has fallen short because it has not yet advanced a line of argument that more compellingly addresses the major issues of security, structure, and power that animate Realism.

Contemporary Liberal international theory is also extensive and diverse. As is the case with Realism, contemporary Liberal international theory encompasses social science arguments, policy-relevant analysis, and interpretations of earlier theorists. On the social science side, Liberal international theorists have been especially enthusiastic participants in the scientific and methodological ferment of the 'behavioral revolution.'[31] Despite aspirations toward common methodology and cumulation of knowledge, contemporary Liberal international theory has produced a bewildering proliferation of new concepts, theories, and schools: Functionalism, neofunctionalism, pluralistic security communities, pluralism, integration, transnational relations, preferred world orders, interdependence, complex interdependence, democratic peace, regimes, and cooperation—to mention only some of the most prominent and extensively developed.[32] This theoretical situation is paralleled by a great diversity of practical agendas regarding democracy promotion, international organizations, international regimes, international law, arms control, and human rights.

This theoretical explosion has produced the great fragmentation of Liberal theory, creating uncertainty about the relationship among these new conceptual vocabularies and theories, and about their novelty or superiority to earlier Liberal arguments, with the result that contemporary Liberal international theory appears to be less than the sum of its parts. Even more fundamentally, however, the main drift of this polymorphous tide has been away from a direct challenge to Realism: away from security-from-violence and toward nonsecurity issue areas (notably economics and environment); away from political structure and toward process; and away from material variables and toward norms, common understandings, and other ideational factors.[33] Lacking Liberal arguments that directly and effectively address the pivotal Realist arguments about security, structure, and material context, Liberals often cast their arguments as adjunct or special case modifications of Realism.[34]

Despite this diversity and these tendencies, the Liberal theoretical tent, particularly regarding security, also has three tall poles: *democratic peace*, *commercial peace*, and *international institutions*, which together constitute the most intellectually potent elements in the Liberal camp.[35] The first polar idea, democratic peace, holds that democracies will not make war against other democracies, due to domestic structural or normative restraints, and has been labeled "as close as anything we have to an empirical law in international relations."[36] The second polar idea, commercial peace, holds that rising levels of international economic interdependence through trade will tend to produce peace among states by raising the cost of war to irrational levels and by providing an alternative to conquest as a path for national gain. Contemporary international Liberalism's third polar idea, international institutions, holds that the presence of various forms of international organizations, law, and regimes (extending beyond the traditional institutions of the society of states) moderates interstate relations and that Liberal states have a particular affinity for such institutions.

The origins of these three Liberal polar ideas is also straightforwardly republican and often attributed to republican theorists cast as 'early liberals.' Democratic peace is widely attributed to Immanuel Kant, who spoke of 'republics' and specifically condemned majoritarian democracy without restraints as despotic.[37] The idea of commercial peace makes its appearance in early modern thought, particularly Montesquieu, and is commonly attributed by Liberals to Adam Smith, Jeremy Bentham, and Richard Cobden. Similarly, the idea of international institutions, cast as various forms of unions, leagues, and federal arrangements, is a staple of early modern republican thought. Recent readings of these early modern theorists, most prominently by Michael Doyle, have created a fuller sense of a 'tradition' of Liberal, or 'neoclassical Liberal,' theorizing with deeper roots and greater authority and have provided an important step toward unity and historical depth in contemporary Liberal international theory.[38]

These readings are compelling as far as they go, but as a mining of the past to add pedigree and depth to contemporary international Liberalism's three polar ideas, they miss central issues of early republican security theorizing and neglect several substantial bodies of pivotal literature. As with the Realist reading, the Liberal projection of current concerns on the past produces an odd pattern of incomplete appropriation, misappropriation, and nonappropriation of earlier lines of argument. Earlier theorists certainly made arguments that are substantively similar to contemporary Liberal claims, but these arguments were formulated in different conceptual languages and were parts of larger arguments different from contemporary Liberal claims. To see how this is so, it is useful to examine four unsatisfactory features of the contemporary formulation of international Liberalism as a tradition.

First, the formulation of neoclassical Liberalism largely neglects earlier republican arguments about security, political structure, and material context. This omission in part reflects the impact of what is widely referred to as the 'republican revival' among political theorists and intellectual historians over the last quarter century.[39] The revivalists advance the view that there is a sharp conceptual divide between republicanism, centered on community and virtue and derived from Aristotle's 'civic humanism,' and Liberalism, centered on individualism and interest. In this narrative, Liberalism slowly emerges in the early modern period and then supplants republicanism by the early-nineteenth century. The focus of the republican revival has been mainly domestic, but the most substantial treatment of republicanism and international theory, provided by Nicholas Onuf, asserts a particularly strong version of the republican-Liberal divide.[40] The emphasis on Kant by neoclassical Liberalism has also reinforced idealist over materialist arguments. As a result, the Enlightenment culmination of republican structural-materialist security theory, Montesquieu's *Spirit of the Laws*, occupies a marginal status in the contemporary formulations of Liberalism as a tradition of international and security theorizing, despite being a continuing epicenter of scholarly analysis.[41] When these security, structural, and material arguments are brought back into the narrative, the primary novelty of early modern thought is not the claim that democracy and commerce have pacific effects, but rather an analysis of the circumstances in which such political forms are compatible with interstate survival.

The three Liberal polar arguments emerge from republican thought, but they are secondary to the one topic that stands out as overwhelmingly central in this body of thought: the Roman Republic. Interpretations of the Roman republican experience are present in virtually every thinker, and are central to most, and here Kant stands out as nearly unique in not addressing it at all. For friends of political liberty, the Roman record was tragically pessimistic. Roman survival in a harshly competitive security environment was achieved through expansion, but expansion created internal imbalances that were nearly universally understood to be the root cause of the violent transformation of the Republic into the monarchical and ultimately despotic principate.[42] It is against this experience that the early moderns defined their problems and measured their innovations.

The third omission, the founding of the United States of America as an alternative to both the hierarchical state and the anarchic state system, follows logically from the second. The Roman experience posed for the American founders the problem that federal union is advanced to solve: how can political freedom be combined with the large size, and hence interstate security, associated with despotically governed empires? The first dozen or so papers of the *Federalist* in many ways mark the culmination of ancient and modern Enlightenment republican security theory. They expound in crystalline clarity the security project of simultaneously avoiding hierarchy and anarchy both internally and externally, and advance federal union as the solution to the debilitating impasse posed by the Roman record. Despite this, the *Federalist* is almost invisible in contemporary formulations of international Liberalism.[43]

Fourth, the neoclassical Liberal narrative oddly jumps from the early-nineteenth century to the present, largely overlooking late-nineteenth- and early-twentieth-century arguments about the interplay between federal forms and the emerging global-scope security environment produced by the industrial revolution. Here Liberals have largely accepted the conventional view that the strong materialist arguments of fin de siècle 'social Darwinism' and 'geopolitics' are thoroughly and harshly Realist. As a result many Liberal figures and arguments are omitted from the narratives and attention of international theorists. Most notable are H. G. Wells and John Dewey, who pioneered the reformulation of the earlier static geographic contextual-materialist arguments to deal with a dynamic industrial technological-material context.[44] In sum, neoclassical Liberalism has neglected major parts of republican theory that deal with security, structure, and material-context, topics now largely ceded to Realism.

These significant problems in the contemporary constructions of both Realism and Liberalism as traditions, in combination with the powerful underacknowledged legacies of republicanism in both Realism and Liberalism, indicate the need for a fresh reading of republican security thought on its own terms. It should be emphasized that the purpose of this reconstruction and exegesis is not to challenge the value or accuracy of the six polar concepts of contemporary Realism and Liberalism, but rather to put them in their proper place. Indeed, to the extent that the six polar ideas are judged to be persuasive, a fuller recovery of republicanism becomes appealing. Nor is this reading intended to be a prehistory of Realist and Liberal international theory. Rather, it is a reconstruction and exegesis of the republican security theory from which Realism and Liberalism have found some of their most important arguments. Its primary goal is not to establish that the six polar ideas of Realism and Liberalism derive from republicanism, although the junctures where they emerge are highlighted closely. Nor is the goal to engage the intricate contemporary debates about the six polar legacies. Because of what Realism and Liberalism have not appropriated from republicanism, republican security theory is more than the sum of the Realist and Liberal arguments derived from republicanism. When we view the past in this way, rather than as 'early Realism' or 'early Liberalism,' we acquire not only a very different past, but also a body of future-relevant theory better suited to grapple with security globalization and the Liberal ascent than either Realism or Liberalism.

THE FIRST FREEDOM AND REPUBLICAN SECURITY THEORY

Few political terms are as widely used and theoretically significant, but as vaguely defined, as 'republic' and its cognates.[45] John Adams, second president of the United States and author of a major theoretical exposition on the U.S. Constitution, despairingly declared that 'republic' meant "anything, everything or nothing."[46] Over the course of Western history, republican terminology has been used by theorists and practitioners to label a bewildering diversity of phenomena: Plato's picture of a small city-state ruled by a philosopher-king, popular government in city-states, Rome between the kings and the principate, the European state system, and many contemporary political regimes such as the United States of America, and the People's Republic of China.[47] To further compound the confusion, numerous 'republican' political parties hawk a variety of conflicting agendas. Within political theory the situation is even more profoundly complex, because the term 'republic' and its cognates have been used in various, often important, ways by most major theorists, making a full understanding of republicanism tantamount to reaching an understanding of most of Western political thought.

In simple terms, a 'republic' is a plural political order marked by political freedom, popular sovereignty, and limited government, and the modern liberal democracies come closer to realizing this from of government than its earlier versions. Due to its attention to the interplay of material contexts and the simultaneous avoidance of the extremes of hierarchy and anarchy, republican security theory encompasses far more than simply a variant of the internal or domestic forms of a 'state.' Many of the contemporary uses of 'republic' are attempts to disguise essentially antirepublican forms with the prestige of this label. Many other republican arguments are marked by one element of republican government being exaggerated at the expense of others to the point where an essentially nonrepublic is present. Many of the earlier and more philosophical usages, which are sorted in chapter 2, are rival siblings of the arguments of security-restraint republicanism. Security-restraint republicanism, composed of two problematiques (anarchy-interdependence and hierarchy-restraint), has not been adequately appreciated or mapped. Despite the vast amount that has been written on the sprawling topic of republicanism by political theorists,[48] intellectual historians,[49] and international theorists,[50] a central line of argument has not been adequately appreciated. To recover and reconstruct this lost and fragmented structural-materialist security theory requires following a line of argument as it runs through the works of a wide array of theorists, some well known, some largely forgotten, stretching from antiquity to the American founding and beyond.

Security from political violence is the *first freedom*, the minimum vital task of all primary political associations, and achieving security requires restraint of the application of violent power upon individual bodies. Insecurity results from extremes of both anarchy and hierarchy, because both are characterized by the absence of restraints on the application of violent power. The material context composed of geography and technology defines which powers must be restrained and which security practices and structures are appropriate for doing so. Thus security problems and solutions are not fixed and immutable, but spatially and temporally variable.

This set of concerns is not antiliberal or nonliberal; it is *first Liberal*. Contrary to the contemporary emphasis on the difference between republicanism and Liberalism, the republican arguments about security, political structure, and material context here excavated and reconstructed are not only compatible with Liberalism, they are Liberalism's primary concern—liberty—at its most primal and vital level—the application of violence to bodies. The 'liberty' that ancient and early modern republicans were first and foremost seeking to achieve was freedom from violence.[51] The Romans were obsessively concerned with achieving *publica salus* (public safety) by restraining violence in multiple directions, both inside and outside. Similarly, the 'right' that repeatedly appears as most central in early modern 'rights' theory is protection of life from violence,[52] and the earlier language of republics as 'free states' marked by 'liberty' is often (but not always) intermingled with talk of 'rights.'[53]

What distinguishes the first Liberalism of republican security theory from simple libertarianism or simple anarchism is its concern for political structures of restraint, of authoritative political arrangements that restrain violence among large numbers of people. The centrality of this concern for political structure emerges from the sober and at times pessimistic recognition that achieving protection from political violence is a daunting and difficult—and often impossible—task. Security from violence is a 'negative' freedom, but realizing it often entails a demanding set of 'positive' tasks. With this instrumental view of political arrangements, the republican security theorists have focused on a wide array of power restraint arrangements, their appropriateness in different settings, and their evolution. As such, the first Liberalism of republican security theory is about the positive tasks entailed in protecting negative freedom and avoiding certain evils, rather than about the realization of particular goods.[54] In this view, which Quentin Skinner usefully characterizes as 'neo-Roman republicanism,' political participation and civic virtue are means, not ends,[55] suited to particular contexts, and thus inappropriately identified as intrinsically or distinctively republican. In sum, republican security theory contains the first and most foundational arguments of Liberalism—its core devoted to the protection and preservation of free peoples and individuals—upon which other less vital but still important concerns and arguments have been added. Contemporary Liberalism is not the enemy of republican security theory, but its privileged—if forgetful and not always grateful—child.[56]

The relationship between republican security theory and the ideas now known as Realist is also intimate, but in a very different way. Among the many ideas Realism inherited from republicanism, the most conceptually foundational concern the 'state of nature.' These arguments are about anarchy, but only secondarily or by analogy about interstate anarchy. In simplest terms, these 'state of nature' arguments delineate the first set of problems that must be solved, the first set of unrestrained powers that must be restrained, in order for security to be achieved. As a realm lacking in political structural restraints, the anarchy of the 'state of nature' is potentially a realm of 'pure power politics.' For the project of republican security theory, 'pure power politics' is foundational, but in a completely negative way. Republican political orders are defined and configured as the systematic negation of pure power politics that mark the extremes of anarchy and hierarchy. To the extent Realism contains ideas about power restraint, most notably the 'balance of power,' a large indifference to unrestrained hierarchical power, and an affirmation of 'pure power politics,' it emerges as both incoherent and incomplete as a successor to first Liberal republican security theory.

Reading the main axis of Western structural-material security theorizing in this manner encompasses a large array of figures, some well known, others largely forgotten, stretching from antiquity to late modernity. Instead of seeing various 'early Realists' or 'early Liberals,' we see many of these key figures making parts of one argument, and we see many of them as either important in different ways or as less important than now thought. The first major vein of security restraint republicanism was produced by Graeco-Roman analysts of Athenian Democracy and the Roman Republic. Early modern revivalists of self-governing city-states mainly in Northern Italy, particularly Florence and Venice, continued and deepened this analysis. In Northern Europe (Holland, Germany, France, and most importantly, England and Scotland), republican security theory reached critical mass both in practice and theory, and sharply defined itself against oriental despotism, papal supremacy, Spanish imperialism, and French absolutism.[57]

Republican security theory is not, however, confined to the 'domestic,' but also addresses the issues of large-scale or 'international' security governance, as part of what J.G.A. Pocock refers to as "the problem of extent."[58] Republican security theory subsumes the 'domestic' and the 'international' by offering a sustained analysis of the *size of different political forms*. It is within this analysis of extent that the polar ideas of Realist and Liberal international theory about the dynamics of international anarchy were first clearly formulated by Enlightenment republican theorists. The primary locus of this innovation was the practice of referring to Europe as a whole as a 'republic,' by which they meant both to describe it as a complex system characterized by division, balance, and mixture and to praise it as a system for restraining the extremes of both anarchy and hierarchy.[59] The culmination of Enlightenment republican international theory is the U.S. Constitution of 1787, which its architects characterized as a 'compound republic' or 'federal union.' It was explicitly designed to prevent North America from becoming a Westphalian system of hierarchic units lodged in anarchy. In the wake of the industrial revolution 'Liberal internationalist' agendas ranging from binding international law, the League of Nations, world federal union, Atlantic Union, and nuclear arms control (which are central to the Realist depiction of its rival as utopian) are advanced as extensions of mutual restraint structures made necessary for security by material contextual changes. In sum, republican security theory, understood as the project of simultaneously avoiding the extremes of anarchy and hierarchy across different spatial scales, originates the theory of state systems now so elemental to Realism, alongside ideas about large-scale postanarchic and nonhierarchical orders now ignored by Realism.

MATERIAL CONTEXT: PHYSIOPOLITICS AND GEOPOLITICS

This preliminary sketch of the contours of republican security theory clearly suggests the presence of a 'geopolitics,' not only in the sense of an 'international' argument, but also in the sense of an argument about *material contexts composed of geography and technology as restraining and empowering forces*.[60] Arguments about the influence of material-contextual factors, usually cast in terms of 'nature,' are ubiquitous in early political thought and have been intimately woven into republican security theory since its inception.[61] Far from being incidental or ancillary, claims

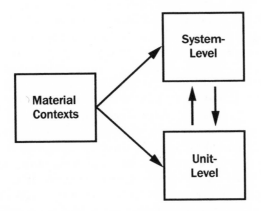

I.1 Material Context Shapes Unit-Level and System-Level

about material context sit at the center of republican security theory because material contexts in general, and violence interdependence in particular, delineate the scope and forms of violence potential that must be
restrained in order to achieve security. Arguments about material contexts
and their relationship to political structure and security-from-violence are
not confined to either the 'unit' or the 'system' level, but rather address
both (see figure I.1). Indeed, material-contextual arguments were first deployed to understand the political constitutions of particular republican
polities and then gradually applied to larger, less ordered 'international'
spaces by a process of analogy and extension.

Despite the ubiquity and importance of material-contextual arguments,
there is no generally accepted label for them. The term 'geopolitics' is of
early-twentieth-century vintage, has a lingering aura of conflictual and
Realist connotations, and recently has become a useful, if otherwise
empty, term for international relations generally.[62] To provide a clear
label, I shall refer to these material-contextual arguments as *physiopolitical*—about the relationship between nature (*physis*) and politics.

Ancient and early modern physiopolitical arguments rest on the simple
assumption that the physical world is not completely or even primarily
subject to effective human control and that natural material-contextual
realities impede or enable vital and recurring human goals. Such arguments attempt to link specific physical constraints and opportunities given
by nature (such as the presence of fertile soil, good weather, access to the
sea, and mountain ranges, etc.) to alterations in the performance of very
basic functional tasks universal to human groups (most notably protection from violence and biological sustenance). Because humans conceive
and carry out their projects in differing material environments, the vari-

ous ways in which these environments present themselves to humans heavily shape the viability of various human projects.[63]

Narrowing the focus to security-from-violence, one still finds a myriad of variables, but by far the most central is *violence interdependence*, a rough and basic measure of the capacity of actors to wreak destruction upon one another. This idea, explored at length in the pages ahead, is clearly an oddity from the standpoint of contemporary international theory. On one side, Liberals attach great importance to interdependence, but focus almost exclusively on economics and ecology rather than violence. On the other side, Realists focus on violence, but not violence interdependence. They view economic interdependence as exaggerated in its occurrence and effects, and think powerful states should, and largely do, avoid it. In reality, however, interdependence as it concerns violence is the core notion of 'state of nature' arguments, sometimes explicitly, but always powerfully. As we shall see, it is the presence of stronger degrees of violence interdependence that makes anarchy incompatible with security in such arguments. And it is an argument about changes in spatial scope of stronger degrees of violence interdependence that underpins the globalist case for the abridgment of anarchy across progressively larger spaces. Despite the 'materialism' of many contemporary international arguments, republican security theory's core arguments about material context as geography and technology as restraining and empowering have an attenuated and marginalized contemporary presence.[64] Two major waves of work and argument have been neglected.[65]

The first wave begins with the arguments of the ancient Greeks, particularly various pre-Socratic naturalists and Aristotle, and is recovered and extended by numerous early modern and Enlightenment theorists culminating in Montesquieu. These first-wave arguments, usually cast in the language of 'nature,' concern geographic factors like climate, soil fertility, topography, and land-sea interactions. These arguments are about 'nature' in the 'state of nature,' thus specifying which restraints must constitute the 'civil state.' Claims about natural material contexts are at the root of the pessimism of the ancients (and very circumscribed optimism of the early moderns) about the prospects for political liberty. At the same time, the actual islands of republican government are understood to be shaped internally by various material divisions and balances, and heavily dependent upon restraints on violent power deriving from nature, particularly geographical topography and land-sea interactions. Similarly, the first international theory of the early moderns, casting Europe as a 'republic,' locates the basis of this plural order in material-contextual nature.

The second wave of neglected early contextual materialist theorizing, often referred to as 'global geopolitics,' emerges in the period stretching roughly from the middle of the nineteenth to the middle of the twentieth century. This group of theorists is distinguished from its predecessors in its much more explicit treatment of technology and change, and its focus on global-scale patterns. Building from their predecessors, second-wave theorists sought to understand how the new capabilities of transportation, communication, and destruction produced by the industrial revolution (most notably railroads, steamships, telegraphy, chemical high explosives, and airplanes), when interacting with the largest-scale geographic features of the earth, would shape the character, number, and location of viable security units in the emerging global-scope security system. In assessing whether the global-scale material context was so configured to support a plural state system (comparable to early modern Europe) or a centralized world empire (comparable to the earlier widespread regional 'universal monarchies'), these theorists shed light on the epochal shift from the preglobal archipelago of regional state systems (or empires) to the contemporary intensely interactive global system, a shift curiously undertheorized in the Realist narrative of 'anarchy from time immemorial.' Within this matrix are found assessments of the contribution of American federal union to the project of political liberty in the era of global total wars, and arguments about the increasing security necessity of postanarchic and nonhierarchic world federal government.

Within this second-wave literature, a few of the major figures, most notably Alfred Thayer Mahan and Halford Mackinder, are occasionally noted or engaged, particularly by Realist grand strategic theorizing. But a large number of their arguments and those of many other largely forgotten theorists, ranging from the German *Geopolitik* school to Liberal cosmopolitans such as H. G. Wells, are almost invisible in both Realist and Liberal narratives. These theorists were the first globalists, and their neglect is glaring in light of the contemporary preoccupation with globalization and the global.[66]

The omission of earlier contextual-materialism in the contemporary formulations of Realism and Liberalism as traditions can reasonably be attributed to the political situation and agendas of Realism and Liberalism during the middle of the twentieth century.[67] The association of materialist geopolitics with the crimes of Nazi Germany made Anglo-American Realists of the era eager to distance themselves from this literature. For Liberals, this neglect stems from an acceptance of the general association of late-nineteenth- and early-twentieth-century geopolitics with extremely conflictual, materialist, and antiliberal perspectives, and the general tendency of contemporary Liberals to focus on nonsecurity domains and nonmaterial variables. This lacuna is reflected in the widespread—but largely mythical—Realist view that the study of international politics was dominated by 'idealism' prior to the emergence of Realism during the period of the Second World War.

Overall, when these neglected material-contextual arguments are reassembled as a component of republican security theory, we find ourselves in possession of an approach well suited for grappling with security globalization and the Liberal ascent. The five-century and four-dimensional (military, economic, ecological, and cultural) process of globalization has impacted every aspect of human life, but it first and foremost has been a transformation of the material condition of the human species. Given this, only an approach theorizing variations and changes in material context across space and time can fully register its first-order implications for security. From the perspective of this expanded and recentered structural-material theory, the Liberal ascent, and the role of the American founding and the United States in it, are transformed from an eccentric domestic event into *the* pivotal development in the enduring project of simultaneously avoiding the extremes of anarchy and hierarchy over larger spaces. This recovered theoretical approach also offers to provide firmer foundations for the beleaguered and fragmented Liberal international project of abridging interstate anarchy with institutional restraints on state power, especially arms control. It also enables us to see that suitably crafted international restraints preserve domestic liberty by foreclosing the erection of domestic hierarchy to cope with international anarchy. Looking ahead at the cascading interdependences that mark the global village with this recovered approach also provides the basis for reversing the presumption that the erection of substantive world government is unprecedented, while at the same time suggesting templates for the design of fully nonhierarchical, fully republican, world federal government.

EXEGESIS AND RECONSTRUCTION

This investigation is a theoretical exegesis and reconstruction. As such, it is appropriate to specify the nature and limits of such an enterprise. It is not a full intellectual history of all arguments about republics. Nor is it a history of all republics, or a history of all the ways in which the actual political controversies of actual republics used or abused republican theoretical arguments. It does not advance or test positive social science propositions, although the reconstructed overall argument could be further articulated and so treated. As an exegesis it seeks to trace a set of theoretical arguments as they appear across many centuries and in several conceptual idioms. The line of argument concerns the interplay between material context and political structures, but I am neither assuming nor defending claims that material contexts and political structures caused these theoretical arguments or that these ideas caused any political arrangement. These theoretical arguments, however, are commonly cast as reflections on the practical security problems of historically specific republican polities, and as such are unintelligible without reference to their situations. Instead of reading previous great thinkers in terms of contemporary competing schools of thought, I seek to unearth common problematiques subsuming contemporary divisions in previous thinkers of varied standing, and in doing so suggest that several currently venerated great thinkers (most notably Machiavelli and Kant) are less important than several less esteemed figures (most notably Montesquieu, Publius, Dewey, and Wells).

In this exegesis and reconstruction, I make three interpretative assumptions: security-restraint republicanism is a *tradition* that is *practical* and *progressive*. It is a tradition because it was 'handed down' over an extended period of time among theorists and practitioners who were self-consciously building on the ideas and actions of predecessors with whom they shared normative orientations and theoretical problematiques.[68] It is practical because it contains a set of generalizations drawn from practical experience, is intended to solve important and recurring problems, is in a continual dialectic with the needs and experiences of practitioners, and is valued according to its practical usefulness. It is progressive because its participants understood themselves as advancing, not toward universal and timeless truths, but toward understandings and solutions that were better able to solve timeless security problems by better adjusting to changing constraints and opportunities.

The arguments of republican security theory are formulated in ways alien to contemporary academic social science. They contain a mixture of normative, scientific, and design claims, often combined in complex and obscure ways. Normatively, the security-restraint republican values freedom and opposes tyranny, wants independent actors to self-regulate themselves in order to make centralized control unnecessary, supports centralized political power only where necessary to counterbalance outside threats, and jealously watches minimally necessary centralized power. There are three main analytical and scientific parts of security-restraint republicanism: taxonomic categories useful for describing plural, decentralized, and complex political orders (including certain types of state systems); causal propositions about the relationships between political practices and structures, and between such political factors and material contexts. The policy aspects of republican security theory encompass design features for building and operating political orders able to achieve republican goals.

Mapping the Argument

The exegesis and reconstruction offered here proceeds in nine chapters grouped into three parts. Part I is devoted to overall issues of theory and the relations between republican security theory and other related theories. Chapter 1, "Republican Security Theory," provides the overall theoretical reconstruction, beginning with a statement of the two main problematiques of structural-materialist republican theory and then proceeding to a more detailed exposition of its key arguments concerning human nature, the political structures of anarchy, hierarchy and republican forms, and the material context that defines the types of restraint necessary for security. Chapter 2, "Relatives and Descendants," augments and helps to situate the reconstructed argument by selectively mapping its complex relationships with other types of republicanism, some Realists, Liberals, and constructivists and several key figures and concepts straddling these divisions.

The rest of the volume, divided into two parts and seven chapters, is the exegesis. The four chapters of Part II, "From the Polis to Federal Union," examine four major bodies and episodes of republican security theory stretching from Graeco-Roman antiquity to the American founding. Chapter 3, "The Iron Laws of Polis Republicanism," begins at the beginning, with Greek and Roman arguments about the role of material contexts in shaping security problems and solutions, and the particularly hard trade-offs republican polities faced, with particular attention to the features and evolution of the Roman Republic and Polybius's analysis of it. Of particular concern here are the numerous arguments relating the evolution of the Roman Republic into the Augustan principate, and their pessimistic implications for political freedom. The Roman experiences provide the benchmark against which subsequent developments in republican security theory and practice can be measured.

Chapter 4, "Maritime Whiggery," begins an examination of the emergence of modern European republicanism, focusing on Venice and Britain, and arguments about the role material contexts played in the ability of these polities to survive as republics in a European state system populated by large absolutist monarchies, thus providing a contextual-material and system-structural dimension to the familiar narrative of the rise of 'constitutionalism' in Britain. Also of importance here is the role of material and structural factors that permitted modern republics to survive the softening of intensive citizen military *virtú*, and early arguments about material and systemic structural factors in the novel emergence in Europe of 'the republic of commerce' (or in nineteenth-century terms, 'capitalism') as a central feature of modern republicanism. These arguments provide a substantially different view of these familiar developments than provided by other contemporary interpretations, most notably republican revivalism.

Chapter 5, "The Natural 'Republic' of Europe," explores neglected but creative and influential eighteenth-century arguments about the overall European system as a plural political order constituted by restraints both natural and social. It is here that international system theory begins, and it is here that the 'balance of power' is first extended from the anomalous nonhierarchical republican polities to describe and explain the anomalous absence of a 'universal monarchy' in Europe. But even more important than balance in the arguments of Montesquieu, Rousseau, and others is the restraining power of 'natural division,' the topographical fragmentation of the European physical landscape in constituting the 'republic of Europe.' When all the pieces of this neglected episode in republican security theory are assembled, there emerges an overall picture significantly different from conventional interpretations of the European state system as the paradigmatic interstate anarchy, and the evolution of subsequent international theory is cast in a different light.

Chapter 6, "The Philadelphian System," explores the American founding as the climactic moment in Enlightenment republican security theory. Steeped in earlier republican security theory and history, the American founders, as articulated in the *Federalist*, brought the overall republican security argument to a new level of clarity, and the architecture of the First American Constitution is understood by the founders as an effort simultaneously to avoid or adequately cope with anarchy and hierarchy both domestically and internationally. The founders viewed their innovation of the 'federal union' or 'compound republic' as a decisive advance because it combined republican political forms with the territorial extent previously available only to hierarchical empires, thus giving republican government an unprecedented security viability. The overall view that emerges here is that the United States is an alternative to the Westphalian system of hierarchies in anarchy, rather than an oddly constituted unit within it.

The three chapters of Part III, "Toward the Global Village," continue the examination of the interplay between republican political forms and security across the nineteenth- and twentieth-century industrial divide. This period saw the explosion of diverse theoretical positions, thus ending the relative conceptual unity of Western structural-materialist security theorizing from the ancients through the modern European Enlightenment. Chapter 7, "Liberal Historical Materialism," examines the presence of arguments about Liberal forms in several schools of materialist thought. Although commonly viewed as mainly Marxist or Realist, the first arguments about material contexts changing across time due to technological developments were expounded by Scottish Enlightenment historical stage theorists and then modified by others. Similarly, the large literature of late-nineteenth- and early-twentieth-century social Darwinism, commonly seen as strongly Realist and antiliberal, also contains extensive and powerful analyses favorable to more Liberal political arrangements. This recovery culminates in an examination of the materialist arguments of two of the most prolific and influential figures of the period, H. G. Wells and John Dewey, who provide particularly innovative arguments about the interplay between republican political forms and the constraints and opportunities produced by the industrial revolution.

Chapter 8, "Federalist Global Geopolitics," pursues this line of argument as it is applied to the emerging global-scope interstate system in the late-nineteenth and early-twentieth centuries. The numerous materialist theorists of this period, generally grouped together as 'global geopolitics,' now seen as antiliberal, were actually quite diverse. They provide analyses of the security implications of federal union in the emerging global-scope state system. The exegesis begins with an examination of the common problematiques of global geopolitical theorists, and their areas of agreement and disagreement, thus placing competing Liberal and hierarchical statist political forms into one general framework. Then the treatment narrows to examine more specific arguments about federal union as a possible solution to the British predicament, pessimistic prognoses for the European state system, and a new view of world government. Finally, this chapter assesses the relative contributions of Kant and Publius and explores the republican logic of American internationalism.

Chapter 9, "Anticipations of World Nuclear Government," brings the exegesis into the second half of the twentieth century with an examination of the debates over the implications of nuclear explosives for security in an anarchical state system, with particular emphasis on 'nuclear one world' arguments that nuclear weapons had created a global-scope 'state-of-nature' anarchy that needed to be replaced with authoritative world government. Realist versions of these arguments reach something of a conceptual impasse, as a world hierarchical state is deemed necessary but intrinsically dangerous in its own right. Alternatively, various schemes for mutually reciprocal and authoritative arms control are explored.

A concluding chapter summarizes the revisionist recasting of the tradition of Western structural-material security theory, weighs the free world prospect, and reflects on the tradition and world government.

PART I

Traditions and Theory

Chapter One

REPUBLICAN SECURITY THEORY

No universal history leads from savagery to humanitarianism, but there is one leading from the slingshot to
the megaton bomb.
—Theodor W. Adorno[1]

SECURITY, BOUNDING POWER, AND THE BOUNDING OF POWER

From its inception, republican security theory has been concerned with
what might be termed the *security-political question*: what kinds of political arrangements are necessary for security? Republican security theory
comprises a cluster of interrelated problematiques and substantive arguments, which this chapter reconstructs. In addressing the question of what
kinds of political arrangements are necessary for security, republican security theory has started from the simple assumption that achieving security-
from-violence (security from the application of violent power to human
bodies) is the most basic political problem. Arising from the intersection
of human corporeal vulnerability and the fundamental value of life as a
prerequisite for all other ends, security-from-violence is the primary (but
not sole) purpose of political association.

Thus animated, republican security theory has focused on the relationship between restraints and security. In the broadest terms, *insecurity results from the absence of restraint on violent power, and security results
from the presence of restraints on violent power.* There are logically only
two possible sources of restraints—either in the limits imposed by the
material context or in socially constructed limits provided by political
practices and structures. If either material-contextual or political-structural restraints are present, there is security; if neither material-contextual
nor political restraints are present, there is insecurity.

Looking at the overall sweep of Western structural-materialist theory
from the polis to the contemporary global village, in the idioms of republicanism and its main descendants, both limits imposed by material context
and limits imposed by political arrangements have been in interactive motion, sometimes slowly, sometimes rapidly. The essential dynamic at work
is captured in the interplay between the two different meanings of the
phrase 'bounding power.' As power capability leaps or bounds upward,

the scope and type of political restraints or bounds necessary for security is also altered. Over time the possibilities of violent power have been bounding upward, inexorably growing by leaps and bounds from the bow, arrow, spear, and sword, through gunpowder weapons transported by animal or wind, through steel guns, railroads, and steamships, to thermonuclear intercontinental ballistic missiles. As the material context changes, the permanent problem of security-from-violence reappears in new and different forms, and this in turn means that the political arrangements able to provide security by restraining violence must change if acute insecurity is to be avoided. Providing security in a world of bounding power, of leaping violence possibilities, has thus required changes in the scope and types of bounding power, of socially constructed practices and structures. Bounding power requires the bounding of power.

THE TWO PROBLEMATIQUES

Immediately beneath this canopy metaphor of bounding as leaping and restraining sit the two main problematiques of republican security theory: the *anarchy-interdependence problematique* and the *hierarchy-restraint problematique* (see figure 1.1). The material context plays a pivotal role in the relationship between security and restraint. It conditions the security viability of the three major types of political arrangements—anarchy, hierarchy, and republics. The material context shapes the scope and severity of the application of violent power, thus defining the extent and type of political arrangement needed for security. Parts of these problematiques, and the substantive arguments generated within them, remain salient in contemporary Realism and Liberalism, but in an incomplete and fragmented form.

The anarchy-interdependence problematique examines the relationship between variations in material context, the scope of security-compatible anarchy, and the scope of authoritative government necessary for security. Today the expression 'the anarchy problematique' stands as the label for a rich body of arguments produced by neorealist international theorists and their critics about the dynamic logic of interstate anarchic systems. These arguments, often quite powerful so far as they go, are a truncated version of the anarchy-interdependence problematique because they employ an impoverished conceptualization of material context as a factor in security politics. Contemporary Realist international theory, reflecting major (if unacknowledged) republican legacies, centers its analysis upon the distribution ('balance') of power, largely neglecting the previous centrality of interdependence as it relates to violence.

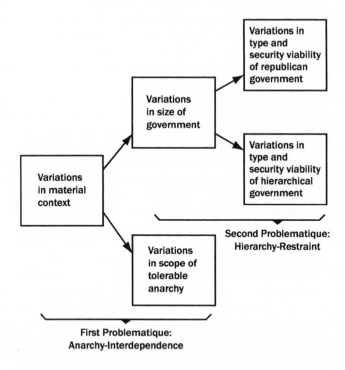

Figure 1.1 Main Problematiques of Republican Security Theory

In republican security theory, many different material contextual factors make their appearance, but one variable stands out throughout as first in importance: *violence interdependence*. Pivotal in all state-of-nature and most origin-of-civilization narratives, in naturalist and materialist analysis of the role of geography, and appearing more recently in a variety of different terminologies, analysis of this variable is the central axis of Western structural-material security theory. Through all the variants of terminology and modes of argument, there is a near consensus that situations of intense or extreme violence interdependence combined with anarchy are incompatible with security, which is to say that without authoritative political restraints such situations are intrinsically insecure. From this basic insight flows the realization that the first task of both security theory and practice is to escape this situation and establish at least minimally authoritative government. When the material context is severely limiting—when the possibilities of violent power are restrained by geography and technology—authoritative political arrangements are not needed for security, which is to say that the absence of government—anarchy—is compatible with security. Conversely, when the material context is not limiting—when extreme violent power is unrestrained by geography and technology—then the absence of government—anarchy—is incompatible with security. Because the material context varies across space, the size of the area within which intense violence interdependence is present—and thus the size of the area in which effective government is needed—varies as well.

Initially this insight was developed along with the assumption that material contexts, while different from place to place, did not change over time, but were naturally static, an expression of diverse but unchanging geography. In the idiom of early modern state-of-nature arguments, the size of the area characterized by a security-incompatible state-of-nature— and thus the size of security-necessary minimum government—is different in different material contexts. The scope of security-compatible anarchy varied across space, but not across time. The initial physiopolitical stages of the application of this insight produced an empirical political science of the relationship between the size of political associations and their natural-material, particularly geographic, environments.

In later stages of the elaboration of this insight, in the nineteenth and twentieth centuries, the previously implicit role of technology as part of the material context comes into prominence, reflecting the fact that major changes in basic technologies of communication, transportation, and destruction were expanding rapidly the size of the area within which intense violence interdependence was present, and thus authoritative government needed. As this happened, the *naturalist* contextual-materialist security arguments of the ancients and early moderns evolve into *historical* contextual-materialist security arguments, beginning with the Scottish Enlightenment and blooming in the late-nineteenth and early-twentieth centuries. Thus, stretching from the polis to the global village, the material context shaping security problems and solutions has not only *varied across space*, it has *changed across time*. In reading the arguments of the first problematique evolving in this way, we find ourselves in possession of a sophisticated treatment of security-military globalization. Very different, even opposing, bodies of literature and lines of argument can be seen as one single argument evolving and adapting in response to changing material contexts from the ancient polis to the contemporary global village.

Unfortunately for human security, all governments are not created equal, as evidenced by the historical prevalence of 'death by government,' the extensive violent predation of some governments upon their own people. Thus arises the second main problematique of Western structural-materialist security theory: what is the relationship between variations in the size of government needed and variations in the security viability and types of hierarchical and republican government? In thinking about types of government and security, republican security theory maintains that *the extremes of anarchy and hierarchy are fundamentally alike because nei-*

ther provides adequate restraints upon the application of violence to human bodies. Building on this insight, republican security theory holds that security requires avoiding the extremes of both anarchy and hierarchy, and that republics entail the simultaneous negation of anarchy and hierarchy. Republics have authoritative government, and thus are not anarchies, and they are simultaneously antihierarchies. A corollary claim is that the full insecurity potential of hierarchies is often unrealized due either to material contextual limitations or republican restraints grafted onto otherwise hierarchical forms.

HUMAN NATURE AND SECURITY FROM VIOLENCE

The main problematiques of Western structural-materialist security theory are concerned with the interplay between political structures (anarchy, hierarchy, and republics) and material context, but these problematiques rest on a series of simple assumptions about human nature—a set of largely fixed and recurrent attributes, tendencies, and needs—without which these problematiques are unintelligible. Although now marginal in international theory, Western structural-materialist security theory began within a context of theorizing about human nature, and the numerous vociferous debates of philosophical anthropology about many secondary aspects of human nature have obscured a core of robust consensus about more primary issues.[2]

The primary assumption about human nature is conceptually foundational and pervasively articulated: *security from violence is a basic human interest*. Protection from physical violence is a fundamental human need because without it all other human goods or ends cannot be enjoyed. The fact that humans are perishable corporeal beings means that they must be concerned with the avoidance of lethal and incapacitating violence or harm. To suffer such violence is almost universally viewed as an evil because life is a good, both in its own right and as a prerequisite to other goods. Life is a primary value, and protection from violence is essential for life. This desire to protect and preserve life is, of course, not unique to humans, but extends throughout the world of animate and sentient beings. In short, Western structural-materialist security theory assumes *normative survivalism*: the provision of protection from destructive violence is an essential human need and the most primary and essential—but certainly not the only—goal of human collective association. In a lucid modern formulation, John Stuart Mill describes the attainment of security as the point where "*ought* and *should* grow into *must*, and recognized indispensability becomes a moral necessity, analogous to physical, and

often not inferior to it as a binding force."[3] Even when normative survivalism seems to be rejected, it persists in reconfigured form.

Given the importance of security from violence, why is there so much
insecurity? Why is history littered with mountains of corpses? Part of the
answer to this question lies in the scarcity of nature and the dynamics of
structural situations, but these factors only come into play because of
three additional features of human nature and character: the presence of
power-seeking risk averse individuals, the *limited and compromised nature of human rationality*, and the universal human acquisition of *social
identities and interests*.

First, from its inception, structural-materialist security thinking about
human nature has recognized that while most individuals place a high
premium on security, there are some who are either willing to risk death
and other deprivations to achieve power (natural devils) or who conversely are particularly virtuous (natural angels). Thus humanity naturally distributes itself into a familiar 'bell curve' figure, with a great middle
majority of security seekers and outlier minorities of natural angels and
natural devils. In conceptualizing the types of arrangements necessary for
security, the natural devils pose a recurring significant problem. They
make the governmentless situation of anarchy perilous for security seekers; and their *animus dominindi* generates hierarchies and helps actualize
their intrinsically predatory potential.

Second, ancient and early modern analyses of human nature, while differing in many regards, held that human rationality is a relatively frail
faculty of the human psyche and easily overpowered by various emotions,
most notably fear and anger.[4] Fear is the emotion most intimately linked
to security, and how fear is managed—expressed, repressed, directed, or
cultivated—is among the most elemental issues of security politics. The
dynamics of fear are central to many of the most influential analyses of
political security, from Thucydides' portrait of how fear inspired Sparta
to make war and then how panic led Athens to ruin, through Hobbes's
claim that fear of violent death motivates the establishment of civil society
and Montesquieu's claim that fear is the active principle of despotism to
the contemporary focus on rational absolute fear as 'nuclear deterrence.'[5]

Like most emotions, fear is both a vital and potentially dangerous part
of the human psyche. It connects the body's survival imperative to human
actions. A completely fearless person would be completely indifferent to
risk, and would be dangerous both to himself and others. All sound security practice must be architectonically animated by fear, combining an
anticipation of outcomes with an aversion to the outcome of death. But
fear also has a self-destructive and irrational side. When human beings
are gripped by the emotion of fear, their capacity for instrumental (means-
ends) rationality is often impaired. As Thucydides so vividly shows, fear

can lead individuals and groups to take actions that are panicked and ill-conceived. When fear distorts judgment and behavior, the pursuit of the goal of security can be disastrously subverted. In sum, the absence of sufficient fear deprives cognition of proper direction, but too much fear can disrupt and distort it.

Third, structural-materialist theorizing about security has recognized that humans have a 'second nature' of identities and affiliations produced by social interactions, the reflection of the fact that humans are by nature social animals.[6] While arguments about the actual and appropriate contours of human second nature are numerous and varied, they all point to the fact that humans act not simply on the basis of natural needs, but on the basis of particular socially generated identities and group interests. Much of the security dysfunctional behavior exhibited by humans derives from these socially generated identities and interests: groups of humans violently hurl themselves against one another to protect or realize a wide range of goals—prestige, honor, and wealth—and in doing so suffer grievous security deprivations.

Taken together, the biologically based natural need for security, the existence of risk-taking power seekers, emotional compromises of rationality, and the immensely varied forms of group identification suggest it is the presence—not the absence—of security that is surprising. It is against this background of somber assumptions about natural human needs and tendencies that the fundamental structural political project of republican security theory emerges: *what kind of restraints are necessary in which situations in order to achieve security?*

THE TWO ANARCHIES AND VIOLENCE INTERDEPENDENCE

The first problematique of republican security theory concerns anarchy. Arguments about anarchy appear in a variety of idioms and formats, beginning with ancient discussions of the origins of civilization and continuing in early modern European state-of-nature and social contract theories.[7] There are many complex and important differences regarding many secondary issues, but there is an overwhelming consensus that anarchical situations combined with actors who are in a relationship of intense violence interdependence are intrinsically perilous for security.[8]

These arguments distinguish between three fundamentally different situations: a *pre-state anarchy* (multiple individuals or small groups interacting without common government), and *authoritative government* (multiple individuals and groups whose relations are ordered by authoritative law), and an *anarchic state system* (multiple governments inter-

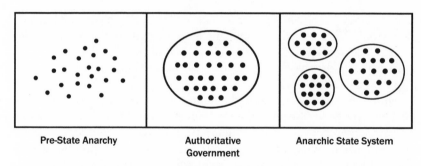

Pre-State Anarchy   Authoritative   Anarchic State System
Government

Figure 1.2 Anarchy, Government, and Anarchy

acting without common government) (see figure 1.2). Since early modern times, these three situations have also been referred to as a *state-of-nature*, a *sovereignty*, and a *state-of-war*. Life in the state-of-nature is, in Hobbes's often repeated formulation, "solitary, poor, nasty, brutish, and short."[9] In the state-of-nature each individual or small group is self-governing, but life is insecure. This vulnerability induces individuals or small groups to trade their absolute freedom for a minimum of security, provided by the "sovereign." In contrast, the state-of-war (not to be confused with actual war) exists between separate sovereign governments. Both the state-of-nature and the state-of-war are characterized as 'nasty and brutish.' But, unlike individuals or groups in the state-of-nature, sovereign governments in the state-of-war are not subject to sudden death at each other's hands: they are in an anarchy vis-à-vis one another, but are not so vulnerable. With their survival more assured than the atomized individual or small group in the state-of-nature, the sovereign governments in the state-of-war need not submit themselves to an even greater sovereign.

The relationship between these two anarchic situations and acute insecurity (and thus the imperative need for government) is commonly seen as vastly different. Government is needed in one, but not the other. It is a fundamental security imperative to leave the state-of-nature and find protection in government. In contrast, replacing state-of-war commonly associated with state systems with government might yield many security benefits, but is not a fundamental security imperative. The radically different security implications of the two anarchic situations is reflected in the Janus-faced posture of Realist international theorists: internal government is vital to security, but 'international' government is utopian, unprecedented, and not vital for security.

The presence of these two radically different anarchic situations thus poses a fundamental question: Why is pre-state anarchy so insecure while interstate anarchy, while at times perilous, is not generally so acutely insecure as to require government? The simple answer to this question is the material-contextual variable of *violence interdependence*, the capacity of actors to do violent harm to one another. This variable is present in an underdeveloped form in Hobbes, but appears explicitly in many other accounts. Although it plays a pivotal role in the Western structural-materialist security, it has gone under a bewilderingly large number of labels, none of which has achieved authoritative intellectual status. A situation of violence interdependence (when two actors can wreak violence upon one another) inherently poses the issue of restraining violence for security as a primordial and fundamental problem. Once some violence interdependence is present, the way in which this reality is dealt with becomes an inescapable political issue.

This variable attempts to capture one of the most central notions in political science and international theory, and not surprisingly, it appears under many different labels: 'position' and 'accessibility' and 'effective distance' in traditional geopolitics; 'loss-of-strength gradient' in recent quantitative geopolitics; 'offense-defense balance' in security studies; 'interdependence' in early-twentieth-century international relations theory; and 'dynamic density' in late-nineteenth-century social theory; and most recently 'interaction capacity' and 'violence interaction capacity.'[10] Each formulation is embedded in different models and has different connotations, but all are attempting to express the same commonsense insight that the capacity of actors to interact violently with one another has profound implications for security that are independent of the distribution (or balance) of power among them.

Aside from its importance (and diverse labeling), the next most important fact about violence interdependence is that it varies across space and time. At its most elemental level this factor can be divided into a simple four-part spectrum running from *absent*, through *weak* and *strong*, to *intense* (see figure 1.3). Thus schematized, the main argument of Western structural-materialist theory regarding anarchy and security is quite straightforward. At one extreme, government is largely impossible, and certainly unnecessary, when violence interdependence is absent. At the other extreme, government is necessary for security (but not necessarily politically possible) in situations of intense violence interdependence. In between, government is largely unnecessary for security (but potentially beneficial) in situations of weak or strong violence interdependence. It is thus the core claim of republican security theory that situations of anarchy combined with intense violence interdependence are fundamentally perilous for security, and that in this situation government, some authoritatively binding arrangement of restraint, is necessary for security.

Variations in the degree of violence interdependence play a pivotal role in determining the relationship between anarchy and security, but the commonly employed terms to refer to different anarchic situations do not

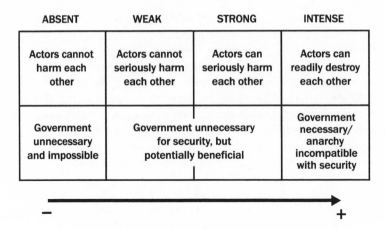

Figure 1.3 Degrees of Violence Interdependence

clearly and explicitly register the difference between anarchies marked by different degrees of violence interdependence. The terms 'state system' and 'state-of-war' imply or implicitly assume the presence of a weak or strong, rather than intense, degree of violence interdependence, but it is possible for a state system to be accompanied by either weak/strong or intense violence interdependence. Therefore, to capture directly this powerful but only implicitly registered, and thus easily overlooked, relationship between anarchy and violence interdependence, it is useful to speak of *first anarchy* as a situation marked by intense violence interdependence and of *second anarchy* as a situation marked by weak or strong violence interdependence.

With these distinctions it is possible to problematize clearly the relationship between state-systems and the degree of violence interdependence, a relationship that the truncated anarchy problematique of neorealism silently elides. Across historical time, the pre-state anarchy of individuals or small groups has almost always been a first anarchy, because it is marked by intense violence interdependence. However, depending on the degree of violence interdependence present, a state system can be in either a first or a second anarchy. Indeed, the crucial lesson of security globalization is that state systems have been undermined catastrophically by being thrown from a second anarchy to a first anarchy. Given this, the clear formulation of the main substantive claim of the anarchy-interdependence problematique is that *actors in first anarchies require substantive government for security, while actors in second anarchies do not.*

Once the importance of this material-contextual variable of violence interdependence has been recognized, my formulation of the first main problematique of Western structural-material security theory (recall figure 1.1) becomes fully intelligible: what is the size of the area within which government is necessary and anarchy intolerable? The attempt to answer this core question, which we shall examine at length, has basically entailed various arguments about the material context in shaping the degree of violence interdependence present in different spaces. Against this backdrop, contemporary Realism (particularly neorealism), despite its intense focus on anarchy, emerges as a significantly truncated descendant of republican security theory because it has largely dropped, or treated in an ancillary fashion, the interdependence part of the anarchy-interdependence problematique.

Violence Interdependence across Space and Time

As noted earlier, material contextual analyses divide into two relatively distinct bodies, ancient and early modern physiopolitics and late modern global geopolitics. The first, stretching from the ancients through the modern Enlightenment, examined variations in material context across space. In the second, beginning with the industrial era and extending to the present, changes in technology are understood to be producing changes in material context across time. The first, naturalist or physiopolitical, phase of material contextual analysis was formulated in the idioms of geographic spatial analysis, and was focused on the ways in which violence interdependence *differed from place to place.* Crossing the industrial divide in the nineteenth and twentieth centuries, these lines of argument continue, while losing their unifying vocabularies. What is most distinctive of the last two centuries of global geopolitical contextual-materialist security theorizing is the effort to grapple with *changes in material context driven by technological change* and the resulting increase in the size of areas marked by strong and intense degrees of violence interdependence.[11]

In order to bring the overall trend in the material context, captured in the term globalization, into a unified framework within which the development of republican and other structures can be analyzed, it is useful to map patterns in the *degree of violence interdependence across space and time* (see figure 1.4). On the vertical axis, four grades of spatial area are sequenced as rough order-of-magnitude increases: *micro* (the area of a city-state, such as ancient Athens), *meso* (the area of a modern European nation-state, such as France), *macro* (the area of a continental federal or imperial state such as the United States or the Soviet Union), and *mega* (the entire habitable territory of the earth). On the horizontal axis, four rough periods of technological capability as the main determinant of violence interdependence are specified: the *premodern* period stretching back to the agricultural revolution (marked by the destructive technologies of swords, bows and arrows, and the transport technologies of the horse and coastal vessels), the *early-modern* period beginning around 1500 (marked by the 'gunpowder revolution' and the advent of oceanic communication and navigation capabilities), the *industrial* period stretching from the middle of the nineteenth to the middle of the twentieth centuries (marked by steel weapons and high explosives and railroads, steamships, and airplanes), and the *nuclear* period of the last half century (marked by nuclear explosives and ballistic missiles).[12] Within this matrix of spatial variation in size and temporal change in capability, it is possible roughly to map the occurrence of the four grades of violence interdependence (absent, weak, strong, intense) (recall figure 1.3). Within this framework we can see the two problematiques concerning anarchy and republican and hierarchical forms (recall figure 1.1) in their major stages of development. Because this figure serves as an organizing framework for the detailed exegesis ahead, it is useful to observe six major facets of the argument it summarizes.

First, concerning violence interdependence and anarchy (moving up the diagonal sequence of A1–4), there appears to be a striking trend of increase in the sizes of the areas subject to intense violence interdependence, culminating in the nuclear era with the presence of intense violence interdependence on a global scale. Within this trend, we see the core argument of the first problematique about the security incompatibility of intense violence interdependence and anarchy being repeated and applied to successively larger spatial scales. In the premodern period, Thucydides' account of the civil war in Corcyra provides an image of the perils of first anarchy in a microsized area.[13] In the early modern era, Bodin's and Hobbes's depictions of religious civil wars, culminating in the Thirty Years' War in Germany, provide an image of the perils of first anarchy in a mesosized area subject to intense violence interdependence. In the industrial era the accounts of E. H. Carr and others of the 'European Civil War' of the First and Second World Wars provide an image of the security perils of first anarchy in a macrosized continental area of Europe as a whole. In the nuclear era, Herz's and Morgenthau's anticipations of a global nuclear war, a total war on worldwide scale, convey the perils of anarchy combined with intense violence interdependence in the megasized area of the entire planet. In each of these steps, the security perils of a first anarchy are seen occurring or potentially occurring on a larger scale, and some form of authoritative government is deemed necessary for security.

Second, a central feature of the first three steps up the A diagonal (figure 1.4) is that the consolidated political authorities required to avoid the perils of first anarchy are themselves units within an even larger area characterized by strong violence interdependence (sequenced on the B diagonal) and are thus also subjected to the incentives and restraints inherent in a second anarchy. Thus the consolidated political authorities of a mi-

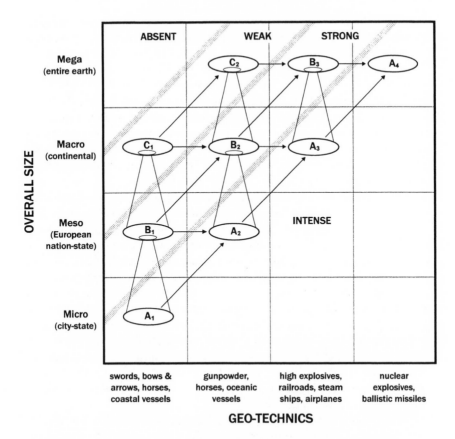

Figure 1.4 Degrees of Violence Interdependence across Space and Time

crosized Greek city-state are in the demanding but tractable second anarchy of the Greek city-state system. In the early modern era, the consolidated political authorities of a mesosized nation-state such as France or
Britain are in the demanding but tractable second anarchy of the European state system. In the industrial era, the consolidated political authority of a continental, macrosized multinational state, such as Russia or the
United States, experiences the security imperatives of a second anarchy
on a global scale, as would a unified Europe, whether as a Hitlerian panregional empire or a federal union. Thus, in each of the first three periods,
a larger second anarchy was forming at the same time that a smaller first
anarchy was creating security imperatives for authoritative government
in an area previously characterized by strong violence interdependence.

Third, the evolution in the size of republican polities can also be seen
as a series of steps along the A diagonal (figure 1.4). In the premodern era,

the nearly direct democracy of Athens had the minimum size necessary to be potentially viable in the Greek city-state system. In the early modern period such city-state republics were decreasingly viable in a system of nation-states, and only the innovations of representative constitutional republicanism, most prominently in Britain, enabled republics to be large enough to be viable. In the global industrial era, republican nation-states such as Britain and France were decreasingly viable in a system of continental-sized powers, and only the American innovation of federal republicanism enabled republics to be viable. It is this movement up the A diagonal that constitutes what I shall refer to as the 'the main axis of republican security theory.'

Fourth, bringing violence interdependence back into the analysis of anarchy underscores a key fact, somewhat obvious, but easily overlooked by the Realist assumption of 'anarchy from time immemorial': the relationship between actors or units with absent violence interdependence (empty upper-left-hand corner, figure 1.4) is fundamentally different from the relationship between actors or units with violence interdependence. Thus, for example, the security relationship between the Romans and the Mayans in the second century is fundamentally different from the relationship between, say, France and Britain in the eighteenth century. For a situation to be an anarchy (literally 'no rule') there must be enough violence interdependence for rule to be possible in principle. In order to capture this distinction, and register the historically circumscribed occurrence of anarchy, it is useful to refer to a situation with absent violence interdependence as a *nullarchy*.

Fifth, globalization, understood as rising levels of interdependence, divides roughly into three distinctive periods (C2, B3, A4). The first phase (C2), stretching from the European reconnaissance of the global ocean and its littorals until the onset of the industrial revolution, is marked by weak violence interdependence on a megascale and spawned the first, albeit slow motion, 'world' wars. Due to the previous near absence of technological diffusion (particularly between the 'old' and the 'new' worlds), this phase of globalization is marked by highly asymmetrical distribution of capabilities and the erection of light and loose predatory empires. The second phase (B3), stretching from roughly the industrial railroad penetration of the continental interiors through World War II, is marked by strong violence interdependence on a megascale and the emergence (as well as failed coalescence) of continental-sized units interacting in a highly competitive interstate system in second anarchy spanning the entire planet. The third phase (A4), stretching from the development of nuclear explosives and global-reach delivery vehicles to the present, and experiencing intense violence interdependence on a planetwide scale, generates the violence global village whose implications for security remains at the center of contemporary dispute.

Finally, the contemporary period of the planetary or nuclear era emerges as partially similar to and partially different from the preceding steps. The formation of authoritative world government, now cast by contemporary Realist international theorists as utopian and unprecedented, would *not* be novel in a fundamental way: where anarchies are combined with intense violence interdependence, authoritative government is needed for security, and the establishment of an authoritative world government would be simply doing again what has been done many times before. What is fundamentally novel about the present situation, however, is that the expansion of the area marked by intense violence interdependence has not been accompanied by the simultaneous emergence of an even larger area within which strong violence interdependence is present. Barring an invasion by extraterrestrials or substantial colonization in outer space, a world government would be unlike all previous governments because it would not need to cope simultaneously with the threats emerging from both internal and external anarchy, and therefore would not need to have foreign policy. A world government would need to address only the problems of internal anarchy and hierarchy. This suggests that a world government along federal-republican lines could be more purely constituted by mutual restraints than any previous republic because it would not require hierarchical elements necessary to balance against outside threats. Thus a political form previously marginal and incomplete due to its difficulties in coping with external anarchical threats would be for the first time fully appropriate for a security situation.

Second Anarchy, Hierarchy, and Material Contexts

The *main* argument of the anarchy-interdependence problematique, as we have seen, is that situations of intense violence interdependence combined with anarchy are a first anarchy. First anarchies are incompatible with security, and the size of the space with intense violence interdependence has expanded over time with far-reaching implications for security. As such, the main argument of the first problematique is of particular relevance when changes in material contexts transform a second anarchy into a first anarchy. But it offers little insight about the routine interstate relations commonly occurring in situations marked by weak or strong violence interdependence, or about whether contexts marked by the middle degrees of violence interdependence will tend to be anarchic or hierarchic. Anarchies in situations of weak and strong violence interdependence are, by definition, second anarchies. But not all situations of weak and strong violence interdependence are anarchies; some are hierarchical (empires). This poses the question of whether other material contextual factors in situations of weak and strong violence interdependence will favor hierar-

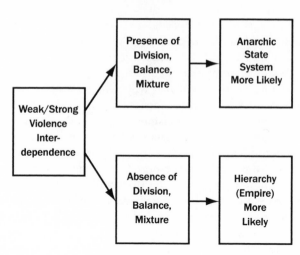

Figure 1.5 Material Contexts, Anarchic State Systems, and Hierarchy

chy or second anarchy. In this nested and subordinate way we encounter the main ideas now associated with a truncated version of the first problematique, the 'anarchy problematique' of neorealism.

Material contexts are the prime movers in structural-material arguments, and the most important such factor is the degree of violence interdependence. To move beyond the general proposition that government is not a security imperative in situations of weak or strong violence interdependence to arguments about whether second anarchy or hierarchy will be favored in such contexts requires a finer-grained examination of material context. The three most important factors are (in rough ranking of significance): *division, balance,* and *mixture* (see figure 1.5). Cast in republican language, these three factors specify material contextual restraints that impede the formation of hierarchy.

First, material contextual *division* refers to a situation marked by a fragmented topography. It is possible to speak of broad patterns of violence interdependence along the four-part spectrum (absent, weak, strong, and intense), but such specifications are averages and aggregates of often more complex configurations. Division stems from topography, the shape of the physical environment as it impedes or facilitates human mobility and thus interaction. Natural geographic material environments with smooth topographies, such as are present in plains, facilitate mobility, and thus interaction and interdependence, in effect enlarging the size of the space within which anarchy is intolerable for security. Conversely, uneven topographies, such as those marked by mountains or land interspersed by bodies of water, impede military mobility, and thus violence interdependence, in effect shrinking the size of the space within which anarchy is intolerable for security. Stretching from the Greeks through the Enlightenment to global geopolitics, there is a fairly robust consensus on the relationship between topographical division and political order that was inductively developed through a comparative examination of actual geographies and political arrangements.[14] The topographic fragmentation of Greece was seen as the natural setting for its numerous small polities in a systemic anarchy. In contrast, the topographic continuities of the river basins and plains of Egypt and Mesopotamia were the natural seats for larger, more hierarchic regimes that had submerged numerous smaller polities into an imperial peace. In the early modern period this line of thinking was applied to the larger space of Europe and comparably sized regions elsewhere in Eurasia that had come into European view. The fragmented topography of Europe was seen as the natural seat of a fragmented anarchical political order, in contrast to regionwide universal monarchies elsewhere.[15]

Second, the *balance* of power also shapes whether situations of weak and strong violence interdependence will tend toward hierarchies or anarchies. The main republican view is that hierarchies are avoided, whether internally within a polity or externally between different polities, by the presence of an at least roughly balanced distribution of capabilities between actors. A situation in which the distribution of capability is roughly equal, or balanced, restrains the formation of hierarchy because any actor seeking domination over others is potentially checked by the power of others. This idea, as even the most casual student of contemporary international theory cannot help but know, is central to what has come to be called Realism and particularly neorealism. However, as we shall see at length (chapter 5) this idea was among the basic ideas of republican political theory from its inception, and this idea came to be applied to international systems during the Renaissance and Enlightenment by numerous republican theorists who widely voiced the view that state systems were 'republics' precisely because the balance of power (and other power restraint situations and practices) prevented the emergence of a hierarchical 'universal monarchy.' The concept of the balance of power as a restraint on hierarchy is both unmistakably a legacy of republican security theory and central to what contemporary Realism, particularly neorealism, takes to be its major theoretical insight, thus justifying the claim that much of Realism is derivative of republican security theory.

Third, a *mixture* of power restrains hierarchy. Mixture refers to a situation with a material context marked by a combination of both naval-maritime and military-landed capabilities. Such arguments appear prominently from the Greeks onward. The underlying notion here is that capabilities sometimes exhibit variable commensurability and fungibility.[16]

When power assets are significantly incommensurate, they cannot simply be added up or compared like units of money. Instead, power assets have built-in strengths and weaknesses that shape political outcomes independently of their distribution. This entails a 'toolbox' image of power assets: just as tools like hammers, saws, and screwdrivers vary in their ability to perform different tasks, so too power assets have various strengths and weaknesses shaping the tasks they can perform. States with their power assets concentrated in land power cannot readily bring their power to bear across water to insular naval states. At the same time, naval power, even if largely concentrated in the hands of one state, cannot readily be used to create a systemwide hierarchy because naval power cannot be used readily to conquer and occupy land. As we shall see, the two historical state systems that have been most robustly persistent as second anarchies (the modern European and the global-industrial) were both characterized by substantial mixture.

Three general points emerge regarding this summation of arguments about material context, second anarchy, and hierarchy. First, there is no general presumption that anarchic state systems (state-of-war second anarchies) characterize political structure at the broadest spatial scale of a security system. Empires (system-level hierarchies) that swallowed numerous states and entire state systems were expected in material contexts with high military mobility. Second, where anarchic state systems did persist, they were understood to be dependent upon restraints present in nature, upon the topographical fragmentation of the geographic space. Third, only within such anarchic systems were smaller units capable of being republics potentially viable. Overall, nature as a source of restraint was rarely a friend of political freedom.

Axiality, Integrality, and Distinctiveness

No analysis of arguments about material contexts and restraints on power would be complete without incorporating claims about special places or master assets that have the potential to dominate the entire system due to their special character and tendencies. Largely ignored by contemporary international theory, these arguments are commonly formulated about specific material contexts and lack a common conceptual vocabulary. These arguments can be captured by three terms: *axiality*, *integrality*, and *distinctiveness*.

Arguments about some particular place or capability with an influence vastly disproportionate to its size assert the existence of an *axial* quality, potentially capable of setting all else into dependent rotation. For example, Mahan claims that control of the Ocean would lead to control of the world, Mackinder claims this about the Heartland of Eurasia, and theorists of airpower and space power make comparable claims for the atmosphere and orbital space. Some observers of the nuclear era characterize fissionable material in a similar manner. In one sense these are claims about the balance or distribution of power, but they also presume, unlike most arguments about distribution, that there is a strong incommensurability between the axial asset and more mundane capabilities. The axial asset is so special and so different that it potentially outweighs much else.

Closely related and often conflated with axiality is *integrality*, the notion that a special place or asset has the tendency to consolidate into the hands of one actor. Thus Mahan not only held that the Ocean was an axial region, but also held that seapower would tend to consolidate into the hands of one state. Similarly, Mackinder not only held that the Heartland of Eurasia held the key to world domination, but also thought that it would tend, unless restrained appropriately, toward political consolidation. Theorists of outer space power similarly combine claims of axiality and integrality. These claims of a tendency to consolidate generally hinge upon claims about the lack of division, and a consequent tendency for the offense to dominate and for distributional advantages to snowball rapidly into complete asymmetry.

Another variant of this general approach concerns the *distinctiveness* of particular assets and capabilities, a measure of how different a particular militarily important violence capability is from routine activities prevalent in particular societies. Thus understood, distinctiveness has varied greatly. At one extreme, the military prowess of the Mongols, based on their superb riding and archery, was virtually indistinguishable from their main economic activities of hunting and herding, and so distinctiveness was low. At the other extreme, the technologies and materials of nuclear and space power, although not completely lacking civilian application, are highly distinctive from the mundane world of even advanced industrial societies. In between, the heavy industrial capacities for civilian and military activities, for example a truck and tank factory, are of medium distinctiveness because they convertible to one another but not without considerable time and effort.

Arguments about material contexts with special features are employed by advocates of political pluralism and power restraint, as well as by their opponents. If there are such special places marked by such tendencies, then restraints for preventing hierarchy must be configured appropriately and their prospects for success are shaped by the features of what they seek to restrain. Perhaps the most prevalent scheme for restraint is what might be termed *strategic neutralization*: a special place capable of dominating all actors is systematically removed or neutralized from interstate competition. Perhaps the best examples of this approach are proposals to comprehensively contain and separate nuclear material and to neutralize orbital space, although earlier examples also embody this approach. The prospects for successful strategic neutralization are likely to be greater when the special capability is highly distinctive, the axial asset is an uninhabited extraterritorial medium, and no actor has privileged access to it. Conversely, the prospects for successful strategic neutralization are likely to be diminished when the special capability has low distinctiveness, the axial asset is an inhabited territory, and one actor has privileged access to it.

SECURITY AND HIERARCHICAL AND REPUBLICAN STRUCTURES

Nested within the main argument about violence interdependence, anarchy, and government sits the second main problematique of Western structural-materialist security theory, the *hierarchy-restraint problematique*. The animating insight of the second problematique is the realization that *governments can themselves pose as severe a security threat as first anarchy*. Thus republican security theory holds that extremes of hierarchy can be as much a source of insecurity as first anarchy. Although republican analysis of political arrangements and their relationship to security becomes, as we shall see, complex in its articulation and application, there is a very simple schema (see figure 1.6) encapsulating the republican view of the relationship between political structures and security-from-violence. At its most elemental level, republican security theory holds that insecurity results from the extremes of both anarchy and hierarchy, both of which can manifest themselves internally and externally, thus producing four situations of gross insecurity: the internal anarchy of civil war (*stasis*), the external anarchy of total or annihilative war, the internal full hierarchy of tyranny, despotism, and totalitarianism, and the full external hierarchy of imperial rule. Thus framed, republican security theory is in a second way more complete than its Realist descendant because it includes analyses of hierarchy as a source of insecurity and practical solutions to this threat.

The genesis narratives and theoretical texts of Western political thought emphasize that republican forms emerge in reaction to the abuses of excessively hierarchical government. The Athenian democracy emerges as a mechanism for the prevention of tyranny, and the Roman Republic emerges through a series of popular rebellions against the abuses of kingship. In Polybius's seminal version of the cycle of regimes, a sequence of change proceeds from virtuous kingship to despotic democracy propelled by abuses of power, and here appears the first (extant) analysis of republican constitutions as a system of mutual checks and balances simultaneously

	Inside	Outside
Anarchy	Stasis & Civil War	Total War/ Annihilation
Hierarchy	Tyranny/ Despotism	Imperial Conquest & Subordination

Figure 1.6 Anarchy, Hierarchy, and Insecurity

restraining the abusive tendencies of all elements in the polity. Similarly, it is the fear that the Hobbesian sovereign erected to escape the anarchic state-of-nature would in turn become a security predator that conceptually animates the early modern republican 'constitutional' project.[17] As Locke puts it, an individual is "in much worse condition, who is exposed to the arbitrary power of a man, who has the command of 100,000, than he that is exposed to the arbitrary power of 100,000 single men."[18]

In asserting that the security threats of both anarchy and hierarchy must be addressed to achieve security, republicans posit that all legitimate government derives from *popular sovereignty*. Such popular sovereignty is understood not as majority rule but rather that all legitimate government is constituted by delegations of authority from the people as a whole. The emphasis upon mutual restraints and overall public sovereignty means that republics entail at least roughly symmetrically reciprocal relations of restraint among all the members of a legitimate political association.[19] While defenders and theorists of virtually all forms of political arrangements acknowledge that government in some ultimate sense should serve the public interest, republicans have been concerned with the theory and practice of sustainable arrangements of political authority to guarantee that the public's fundamental security interests actually are served.

Given this set of claims, republican theorists insist that hierarchical and republican political orders are fundamentally dissimilar structurally, as different from one another as both are from anarchy[20] (see figure 1.7). Authority in hierarchical polities flows 'down' from a unified center, but authority in republics is constituted by an 'upward' delegation of legitimate governmental authority from the people as a whole. In both hierarchical and republican polities, the delegation of authority from the sovereign must serve the sovereign's interests while at the same time preserving

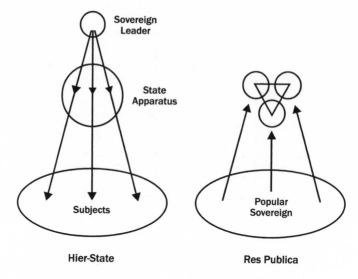

Figure 1.7 Hier-State versus Res Publica

sovereignty from usurpation. In republican forms, the pattern of authority is arranged so as to meet public needs, while at the same time preventing popularly delegated authorities from appropriating sovereignty from the people. In achieving these ends republican political theorists have identified a wide range of mechanisms or arrangements of restraint that are combined in different ways in different contexts.[21]

Despite the foundational and ubiquitous presence of this distinction between hierarchical and nonhierarchical forms of political order, contemporary structural and system structural international theory, now largely an enterprise of Realism, has refused to register republican forms in its basic conceptual vocabulary of structural types. Weber's influential division of forms of "legitimate authority" (traditional, charismatic, and bureaucratic) fails to include reciprocal or democratic arrangements as a fundamental type.[22] Similarly, Waltz's neorealist analysis of 'structural ordering principles' insists that all political orders are either anarchies, hierarchies, or their mixtures.[23] Therefore, in order to help better register the distinctive republican structural form, it is useful to expand the Realist dyad-spectrum typology into a triad-triangle typology by adding what might be termed *negarchy,* to capture the primacy of full and rounded restraints, or negatives, in republican political associations (see figure 1.8). Actors in hierarchies are in ordinate and subordinate relation; actors in anarchies are not authoritatively ordered; and actors in negarchies are authoritatively ordered by relations of mutual restraint. Just as there may exist both unit- and system-level anarchies and hierarchies, negarchic

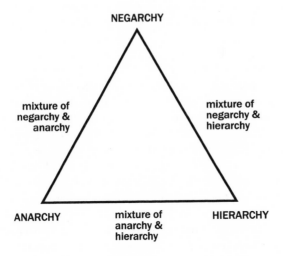

Figure 1.8 Three Structural Ordering Principles

forms also may exist as units (republics) and as systems (unions).[24] And just as there are a variety of ways in which hierarchies and anarchies can be combined, there also can be various mixtures of anarchy and negarchy, and of hierarchy and negarchy. By examining the ways in which the three structural forms relate to security and material contexts across space and time, republican security theory softens the hard analytic divide between 'unit' and 'system.' It provides a framework for analyzing all three forms 'all the way up' and 'all the way down,' to replace the Realist view of world politics as state units as hierarchies waxing and waning in a timeless and boundless ocean of anarchy.

As part of this program, republican security theory sees 'balances all the way up and down,' and conceptualizes 'balance of power' phenomena operating both internally and externally. When *interior* balances and balancing are brought back into security theory, the Realist ideas (appropriated from republicanism) of *exterior* balances and balancing are but parts of a richer matrix of balance arguments. Both negarchies and hierarchies are marked by *embedded* balance-of-power patterns. Republican negarchies are marked by varying degrees of muffled and *channeled balancing* and symmetrical and *recessed balances*. Conversely, hierarchies exhibit varying degrees of *asymmetric balances* and *suppressed balancing*, and often collapse when the coercive center weakens. As such, it is appropriate to speak of anarchies as exhibiting not balances and balancing per se, but rather *raw balancing* and *unmediated balances*.[25] A powerful indicator of a shift from one structural arrangement to another is the emergence of balance and balancing patterns common to another structure. The rise of gross imbalances of power capabilities between groups in a republic and the increasingly raw coercive use of concentrated power indicate a shift toward hierarchy. Similarly, the shift from an anarchy to a negarchy is indicated by the shift from the raw balancing toward balancing muffled and channeled through mutually accepted political processes.

Similarly, 'arms control' of differing types is constitutive of both hierarchies and negarchies, rather than a fleeting occurrence in interstate anarchies.[26] In hierarchies, arms control takes the form of a centralized monopoly of violence achieved and maintained through the systematic (and often coercive) disarmament of rival internal actors. In republics, arms are controlled by the people as a whole, either directly or indirectly.[27] Over time, the early republican approach of direct citizen control of arms through militias has gradually been supplemented and supplanted by institutional checks and balances. A strong indicator that a negarchy is evolving into a hierarchy is the emergence of a state apparatus with both autonomy and armed capacity to coerce the public. And a strong indicator that an anarchy is evolving into a negarchy is the establishment of increasingly cobinding mutual restraints on armed force.

Sovereignty, Authority, Democracy, and Unions

A brief examination of the vexed topic of sovereignty can shed further light on the characteristics of republican political forms. Sovereignty is often characterized as a 'fundamentally contested concept,' but semantic confusions masking straightforward political differences envelop this topic.[28] Some identify a particular disposition toward sovereignty as foundational in conceptualizing republican polities, while others see sovereignty and republics (particularly federal-republics) as essentially antithetical.[29] Properly understood, the concept of sovereignty invented by the early moderns serves as a useful heuristic device for conceptualizing the architectures of different political orders, particularly negarchical republican ones.

The basic meaning of sovereignty, as developed by Bodin, Hobbes, and William Blackstone, is that there is an ultimate and undivided *source* of legitimate authority in a polity. As Blackstone put it in his widely read *Commentaries*, "there is and must be in all [forms of government] a supreme, irresistible, absolute, uncontrolled authority, in which the *jura summi imperii*, or the rights of sovereignty, reside."[30] This meaning of sovereignty is often conflated with the related question of the locus of *authority*, which refers to the actual exercise of legitimate power; *autonomy*, which refers to the political independence of a polity vis-à-vis other

Location

The State   The People

Engaged	Hierarchy without Delegation	Direct Rule of the Whole People
Recessed	Hierarchy with Delegation	Compound Republic

Salience

Figure 1.9 Configurations of Sovereignty

polities; and *recognized autonomy* (or Westphalian sovereignty), which involves a polity's assumption of the rights, roles, and responsibilities of membership in a society of states.

Employing the distinction between sovereignty and authority allows us to capture two different dimensions of variation: *location* (where the ultimate source of legitimate authority lies) and *salience* (whether the sovereign actually exercises all political authority). Sovereignty can in both principle and practice be located or situated in any number of the components of a polity, but the two most important are sovereignty situated in one individual, or in all individuals as one group—'the people.'[31] The relation between the sovereign and the exerciser of authority is one of salience: to what extent does the sovereign body actually wield authority? The sovereign body may be either *engaged* or *recessed* in its exercise of authority. The sovereign is engaged when the sovereign and the actual wielder of governmental authority in a polity are one and the same. The sovereign of a polity is recessed when the actual exercise of authority has been *delegated* to some other body or bodies. With these distinctions we see four fundamentally different types of polities (see figure 1.9). It is important to note the central role that size plays in determining the salience of sovereignty. It is impossible for an engaged sovereign (whether monarchical or popular) to exist in a political order that is extensive in its size and number of members. Similarly, it is difficult for a recessed sovereign to exist in small-sized political orders.

The first and second configurations of sovereignty generate hierarchical political structures. In the second configuration, sovereignty is situated in a single individual who is not directly engaged in the exercise of political power. This 'top-down' vision of political order was inherited from the dominant medieval and Roman imperial models and was repeatedly asserted by early modern European absolute monarchs.[32] A great deal of energy was expended to assure that the delegations of authority necessary to operate such polities was distinguished from sharing in the royal sovereignty. It was against this conceptualization of political order that early modern republican and constitutional theorists began to employ an inverted assertion of 'bottom-up' sovereignty.

In the third and fourth configurations sovereignty is popular, which means it is situated in the whole people. As James Madison puts it, "the ultimate authority, wherever the derivative may be found, resides in the people alone."[33] It is important to emphasize that *popular sovereignty is not democracy*, in the sense of majority rule. It is impossible for a majority to be the embodiment of a popular sovereign, because this entails a division of the people into at least two parts (the majority and the minority), and sovereignty is by definition indivisible. If a democratic majority has all the authority in a political order, a hierarchy (a 'tyranny of the majority') exists between the majority and minorities. Hence substantial restraints on a popular majority are solely consistent with popular sovereignty. The third configuration of sovereignty—popular and engaged—constitutes a simple republic.[34] A necessary practical feature of such simple republican polities is that they must be small and homogenous, for otherwise it would not be possible for the sovereign—the people—directly to exercise political power.[35] The fourth combination—sovereignty located in the people but recessed—provides a heuristic to conceptualize negarchical political structures, patterns of authority marked by mutual restraints. The actual governance of a recessed sovereign public must be carried out by authorities with power delegated by the people rather than directly by the people, a move laden with both possibilities and perils. A larger popular sovereign is potentially more secure from external predation and is less threatened by the debilitating effects of internal faction. But the danger of usurpation increases as the exercise of political authority becomes more remote from the popular sovereign. The essential remedy is to construct more structural restraints on the exercisers of governmental authority. As a popular sovereign becomes larger and more extensive, it necessarily becomes more recessed, and as this happens structural restraints grow in importance. This combination of further delegation and added restraints is sufficiently different in its overall architecture to warrant a new label, what Madison termed a 'compound republic.' This arrangement contrasts with both the *simple republic* analyzed by city-state republican theorists and what Montesquieu termed a *confederate republic*, a union of republican units (an anarchy-negarchy mixture). This way of framing the issue of sovereignty helps dispel a number of confusions among some republicans and statists that result from conflating sovereignty and authority. The claim of some republicans that sovereignty must be divided to preserve public security is a confused formulation of the axiom that in a republic parts of political authority are exercised by several distinct bodies, and that the parts composing such polities retain some autonomy vis-à-vis one another. Similarly failing to distinguish sufficiently between authority and sovereignty, many statists and Realists tend to make the leap from the definitional point that divided sovereignty is impossible to the erroneous conclusion that a divided configuration of authority structures is impossible or inconsistent with sovereignty.

Finally, interstate unions, which entail the delegation of specified authorities to international organs, are expressions rather than violations of sovereignty for republican polities founded on popular sovereignty. To deny the intrinsic republican constitutionality of such unions (as do American neoconservative and Realist 'new-sovereigntists') is to confuse interstate autonomy with republican sovereignty, and to implicitly situate sovereignty in the state apparatus rather than the people, in the tradition of European absolutist statecraft. Most importantly, such unions can serve and conserve a popular sovereign as a potentially vital tool to exit anarchy and diminish pressures for the erection of a hierarchical state apparatus deformative of interior balances favorable to political liberty.

Republican Size, Interior Balances, and Type Change

These observations about republican unions point toward the topic of size and structure.[36] A central contribution of Greek and modern Enlightenment political science, particularly Aristotle and Montesquieu, was efforts to categorize regime types and empirically catalog the constitutions of actual political associations. The nomenclature of these systematic investigations—various types labeled as different 'archies' (democracy, oligarchy, monarchy, etc.)—are still the working vocabulary of contemporary political science and political discourse. But an important set of arguments developed by Aristotle, Montesquieu, and others relating variations in size with variations in structure has largely disappeared.[37] In the pervasive natural-biological metaphors of the 'body politic' early political science sought to relate observed variations in overall size with variations in internal structure. The early view was that republics tended to be small, monarchies medium sized, and despotic empires large, a schema apparently confirmed by the much-studied evolution of the ancient Roman constitution.

Underlying these arguments about the relationship between size and regime type is the idea of *scale effect*. Articulated by Aristotle and formulated more clearly by Galileo in the sixteenth century, scale effect has

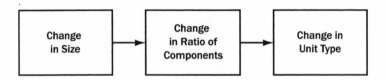

Figure 1.10 Scale Effects

been incorporated as a basic working concept in engineering, biology, and other disciplines concerned with morphological architectures and whole-part relationships.[38] The central notion of scale effect is that if the size of a multipart entity changes (increases or decreases), then the proportion between its parts also inevitably changes, producing a different type of entity (see figure 1.10). The scale effect thus helps explains how changes in quantity produce changes in quality.

In relating this general logic of scale effect to political phenomena, the crucial insight, most fully articulated by Hume and Montesquieu, is that increases in the size of a polity alter its interior balance of power.[39] As this happens some problems are ameliorated and some are exacerbated, but the overall *structural configurations needed to prevent simultaneously hierarchy and anarchy internally and externally vary with size*. Changes in size alter interior balances in two ways. First, assuming that there must be a roughly constant ratio between the size of the government and the size of the polity, a change in overall size shifts the balance between the power of the government and power of any individual or group in directions unfavorable for liberty. Second, a change in overall size exacerbates the collective action problem faced by individuals and groups in coordinating enough power to balance against the center.[40] In a small polity where citizens can gather in one place, the collective action problem entailed in interior balancing is negligible compared to a large and extended polity where such assemblies are impossible.

Understood in the light of scale effects, the main internal structural innovations of security-restraint republicanism moving from the city-state polis to the continental federal union can be understood as compensations for republic-threatening alterations in interior balances caused by scale-ups related to changes in material and systemic contexts (see figure 1.11). In the shift from the nearly direct democracy of the city-state polis to the representative constitutional nation-state, the innovation of *representation* (the delegation of authority by groups of citizens to individuals who can assemble in one place) addresses the collective action problem, and the articulation of various divisions and separations of power erects barriers to the employment of the greater absolute power of the government.

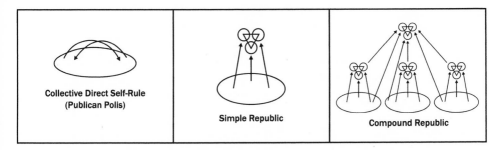

Figure 1.11 Republican Forms and Size

Moving from the representative constitutional nation-state to the federal union, the innovation of *federalism* (the division of government into two tiers) is combined with representation and a further articulation of the separation of power to achieve similar ends. Against the baseline of the original three types (republics, monarchies, and empires), these two modern republican forms constitute new types. Representative constitutional republics are structurally antiabsolutist states, and federal unions are structurally antidespotic empires, new types or arrangements of structures preserving public security from hierarchy.

EXTERNAL BALANCING, DOMINATING, HIDING, AND COBINDING

Whatever the sources of restraint that produce second anarchies, units configured as republics throughout history have had to eke out security in them. Like all other types of political associations, republics have had to grapple with security threats posed by the external interstate anarchy, but their foreign policies face distinctive issues. The republican project of providing security by simultaneously avoiding the extremes of anarchy and hierarchy, both internally and externally, is both given added importance and complicated by the republican claim that *extremes of hierarchy and anarchy feed upon one another.* Extreme domestic hierarchy provokes rebellion, propelling a polity into the anarchy of civil war and revolution, while the threats posed by external anarchy tend to stimulate the creation of domestic hierarchy. From the dual aversion to hierarchy and anarchy and their mutually reinforcing tendencies arises a set of foreign policy concerns and practices distinctive to republics. Republics are seen as having distinctive relationships with the four main foreign policy practices of *hiding, balancing, dominating,* and *cobinding*[41] (see figure 1.12).

Despite the fact that various concepts of 'balance' in international theory largely derive from republican security theory, significant aspects of

---

	Main Material-Contextual Prerequisites	Effect on Unit Structure	Effect on System Structure
HIDING	Weak Violence Interdependence	Reinforces Negarchy	Reinforces Anarchy
BALANCING	Roughly Symmetrical Distribution	Reinforces Hierarchy	Reinforces Anarchy
DOMINATING	Asymmetrical Distribution	Reinforces Hierarchy	Generates Hierarchy
CO-BINDING	Roughly Symmetrical Distribution & Intense Violence Interdependence	Reinforces Negarchy	Generates Negarchy

Figure 1.12 Foreign Policies, Material Contexts, and Structural Effects

the interstate practice of 'balancing' subvert republican polities. Republican polities do have some advantages in interstate anarchies. They are recognized as having particular affinity for interstate alliances, or *external balancing*, and their high levels of internal legitimacy add to their ability to mobilize power internally.[42] More importantly, however, they are seen as fundamentally compromised by the ways in which significant *internal balancing* (the domestic mobilization of resources to counteract external threats) alters *interior balances* (the relative capacities and authorities of domestic actors). Specifically, republican theorists argue that successful competition in an interstate anarchy tends to deform and ultimately destroy internal republican structures of mutual restraint. Faced with external threats, republics must mobilize their resources and centralize their authority structures. If external threats are significant and persistent, these responsive measures tend to become permanent, pushing domestic structures away from republican negarchy and toward hierarchy. Until very recently, the problems of securing republics in interstate anarchies have been particularly acute due to the severe limits on the size of republics. Even when republics have been large enough relative to their rivals in interstate anarchy to enjoy a plausible security viability, they have suffered severe security problems not shared by hierarchical polities.

Unfortunately, if a republic is strong enough to escape chronic interstate threats by *dominating* (conquering its rivals and establishing an empire), then imperial rule also tends to deform and ultimately to destroy domestic republican arrangements. To cope with external anarchy by dominating, interior balances are deformed, and internal negarchy gives way to internal hierarchy. Within the confines of the choice between defending from conquest or conquering, failure is immediate failure and success is eventual failure. Thus arises one of the most central and extensively analyzed problems of republican theory, beginning with reflections on the expansion and fall of the Roman Republic, continuing in the early modern republican obsession with the perils of the standing army, and culminating in twentieth-century American fears that successful competition in the global state system would require the erection of a totalitarian 'garrison state.'[43]

Given these unfavorable dynamics, republics are seen as having a proclivity to pursue, where possible, *hiding* (policies of isolationism) and to be more viable in settings of relative isolation. To the extent policies of hiding are feasible, they diminish the need to deform interior balances through internal balancing. Unfortunately, the successful pursuit of isolationism depends upon a degree of isolation that is often exceptional in interstate systems. From its earliest inception, republican security theory has observed that republican viability in second anarchies is significantly enhanced by the presence of various natural-material restraints, most notably bodies of water and mountainous terrain, which have the effect of reducing the violence interdependence between these naturally protected areas and other parts of the system. In antiquity the Greek city-state republics are seen as gaining security viability due to the mountainous and broken land-sea terrain of Greece. In early modern Europe the anomalous republican polities of Venice and then Holland and Britain gained viability in their respective state systems due to the barriers of insularity or near insularity, and the Swiss confederation emerged and persisted long after other landed areas in Europe had either been conquered or transformed into hierarchical units. And the organization of the United States as a republic is widely seen as possible due to the fact that the Atlantic Ocean reduced the threat posed by initially much more powerful European states.[44] The importance of these widely discussed geographical facts in the history of republican polities can be cast in terms of violence interdependence: republican viability is enhanced when geography creates enclaves in which actors face weak violence interdependence with other actors in a system generally characterized by strong violence interdependence.

Cobinding, the final option for restraining the threatening and corrosive effects of external anarchy, entails republics joining together with other republics in various forms of unions (alliances, leagues, confederations, and federations). Such arrangements aggregate power in order to enhance their ability to survive without deforming and destroying their domestic balance-of-power systems. Such unions do not reduce threats

58 CHAPTER 1

from other polities, but rather they alter the aggregate balance of power between republics and their rivals. All polities, regardless of their internal patterns of authority, have the incentive and have shown the ability to form various ad hoc alliances in order to counterbalance outside common threats, but republics have both particularly strong incentives and abilities to cobind in order to form temporary alliances and more lasting confederations and federal unions.[45] Republics have a greater incentive to form interstate unions because such unions make less necessary the centralization of authority, and thus less likely the deformation of domestic republican forms. At the same time, republics have a particularly strong ability to create such unions, because the structure of the union extends their fundamental constitutional arrangements on a more extensive spatial scale. While hierarchical polities operating in interstate anarchies may be driven to make ad hoc alliances against threats, the tendency of republican polities to become more hierarchical in competitive interstate anarchies gives republics an incentive to either escape competitive dynamics where possible or to transcend them through various abridgements of anarchy. Where suitable partners for such unions are absent and republics are forced to survive in an anarchical system populated by hierarchies, situationally tragic trade-offs and dilemmas arise.

Taken as a whole, the arguments of republican security theory about the prospects for republics in anarchic state systems are anything but optimistic, and until very recently, tragic. Given the aversion of republics to interstate anarchies, a central concern for republican security theorists has been finding or creating restraints in anarchies, situations or arrangements in which the security challenges posed by systemic anarchies have been moderated or limited either by the material context or by mutually restraining political arrangements. Unfortunately for republican security, neither of these options for restraining the security threats of external anarchy are universally available. The number of geographical enclaves affording a measure of natural security is obviously shaped and limited by geographic realities uncontrolled by human agency. While the creation of a union of republics is an act of human politics, such unions are viable only when there are enough proximate republics to be suitable partners for union.

DETERMINISM, AGENCY, AND PRACTICAL POLITICAL SCIENCE

In closing this brief reconstruction of the arguments of the two problematiques of republican security theory, it is appropriate to reflect on the implicit 'ontology' (understandings of social primitives) underlying these substantive arguments. In recent years, international theorists have become much more self-conscious and sophisticated in treating such 'meta-theoretical' issues, but these debates have tended to pit advocates of very pure and simple ontologies, most notably 'rationalism' and 'constructivism,' against one another. Unfortunately, such pure ontologies—however gratifying for their coherence—contradict our commonsense experience of the world as a complex and shifting amalgam of very ontologically different dimensions. Like the proverbial story of the blind men insisting that the elephant is like its leg, trunk, side, ear, and so forth, contemporary pure ontologizing provides radically incommensurate views that we intuit must somehow be synthesized or at least combined.

In contrast to this contemporary quest for ontological purity and coherence, republican security theory operates with a *mixed ontology* that incorporates in one rough model a diversity of fundamental insights often taken to be antagonistic or inconsistent with one another. Insights about human nature and the natural-material context are combined with the structuralist image of human agency as a free but contextually constrained force with the constructivist view of political practices as generating political structures. But all combinations of elephant parts do not an elephant make. Republican security theory specifies a particular combination of these elements to form an understanding of the world within which the pursuit of security necessarily takes place.

In this understanding, human political security arrangements are practically constructed mediations between the unchanging natural need for security and the variable and changing constraints and opportunities of the material context. Other aspects of human nature can impede or facilitate these efforts, as can existing political arrangements and material contexts, but the goal of security is the measure against which security practices are judged successes or failures. Political practices and structures are not part of nature. They are created by humans with diverse identities, interests, capabilities, and understandings. But *which* political arrangements and structures are security-viable in a particular context is not socially constructed. The material context presents varying and changing practical violence possibilities that shape which sets of restraints are needed or not needed for security to be achieved. The material environment composed of the interaction of geography and technology are for human *practical* purposes effectively revelations of natural possibilities not primarily constructed by humans.[46] But which arrangements humans actually arrive upon can be impeded or facilitated by material contexts (along with numerous other factors) but are not fully determined by them.

Within this worldview the nexus of determination and agency pivots around the notion of function. Two different, related and often conflated, types of function arguments appear: *functionality arguments* (claims about which arrangements are functional in meeting some goal or purpose) and *functionalist arguments* (claims that outcomes emerge *because* they meet some goal or purpose). Of these, it is the older functionality arguments that are most central to the main lines of argument in republican security theory. Its core arguments about the relationships between the material contextual variables of violence interdependence and the security viability of anarchy, hierarchy, and republican negarchies are typically posed as arguments about what is functional, rather than about explaining what exists by its superior functional fit. Hobbes, for example, does not say that a state-of-nature anarchy will always give way to a sovereign state or that a state-of-nature necessarily causes the creation of a state. Rather he says that if there is going to be security, then a state-of-nature anarchy must give way to a sovereign state order. Similarly, the arguments of the global-industrial and planetary-nuclear era about the growing inviability of the anarchic state system, first at the continental scale in Europe and then at a worldwide scope, do not maintain that a European and then a global consolidation *will* happen, but that it *must* happen to achieve security.[47]

This understanding of the world, combined with the animating goals of normative survivalism, produces a political science that is practical in character and more inspired by medicine than physics, economics, or cybernetics. Political science seeks knowledge with practical use-value for security seekers. Political science knowledge is sought to preserve the survival, health, and well-being of the 'body politic.' Sound practical knowledge is that which is useful in protecting human animal corporeality from destruction in an indifferent and complex natural-material environment.[48]

Chapter Two

RELATIVES AND DESCENDANTS

Only something with no history can be defined.
—Friedrich Nietzsche[1]

SITUATING REPUBLICAN SECURITY THEORY

Due to their scope and antiquity, the arguments of republican security theory find partial articulation in a vast number of theorists stretching from the Greek Enlightenment to the present. No one theorist makes all these arguments, and some part of these arguments appears, if sometimes faintly, in virtually every theorist who attempts to shed light on the politics of security. Given this, it is useful to sketch some of the ways in which the arguments of republican security theory relate to and differ from other bodies of 'republican' thought and Realism and Liberalism. These general relationships are usefully visualized as a set of partially overlapping sets (see figure 2.1) in which republican security theory is a subset of all republicanism, and Realism and Liberalism are partial (and partially overlapping) subsets of republican security theory. Overall, security restraint republicanism is the rival sibling of other early varieties of republican thought, while Realism and Liberalism are in significant measure its forgetful incomplete descendants.

Fully sketching these relationships is an undertaking beyond the scope of this reconstruction and exegesis. This chapter offers a series of selective encounters with rivals and descendants, stretching from the beginning to the present. These encounters do not provide a full explication of the complexities of the different ideas and thinkers, but rather focus on how they derive and differ from republican security theory in their treatment of security-from-violence, mutually restraining political structures, and natural-material contexts. The first three sections survey other varieties of republicanism, the middle six sections examine hierarchy-restraint and anarchy-interdependence among select Realists, and the next two sections look at contemporary Liberalisms. The concluding section assembles these sketches to finish the overall mapping of where different arguments sit.

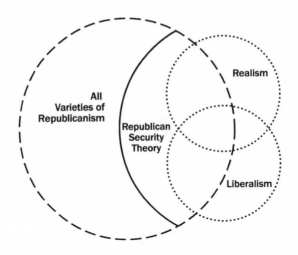

Figure 2.1 Situating Republican Security Theory

Classical Natural Law and Cosmopolitanism

Within the broad body of Western political thought, Plato and Aristotle, the two greatest extant political theorists of the Greek Enlightenment, are commonly associated with 'republicanism.' Both are major figures in the broader tradition of 'natural law' theorizing, which is further developed by Stoic and Christian metaphysical, ethical, and political thought.[2] Three central notions form the heart of the natural law tradition. First, the cosmos is a hierarchical 'great chain of being' in which humans have an appropriate position, and there exists a natural or divine template to guide human activity that human reason can apprehend. Second, natural law ethical thought holds that human happiness depends upon individual virtue whose achievement can be aided by philosophy and education. Finally, although natural law theorists often speak of the cosmos and the soul of the individual as 'republics' marked by equilibrium and restraint, good polities are characterized by hierarchy and virtue, rather than by political freedom and popular sovereignty.

Natural law and republicanism seem intimately related because Plato's most famous dialogue, the *Republic*, is one of the greatest works in the natural law tradition.[3] Here Socrates' quest to understand the nature of justice produces a lengthy analogy between the individual psyche and the constitution of the polis. Although concern for restraint, particularly of the appetites and of the warriors, is prominent, Plato evinces little interest in either individual or public freedom. Although there is dispute about

Plato's intended teaching in the *Republic*, the main governance idea commonly associated with it—the absolute rule of philosophical wise men—has much more in common with enlightened despotism than with security-restraint republicanism. The ideal regime described by Socrates is a dictatorship of wisdom, and so might more accurately be called a 'sophocracy' or a 'solonocracy' than a republic.

The relationship between Aristotle's political theory and the arguments of security-restraint republicanism are more intimate and complex, but still substantially removed. Many recent theorists of 'civic humanism' and the 'republican revival' emphasize the Aristotelian roots of the ideas they take to be distinctively 'republican.'[4] Aristotle's general concern with moderation, his analysis of the mixed constitution or 'polity' as the best practical regime, and his many arguments about the interplay of political structures and material contexts (explored in the next chapter) are consistent with the concerns of republican security theory. But central for most 'republican' appropriations of Aristotle is his emphasis on the centrality of political participation as an end in itself and as necessary for the good human life. Beyond these links, there are major differences, most importantly Aristotle's insistence on the primacy of political domination and hierarchy.[5]

Far wider in influence in antiquity, Greek and Roman Stoics provided the dominant ideology of the Hellenistic and Roman political elites during the centuries after the political eclipse of the polis city-state and enjoyed a major revival in early modern Europe. Most of the early major texts of ancient Stoicism are lost, but in its Roman and subsequent incarnations Stoicism appears to have focused far more on the psyche of the individual rather than political structures.[6] The entire universe, or cosmos, was conceptualized as the city or polis of the just man, and the Stoics' strong cosmopolitanism anticipates radical internationalist thought of the late modern era.[7] Classical Stoicism gave little attention to either political structures or material context, and so tended toward philosophical and moral idealism. The Stoics viewed freedom as mastery of the psyche's enslaving desires and passions rather than the absence of political domination. To the extent the Stoics conceptualized political orders, they emphasized appropriate hierarchy and the enlightenment of monarchical power rather than its overthrow, and they neglected individual political freedom and popular rule.[8] But the central role of temperance in Stoic conceptions of virtuous kingship clearly demonstrates the central role of restraint in even this largely apolitical and idealistic 'republican' tradition. Beyond these limited similarities and great differences, the main classical statements of republican security theory are not to be found in natural law, but rather in the theory and practice of Athenian democracy and the Roman Republic.

Civic Humanism and Neo-Spartan Republicanism

Another large and old body of thought that goes under the name 'republican' attaches central importance to political participation. Variously known as 'civic humanism,' 'communitarianism,' or 'neo-Athenian republicanism,' and central to the recent literature of 'republican revivalism,' this variety of republicanism traces back to the Aristotelian idea that man is a *zoon politicon*, a political animal, for whom political participation is an essential component of the good life.[9]

Political participation played a prominent role in the theory and practice of the polis, but plays a much diminished role in modern republics due to their enlarged size and devotion to commerce. Beginning with particular force in the later-eighteenth century, critics of modern extended commercial republican polities have idealized and radicalized various aspects of the ancient city-state as a model of the ideal political association and a basis for criticizing modern arrangements. Thus some of the most potent critics of modern republics launch their attacks in the name of ancient republics. As this happened, modern political republicanism split into two distinct branches, one exemplified by Rousseau and the radical democrats of the French Revolution such as Robespierre, another by Montesquieu and the moderates of the American Constitutional Convention of 1787 such as James Madison.[10]

Rousseau provides the most powerful modern evocation of the ghost of the polis as a guiding spirit for political renewal. Rousseau is both a strong democrat and a major source of ideas now seen as distinctively Realist, and he will be encountered again here. Despite the burning clarity of many of his formulations, Rousseau's sprawling corpus seems riddled with contradictions, and he has served as an inspiration for an amazingly wide variety of groups.[11] However, the conceptual center of gravity of Rousseau's system is a simple and powerful argument about the negative psychological impact of modernity. The problem for Rousseau is the alienation of each individual from his or her own true self, dooming modern humanity to unhappiness. The modern individualism of emergent capitalism and representative pluralistic democracy are implicated in this malaise, and this alienation marks the decaying ancien regime monarchies with their veneer of 'enlightenment' as well as the bustling commercial new form republics of the Dutch and British.

The solution for Rousseau is radical and unlikely to be realized except in exceptional circumstances. The natural freedom of early humans, marked by lack of interaction and dependence, cannot be recovered. But human freedom can be realized by "the total alienation of each associate with all his rights to the whole community."[12] Only through the complete self-subordination of each individual to the community can the individual be free of paralyzing internal division. As a model for this solution, Rousseau looks to ancient Sparta and early Rome, devoted to political equality, martial virtue, economic frugality, cultural isolation, and an all-pervading patriotic piety.[13] Thus the core of Rousseau's politics is a radically new case for the very old publican polity emphasizing the intrinsic value of strong communal solidarity and the systematic socialization of the individual into elaborate common mores.[14]

In the course of making this psychological critique of modernity, and in formulating his political solution, Rousseau draws extensively upon many of the ideas of republican security theory, particularly concerning size, material context, and political structures, as well as the logics of interstate anarchy, division, and balance. Despite the power of his overall argument and his many intersections with security-restraint republicanism, the core of his political view is oppositional to the 'first Liberalism' at the heart of republican security theory. Although Rousseau passionately proclaimed his devotion to 'freedom,' the communal participation he championed can be sharply antithetical to individual liberty as understood by the 'first Liberalism' of republican security theory.

After Rousseau's death, the radical French revolutionaries applied a simplistic version of Rousseau's neo-Spartan publican program for the comprehensive transformation of France. In their quest to realize the participation, virtue, and homogeneity of Rousseau's ideal publican polis, they launched a 'reign of terror' against nonconforming elements of French society.[15] Thus began a distinctively modern type of revolutionary publicanism in which an inspired revolutionary elite acting in the 'true interests' of the 'oppressed' majority produces despotism and the complete elimination of restraining structures to divide and balance power while rhetorically appealing to liberation.[16] Despite the disastrous record of modern revolutionary publican politics, nostalgia for the participatory polis remains strong among many intellectuals and political theorists who insist that the publican polis of ancient Greece provided the best political life and that the progress of the moderns has failed by comparison.[17] Nostalgia for the publican polity occurs on both the political right and the left, among Marxists as well as antiliberal conservatives, and it continues to serve for many as a powerful ideal against which the failings of modernity can be gauged.

Overall the antimodern publican program of the neo-Spartan republicans is a dead end. While the reinvigoration of public and community participation in contemporary liberal democracies is much needed, the more radical publican ideal is straightforwardly archaic. This program rests, as we shall see in the next chapter, on a flawed understanding of ancient republics because it fails to see the extent to which the illiberal

elements of ancient republics were necessary adaptations to their severe
security situations rather than ends in their own right. More importantly,
publican programs are radically utopian in the contemporary global village
created by intensifying globalization, a situation that demands substantive
cosmopolitan rather than parochial forms of community and identity.

REPUBLICAN REVIVALISM

Aside from the casual use of 'republic' as a synonym for liberal democracies, the most substantial contemporary presence of 'republicanism' is
among the recent school of intellectual historians known as the 'republican revisionists.' Prior to republican revisionism, which begins in the late
1960s, the two dominant interpretive traditions, Liberalism and Marxism, both tended to treat the rise of democracy and constitutional states
as derivative of the rise of capitalism and the bourgeoisie. Both Liberalism
and Marxism emphasized the rise to political primacy of 'possessive individualism,' the leading roles of Hobbes and Locke in the rise of Liberalism, and the progressive power of economic changes in displacing feudalism with liberal democratic capitalism.[18]

The revisionist's main claim is that a great deal of European and American political language in the eighteenth century concerned virtue, corruption, and participation, and was deeply hostile to market exchange and
the inequalities it produced. In the case of England this meant seeing the
axis of eighteenth-century political conflict between 'country and court'
rather than between the capitalist bourgeoisie and the feudal aristocracy.[19]
In the case of the American Revolution, this meant seeing grievances and
fears of monarchical conspiracies and usurpations expressed in the language of civic humanist republicanism rather than individual rights and
social contract theory.[20] Although critics have countered that individualistic and capitalistic Liberalism were also strong in the eighteenth century,
there is widespread agreement that civic humanist republicanism was very
strong.[21]

The republican revivalists do not, however, claim that the republicanism of the eighteenth century survived into the nineteenth. Civic humanist
republicanism died in the late-eighteenth century and was replaced by
individualistic and capitalistic Liberalism and representational constitutional democracy: "republicanism swooned; out of the Constitution's side
stepped liberalism."[22] Far from contesting the death of civic humanist
republicanism, the revivalists documented the exact date of its demise:
the years between the beginning of the American Revolution and the ratification of the Constitution saw the transformation of American expectations and discourse from the older civic humanism to an altogether new
type of political order.[23] The grievances of the Revolution had been framed

in the language of the public good, virtue, and the ideal of disinterested publics and leaders, but the actual politics of the newly independent American states was too centered upon interest, riven by faction, and bereft of a virtuous aristocracy to support a political order along civic humanist lines. The most the founders could hope to do was moderate and channel these interests. Within the triumphant mainstream tradition of Liberalism, republicanism ceased to carry any distinctive meaning, and soon became a casual synonym for democratic.

Republican security theory provides a significantly different account of the character and trajectory of early modern republicanism. The revivalists' emphasis upon ideology, language, and discourse does not adequately recognize the importance of practical problem-solving in republican thought. A highly idealistic image of politics results when discourses and institutions are analyzed without primary reference to the daunting security problems of early republics. Neglecting the security problem, the revivalists miss the really crucial early modern development, which is that free polities devoted to commerce are no longer vulnerable because of their wealth, but instead were increasingly secure and powerful because of it.

Because the revivalists focus upon words rather than institutional forms and functions, they see the eighteenth century as the final act of republicanism. In actuality early modern republicanism innovated new solutions to the problem of securing freedom that enabled republics to begin to transcend the severe strictures that had previously bound free polities. The rise of capitalist and individualistic free societies marks not the end of republicanism, but is rather the result of the new material contexts and institutional innovations that permitted free polities to secure themselves without the pervasive militarization of civil life. The virtues necessary for the security of freedom no longer needed to be primarily imprinted in the characters of the citizens, but were increasingly in the power restraint machinery of constitutions and in the physical machinery of nascent industrial-military technology. Missing the progressive character of republican power restraint practices, the revivalists erroneously assume that the particular complex of civic humanist political preoccupations (virtue, anticommerce) are equivalent to republicanism, when in fact they were historically particular forms required to secure freedom in particular material contexts.

ABSOLUTIST STATECRAFT AND ENLIGHTENED DESPOTISM

The project of security-restraint republicanism, particularly in early modernity, developed alongside and in opposition to hierarchical forms of government and their advocates. Beginning with Machiavelli (in *The Prince*), extending though Bodin and Hobbes, and culminating in the twentieth century with Carl Schmitt, a well-developed line of 'reason of state' thought deals with the internal logic and operation of statist hierarchies.[24] Here is found not only a straightforward embrace of hierarchy, but also an antiidealist and antiutopian rhetoric purporting to treat people and politics 'as they really are.' Despite its fundamental antagonism to the republican assumptions of popular sovereignty and structural restraint on hierarchy, the absolutist state building project found itself wrestling with the problem of restraint in an especially acute form: how can power, once concentrated and rendered autonomous, be controlled and directed for the security benefit of the entire polity?

Early absolutist statecraft was geared to the problem, particularly acute in early modern Europe, of providing security and public order in the face of the new power possibilities and the decay of the feudal order of Latin Christendom.[25] The theorists and practitioners of absolutist statecraft formulated the security problem as minimizing internal anarchy through the erection of a hierarchical state, which they argued was a path to greater security for the many and power for the few. The central organizing concept, illuminated most clearly by Bodin in the sixteenth century and Hobbes in the seventeenth, was the establishment of a central political actor invested with 'sovereignty.' In practice the absolutist solution entailed the disarmament and subordination of feudal lords and popular militias and concentration of violence capability in rationalized organizations subject only to the sovereign's authority.

Absolutist statecraft faced a theoretical and practical puzzle: how conceptually and practically to distinguish absolute monarchy from tyranny. From its Greek beginnings, Western political thought has universally viewed concentrated power used abusively, 'tyranny' or 'despotism,' as a severe political malady.[26] Advocates of highly concentrated and autonomous power have never sought to defend tyranny or simple despotism, but instead have sought to distinguish absolute monarchy and enlightened despotism from tyranny and despotism.

The problem of leader restraint inherent in all hierarchical forms of government was particularly acute for absolutist statecraft because it rejected the restraining influences of custom and religion, which had traditionally been widely held to be essential for preventing concentrated power from becoming arbitrary and tyrannical. Absolutist theory and practice sought to move beyond the feudal monarchical model in which the king was understood to be severely limited in power by custom and religion as well as the substantial powers held by the aristocracy and parliaments, and sought to turn religion into an agent of monarchical power rather than a limit on it.[27] In practice, absolutist states fell far short of achieving absolute power, but the restraint problem became more acute as the hierarchical ideal was approached.

To republican critics of the absolute state, these problems are inherent and unresolvable without fundamental departures from statist approaches. But theorists of absolutist statecraft developed a set of distinctive solutions to this problem that did not entail the compromise of hierarchy. To do this, some means had to be found to insure that the leader is internally restrained in the absence of external restraints. Three overlapping solutions were advanced: *reason of state* (conceptualize an objective rational state interest that is simple and easy to follow); *princely virtue* (improve the leader with internal self-restraint); and *enlightened despotism* (educate concentrated power about its true long-term self-interest in the exercise of power for the general good).

The terminology of 'reason of state' is an early modern invention, but it had many precursors, particularly among the Romans (whose works were intently mined by 'humanist' scholars). The distinguishing feature of early modern absolutist statecraft was the claim that there was an objective and rational interest that rulers could and should apprehend and follow. As Meinecke demonstrated in his classic treatment, the notion of a 'reason of state' was advanced as an objective standard that the state leader should pursue, transforming a ruler into the first servant of his own power, "serving some higher entity which rises far above individual life."[28] As the feudal constraints on kingship diminished, the state machine needed direction from a leader who was more than the head of clan or family and who had purged individual caprice and subjectivity from his public decision making. In this vein, Frederick II of Prussia, the fervent proponent and exemplar of this doctrine, proclaimed himself as much a servant of the state as its lowest functionary.[29]

The solution of princely virtue also long predated absolutism, and its cultivation was especially elaborate and sophisticated in ancient Stoic political theory, which the modern absolutists assiduously mined.[30] The literary vehicle for the cultivation of virtue in the prince was the 'mirrors of princes,' the numerous practical 'how-to-do' manuals that were produced in vast number.[31] The best known of these—Machievelli's *Prince*, Giovanni Botero's *Reason of State*, Walter Raleigh's *Maxims of State*, Cardinal Richelieu's *Testament*, and Frederick's *Anti-Machiavelli*—are but a small sampling of this genre. Despite the notorious innovations Machiavelli introduced, the essential Stoic theme of virtue as self-restraint remained central to these manuals.[32]

The third absolutist solution to the problem of leader restraint is 'enlightened despotism.' As far back as there have been intellectuals, there has burned the aspiration to cultivate and tame rulers, ideally into agents for their own highly particular vision of the ideal polity.[33] The subsequent association of the modern Enlightenment with Liberalism has tended to obscure the fact that the political theory and practice of the continental *philosophes* was often oriented toward 'enlightening' absolutist monarchies, such as Voltaire's attempt to enlighten Frederick II.[34]

Looking at absolutism's leader restraint program from the perspective of republican security theory, what is most striking is not its poor success rate, but rather the extent to which the absolutist project is understood by its advocates to hinge upon establishing a highly idealistic and utopian arrangement of rationalization, virtue, and enlightenment in the character of one individual. Only by building a psychic 'republic' of restraint in the character of externally unrestrained rulers can the universally recognized evils of tyranny be avoided. Whatever the prospects for such focused 'human engineering,' this dimension of the absolutist project rests upon its own hidden idealist and optimistic, if not utopian, program.[35] Nontyrannical hierarchies are revealed to depend upon a particularly utopian form of republicanism.

German Nationalist Statism and *Machtpolitik*

A brief survey of nineteenth- and early-twentieth-century German thought on the nation and the hierarchical state devoted to power politics will help illuminate the nonrepublican elements in Realism. Virtually all contemporary Realists identify the nation as a primary form of group association, think states are hierarchies, and view power politics as central to interstate life, but these views are commonly coupled with and circumscribed by the three polar ideas derived from republicanism. In order to help understand what a Realism without these republican elements might be like, it is instructive to examine these ideas as developed largely without the republican elements by the German writers so uniformly ignored by contemporary Realists.

In the historical development of political order in the German-speaking lands of middle Europe, the predations of French republican and imperial armies during the revolutionary and Napoleonic periods not only destroyed the ramshackle, if serviceable, edifice of the 'German Confederation' or 'Holy Roman Empire,' but also set in motion a process of national awakening and state-building whose eventual culminations proved so disastrous.

The move to elevate the nation as the primary form of political association, partially begun by Rousseau, finds fuller development in the thought of Herder. Breaking from his teacher Kant, the paragon of cosmopolitan Enlightenment in Germany, Herder developed a notion of progress culminating not in cosmopolitan peace, but rather in the increasing diversity of peoples and customs. For Herder variations in a myriad of natural-material factors, most notably 'soil' and climate, drive different parts of humanity toward a "form of human perfection" that is "national and time-bound, and considered more specifically, individual."[36] Echoing Rousseau, Herder declares that "prejudice is good, in its time and place," because it "urges nations to converge upon their centre, attaches them more firmly to their roots," and he observes that "the most ignorant, most prejudiced nation is often superior in this respect."[37]

This theme is further developed and more directly connected to politics by Fichte, who also began as a Kantian cosmopolitan before firmly embracing, in his passionate *Addresses to the German Nation*, the nation as the foundation for political community and the state. He declares that "love of fatherland" must govern the state, and that the state must pursue a "higher object than the usual [i.e., liberal] one of maintaining internal peace, property, personal freedom, and the life and well-being of all."[38] Much of this nationalist animus is directed against capitalist individualism and materialism corrosive of community, against rising international economic interdependence and against any form of international governance.

These ideas also appear in Hegel's grand philosophical edifice. Also criticizing the limitations of Kantian morality and individualistic civil society, Hegel looks to the state and the sacrifices it demands in war as the embodiment of a higher communal morality. In his view of states as moral entities, war serves as a corrective to the ills of peace, specifically excessive self-regarding individualism. Governments must periodically "shake them to the very center by war" in order that citizens do not become "rooted and settled" and "let the common spirit evaporate."[39] As ethical persons, states require other states against which to define themselves, and "even if a number of states make themselves into a family, this group as an individual must engender an opposite and create an enemy."[40] The state is thus more than a protector and provider, and war makes a necessary positive contribution to communal life that goes beyond protection.

This line of thought is further developed by Trietschke, whose *Politics* and lectures at the University of Berlin exerted wide influence in Bismark's Second Reich. In Trietschke's work the radicalized claims of national particularism are firmly wedded to Prussian militarism and authoritarianism to produce a harshly Realist *Machtpolitik*. For Trietschke, modern wars are not "waged for the sake of material advantage" but rather for the "high moral idea of national honour."[41] War enshrines "something positively sacred" and it compels "the individual to sacrifice himself to it." It also "fosters the political idealism which the materialist rejects" by producing the "heroes of a nation" who "rejoice and inspire the spirit of it in youth."[42] This idealistic and Romantic militaristic nationalism must be served by a powerful authoritarian state devoted to the successful pursuit of international power politics. The state "protects and embraces the people's life," and it "does not ask primarily for opinion, but demands obedience."[43] The cold rational *Machtpolitik* of the state, analyzed at length by Trietschke, serves not its own ends, but the particularistic nation. Or as Meinecke, his successor at the University of Berlin, puts it, when "the full consciousness of a great national community is once awakened," it "is not satisfied until everything is nationalized that is at all capable of nationalization."[44]

As the century turns, this line of argument, nourished by irrationalist and decisionist currents in European and German culture, comes to identify lust for power and domination, or *animus dominindi*, as natural to all humans and national states. As Meinecke puts it, this "striving for power is an aboriginal human impulse, perhaps even an animal impulse, which blindly snatches at everything around until it comes up against some external barriers." Such an "impulse is not restricted solely to what is directly necessary for life and health," and "man takes a wholehearted pleasure in power itself."[45]

Germany's defeats and devastations in the world wars stimulated chastised reflections among German nationalist statist theorists. In the wake of World War I, Meinecke's *Reason of State* continues his predecessors' themes, but he adds that the power drive of the nationalized masses must be tempered and channeled by a powerful and autonomous state following the cold calculus of 'reason of state.'[46] After the much more complete disaster of the Third Reich and World War II, Meinecke in *The German Catastrophe* becomes completely disillusioned with the political nation and nationalism and offers something of an autopsy of the radicalized national statist line of argument. He acknowledges that the "German power-state idea" finds "in Hitler its worst and most fatal application and extension" and says that "our conception of power must be purified from the filth which came into it during the Third Reich" and that "the purpose of power must be reflected upon and wisely limited."[47] Rejecting the "fighting folk character" culminating in Hitlerism, he urges a return to the cultural nationalism of "the peaceful volk character" with its "genuine Romanticism."[48] He looks to its protection not from an autonomous power state but rather as a "member of a future federation, voluntarily concluded, of the central and west European states," which would be a "United Nations of Europe."[49]

Often subterranean in Realist narratives, the idea of the primacy of the nation as a form of political community and of the hierarchical state are rarely far beneath the surface. Of course, few if any contemporary Realists subscribe to the extreme formulations of these ideas developed in late modern German thought. Nevertheless, a commitment to these two 'unit-level' arrangements plays a powerful role in Realist thought and helps explain why Realists have tended to drop the interdependence component of the anarchy-interdependence problematique when its analysis indicates the need to leave anarchy on larger scales to achieve security.

Turning from the topics of hierarchy and restraint to that of anarchy and material context, the next four sections scrutinize the progressive truncating of the anarchy-interdependence problematique into the anarchy problematique from early modern 'state of nature' arguments to contemporary Realism.

The Princess and the Pea: Nature and the State-of-Nature

Given the importance of the distinction between first and second anarchy in republican security theory, it is appropriate to examine the role of material contexts and violence interdependence in early modern state-of-nature arguments. A particularly pivotal version of the state-of-nature argument is found in Hobbes, who apparently coined the expression and whose argument serves as a summation of the ancient as well as the starting point for the modern analyses on this topic. Purporting to be a systematic recasting of Thucydides, Hobbes's formulation in turn stimulated widespread commentaries and modifications by many other early modern state-of-nature theorists, and readings of Hobbes's argument have been widely embraced by Realist international theory.[50]

Within state-of-nature arguments the importance of material-contextual factors are pivotal but easy to overlook. At first glance, these arguments seem to differ from ancient naturalist origin-of-civilization narratives by seeming to purge themselves of merely contingent nature in order to illuminate basic dynamics of human interaction. But in actuality, nature as the material context still plays a pivotal role. Assumptions about material context in state-of-nature arguments play a role much like the pea in the Brothers Grimm story of the "Princess and the Pea." No matter how many mattresses are piled upon the pea, the princess awakes with bruises. And no matter how many layers of deductive argument intervene between the natural fact (however arbitrarily chosen and underarticulated) and the argument's conclusion, the assumptions about nature leave their strong imprint. State-of-nature arguments may thus be read as abstract and somewhat cryptic structural-materialist security arguments in which the 'state' is formed to solve the predicaments posed by 'nature.' The formation of the 'civil state' can be seen as a compensation for vulnerabilities in nature as material context and the structural features of the civil state serve as solutions to these vulnerabilities. Thus, which natural facts a theorist uses to define the state-of-nature determine which particular arrangements of civil society are needed. Nature, far from disappearing, holds in thrall the entire state-of-nature argument.

In Hobbes's version of this kind of argument, he deploys the now common distinctions between the state-of-nature, the sovereign, and the state-of-war. Life in the state-of-nature is "solitary, poor, nasty, brutish and short."[51] In the state-of-nature each individual is his own master, but life is insecure. This vulnerability induces individuals to trade their absolute freedom for a minimum of security, provided by the "sovereign." In contrast, the state-of-war (not to be confused with actual war) exists between separate sovereigns.[52] Both the state-of-nature and the state-of-war are 'nasty and brutish.' Unlike individuals in the state-of-nature, however, sovereigns in the state-of-war are not subject to sudden death at each other's hands: they are in an anarchy vis-à-vis one another, but are not so vulnerable.[53] In short, what makes the state-of-nature unlike the state-of-war and less tolerable for security purposes is the presence of heightened levels of violence interdependence.

Viewed in this way, Hobbes's argument differs significantly from Realist readings. Realists have two radically opposed interpretations, both of which are incorrect. The dominant view is that Hobbes's state-of-nature and the interstate system are alike and that international life is *always* a state-of-nature.[54] A second interpretation holds that Hobbes's state-of-nature is *never* like interstate life because states are able to secure themselves in ways that individual humans cannot.[55] Both interpretations are incorrect because they fail to recognize that Hobbes's state-of-nature and state-of-war are ahistorical categories rather than propositions about actual historical entities. Hobbes provides criteria for assessing the security viability of different political arrangements, but the two erroneous readings make an unwarranted leap from Hobbes's ahistorical criteria to universal historical generalizations. Hobbes never says such-and-such a political entity is a state, and he never says how big or how inclusive a sovereign must be in order to be out of the state-of-nature.[56] Thus one can only ascertain whether a system with entities of x size with y capabilities are or are not in an Hobbesian state-of-nature after measuring those sizes and capabilities against the standards Hobbes sets forth: is their life precarious, and is this precariousness generally shared?

Hobbes's argument thus raises a crucial question that he does not address: why are particular sovereigns merely in a state-of-war and not in a state-of-nature vis-à-vis one another? Stated differently, how large must a Hobbesian sovereign be in order effectively to leave the state-of-nature? The answer to this question is outside the logic of Hobbes's model and implicitly assigned to the contingent natural-material context and the level of violence interdependence it presents. Whether entities claiming to be states can preserve themselves by their own efforts or whether they must band together as individuals in the state-of-nature are driven to do cannot be determined once and for all. The most one can conclude on the basis of Hobbes's categories is that sometimes interstate anarchical systems are like his description of the state-of-nature and sometimes not. When the relationship between the sovereigns becomes like that of individuals, then the logic of Hobbes's argument points inexorably toward the establishment of a more encompassing sovereign, even possibly a world state. To the extent contemporary Realists base their understanding of interstate systems on these two flawed interpretations of Hobbes, they have narrowed the anarchy-interdependence problematique into the anarchy problematique.

In contrast to Hobbes's ahistorical criteria, Rousseau's version of these arguments (examined in chapter 5) is much more historically situated. For Rousseau, the states in Europe are in a state-of-war, which despite its various privations does not pose a fundamental threat to unit survival. Rousseau locates the restraints in this anarchy in a material context, particularly in the division produced by topographical fragmentation.[57] Writing before the industrial revolution began the rapid change in the scope of intense violence interdependence, neither Hobbes nor Rousseau needed to seriously entertain the implications of a second anarchy being transformed into a first anarchy, a project that would come to dominate late-nineteenth- and early-twentieth-century geopolitics.

'CLASSICAL' MID-TWENTIETH-CENTURY REALISM

Whatever the actual origins of its ideas, contemporary Realists routinely attribute the beginnings of their late-twentieth-century ascendancy to the influential works of E. H. Carr and Hans Morgenthau produced during the period of the Second World War. Within their sprawling and complex works, the variable of violence interdependence plays an at-times prominent role but has largely been ignored or misunderstood in subsequent Realist accounts and appropriations.

Widely hailed as a 'father' of modern Realism, E. H. Carr and his works enjoy an oddly selective canonical status in American Realism.[58] His advocacy of appeasing Hitler and his admiration of Soviet Russia made him a decidedly ambivalent founding figure for American Realists. More important than these political indiscretions, the role of violence interdependence in Carr's theory of world politics has been almost completely ignored. Carr's *The Twenty Years' Crisis* analyzes the role of hegemony in international order and it (purged of its appeasement punch line in later editions) remains one of the most widely used textbooks in the instruction of international theory. His next works, most notably *Conditions of Peace* and *Nationalism and After*, analyze the consequences of changes in violence interdependence, but they are long out of print and almost never

cited. It appears that Carr has "at least two different theories," one famous, one ignored.[59]

The well-known main argument of *The Twenty Years' Crisis* is that the
disarray culminating in World War II was caused by the idealist harmony-
of-interests doctrine and the inability of Britain's power resources to sustain her role as international hegemon.[60] In *Nationalism and After*, however, and to a lesser extent *Conditions of Peace*, the crisis is attributed to
the tension between technological interdependence and political parochi-
alism. The first theory sees a systemic crisis in the reigning ideology and
in the relative power positions of leading states in the system; the second
posits a much more fundamental system crisis of the national state and
anarchic state system.

The central claim of Carr's second theory is that a change in violence
interdependence has produced the obsolescence of the European nation-
state and state system as an arrangement for providing military security
and organizing production.[61] Carr argues that "modern technological developments" are making the nation-state "obsolescent as the unit of military and economic organization."[62] Carr sees the emergence of a "few
great multinational units" that are culturally "civilizations," economically what the German geopoliticians referred to as *Grossraum* (great
space), and militarily characterized by "strategic integration," a vision
widely held by global geopoliticians.[63] Carr sees the emergence of multinational units in both the United States and the Soviet Union and observes
about the Second World War that "none of the main forces that have gone
to make the victory is nationalist in the older sense."[64] The emergent
global order composed of "a small number of large multi- national units
exercising effective control over vast territories" promises to replicate the
patterns of the eclipsed European system, with "competition and conflict"
and a "new imperialism" that would be "simply the old nationalism writ
large" and would produce "more titanic and devastating wars."[65] Carr's
slim hopes for peace rest on the decoupling of national sovereignty from
military security, great power self-restraint, and international functional
agencies.[66]

CONTEMPORARY REALIST INTERNATIONAL THEORY

Of the three polar ideas contemporary Realism derives from republicanism, the anarchy problematique is both analytically central and a truncated version of the anarchy-interdependence problematique. To the see
the contours and consequences of this narrowing, it is instructive to examine the role of material context and especially violence interdependence in

the four prominent contemporary Realist theories—neorealism, offense-defense theory, offensive Realism, and structural Realism.

In the quarter century since Waltz refined the "thought" of earlier writers, most notably Hobbes and Rousseau, into the "theory" of neorealism, his lucid arguments about how anarchy shapes the politics of international systems have dominated Realist international theorizing.[67] Waltz's reformulation has stimulated a large body of neorealist routine science on topics such as polarity, balancing, alliances, the security dilemma, relative versus absolute gains, and grand strategy. It also has evoked a wide array of attacks from neoliberal institutionalists, constructivists, Marxists, and others. For better or worse, Waltz's neorealist argument has served as the common lodestone of international theory, attracting some while repelling others. These wide-ranging debates have largely ignored the crucial fact that Waltz almost completely drops the variable of violence interdependence that played such as central role in the arguments of Hobbes and Rousseau. Far from being too focused on material variables, as numerous critics maintain, Waltz actually employed a rather impoverished argument about material context.

The absence of violence interdependence marks both Waltz's early 'three images' analysis and his later systematic formulation of neorealism. His three-image schema of human nature (first image), domestic structure (second image), and system structure (third image) drops the physiopolitical original 'ground image' of a material context composed of geography and technology.[68] Although his favored third-image theory is derived from Rousseau and Hobbes, he makes no mention of the important role Rousseau assigned to topographical fragmentation in determining that Europe was a plural and thus potentially anarchic system.[69] In refining earlier arguments about anarchy and balance, but not division and violence interdependence, Waltz narrows the anarchy-interdependence problematique into the anarchy problematique.[70]

Waltz's formulation of neorealism in *Theory of International Politics* develops into a social scientific theory the ideas on anarchy unearthed in the exegesis of *Man, the State, and War* and continues the narrow treatment of material context. In the three-tiered conceptual apparatus of his neorealism (ordering principle, extent of functional differentiation, and distribution), material factors register only as distribution. Waltz's claims about interdependence address economic interdependence, which he holds has been exaggerated and which he holds states should and will seek to minimize.[71] Regarding violence interdependence, he ignores geography and generally downplays the importance of technology, arguing that the "perennial forces of politics are more important than new military technology."[72] He also observes that "nuclear weapons do not equalize the power of nations because they do not change the economic bases of a nation's power" and because they neither caused nor changed the bipolarity of the post–World War II system.[73]

In subsequent essays Waltz sketched a very different view, in which nuclear weapons seem to negate the perennial political force of anarchy by producing a peace in the anarchic state system more robust than could be reasonably provided by a global sovereign.[74] Nuclear weapons are clearly a material variable and the effects of nuclear weapons are explicitly held to be unrelated to distribution, the only material variable in the neo-realist model.[75] As a result, Waltz's claims about nuclear weapons are unrelated to the conceptual apparatus and claims of neorealism, and are essentially ad hoc, whatever their substantive merit.[76]

Attempting to overcome perceived limitations of Waltz's argument, the 'offense-defense theory' of Stephen van Evera and the 'offensive realism' of John Mearsheimer have partially reintroduced a broader conceptual-ization of material context, but still in a fairly circumscribed and impover-ished manner. Pursuing the problem of war causation, van Evra argues that "the gross structure of power" and anarchy are largely indetermi-nate, and he provides an analysis of the "fine grained" structure of power.[77] In this circumscribed way, van Evera points to the compositional contextual-material factors of topography and technology as among the factors shaping the offense-defense balance. The larger and more basic relationships between system structure and a more generalized version of these material-contextual factors remains unexplored, as are pre-twenti-eth-century versions of these arguments.[78]

Cast as a more full-bodied challenge to Waltz rather than an internal modification, Mearsheimer's 'offensive realism' postulates that all states seek hegemony in their "region," but maintains that this aspiration is im-peded globally by the "stopping power of water."[79] Curiously detached from the long lineage of maritime geopolitics and parallel analyses of land impediments, particularly the global geopolitical literature, Mearsheim-er's introduction of the long familiar variant of division is unattached to a more general treatment of violence interdependence and anarchy. With a strong emphasis upon ground conquest, Mearsheimer largely sidesteps the need to grapple with the implications of nuclear weapons. Despite his rejection of Waltz's optimism about the balance of power as a restraint, Mearsheimer ends with an international system whose plurality is firmly fixed by a form of division.[80] Overall, neither van Evera or Mearsheimer relate their variables to the core of the anarchy-interdependence problema-tique, being content to follow Waltz in not distinguishing between first and second anarchy. Changes occur *within* anarchy rather than *to* anar-chy. And their disengagement from earlier versions of similar arguments makes it difficult to assess their contribution to cumulative knowledge.

Finally, the 'structural Realism' of Barry Buzan and Richard Little marks a major attempt to recover the variable of violence interdependence.[81] Their analysis of 'interaction capacity' (which encompasses a range of material factors including destruction, communication, and transportation as well as societal factors) emphasizes that the existence of a system presupposes a certain capacity for interaction and that this capacity varies in several dimensions with great impact on political outcomes. In their major work attempting to integrate world history with international theory, they argue that change in interaction capacity has been the major driver of the globalization of the state system, creating a situation in which all previously isolated or loosely interactive groups are now capable of extensive interaction.[82] However, they stop short of fully employing this variable because their treatment is almost entirely directed to understanding the consequences of change from situations of absent or negligible interaction capacity to situations of moderate interaction capacity, thus dropping out the core argument of the anarchy-interdependence problematique that situations of intense violence interdependence combined with anarchy require government for security.

ARCHAIC AND POSTMODERN GEOPOLITICS

Finally, at the edges of contemporary Realism and beyond there is contemporary 'geopolitics.' As the material contextual arguments of physiopolitics and global geopolitics have become marginalized in the mainstreams of contemporary international theory, the term 'geopolitics' has enjoyed a ghostly afterlife, becoming the ubiquitous vernacular synonym for high interstate politics generally while being largely drained of distinctive theoretical content.[83] More substantively, self-described contemporary 'geopolitics' has the odd status of being done by two ideologically antithetical groups operating at the margins of the mainstreams of international theory. On one end of the political spectrum is the geopolitics of the more hardened elements of the Realist security studies community, most notably Colin Gray, who employs ideas drawn from the global geopolitical literature to advance 'hawkish' advice on a wide range of American military policy questions. At the other end of the political spectrum, the prolific school of postmodern, antimaterialist, and politically left-leaning 'critical geopolitics' has sought to 'deconstruct' geopolitical concepts and theories as power-serving ideologies of domination and violence.

Over the last several decades Gray has produced a small library of works attempting to apply what he takes to be the ideas of the classical global geopoliticians to illuminate contemporary strategic issues, most notably the role of nuclear weapons in the Soviet-American competition.[84]

Gray argues that "geopolitics is not simply one set of ideas among many competing sets that might help illuminate the structure of the policy problems," but is a "meta- or master framework." Regarding nuclear weapons he argues that "the very totality with which mutual vulnerability has emerged has served to minimize its significance." In this situation, "the concepts contained in the classic literature of geopolitics were never so relevant to the international reality as they are today." Once back in the world charted by the global geopoliticians, the permanent features of geography impart a permanent character to the American-Soviet rivalry: "East-west political relations may be fruitfully considered as a long-term and inalienable struggle between the insular *imperium* of the United States and the 'Heartland' *imperium* of the Soviet Union."[85]

At its heart, Gray's geopolitics is archaic, flawed by its inconsistent treatment of technology. Inherent in Gray's argument is the view that technology has ceased to play the role it once did. Gray acknowledges that "the meaning of physical geography" is "altered by technology,"[86] but this general recognition is never consistently integrated into his argument, because he treats contemporary technological developments very differently from how he treats past technological developments. Following the global geopoliticians, Gray treats the technologies of the global era as part of the material context that condition the character and viability of the main actors. The oceangoing vessel and the railroad interacting with geography create the clusters of power potential and military viability that the geopoliticians labeled the Heartland and the Rimland. But Gray treats contemporary nuclear technologies completely differently, as instrumentalities in conflicts between states rather than capabilities that might alter the viability of states as states. In effect, Gray refuses to grant contemporary technologies the status he grants to technologies of the past, thus producing an elaborately archaic geopolitics.

At the other end of the political spectrum, and quite outside contemporary Realism, is recent postmodern or critical geopolitics.[87] Such theorists advance a critical and deconstructive theory about the illusions of geopolitical constructs, ideas, and theories rather than claims about the actual influence of material contexts upon politics. In viewing geopolitical constructs as power-serving ideologies, critical geopolitics offers a valuable corrective to the tendency, particularly pronounced in classical global geopolitics, to naturalize imperial projects of domination. However, in viewing the claims of classical geopolitics solely as ideologies rather than serious claims about reality, critical theorists risk producing a completely ideational worldview completely devoid of material contextual influences. The closely related approach of postmodern geopolitics tends to be strongly antimaterialistic in its general formulations, but much of its specific analysis is directed toward assessing the impacts of newly emerging information technologies, a task for which a more conceptually developed contextual materialist theory is needed.[88]

CONTEMPORARY LIBERAL INTERNATIONAL THEORY

Contemporary Liberal international theory is vast, sophisticated, and heterogeneous, and many theorists working with such arguments eschew the Liberal label, so there are sure to be exceptions to any generalization. Nevertheless, it is instructive to examine some of the ways in which Liberal international theory has shifted its attention away from security-from-violence and toward nonsecurity issues areas (notably economics and environment); away from political structure and toward process; and away from material variables and toward norms, common understandings, and other ideational factors. With the notable exception of the recent 'democratic peace' argument, which is clearly security-related, the overall pattern of international theory has been bifurcated, with Liberal theorists largely ceding the topic of interstate security to Realists and directing their considerable energies to the issues of economics, human rights, and, more recently, environment.

This tendency away from security and toward nonsecurity issues finds an influential opening move in David Mitrany's 'Functionalist' program. Deeming the 'high politics' of interstate war, diplomacy, and sovereignty to be intractable to direct change, Mitrany proposes to concentrate efforts at reform toward the 'low politics' of 'welfare' cooperation. Perhaps also at work here is a broadly idealist view that how peoples and states think of themselves and their relations to others has consequences, in which case reduced attention to security-from-violence could actually itself contribute to security.[89] A quite different pattern of Liberal relation to traditional issues of security-from-violence is found in the current Liberal effort to define and protect 'human rights.' Here the early Liberal and republican opposition to arbitrary state violence against individuals is intermingled with a much broader and more heterogeneous (and thus culturally relative and controversial) set of 'rights' relating to economic development, and racial, religious, and gender discrimination.

The next two tendencies—the turn from structure toward process, and the turn from material variables toward ideational factors—are related, and mark a distinct shift from the main concerns of republican security theory.

The move away from structure has occurred in several ways. Again Mitrany's Functionalism provides the opening move, which has been re-

produced and elaborated in subsequent work that rejects or moves beyond many of his specific formulations. Plans for federal political structural alternatives serve as a foil in Mitrany's argument. He argues that
the effort to escape anarchy through the creation of federal arrangements
of authority is a practical and conceptual dead end, and he proposes instead the creation of issue-specific 'functional authorities' that cumulatively would moderate or supplant the anarchical state system.[90] Subsequent moves in this pattern, most notably the large literature on 'regimes'
and 'cooperation,' pull back from this model of authority transfer, in
favor of a concept of common problem solving in various issue areas
driven by the convergence of interests of state and other actors mainly
working through states. While a valuable tool to understand a growing
domain of world political activity, regime and cooperation theory do not
address whether the cumulative weight of such cooperative decision-making produces a political structure that is other than anarchical. Thus the
vast regime literature seeks to explain the causes and behavioral consequences of regimes, but contains no typologies or benchmarks for postanarchic structures.[91] While almost vanishing at the system level, political
structural variables have become concentrated at the unit level, where
they play major roles in Liberal arguments. Thus the main sweep of neoliberal theory operates within the Realist assumption that anarchy is present until and unless some form of hierarchical authoritative governance
replaces it. Changes occur *within* anarchic settings *despite* anarchy, but
never *to* anarchy. Perhaps, as Realist critics maintain, this omission reflects the actual unimportance of such international cooperative arrangements, but at a minimum it indicates the absence of a metric or yardstick
for measuring the extent of change.

The third general tendency in the last fifty years of Liberal international
theory has been its neglect of material contextual factors. Much Liberal
research and argument about processes, norms, and identities is explicitly
advanced as alternatives to 'materialist' theorizing. The important exception is interdependence. But theorists have focused on nonsecurity interdependence to the almost complete neglect of violence interdependence.
The large 'interdependence' literature from the 1960s and 1970s emphasizes the growth in economic, environmental, and other forms of interdependence and commonly argues, continuing Mitrany's theme, that these
'low political' issues are or should replace or alter the 'high politics' sphere
dominated by security.[92]

The analytic quality of this literature varies, with Robert Koehane and
Joseph Nye's *Power and Interdependence* generally recognized as the
most conceptually sophisticated.[93] Employing a formulation of two 'ideal
type' models (one a standard Realist view, the other what they call 'com-

plex interdependence'), they posit various propositions about how politics operates in complex interdependence, and argue that such patterns at least partially characterize politics in the three 'issue areas' of trade, oceans, and international monetary policy. Whatever the merits of these claims, it is notable that the simple violence interdependence of the American-Soviet political relationship in a world with abundant nuclear violence capability falls outside their model and attention. Thus, while neorealists tend to ignore or discount the role of interdependence in their continuing analysis of violence, neoliberal theorists tend to drop violence in their analysis of interdependence. Thus emerges the situation in which one school of international theory focuses on violence, the other on interdependence, and neither on violence interdependence.

CONSTRUCTIVISM AND COMMUNITARIANISM

The conventional picture of international theory centered on Realism and its Liberal challenger has been increasingly complicated and contested by the emergence of constructivist and communitarian international theory, some of whose core notions are explicitly advanced as applications of republican legacies.[94]

Constructivism in international theory builds from and parallels the broader movement of communitarianism in political theory that claims inspiration from ancient and early modern republicanism. The core idea is community, whose presence or value is advanced as 'republican' in opposition to the asocial atomistic individualism of 'Liberalism.' Inspired by Aristotle, Machiavelli, and Rousseau, and often casting themselves as 'republican revivalists,' communitarians assert the importance of the active involvement of citizens in politics, particularly at the local or 'community' level. They also argue that modern rights-centered Liberalism fails to grasp the importance of extensive citizen participation in politics and that market capitalism undermines the possibilities of genuine community and participation. Blending into the revivalist anarcho-syndicalism of the antiglobalization movement, communitarians oppose hierarchy that is seen as linked to large size.[95] Communitarian republicanism is clearly a descendant of polis and civic humanist republicanism, but is fundamentally different from republican security theory because it gives little attention to security-from-violence, lacks a positive agenda for large political structures, and has no contextual materialist dimension.

A powerful and elaborate international version of constructivism and communitarianism as a type of republicanism has been advanced by Onuf, who is widely credited as a founder of international constructivism and who also offers the most sustained analysis to date of the intersection of republicanism and international theory.[96] Drawing on both natural law and publican communal notions abundantly present in early republican thought, he claims that "before the world of states took form, the world itself formed a republic," thus emphasizing the logical and historical priority of international society and community over the individual atomistic self-regarding sovereign state dominant in Realist theory and in modern public international law.[97] He also refers to "realism as liberal theory," rather than the rival of Liberalism, because Realism transposes the model of the 'atomic individual' in modern Liberal theory onto the interstate realm, thus emphasizing rights over responsibilities, and downplaying the ways in which states, like individuals in society, are constituted by their place in international society.[98] The main practical implication of this international communitarianism cast as republicanism is to undermine the absolute prerogatives of state sovereignty and to support more robust international responsibilities and solidarities.

Another powerful and elaborate treatment of these themes is advanced by Alexander Wendt, whose formulations are cast as positive social scientific theory rather than as political theory. Attempting to provide a 'sociological' alternative to neorealist 'economistic' systemic theory, Wendt seeks to establish through conceptual argument the importance of ideational and the insignificance of material factors, and to argue that three different patterns of mutual identity (which he terms 'cultures of anarchy') rather than either anarchy itself or material factors, constitute the structure of interstate systems.[99] Wendt's vigorous and elaborate assault on 'materialism' is aimed at ontologically pure, reductionistic, and deterministic varieties of materialism, and as such does not address the practical contextual materialism of republican security theory that employs a hybrid ontology encompassing the constructivist claim that patterns of authority are produced by the practices of agents. Despite its unconventional features, Wendt's argument incorporates key features of the neorealist model, and thus its narrowings and limitations. With states conceptualized as personlike corporate agents, the logics of popular sovereignty, tiered delegation of authority, and federal union become difficult to conceive. Operating with the Realist spectrum of hierarchy and anarchy, Wendt theorizes different types of anarchies, but no alternative to anarchy except hierarchy.[100] Despite his attempt to broaden appreciation of varieties of anarchy, the basic distinction between first and second anarchies disappears due to the absence of the material contextual variable of violence interdependence. But, in princess-and-the-pea fashion common to idealistic theories, material factors eventually reappear to play major roles in the argument.[101]

Republicanism and Realism and Liberalism

Having examined some of republican security theory's early rival siblings and later forgetful descendants, it is possible to specify in more detail the mapping (recall figure 2.1) of the relationships between republican security theory and other varieties of republicanism and Realism and Liberalism.

Because the origins of the rival siblings are equally ancient, the arguments of natural law, civic humanism, and republican security theory are often intermingled and frequently employ common conceptual vocabularies. But at their core, natural law and civic humanism are quite distinct from security-restraint republicanism because they are not much concerned with security-from-violence, mutually restraining political structures, and natural-material contexts. The commitment of natural law to hierarchy means that its politics are essentially oppositional to the mutual restraints and popular sovereignty of security-restraint republicanism. Although both share the recognition that restraints are vital for political order, the types of restraints they envision as appropriate are quite different. Plato's misleadingly titled *Republic* is, at last in its surface teaching, an argument for an improbable dictatorship of the wise, and it is overtly hostile to political liberty and democracy. Aristotle's subtle and complex political theories have more points of intersection with security-restraint republicanism, but he too remains far too committed to hierarchy to be counted as much of a republican security theorist. From what is known about the political theory of Stoicism, it too has a politics more of enlightened kingship than mutually constituted plurality, although its precocious embrace of cosmopolitanism makes it a visionary anticipation of late modern globalism's program for political identity. Of these ancient positions, only Aristotle's has a significant material contextual dimension, to be examined shortly.

The widespread view among political theorists and intellectual historians that an emphasis on political participation is quintessentially republican and in opposition to Liberalism is more misleading than accurate. 'Civic humanism' or 'communitarianism' confuses one element of an historically variable set of power restraint arrangements with republicanism generally. In the case of Rousseau, ancient forms originally necessitated by the straitened circumstances of ancient republics are exaggerated and embraced for the realization of a freedom from freedom.

For the forgetful descendants—Realism and Liberalism—the relationship with republican security theory is much more intimate and thus much more complex. In terms of conceptual language, the problem here is nearly the opposite of distinguishing security-restraint republicanism from its rival siblings. Instead of different points being made in similar vocabularies, similar points are made in different vocabularies. The picture is further complicated by the fact that the descendants of security-restraint republicanism are not completely derivative of it, and the ways in which they are not derivative are very different. While much of Realism is republican, most of its nonrepublican parts are antirepublican. In contrast, those parts of Liberalism not descended from republicanism are not antithetical to it, but are progressive extensions of core republican concerns to nonsecurity domains.

Since the term 'Realism' made its appearance in the middle of the nineteenth century, an astonishingly large number of concepts and theories have been advanced under its guise. Three of the tall poles in the Realist tent, the anarchy problematique, balance of power, and the society of states, straightforwardly derive from earlier republican theorists. To the extent Realism is hegemonic in international theory, much of its theoretical power derives from unacknowledged republican sources. These three ideas that play such prominent roles in neorealism and the English School have been much refined and developed over the last half century and taken together, they provide an extremely powerful model of interstate systems.

This inheritance from republican security theory is, however, significantly incomplete. Most importantly, contemporary Realism, despite its avowed 'materialism,' has largely dropped violence interdependence as a variable, thus narrowing the anarchy-interdependence problematique into the anarchy problematique. This narrowing, which occurred in the transition from the 'prescientific' 'classical' Realism of Carr, Morgenthau, and Herz to the 'scientific' neorealism of the last several decades, has had far-reaching theoretical consequences. Most importantly, it has deprived contemporary Realism of the conceptual tools to grapple with security globalization (except as it effects distribution). This has left contemporary Realism with a largely static model of international politics as 'anarchy from time immemorial,' and largely blinded Realism to the more dynamic developments regarding anarchy produced by shifts in the size of the space marked by intense violence interdependence.

Contemporary Realism is not, however, only a narrowed and refined version of security republican arguments, because it also contains powerful concepts that are nonrepublican and antirepublican. Most importantly are the Realist commitments to the state as a hierarchical arrangement of authority and the 'nation' as the primary form of political community. These two powerful ideas exist alongside, and in underacknowledged tension with, the three polar ideas from republicanism.

In early modern theories of reason of state and enlightened despotism, contemporary Realism finds a precursor with a strong view of the state as hierarchy that is explicitly antirepublican. Here is the state struggling to become a 'unitary rational actor' rather than presumptively designated as such. Upon closer examination, this project of rationalizing hierarchy turns out to hinge on a quite utopian vison of restraint at the apex of an otherwise (at least ideally) unrestrained 'absolute' hierarchy. This most antirepublican of forms is saved from sliding into the universally recognized malady of tyranny only by erecting a psychic 'republic' of self-restraint in an individual subject to the maximum opportunities for immoderation of every form. The antirepublican form of absolutist hierarchy secretly depends on a quite utopian republicanism.

Curiously ignored in contemporary accounts of Realism as a tradition, the German nationalist and power-state theorists of the nineteenth and early-twentieth centuries provide a revealing image and cautionary lesson of a Realism without republican elements. From the standpoint of security-restraint republicanism, the conceptual slide from hyperstatism and hypernationalism to the tortured apologetics for the Hitler tyranny and mass murders is an all too easy target. Of course, few contemporary Realists would claim to be neo-Trietschkians and few are committed to such an extreme nationalism and statism. Nevertheless, contemporary Realism's rarely reflected upon 'unit-level' assumptions about these forms contribute to its inability or willingness to conceive of a postanarchic arrangement that is other than anarchical. Furthermore, contemporary Realism's insistence that the only alternative to anarchy is some form of hierarchy contributes to its failure to acknowledge the security accomplishment produced by the expansion of republican government over successively larger spaces. When all nonanarchical political structures are viewed as hierarchical, the internal security-from-violence difference between modern liberal democracies, such as the United States, and modern totalitarian states, such as the Soviet Union, simply vanishes from the domain of security theory and practice.

The relationship between Liberal international theory and republican security theory is also intimate and complex. The three polar Liberal ideas of democratic peace, commercial peace, and international unions are straightforwardly from republican security theory. In addition to developing and refining these ideas, contemporary Liberals have also contributed to security theory in ways complementary to the structural-materialist arguments of republican security theory by developing theories about ideational and process restraints on violent power. Unlike the antirepublican components of contemporary Realism, these elements of contemporary international Liberalism that are not derived from republican security theory are complementary to it.

Despite Liberalism's posture as a challenger to Realism, its relationship to republican security theory partly follows the posture of Realism toward republican security theory. Most importantly, contemporary international Liberalism also operates with a truncated version of the anarchy-interdependence problematique. Where Realists focus on violence and deny that economic interdependence is a powerful force, Liberals generally ignore interdependence with regard to violence and defend the significance of economic interdependence. Similarly, contemporary Liberals have developed many sophisticated arguments about international institutions and their ameliorative effects within anarchy, but they stop short of arguing that such arrangements move interstate politics out of anarchy, since they seem to accept that political orders are only either anarchic of hierarchic (or some mixture thereof).

As with Realism, contemporary Liberalism is an incomplete descendent of republican security theory. Most prominently, the power restraint practice of balance of power has curiously gone from being central to republicanism to being seen as outside or antithetical to Liberalism. Contemporary Liberalism, far more than Realism, suffers from the amnesia effect of repeated bouts of social scientific revolutionary new beginnings. Liberals also have curiously deferred to the Realists' 'first appropriation' of many pivotal republican figures as 'Realists.' Even more of a problem with the Liberal construction of itself as a tradition is that the narrative starts at the end of the Enlightenment, thus missing the central role of the Roman experience in defining the problems and solutions of early modern republican security thought, and thus ignoring Montesquieu and the American founding.

To recover these lost beginnings, we turn to an examination of ancient and early modern thinking about republican security.

PART II

From the Polis to Federal Union

Chapter Three

THE IRON LAWS OF POLIS REPUBLICANISM

If a republic be small, it is destroyed by a foreign force;
if it be large, it is ruined by an internal imperfection.
—Montesquieu[1]

THE ANCIENT CITY-STATE AND REPUBLICAN SECURITY THEORY

The origins and early development of Western political theory and republicanism in particular are intimately connected with the city-states that flourished around the Mediterranean prior to the Roman Imperial ascendency. Actions and words from classical Greece and republican Rome stand enshrined as foundational in the modern conception of the West as a distinct civilization, and ancient writers and events have exercised a startlingly powerful presence in all aspects of Western thought, particularly about politics. The evolution of Western political thought has proceeded as a series of revivals, modifications, commentaries, revisions, and critiques of ancient political theory. For two millennia Western thinking about politics and history has been a long dialogue with the ancient figures of Herodotus, Hippocrates, Socrates, Plato, Thucydides, Aristotle, Livy, Polybius, Cicero, Tacitus, and others. The works of major modern political theorists such as Machiavelli, Montesquieu, and Rousseau are as much about ancient writers and experiences as modern ones. Since the emergence of more scientific and systematic approaches to history in the nineteenth century, generations of classicists, historians, and social scientists have subjected the ancient city-state to intensive scrutiny, cumulatively creating an immense body of scholarship on ancient political theory and practice.[2]

At first glance, the lines of argument embodied in my reconstruction appear to confront extremely inhospitable intellectual terrain across the board—in the bulk of extant ancient texts, in the dominant contemporary readings of these texts, and in the main contemporary views of Greek and Roman political experience. While the reception of so large and varied a topic remains conflicted and contested, the ancients are understood to be theorists of *antimaterialist naturalism, antiliberal republicanism,* and *postsecurity idealism.* The towering figures of Plato and Aristotle are viewed as propounding a powerful version of naturalism that is substantially hostile to materialism of all types. The dominant late modern view of ancient politics, forged by Rousseau and the French Revolutionaries (as well as early-nineteenth century Liberal reactions to them), holds that ancient city-state republicanism is fundamentally antiliberal in character. This view is expressed with particular clarity in Benjamin Constant's claim that the "liberty of the ancients" entailed the "complete subjugation of the individual to the authority of the community" in contrast to the "liberty of moderns," which entails individual freedom from the collective.[3] This view also informs contemporary 'republican revivalism,' which sees ancient republicans as exponents of a community and virtue-centered political theory and practice and as valuable because of their fundamental differences with the commercial and interest-centered liberalism of modernity. Finally, ancient republics, while understood to be engaged in vigorous international interactions, conventionally are seen as having constitutions that are the realization of some ideal form or vision of political life rather than as heavily shaped by the demands of security competition. In short, ancient republics are held to be *different in kind* from modern liberal polities.

The dominant view of the ancients as antimaterialist naturalists, antiliberal republicans, and postsecurity idealists entails a significant distortion of the actual political arrangements of the ancient city-states and of their theorists. In part this distorted picture results from the fact that the surviving texts of ancient political theory are a very skewed selection of actual ancient thought. Although benefiting from the intellectual ferment and freedom of democratic Athens, both Plato and Aristotle articulated the views of oligarchic critics of Athenian democracy, and there is no surviving theoretical defense of Greek democracy.[4]

Despite this incomplete record, both ancient sources and recent classical scholarship provide ample evidence of significant contextual materialist and structural republican lines of argument. As part of their generally naturalistic understanding of human affairs, the ancients advanced a rich array of arguments about how material contexts shaped political associations. Even more importantly for the development of republican security theory as first Liberalism, democratic Athens afforded individual liberty substantial expression and had highly developed architectures of structural power restraints, and republican Rome had substantial democratic elements in its elaborate constitution of antihierarchical power restraints. When these pieces are reassembled, it is possible to see these two ancient city-state republics as *different in degree* rather than different in kind from modern republics, and then to see how these differences emerged as security-driven adaptations to material contexts and small size.

The core reason ancient republics do differ from modern ones in important ways concerns security. The essence of the security-centered revisionist argument, which I shall refer to as the two *iron laws of polis republicanism*, is compactly formulated by Montesquieu: "If a republic be small, it is destroyed by a foreign force; if it be large, it is ruined by an internal imperfection."[5] Republican city-states were precluded from the fuller pursuit of political liberty by the need to eke out physical security in harshly precarious contexts. Because republics had to be small, they were vulnerable, tended to be rare, and had to be martial to survive. But if they expanded through conquest, as did the Roman Republic, then they would inevitably become despotic monarchies. This line of argument emphasizes that the fundamental character of ancient city-state republics was defined—and severely circumscribed—by the interplay between security requirements, political practices and structures, and material contexts. This understanding of the city-state establishes a baseline for assessing the innovations of early modern European republican security theory and practice, innovations that move beyond the tragic impasses of city-state republicanism.

Despite all that has been written about ancient republican theory and practice, this cluster of arguments has been largely neglected by both political and international theorists. Among recent civic humanist treatments, a focus on virtuous participation has obscured the centrality of war and security in city-state republics, and a focus on ideas and ideologies has led to neglect of material contexts and theorizing about them. Among recent Straussean natural laws theorists, who deploy the ancients as the embodiment of a virtue-centered political life to combat the alleged vices of modern Liberalism, there is little attention to structural-material security arguments. Among international theorists, attention has been focused almost exclusively on Athens and the Peloponnesian War, in part because of Athens's status as a precursor of modern democracy, in part because of the haunting similarities with the bipolar Cold War, and in part because of the theoretical ambition and influence of Thucydides. In contrast, contemporary international theorists have almost completely neglected the Roman Republic, which was intensively examined by virtually every later ancient and early modern theorist as the paradigmatic case of ancient republican politics.

This exegesis proceeds in three main steps. In the following three sections I identify the main features of classical physiopolitics and then examine several specific arguments about climate, land-sea interactions, and fertile land. The next three sections explore first Liberal and negarchic aspects of Athenian and Roman Republican political experience and theory, and the centrality of restraint in Thucydides. Then three sections explore the logic of the two iron laws with particular reference to the Roman experience.

Ancient Naturalism and Contextual Materialism

To approach classical physiopolitical arguments about the influence of material contexts upon human affairs is to immediately enter into a vast and complex intellectual universe about 'nature' that is significantly alien to modern sensibilities.[6] The largest and most influential body of surviving Greek naturalism is the *natural law* tradition in which Plato, Aristotle, the Stoics (largely lost), and Aquinas (a melding of Aristotle and Christianity) provided the dominant vocabulary of classical and medieval Western political theory.[7] In the standard interpretation, this awesomely complex and compelling body of thought began with Socrates' rebellion against the reductive naturalism of the 'nature philosophers' and the reductive ethical utilitarianism of the 'Sophists.' The pre-Socratics distinguished between *physis* (nature) and *nomos* (law), and argued that law and justice were conventional constructions, in contrast to human desires and passions, which were deemed to be natural.[8] These claims supported a relativistic and reductionistic power philosophy similar to both primitive versions of Realism and contemporary postmodernism.[9] Socrates' key move was to assert a distinctive human nature, not totally animallike in character, but marked by the faculty of reason, a teleological affinity for justice, excellence, and wisdom, and a capacity to approach (fleetingly and fully available only to a small minority) a divine transcendent reality, which was more real than lived human experience. While humans were not naturally just, good, and wise, the fullest and highest realization of their natural potentials entails the closest possible ascent to these ends. In building a political science, natural law theorists thus answered the pre-Socratic nature-convention distinction by arguing that the realization of justice and law were natural to humans and their political associations. The main thrust of classical natural law was more normative than explanatory, and emphasized *what* different political associations had in common rather than *why* they were different.

Despite the loss of most pre-Socratic Greek thought, important fragments and scattered texts indicate a complex body of thinking about the role of nature as material context in human affairs. Several extant works by Hippocrates, generally regarded as the founder of scientific medicine, contain strong (if simplistic) material-contextual arguments, particularly about climate. Several of Plato's dialogues, most notably the *Protagoras* and the *Gorgias*, contain elaborate presentations of the arguments of these two major Sophists about politics that are widely viewed as accurate.[10] And the large ancient school of Epicureanism, whose sole surviving work (Lucretius's long expository poem *De rerum natura*) contains a well-developed state-of-nature argument.[11]

The standard natural law account, particularly in the recent formulation of Leo Strauss and his followers, has tended to obscure important continuities between pre-Socratic naturalism and the arguments of post-Socratic natural law theorists.[12] The founding works of Greek natural law theorizing preserve and advance arguments about material context and political structure as components in a much larger 'great chain of being' edifice stretching from Aristotle's divine 'unmoved mover' down through material-contextual nature. Structural-materialist arguments are particularly salient in the practical and empirical aspects of Greek political theory and science. While definitely subordinated and circumscribed compared to the broader claims of the pre-Socratics, arguments about material context are preserved and incorporated in analyses of the interaction between the animal part of the human *zoon politicon* and the material context.

Plato's view of politics, embedded in a vision of the cosmos where order is imposed by divine reason on inert formless matter, is largely hostile to contextual-materialist argument. But even here natural-material processes do not altogether disappear. Although generally neglected by recent natural law commentators, Plato advances several very strong catastrophist arguments, in which human civilization is episodically wiped out by natural cataclysms such as floods, fires, and earthquakes. These disasters leave small remnant human populations lacking any memory of previous civilization, thus setting in motion the long process of reinvention.[13]

The works of Aristotle contain far more contextual-materialist arguments. Aristotle's overall approach is much more inductive and empirical than Plato's, and his general concept of nature has a pervasively functional dimension. Aristotle advances an elaborately teleological view of causality, and he routinely explains the morphological structure of organisms by reference to the contexts within which they live.[14] It is within this matrix of assumptions that Aristotle, commonly regarded as the founder of empirical political science, compiled and comparatively analyzed the constitutions of many polities[15] and advanced numerous arguments relating political structures (as well as numerous other aspects of human life) to their natural-material context. This structural and functional contextualism, the empirical and comparative method of his natural and political science, and his apparent ambition to synthesize the main insights of all his predecessors combine to make Aristotle the major ancient contributor to the development of structural-materialist political science.

Technology and artifacts occupy a curious place in this naturalist worldview. On the one hand, ancient theorists voice clear recognition of the importance of basic technologies like control of fire, agriculture, and metallurgy in fundamentally shaping the human condition.[16] They are also able to imagine technological alternatives, as in Aristotle's hypothetical consideration of an "instrument which could do its own work" such as a shuttle able to "weave of itself."[17] And various technics, ranging from complex ships to siege machines, matter-of-factly make their appearance in various accounts of political affairs. Despite all this, ancient writers do not seem to have reflected in any substantial way on the possibility of further inventions or their possible ramifications, particularly regarding warfare.[18] Far from imagining technologies as potentially dynamic elements in the material context for human action, ancient theorists tended to treat familiar technologies as part of the familiar landscape, not just interacting with nature, particularly geography, but almost as part of nature.

CLIMATE, RESTRAINT, AND RULE

Prior to the industrial revolution, climate is the most analyzed material contextual variable in Western political science.[19] The first surviving work of Greek science, Hippocrates' *Airs, Waters, and Places*,[20] advances such claims, and climate appears as a prominent variable in Aristotle. Summing up the dominant view, Montesquieu observes that "the empire of climate is the first and most powerful of empires."[21] Arguments about climate are as diverse as they are numerous, and many have tangential relation to security-from-violence. But one set of repeatedly advanced and modified climate arguments focuses on explaining the presence and absence of self-restraint and political liberty.

Early climate theories typically divide the earth into temperature zones or belts and then assert that human institutions are shaped powerfully by their climatic position. In the *Politics* Aristotle delineates three zones and argues that political institutions are shaped via the intervening variable of individual psychology.[22] People in the north are given to an excess of *thumos* ('spiritedness,' the middle of the three parts of the psyche) and as a result were ungovernable but free. The dissociative tendencies stemming from their spiritedness produced the neglect of the arts and crafts (*techne*) so northern peoples live in a condition of primitive material life. At the other extreme, people in the torrid zones of Asia and Africa are prone to an excess of *eros*. Pursuing the wants of the body, Asians and Africans live in a condition of material sophistication, but the absence of spiritedness makes them relatively passive politically, and thus more willing to accept despotic rule. Thus the Asians and Africans tend to live in highly civilized despotisms.

In Aristotle's view, the middle temperate zone permitted a balance between the two appetitive parts of the soul, which in turn permitted reason, the weakest part of the psyche, to govern. The Greeks, living in the temperate zone, are thus in Aristotle's view able to strike a balance and could enjoy the benefits of material civilization without despotism. This climatic physiopolitics fits into Aristotle's more general theme that the golden mean was preferable to the extremes, and the general ancient notion of reason as a source of restraint. But reason is sufficiently weak by nature so that a fortuitous set of geographical factors is needed to create a balance among the stronger appetitive parts of the soul. Greek civilization at its foundations is an accident of the geography of climate. Aristotle also took the argument a step further to claim that the Greeks had a natural propensity and right to rule over lesser peoples, thus beginning a long tradition of explaining and justifying the domination of one group over another by reference to natural facts.[23]

Geography, Hoplites, and Triremes

Arguments about topography are also a staple of classical physiopolitical theory. One aspect of topography, the interaction of land and sea, was widely held to have substantial influence on the character of politics, economy, and culture. As part of arguments about fragmented versus uniform topography, the presence of intervening bodies of water is held to retard political consolidation. Another line of argument, beginning with Thucydides and climaxing with Alfred Thayer Mahan, holds that the superior mobility of naval over land transport, combined with the tendency for naval power to concentrate, joined with the important economic role of maritime transport, provide the contextual-material foundations for thalassocracies (sea-based hegemonies and empires) such as Minos's Crete and Themistocles' Athens (and then Venice, Holland, and Britain).[24] Another long-running argument about land-sea interactions holds that naval and maritime polities tend to be less hierarchical, more commercially oriented, and more culturally cosmopolitan than polities primarily dependent on agriculture. In the ancient context, this argument holds that there is a fundamental and recurring difference between commercial and naval polities, which tend to be more democratic, and land-based polities, which tend to be more oligarchic (see figure 3.1).

A particularly sophisticated version of this argument appears in Aristotle's *Politics*, where a combination of topography and military technology and organization is held to explain variation among different city-state constitutions:

> Just as there are four chief divisions of the mass of the population—farmers, mechanics, shopkeepers and day- laborers—so there are four kinds of military forces—cavalry, heavy infantry, light armed troops, and the navy. Where the territory is suitable for the use of cavalry, there is favorable ground for the construction of a strong form of oligarchy: the inhabitants of such a terri-

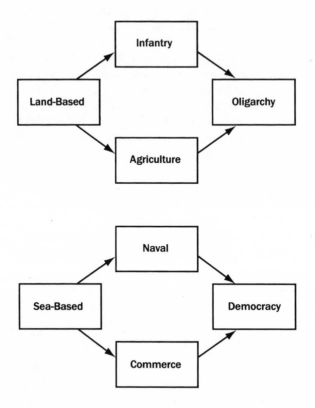

Figure 3.1 Landed Oligarchic versus Naval Democratic

tory need a cavalry force for security, and it is only men of large means who can afford to breed and keep horses. Where territory is suitable for the use of heavy infantry, the next and less exclusive form of oligarchy is natural: service in the heavy infantry is a matter for the well-to-do rather than for the poor. Light armed troops, and the navy are wholly on the side of democracy; and in our days—with light armed troops and naval forces as large as they are—the oligarchical side is generally worsted in any civil dispute.[25]

Similar claims about fundamental political differences between naval and hoplite infantry secured polities appear scattered in other ancient sources and serve as the starting point for a parallel early modern argument. This strikingly material-contextual explanation for variations in domestic regime types connects the relative strength of the different sociopolitical groups in city-states not in terms of their position in the political economy, or mode of production, but rather in terms of their position in the mode of protection, and then attributes the viability of different protection modes to the interaction of topography and military technology.[26] The key assumption of this argument, that those who defend the polis rule the polis, points to the extremity and influence of the security problem and treats unit-level constitutions as the outcome of an internal balance of power heavily shaped by compositional material factors. This basic division in the Greek city-state system between hoplite-based oligarchies and naval democracies is, of course, the difference between Sparta and the Peloponnesian League, and Athens and the Delian League. To the extent that one underlying cause of the Peloponnesian War is the different domestic regime types of the Spartan and Athenian camps, this argument points to the conflictual consequences of domestic variations rooted in material contexts shaping the unit-level rather than directly at the system level. Thus 'geopolitics' begins all the way 'down' and then extends all the way 'up.'

FERTILE LAND, WEALTH, AND MILITARY INSECURITY

Classical physiopolitical theorists also extensively explored *fertility* (arable land) as a factor in security politics, and these arguments shed light on a widely recognized feature of ancient republicanism, its relative antipathy to commerce.[27] Classical republican theorists view wealth and commerce with great suspicion because it saps martial strength, in contrast to poverty, which breeds it. This argument is widely discussed in ancient theory, it looms large in the picture of city-state republicanism drawn by recent scholars, and is widely highlighted as distinguishing ancient from modern republics.[28]

Between the close of the neolithic era and the maturation of the industrial revolution, the overwhelming majority of humankind were farmers and the main source of wealth was agricultural. Wars were first and foremostly fought for control of arable land. Surprisingly, almost all physiopolitical theorists thought peoples in more fertile regions suffered from grievous security problems that were directly linked to their agricultural way of life: more fertile regions are wealthier, which saps martial virtue until military collapse occurs. In contrast, infertile regions produce poor inhabitants who make hardy warriors with incentives to plunder who then conquer richer and militarily softer peoples in fertile regions. This argument appears in Thucydides, Machiavelli, and Gibbon,[29] and is most developed by Ibn Khaldûn, the fourteenth-century North African Islamic philosopher, whose *Muqaddimah* is widely recognized as the first comprehensive theory of history.[30] Ibn Khaldûn argues that when "people settle in fertile plains and amass luxuries and become accustomed to a life of abundance and refinement, their bravery deceases." In contrast, "desert life is the source of bravery, [and] savage groups are braver than others," and they are therefore, "better able to achieve superiority and to take the things that are in the hands of other nations."[31] He sees history as a cycle in which steppe peoples conquer sedentary peoples, only to themselves succumb to softening and eventual conquest.

For long stretches of human history, almost all combat was at close quarters, and the military prowess of warriors depended largely on individual strength, endurance, bravery, and small unit cohesion. Early armies were also dependent on the feet of soldiers for mobility, or upon horses and camels, thus placing a premium on physical endurance and conditioning. Martial virtue mattered more when technological changes, while important and far-reaching when they occurred, were relatively rare and were rarely monopolized by one group for long. Living close to nature, poor nomadic peoples were accustomed to deprivation and hardship, and so the rigors of war were not so onerous to them. Poor peoples in infertile regions also tended to hunt frequently and to settle their disputes violently, while sedentary peoples did not use arms or have recourse to violence in the course of their ordinary living. Prosperity served as a magnet for plunder, drawing the poor to attack the inhabitants of rich agricultural regions.

This pattern was dominant for many centuries, but was moderated by the military disadvantages of poverty and the countervailing advantages of wealth. Poor infertile regions supported limited populations, a product of the very infertility that kept them in poverty, but this disadvantage was not as great as the differences in aggregate population figures would suggest. Most of the population in sedentary agricultural regions was unarmed and unprepared for war because the martial arts were monopolized by elites. In contrast, virtually the entire male population of nomadic peoples could be counted as capable warriors. The smallness of population in infertile regions did, however, make it much easier for conquerors eventually to be absorbed by the sedentary peoples. The wealth of fertile areas may have been a magnet attracting plunderers and a cause of decay of military prowess, but it also had some compensating advantages: bribes could be offered, mercenaries hired, and better weapons procured.[32]

Wealthy and sedentary peoples also gradually developed institutional and cultural mechanisms to compensate for their materially rooted disadvantages, most notably sumptuary laws and martial education. Sumptuary laws discouraged excess private consumption and ostentatious display. The legendary military prowess of Sparta and early Rome was thought to derive from their success in maintaining a citizen-body in which the corrupting effects of commerce, wealth, and soft living were systemically suppressed through sumptuary laws and intensive military training.[33] However effective such institutions might be, they required great effort to create and maintain, and when they decayed, the cycle was free to run its course.

The ultimate solution to the security problem of sedentary peoples was technological. Walls and fortresses helped because the complexity of siege warfare was often beyond the abilities of nomadic peoples to master. But the really epochal change was the development of gunpowder weapons, which early modern theorists would celebrate for eliminating the predation of nomadic upon sedentary peoples.[34]

The ancient republican antipathy to commerce and luxury thus emerges as a necessary adaptation to the precarious security environment of ancient republics, rather than as an intrinsic feature of republican political association. These antipathies are means to the end of security, rather than ends in themselves. When better and less politically strenuous means are found, it will be possible for republican polities to abandon these practices and attitudes that were previously vital to their survival.

THE ATHENIAN *DEMOKRATIA*

In order to establish that ancient city-state republics differed in degree rather than in kind from modern liberal constitutional republics, it is instructive to briefly examine some of the key features of Athenian democracy, and the ways in which they have been misunderstood. As already noted, the ancient city-state, and particularly the Greek polis, has been widely viewed as fundamentally illiberal in character by the dominant modern readings, and this tendency has been amplified due to the salience of the antidemocratic and antiliberal political theories of Plato and Aristotle in the modern reception of Greek political thought.[35] Athens, because of its vibrantly democratic character, has also been subject to special condemnation from critics of democracy, who until recently have been overwhelmingly dominant in Western political thinking.[36] Athens has stood for centuries in Western thought as a dangerous and failed experiment in the direct and unchecked rule of democratic majorities governed by passions and rapacious lower-class envy.

A remarkable feature of Western thinking about Athenian democracy is that actual knowledge of the operation of the Athenian democratic constitution has been largely absent until well into the twentieth century. Although the events and characters of the golden age of Athenian democracy have long occupied a larger-than-life role in the Western historical memory, it is only recently that classical historians, building from the rediscovery of Aristotle's long lost treatise, *Athenion Politeia* (The Athenian Constitution) in an ancient Egyptian garbage dump in 1891 and the careful sifting of other scattered evidence, have provided an adequate picture of its main features.[37]

As recently reconstructed by classicists, the Athenian constitution had several major mechanisms for power restraint, both of democratic majori-

ties and elected officials.[38] The Assembly, composed of about 15 percent
of the total population (women, foreigners, and slaves being excluded)
had no property qualification and met for several hours several times a
month to determine all matters of policy. For changes in laws, approval
of a second smaller body, constituted by lot, was also necessary.[39] Day-
to-day administration and foreign affairs were conducted by the *boule*
(council) and its standing subcommittee, which were also constituted by
lot. Selection of all officials and jurors was also by lot, with the exception
of military commanders, who were elected by the Assembly. All officials
were subject to intensive investigation of their performance (and finances)
upon taking and leaving office. The practice of *ostracism,* in which individuals could be voted into exile for ten years, served as a popular check
on concentration and abuse of power, and is best understood as a mechanism to prevent the emergence of a tyrant.[40] The numerous juries that
ruled on suits of all sorts were also constituted by lot, and any citizen
could sue any public official for perceived misconduct in special judicial
procedures. Far from being an unrestrained 'tyranny of the majority,'
Athenian democracy is more accurately viewed as the "first major polity
in history to have a nonhierarchical system of plural and mutually controlling authorities."[41]

Within this essentially negarchical political structure, individual expression and diversity flourished.[42] The rampant individualism of democratic
Athens was routinely decried by critics such as Plato and Aristotle. Athenians were also notoriously litigious, a further indicator of a robustly indi-
viduated sense of citizen self-interest. Democratic Athens was so hospitable to the expression of heterodox individual views that intellectuals from
all over the Greek world flocked to Athens to expound their ideas, providing the critical mass of intellectual exchange that catalyzed the Greek Enlightenment. Of course, the Liberal features of the Athenian democracy
(particularly the status of women and slaves) fall far short of late-twentieth-century Liberal standards, and the quality of public policy decision
making was often egregiously flawed, particularly in foreign affairs. Con-
sidering, however, that most citizens were illiterate small peasant freehold-
ers or craftsmen, and that Athens lived precariously in a highly violent
and predatory international context, it is the precocity of its first Liberal
republicanism, not its substantial illiberalism, that stands out.

TRAGEDY, RESTRAINT, AND ATHENIAN EMPIRE

Aside from serving as a whipping boy for antidemocrats across the centuries, Athens appears prominently in the canon of Western political
thought, particularly international theory, due to the extraordinary intel-

lectual power of Thucydides' *Peloponnesian War.* As we saw, Realists routinely characterize Thucydides as the father or founder of Realism, and this assertion plays a primary role in the narrative of Realism as the oldest tradition of international theorizing. Realist readings of Thucydides' dense and complex work vary in sophistication, but he is commonly read as advocating the 'pure power philosophy' articulated by the Athenians in the Melian Dialogue (or at least unsentimentally holding that this was the way the world of international politics works).[43] Antidemocrats, including many Realists, look to Thucydides' portrayal of post-Periclean Athenian policies as a canonical indictment of the intrinsic incompetence of democratic foreign policy making.

While Thucydides' work is filled with a breathtaking array of insights, many of which come to play a central role in Realism, the overall message he is attempting to convey is ultimately unclear because he seldom conveys his views directly, and the work is unfinished, breaking off before offering a conclusion. There is no doubt Thucydides is a realist in the sense of an unsentimental secularist (particularly in contrast to the 'fabulous' stories of Homer and Herodotus), but the most convincing reading suggests closer affinities with the main themes of republican security theory than with the 'pure power politics' version of Realism.

Despite Thucydides' reputation as the founder of history, his work is not a straightforward chronicle, but rather is patterned as a tragedy.[44] During Thucydides' life, tragic drama in Athens was highly developed and widely influential, and tragedians routinely addressed political topics. In the standard plot line "success carries with it the seeds of failure" because it "intoxicates heroes and leads them to inflated opinions of themselves and their ability to control man and nature alike."[45] The hubristic hero miscalculates, unexpected events suddenly intervene, and disaster ensues. The tragic cosmology is essentially conservative, with the hero's attempt to break from conventional communal restraints leading to retribution. Unlike the often mythological subject matter of conventional tragic drama, which can be arranged to suit the message, the actual events of the war are much less plastic. Nevertheless, Thucydides' narrative is highly selective and its main progression is one of "success, overconfidence, miscalculation, and catastrophe."[46]

Thus understood, Thucydides essentially tells the story of disasters that result from the failure to recognize and heed restraints and limits. Athens, an "archetypical tragic hero," personified in Pericles, overestimates its strength and virtue, launches a bold war, and is stricken by the unexpected reversal of the plague.[47] In the Melian Dialogue (itself patterned after tragic dramatic dialogue) Athens's disregard for the restraints of convention and morality reaches its zenith. This horrific massacre is immediately followed in Thucydides' narrative by the Sicilian expedition, launched under the influence of the daring, hubristic (and possibly blasphemous) Alcibiades. A classic case of military overreach, the expedition comes to complete disaster, fatally weakening Athens.

The implication of this tragedy-framed and restraint-centered reading is that the amoral pure power philosophy articulated by the Athenian generals in the Melian Dialogue is an extreme articulation of the approach that leads Athens to disaster, rather than a pure expression of Thucydides' view of international politics. Spurred by the increasingly heavy hand of Athens, the allies revolt. Increasingly behaving among themselves as they have toward enemies and allies, the Athenians fall into severe internal discord. Power unrestrained by convention and morality leads to acute disorder and insecurity.

Far from being the first Realist, Thucydides is better thought of as a proto–security republican because his analysis centers on restraint. But his tragic history is too centered upon agents and events and too lacking in structural lines of argument to be straightforwardly republican security theory.

The Roman *Res Publica*

Of all the ancient city-states, the Roman Republic was exceptional, in its military success, in the extent to which its constitution contained an elaborate system of power restraints and in the influence it has exercised over the development of republican thought. The term *res publica*, literally meaning 'the public's thing or affair,' makes its appearance during the fifth century BCE when Rome, then a small and inconsequential town at the edge of the civilized world, expelled the last of its seven petty kings and established a new political order lacking a single ruler. From this origin the term 'republic' and its cognates arose, but only much later, after the wide diffusion of Latin following the Roman conquest of the Greeks, did this term come to be widely used as a general synonym for a popular but restrained city-state government. These arrangements lasted for about five centuries, until Octavian surmounted all rivals, culminating nearly a century of strife and civil war, and assumed the title of Augustus, at which point the Roman constitution is universally viewed as having become a type of monarchy, which the ancients referred to as the principate.[48] During these five centuries, Rome expanded to swallow all the other polities and state-systems of the entire Mediterranean Basin, a domain encompassing a population of one hundred million subjects and an area over a thousand times that of Athens and Attica.

Despite intense scrutiny by scholars over the centuries, there remains much about the Roman constitution that remains unknown, and little that is known is uncontested.⁴⁹ The Roman constitution, like the modern British, does not seem to have been one codified document, but rather a series of major legislative enactments that spelled out basic political processes and authorities. The Roman constitution also evolved considerably over time, and it was as Machiavelli noted, not the work of one founder but rather the product of generations of development. The three major extant sources on the Roman constitution are Titus Livy (a Roman historian whose *Ob Urbe Condita*, "From the Founding of the City," extends through the climactic struggle with North African Phoenician city-state Carthage in the third century BCE), Polybius (an upper-class Greek hostage and intimate of the Scipio family whose *History* covers the period of the Roman ascent over the Greeks),⁵⁰ and Marcus Tullius Cicero (a Roman lawyer, orator, official, and author of numerous works, who wrote during the period of the collapse of the republic).⁵¹ Each of these figures offers substantially different pictures of the Roman republican constitution, reflecting in part the different periods in which they wrote, as well as their own differing political agendas. Their treatments are augmented by a large quantity of other scattered ancient evidence about its features and their evolution that has been painstakingly assembled by classicists and legal scholars over the centuries.

The Roman republican constitution specified an elaborate set of voting assemblies and offices.⁵² At the top of the pyramid of public offices were the two *consuls*, who were annually elected, not renewable, and whose primary responsibility was the exercise of military command. This unusual, and at times dysfunctional, division of executive responsibility reflected the Roman fear that one individual would gain excessive power. For periods of extreme emergency a one-year office of *dictator* was available, but seldom employed. Lesser in importance and authority were the six *praetors* responsible for administration, the twelve *quaestors* who served as judges in law courts, and the two *censors*, who conducted the census of citizens and maintained voting rolls. The Senate, composed of former officeholders, was officially only an advisory body, but exercised great influence, particularly on the conduct of foreign affairs. The combination of rapid rotation, competitive elections, and the large number of officials further helped guard against concentration of power.

The Roman constitution had significant democratic elements, whose extent remains subject to sharp scholarly disagreement.⁵³ According to the main extant account of the early Republic, provided by Livy, the upper class composed of major property owners led in expelling the last king and then dominated the government. Their abuse of the general population led the plebs to conduct a series of general strikes, which were effective because of the importance of their role as soldiers in the army. The result of these strikes was the establishment of two major protections of popular liberty, election through assemblies and the office of tribune.[54] Only members of the upper classes could hold public office, but all offices were elected by a set of assemblies, which also could alone declare war and peace. Although the role of these assemblies insured that differences in policy were competitively debated, the democratic content of these assemblies was diluted because voting was weighted through a complex system that insured that the members of the two upper classes had disproportionate influence. In practical terms a more important protection was the extraordinary office of the plebian *tribune*, elected officials who possessed the *veto* (literally 'I forbid'), which could be exercised to stop any action by any official the tribune deemed abusive of popular liberty and interests. The office of tribune thus constituted a major source of institutional restraint on behalf of the general Roman populace, and the tribunate has entered into the general vocabulary of recurring republican power restraint mechanisms.

The most theoretically penetrating account of the structural logic of the Roman republican constitution is provided by Polybius. He offers a particularly well-developed account of regime formation and decay, known as the *anacyclosis* (the recurring cycle) encompassing three good and three degenerate political regimes of rule by 'one, few, and many,' and of the Roman constitution as a mixture designed to arrest the cycle[55] (see figure 3.2). The initial human condition is characterized as savage, scattered, and insecure. Out of this disorder one man, of particular strength and boldness of character, establishes a hierarchical order, a *kingship*, with the consent of the governed. The king's sons lack the virtue and restraint of the founder and degenerate into abusive *tyranny*, against which the leading citizens rebel and replace with an *aristocracy*. The next generation lacks the virtue and restraint of its predecessor and degenerates into an abusive *oligarchy*, inciting the mass of the people to rebel and establish a *democracy*. Again the virtues of moderation and restraint are lacking in the next generation, which degenerates into an *ochlocracy* (mob rule), which then sinks into savagery, thus returning to the beginning for the cycle to run again. The motor of this cycle is self-restraint in the good regimes, and the repeated inability to replicate and transmit this attribute to the subsequent generations.

Against the backdrop of this stylized model of cyclic political change, Polybius presents his famous explication of the Roman constitution as a system of mutually restraining political structures. Polybius calls the Roman constitution "the best political order yet realized among men" because it combines monarchical, aristocratic, and democratic elements configured so that the virtues of each is preserved and their vices eliminated. Whenever one group "tries to encroach upon the domain of the others, and assumes more power than is due . . . it is checked by the oth-

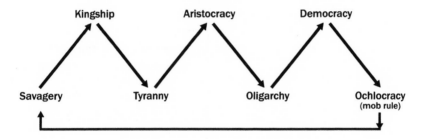

Figure 3.2 The Anacyclosis of Polybius

ers" and its schemes are "counteracted and obstructed by the others," with the result that "every part remains essentially in its once established position."[56] Polybius's portrayal of the Roman constitution also emphasizes the importance of ceremonies, the cult of the dead, and Roman religion,[57] but it is revealing that these mechanisms of acculturation and socialization are not advanced as solutions to the more fundamental problem of regime decay, whose primary solution is to be found in mutually restraining political structures. Although Aristotle's 'polity' is a partial step toward this conceptualization, it is this account by Polybius that seems to be the first theoretical articulation of the logic and virtues of substantially negarchic political structures.[58]

To establish that the protection of individuals from predation through political arrangements of mutual restraint was central to the Athenian and Roman political orders is to establish that ancient and modern republics differ in degree, not in kind. To explain further the origins and features of their significant differences in degree, we turn next to ancient arguments about security, size, and political structure encapsulated in the two iron laws of polis republicanism.

Republican Dwarfdom and Its Consequences

Prior to the modern era, when representation and then federation open new possibilities, political theorists universally held that self-government was confined to small city-states due to limitations upon communication and transportation. For citizen self-government to be viable, all the citizens had to gather within hearing distance of a public speaker.[59] From this pivotal fact, ancient and early modern republican security theorists drew a picture of the entire pattern of ancient city-state republics, captured in

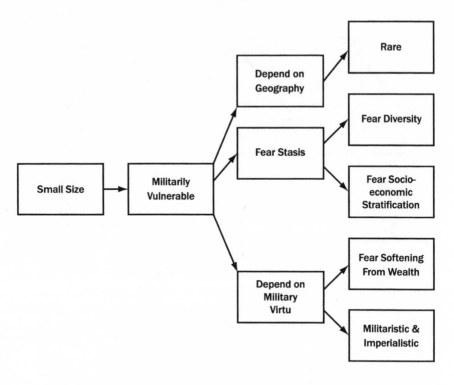

Figure 3.3 The First Iron Law of Polis Republicanism

the first iron law (see figure 3.3). Their intrinsic dwarfdom produces several of their most salient and distinguishing features: their rarity; their chronic fear of diversity, socioeconomic stratification, and the softening effects of wealth; and their militarism.

Small city-state republics were highly vulnerable to conquest by larger neighbors, and their survival was dependent upon geographical circumstances that could compensate for their size-based vulnerabilities. Self-governing city-states survived in Greece where the geography was broken and mountainous, often with a defensible rocky citadel such as the acropolis of Athens.

Even when city-states were situated in a favorable geographical setting, their security was precarious, and city-states had to maintain a heavily militarized posture in order to survive. As Benjamin Constant observed, "as an inevitable consequence of their narrow territory, the spirit of these republics was bellicose."[60] Being small meant continuous threats and endemic war, and much of the citizenry had to be militarily effective. As a result, the political life of the republican city-state was heavily conditioned by the basic fact that military viability and the military *virtù* of the citizens were tightly linked.[61] Prior to the gunpowder and industrial revolutions, military effectiveness was closely linked to the *virtú* of warriors, because almost all combat was at close quarters, where individual strength, endurance, bravery, and small unit cohesion were critical.[62]

In addition to mortal foreign perils, city-state republics were seen as tending to fall into intense and often violent internal conflicts (*stasis*).[63] An intensely participatory political existence required a relatively homogeneous citizen devoted to making extreme sacrifices in military service, and so diversity was perceived to be a threat. Echoing Thucydides' influential portrayal, Publius described city-state republics as "the wretched nurseries of unceasing discord."[64] Commerce and wealth were further viewed as harmful because they contributed to social stratification and class envy. The illiberal elements in the ancient polis republic are thus fundamentally rooted in the strenuous requirements for collective defense.[65]

A Republic for Expansion

The general question that animated Polybius's investigation was why Rome, of all the many polities in the known (Western) world, came to dominate in such a short period. His main answer is that its constitution "did most to enable" the Romans to achieve "the conquest of the whole world"[66] because it seemed to have transcended the syndromes of internal strife that afflicted ancient polities. Beyond this answer, and his detailed accounts of particular wars, Polybius's account is silent about several important features of Roman expansion. Roman foreign and military policy was particularly competent and stable due to the guiding role played by the Senate, composed of many of the most experienced political leaders.

Machiavelli observed that Rome was a "republic for expansion," in contrast to Sparta and Venice, which were "republics for preservation."[67] While it may be doubted that the constitution was designed for expansion, the Republic developed approaches that were highly effective. During the first and most lengthy phase of the conquest of Italy, Roman practices toward defeated adversaries were distinctive. Although Roman policy toward states viewed as particular transgressors, particularly perceived acts of betrayal or revolt, could be harshly savage, the general pattern was quite enlightened by ancient standards. Unlike Athens, Rome permitted ruling groups to remain in power and to enjoy nearly complete internal autonomy, and did not impose direct taxation. In return, alliances with any state but Rome were prohibited, and the allies were required to provide substantial levies of troops to be deployed and commanded by Roman generals. In this way Rome turned defeated enemies into protected clients.

As a result of these arrangements, the Italian allies had little motivation to rebel against Roman hegemony, and Rome was able to tap the military manpower of all Italy without the burdens of direct administration.[68] The security advantages of this pattern of hegemonic alliances was vividly demonstrated in the Second Punic War, the climactic struggle with Carthage for control of the western Mediterranean.[69] Despite the shock of Hannibal's sudden appearance in Italy and annihilation of several Roman armies, he was unable to evoke significant defections from Rome's Italian client-allies, and Rome was able to replenish its armies. In contrast, the Roman general Scipio was able to evoke widespread rebellion of the tribal groups in Carthaginian-dominated eastern Spain who chafed under harsh and exploitative direct Carthaginian rule, and Carthage's dependence on mercenaries made raising additional armies burdensomely expensive.

ROMAN EXPANSION AND THE FALL OF THE REPUBLIC

Despite the virtues of its internal structure, the Roman Republic gave way to the establishment of a monarchical order after a long period of civil war. Many factors were understood to be at work in this revolution, but many commentators in both ancient and modern times believed that the spatial expansion of Roman power was the decisive root cause of the fall of the Roman Republic[70] (see figure 3.4). Expansion offered a solution to the vulnerability associated with smallness, but expansion had the effect of altering the interior balance of power toward the few at the expense of the many. This process of constitutional deformation entailed interrelated processes of both socioeconomic and political-military changes, which together provide the logic of the second iron law of polis republicanism.

On the socioeconomic side, expansion undermined the free peasantry operating small farms that had traditionally provided the economic livelihood of much of the Roman population and from which the soldiers of Roman armies were drawn. The areas acquired by Roman arms outside Italy, beginning with the conquest of Sicily from Carthage in the First Punic War, were directly administered by Roman administrators and generals who had nearly unrestricted authority and frequently abused their positions to amass great private wealth. Ancient wars also typically produced large quantities of slaves, who were brought back to Italy to work large agricultural holdings, against which the small independent agricultural proprietors were uncompetitive economically.[71] The net effect of these tendencies operating over many decades was to increase the socioeconomic stratification among Romans, undermine the free peasantry, and thus to swell the urban proletariat of landless citizens living in Rome dependent on the public dole, which became increasingly generous as Roman wealth grew.

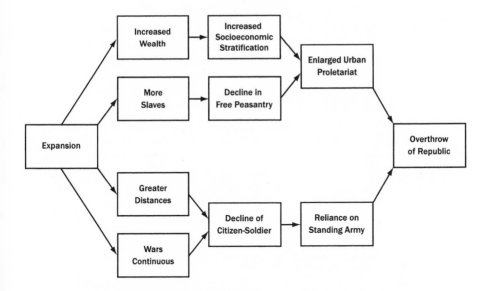

Figure 3.4 The Second Iron Law of Polis Republicanism

Even more erosive of the republican constitutional order were changes in the relationship between the exercise of citizenship and military service and the growing autonomy of Roman generals. Wars during the early period of the republic, while frequent, were fought close to home and waged during periods of agricultural inactivity.[72] Thus it was possible for citizens to be both farmers and soldiers, captured in the famous story of Cincinnatus returning to his farm after serving as a victorious general. As wars become increasingly continuous and were fought at greater distances outside of Italy, military service became a full-time activity at the same time that small farms were being economically marginalized. Lengthy wars fought on distant fronts also required prolongation of military commands. Soldiers increasingly identified politically with their generals, who used their authority to distribute war booty to enhance such loyalties by enriching their soldiers with the fruits of their conquests. With armies loyal to their commanders rather than the Republic, the control of military force passed out of the hands of the Senate and civil authority in Rome, thus setting the stage for ambitious generals such as Marius and Sulla, Caesar and Pompey, and Anthony and Octavian, the larger-than-life figures whose decades of internecine struggle marked the death knell of the Republic.[73]

Efforts to arrest these deformations were not absent but were unsuccessful. The effort by Tiberius and Gaius Graachus to redistribute public lands acquired through conquest to a wider strata were thwarted by their assassinations. Despite the obvious need to introduce mechanisms of representation in order for Roman citizens to have their interests served in governmental deliberations, there is no evidence that such measures were seriously considered. A particularly important alteration in the status of citizenship occurred as a result of the Social War of 91–88, in which a widespread rebellion of non-Roman Italian allied cities occurred, motivated not by the desire to escape Roman rule, but rather to share in it. This convulsion induced the Romans to extend a new class of citizenship, *civitas sine suffrergio* (citizenship without voting), to non-Roman Italians who had lived under indirect Roman rule and served in Roman armies for generations. This new form of citizenship was valued because it entitled protection by Roman courts, but the actual governance of the Republic remained that of a city-state.[74]

The pacification of the Roman world achieved by Augustus marked the end of the negarchical structural restraints that had been the hallmark of the Republic. But the full force of the hierarchical power of the imperial government was substantially tempered in its relation to individuals by the institutions of Roman law, which permitted Roman citizens to challenge abusive actions by Roman officials in Roman courts. With the eventual expansion of Roman citizenship to encompass all free males in the empire, the legacies of the republican tradition of power restraint afforded vast populations across centuries a greater degree of protection from predation than existed in the other large, despotically governed empires that so commonly recurred across the civilized world in Eurasia.

Ancient Pessimism

This reexamination of ancient theory and practice has restored an understanding of the first Liberalism of classical republicanism. Contrary to prevalent contemporary readings, the ancients provide a robust set of arguments about the interplay between material context, structures of political restraint, and security-from-violence. In the naturalistic idioms of classical physiopolitics, 'geopolitics' begins at the smallest scale in an analysis of material context shaping unit-level constitutions. The Athenian democracy and the Roman Republic are at their foundations postanarchic antihierarchic political structures and were understood and celebrated as such.

Despite these innovations and achievements, ancient republican theory was largely pessimistic about the prospect for political liberty. Not only were the benefits of political freedom and security confined to a minority of the total population, but these polities were understood to be severely circumscribed by draconian iron laws. With citizen self-rule seemingly confined to small polities, republics were typically confined to geographic nooks and crannies, where they were likely to be eventually overwhelmed by their larger neighbors. In the exception that proved the rule, the Roman Republic did successfully secure itself through a process of relentless conquest and absorption, only to have its internal constitution fatally deformed and its political liberty lost. Republican government was a rarity and was seemingly destined to always remain so.

Ancient republics were different in degree not in kind from modern liberal republics. The roots of these salient differences—ancient fear of diversity, stratification, enervating wealth, and pervasive militarism—emerge as necessary adaptations to their harsh and confined circumstances. In order to wrest the first freedom from violence from their precarious situations, ancient republics had to employ expedients that modern republics have had the luxury to avoid. Far from being of essentially antiquarian interest, the innovations and compromises of ancient republics posed the set of fundamental problems against which modern republican theory and practice gauged its progress: How could republics transcend the hard trade-offs and limited prospects of the two laws of polis republicanism?

Chapter Four

MARITIME WHIGGERY

[T]he sea is one obstacle to all kinds of evil, and a
means of numerous advantages.
—Destutt de Tracy[1]

MODERN REPUBLICANISM

The period between the late-medieval era and the late-eighteenth century, between the dawn of the Renaissance and the waning of the Enlightenment, witnessed major revivals and innovations in European republican theory and practice. The first waves of revivalist republican theory, most prominently Machiavelli, looked admiringly at the militarism and expansionism of the Roman Republic. But subsequent innovations, first in Venice and then in Holland and Britain, yielded a novel and distinctively modern republicanism that condemned rather than glorified conquest, embraced nascent capitalism, and employed constitutional representation to overcome earlier size barriers.

The legacies of this era are ubiquitous. Key events and theorists from this era have been elevated to canonical status across broad bodies of contemporary practice, theory, and scholarship. The political languages, concepts, and theories of early modern thinking are the dominant vernacular of liberal-democratic capitalist polities across the planet. The historical emergence in Britain of constitutional limited government, most associated with John Locke's *Second Treatise*, and the emergence of market capitalism, most associated with Adam Smith's *Wealth of Nations*, serve as the templates of modern Liberalism. The numerous important events, theorists, and texts of early modern republicanism continue to be reread, reinterpreted, and employed by contemporary theorists and scholars on a wide array of topics and issues, both related and unrelated to international theory.

In recent international theory, the legacies of early modern republican and Liberal thinking have enjoyed a major rebirth of relevance and attention. 'Democratic peace' and 'commercial peace,' two of the most important ideas in contemporary Liberal international theory, are widely recognized as originating in Enlightenment thought.[2] In recent intellectual historiography of early modern Europe, the reevaluation of republicanism by the 'republican revivalists' generally emphasizes the differences between declining 'republicanism' and rising 'Liberalism': republicanism emphasizes public participation over private interest and fears commerce as a threat to military *virtú*, while modern Liberalism eschews participation and embraces commerce.[3]

Despite these living presences and continuing revivals, an important set of early modern international and materialist republican arguments, mainly about Venice, Holland, and Britain, have been neglected by both neoclassical Liberal international and republican revivalist scholarship.[4] I refer to these arguments as *maritime whiggery*. These arguments first appear among analysts of Venice, and then are elaborately developed by many Enlightenment thinkers, most notably Montesquieu and his commentators. They are particularly prominent in the theories of the Scottish and British Enlightenment, in well-known writings of Gibbon, Smith, and Hume, and in lesser-known works by Adam Ferguson, John Millar, Charles Davanent, and John Trenchard and Thomas Gordon. The unifying theme of these writers is that the *restraining and connecting power of water* significantly shapes the emergence of various forms of nonhierarchical political and economic association in early modern Europe. The recovery of maritime whig arguments amends our understanding of the trajectory of early modern republicanism in two significant ways. First, contemporary Liberal international theory is largely a set of claims about the *consequences* of limited constitutional government and capitalism, but the maritime whigs advanced claims about the material contextual *causes* or preconditions for their emergence. Second, the differences between waning republicanism and emerging Liberalism emphasized by republican revivalists appear as innovative continuities when international, material, and security aspects are brought back into the picture.

The development of the argument proceeds in three steps. First I survey the overall early modern situation of republican polities, which remains precarious, thus highlighting the anomalous nature of the Venetian, Dutch, and British polities now taken to be prototypical, and then outline the main features of Enlightenment contextual materialist theory, with particular focus on Montesquieu. The middle five sections explore in detail arguments about the consequences of insularity, the origins of capitalism, the decline of martial *virtú*, the distinctiveness of naval empires, and the relationship between size and regime type. Third, by way of conclusion, to help establish the overall importance of these arguments, and to cast new light on well-known figures, I examine the role of material contextual variables in Machiavelli and Rousseau and compare the arguments of the maritime whigs with major contemporary treatments.

ABSOLUTISM AND THE REPUBLICAN ANOMALIES

To place the arguments of the maritime whigs in appropriate historical context, it is useful to survey the overall situation of republican polities in early modern Europe. Focused on success stories and innovations, we can easily overlook the fact that republican polities continue to be precarious, rare, and confined to geographical nooks and crannies, and are exceptions to the overall trend toward the consolidation of monarchical absolutist states.[5] The state-building of monarchial Leviathans prevailed in France, Prussia, Austria, Spain, Sweden, and Russia. The persisting fragmentation in the German-speaking lands of the Holy Roman Empire and on the Italian peninsula offered possibilities for city-state republics, but even here petty absolutisms, often backed by foreign armies, were common. Early modern republican polities remained acutely vulnerable to external conquest and internal subversion.

The first episodes of the early modern republican story take place in Italy, where the waning power of the Holy Roman Emperor in northern Italy and the rediscovery of texts on ancient history and politics by Humanist scholars combined to produce a revival of self-governing city-states and then republican political theory during the fourteenth century.[6] Here emerged a miniature state system, a prototype of the emerging European state system, with its primary units being Milan, Florence, Venice, Naples, and the Papal States.[7] Two of the three republics in the north were subject to intense internal *stasis* and were either overthrown and replaced with principalities or conquered by their neighbors or the larger Trans-Alpine monarchies.[8] Milan succumbed first, its popular government overthrown in a mercenary-backed coup, and in Florence the republican government that Machiavelli served was replaced by a Medician princedom backed by French armies. Venice alone was able to constrain internal factionalism and avoid external conquest, lasting as an independent polity until Napoleon's armies swept across Europe.[9]

This pattern was reproduced across Europe as the medieval order was replaced by the modern states system, greatly shrinking the total number of independent units.[10] The process of absolutist state-building entailed the subordination of semiindependent feudal aristocrats and mercenaries, the displacement of various regional parliaments, and the elimination of mercantile confederations of city-state republics, such as the Hanseatic League.[11] In the Slavic east, the landed aristocracy in sprawling Lithuania and Poland preserved elaborate checks on monarchical power, producing their severe military enfeeblement and eventual absorption by their predatory monarchical neighbors.[12] Against these trends, the Swiss Confederation, a loose association of city-state cantons, was able to sustain its independence due to its mountainous terrain and strong citizen militia.[13] Most importantly, Holland and then Britain were able both to defeat domestic absolute state-builders and sustain their independence from absolutist predators.

ENLIGHTENMENT NATURALIST POLITICAL SCIENCE

Before turning to the specific arguments of the maritime whigs, it is appropriate to add a few general remarks about the intersection of republicanism and contextual materialism in Montesquieu. Upon its publication in 1748 his major work, *Spirit of the Laws*, was hailed as the landmark work of Enlightenment political science. Reflecting his Enlightenment reputation, D'Alembert eulogized him as the Newton of political science, and Madison averred that Montesquieu had done for political science what Bacon had done for general science.[14] Montesquieu was widely recognized, along with Aristotle and Machiavelli, as one of the major founders of political *science*, and his work has had extensive influences in many branches of the human sciences.[15] Despite its reputation and influence, *Spirit of the Laws* is a sprawling work whose organization is obscure, whose empirical evidence is often suspect, and whose overall argument is not easily evident. Despite these limits Montesquieu advances the project of political science by emphasizing the role of general causes[16] operating across time and space and by reinvigorating the comparative and empirical dimension of Aristotelian political science, but with the much larger 'data sets' generated by the European global reconnaissance.[17]

More important for this investigation, Montesquieu's arguments constitute a synthesis and culmination of the ancient and early modern naturalist phase of contextual materialist theory and of the early modern advances in republican theory and practice. Montesquieu's summation of ancient and early modern physiopolitical claims served as the benchmark against which the subsequent turn to historicist materialist theorizing would measure itself as the topic of technologically driven change became of paramount concern. For republican theorizing, Montesquieu's summation on structure and size served as foundation on which the American project of federal union would build.

Montesquieu advances numerous contextual material arguments about the impact of climate, soil fertility, topography, land-sea interactions, and size. Despite the centrality of these natural-material factors in his argument and the wide influence of his work, recent international theorists have virtually ignored his work, and recent political theory commentaries on his work have studiously ignored his international and contextual-material arguments.[18] Montesquieu's materialist arguments are marshaled as part of a general effort to explain the origins and differences in the mores and laws of particular societies. As his title suggests, Montesquieu seeks to explain how the nonmaterial 'spirit' (or predominant ethos and political culture) are shaped by and interact with political structures and material contexts. The basic approach is clearly articulated by Millar:

> In searching for the causes of those peculiar systems of law and government which have appeared in the world, we must undoubtedly resort, first of all, to the differences of situation, which have suggested different views and motives of action to the inhabitants of particular countries. Of this kind, are the fertility or barrenness of the soil, the nature of its productions, the species of labour requisite for procuring subsistence, the number of individuals collected together in one community, their proficiency in arts, the advantages which they enjoy for entering into mutual transactions, and for maintaining an intimate correspondence. The variety that frequently occurs in these, and such other particulars, must have a prodigious influence upon the great body of a people, as, by giving a peculiar direction to their institutions and pursuits, it must be productive of correspondent habits, dispositions, and ways of thinking.[19]

Within the overall trajectory of republican and Liberal theorizing, Montesquieu occupies a similarly pivotal position, providing the most comprehensive and substantive statement of early modern and Enlightenment republicanism on the eve of its transmutation into Liberalism. Although he shared Machiavelli's political realism, opposition to the Roman church, and embrace of plurality, Montesquieu powerfully registers all of the anti-Machiavellian developments of modern republicanism, particularly the embrace of commerce, abhorrence of war, religious toleration, and rejection of Roman militarism and imperialism as the model of successful republican government. His main allegiances are to the moderate, the restrained, and the antidespotic. Profoundly influenced by his lengthy visit to Britain at the zenith of the Whig ascendency, major parts of his work synthesize and reflect on the emerging commercialism and representative constitutionalism of Britain after the 'Glorious Revolution' of 1688.[20]

Insularity, Navies, and Liberty

Turning to an examination of the specific arguments of the maritime whigs, we first consider claims about the restraining power of water on internal constitutional development. In part because of Machiavelli's towering reputation, the attention of contemporary scholars has been focused more on Florence than Venice.[21] In Venice, as in the Netherlands and England, the emergence of republican forms of governance was associated with insularity and navies.[22] The idea that insular and naval states would tend to be less despotic than states with territorial borders and extensive standing armies was noted by numerous European and particularly British writers. The Venetian Cardinal Gasparo Contarini, in his widely read treatise on the Venetian constitution, argued that Venice was able to avoid the Caesarian coups that destroyed the Roman Republic because it relied primarily upon its navy, thus keeping military force at arms length from the city itself.[23] Botero takes the restraining power of water argument a step further with the suggestion that *serenissima* (most serene) Venice's legendary lack of civil turmoil partially derived from the political effects of its canals.[24] In speaking of the genesis and persistence of the balanced constitution in England, Whig publicists like Charles Davanent[25] (the Huguenot refugee and political economist), and John Trenchard and Thomas Gordon[26] (authors of the widely read *Cato's Letters)* note this relationship, and Montesquieu observes that "conquerors are stopped by the sea; and the islanders, being without the reach of their arms, more easily preserve their own laws."[27]

This argument was made most clearly and forcefully during the Scottish Enlightenment by John Millar, a professor of law at Glasgow University and student of Adam Smith.[28] Millar argues that the failure of monarchical absolutism in Britain and its success on the continent stems from the way in which "accidental" variations in geographic setting shaped otherwise parallel processes of social, economic, and political development (see figure 4.1). As the "opulence" of European states increased in the early modern period, feudal levies and militias are replaced or supplemented with mercenary and professional forces. On the continent, where kingdoms "were greatly exposed to the attacks of neighboring powers," large armies were common. Such armies were "easily diverted from its original destination to that of supporting and enlarging his [the monarch's] power," thus producing "despotical government." But Britain's circumstances were different: its "insular situation" meant it was "little exposed to the attacks of any foreign potentate." And the naval arm was ill-suited for furthering despotism: "The fleets in the service of the crown are, besides, at too great a distance, and their operations of too peculiar a nature, to admit of their being employed occasionally in quelling insurrections at home, or in checking the efforts of the people to maintain their privileges. They are confined to a different element." Thus the "line of separation"[29] between Britain and neighboring countries exerted great influence on the preservation and development of popular liberty in Britain. The Stuart quest for absolutism failed because the English monarch "had no military force upon which he could depend, and was therefore obliged to yield to the growing power of the commons."[30] Parliament was able to counterbalance the weight of a king equipped with a strong navy, but not a general at the head of a large indigenous army, as Oliver Cromwell demonstrated when he established himself as dictator with the large army assembled in the course of civil conflict.[31]

This argument was picked up and repeated by a wide variety of writers. In his commentary on Montesquieu (which was translated into English by Thomas Jefferson), the French political theorist Destutt de Tracy made the link with particular clarity,[32] and then proposed an intriguing counterfactual: that liberty and prosperity would be universal if all the world were divided into islands, and sunk in despotism and poverty if it were all one land mass:

> [I]f we suppose the surface of the globe divided into islands of a proper extent and distance from each other, it would be covered by rich and industrious nations, who would not stand in need of any land armies, consequently ruled by moderate governments only. Having the most convenient communication among themselves, and scarcely any ability to hurt each other without affecting their reciprocal relations, their differences would soon cease by means of their mutual dependence and wants. If, on the other contrary, we suppose the earth without sea, nations would then be without commerce, always in arms, in constant fear of neighboring nations, ignorant of others, and living under military governments: the sea is one obstacle to all kinds of evil, and a means of numerous advantages.[33]

This connection between insularity, navalism, and 'free institutions' was later repeated by Otto Hintze, finds its way into Mackinder's depiction of the genesis of British 'liberty' in his civics textbooks,[34] and is widely noted by recent historians.[35] As a broad historical generalization, this claim is, however, seriously incomplete, for it fails to acknowledge the vulnerability of insular peoples to domination by neighboring larger islands. An Irish or Hawaiin meditation on insularity and liberty would be much less celebratory.

This argument of the maritime whigs can be simply reformulated in the language of recent social science. Britain avoided absolutism because the defense of its territory required a force-structure that was functionally specialized and differentiated in such a way that rendered it useless for purposes of internal coercion. The British success in checking the concentration of power in a centralized state apparatus was rooted in topographical division and the incommensurability of armies and navies. Nature more effectively separated and limited power than did the design of republican institutions and organizations.

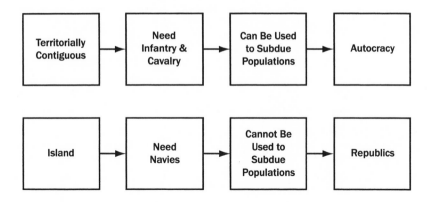

Figure 4.1 Topographical-Positional Impacts upon Regime Type

THE REPUBLIC OF COMMERCE

The maritime whigs also make several arguments linking aspects of the sea with the emergence of capitalism and 'moderate' states (see figure 4.2). Here we are concerned with theories about the nature and presuppositions of 'commerce,' a term used in the eighteenth century to refer to trade, production-for-trade, and the institutions that later came to be called 'capitalist.'[36] The claims of the maritime whigs about the origin of capitalism are 'political economic' explanations in which the political takes prominence over the economic. The maritime whigs present a contextual materialist explanation for these institutional developments that contrasts both with Marxist explanations that emphasize forces and relations of production and the several 'Weberian' explanations that emphasize intellectual and cultural variables.[37]

As virtually all students of the topic note, there is a strikingly high correlation between early capitalist activity and maritime accessibility and activity.[38] In the late Middle Ages, Venice, Genoa, and the Hanseatic League depended heavily upon the sea and helped pioneer capitalist institutions and practices. In the modern era, Holland and then Britain exhibit this correlation on a larger and more successful scale. Three physiopolitical explanations for this correlation are found in early modern writings. First, and most obviously, the sea provided cheap transportation, making exchange possible on a large enough scale to justify production for the market. As Montesquieu observed, Europe was particularly well suited to trade, and thus likely to develop capitalism. Second, the European region was thought to have significant climatic variations, which in turn

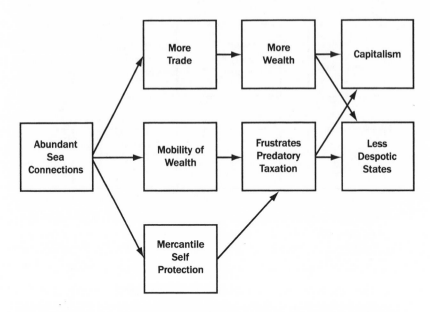

Figure 4.2 The Sea and the Origins of Capitalism and Less Despotic States

contributed to opportunities for trade, since the production of many of the products in commerce (e.g., wine, cork, timber, naval stores, grain, wool, and fish) was limited by climatic conditions to specific regions.[39]

Third, access to the sea provided wealth and productive capability with enough mobility to escape from predatory taxation, thus encouraging capitalism and moderating state behavior. In this argument, the link between the sea and capitalism is through the intervening variable of state ability to tax wealth. Concerning political preconditions to robust market relations, Adam Smith is reported to have held that "[l]ittle else is requisite to carry a state to the highest degree of opulence from the lowest barbarism, but peace, easy taxes, and a tolerable administration justice; all the rest being brought about by the natural course of things."[40] However, such a minimum state was rare and predatory taxation and bureaucratic economic controls were the norm in the great civilizations of China, India, and Islam.

In Europe a different pattern prevailed. In the physiopolitical explanation vividly drawn by Montesquieu, the decisive fact was that wealth was able to become mobile enough to escape from predatory state taxation: "Commerce is sometimes destroyed by conquerors, sometimes cramped by monarchs; it traverses the earth, flies from the places where it is oppressed, and stays where it has liberty to breathe: it reigns at present where nothing was formerly to be seen but deserts, seas, and rocks; and where it once reigned now there are only deserts." Europe was particularly prone to develop commerce because a combination of extensive maritime access and the invention of the "letter of exchange" made commerce "capable of eluding violence."[41] As capital became mobile, states had to reduce their taxation and avoid predatory appropriations of wealth, or else see wealth flee from their grasp. States are tamed, and become less despotic and more respectful of property rights:

> From this time it became necessary that princes should govern with more prudence than they themselves could ever have imagined; for great exertions of authority were, in the event, found to be impolitic; and from experience it is manifest that nothing but the goodness and lenity of a government can make it [commerce] flourish. We begin to be cured of Machiavelism, and recover from it every day. More moderation has become necessary in the councils of princes. What formerly have been called a master-stroke in politics would be now, independent of the horror it might occasion, the greatest imprudence.[42]

In these passages Montesquieu points to two consequences of the mobility of wealth: increased wealth and less despotic states. Those areas where wealth can flee can be expected to be relatively richer and freer than the closed agrarian domains where predatory taxation was less checked. The speed with which Amsterdam and London replaced Antwerp as the leading hub of northern European commerce in the wake of imperial Spanish taxation particularly impressed Millar as a pivotal event in the saga of liberty, and has been characterized in similar terms by several recent political historians and geographers.[43]

The mobility of wealth in the genesis of European capitalism seems to be both the cause and the consequence of the failure of European imperial consolidation in the early modern era. However, it seems plausible to attribute some significant measure of direct and independent causality to maritime accessibility in the genesis of capitalism, because the states in a multistate system lacking significant sea transport might well retard wealth formation nearly as vigorously and effectively as one empire.

Virtú ex Machina

Commentators on the eighteenth century often point to the mildness and moderation of states as a distinguishing feature of the era. Early modern writers sought to explain the rise of moderation as resulting from a new relation between wealthy and commercial states and military viability. As we saw, classical republican theorists had held that commerce, because it sapped the military virtue of the citizen class, would lead to military defeat. To make republics less perishable, ancient republican theorists sought to preserve the military virtue of its citizen-soldiers through sumptuary laws and other customs, a topic that continued to occupy many of the major early modern republican theorists, such as Machiavelli in his *Discourses* and Harrington in *Oceana*.[44] Meeting this requirement, in turn, had ramifications for interstate order: the rudeness of manners and militarism in surviving republics created immoderation in international politics, intensifying the difficulty of maintaining international peace.

Eighteenth-century republican thinkers, following on paths pioneered by Venetians, challenged the old link between minimum military viability and the careful maintenance of a warrior ethos. Their key insight is what might be termed the *mechanization of virtú*, or *virtú ex machina*.[45] They argue this tension between freedom and security had been rendered obsolete by the emergence of capital and technology-intensive warfare. Gibbon makes the argument with striking clarity in his short comparison between the Roman Empire and the modern European 'Republic':

> The military art has been changed by the invention of gunpowder, which enables Man to command the two most powerful agents of Nature, air and fire. Mathematics, chymistry, mechanics, architecture have been applied to the service of war; and the adverse parties oppose to each other the most elaborate modes of attack and defence. Historians may indignantly observe that the preparations of a siege would found and maintain a flourishing colony; yet we cannot be displeased that the subversion of a city should be a work of cost and difficulty; or that *an industrious people should be protected by those arts which survive and supply the decay of military virtue*. Cannon and fortifications now form an impregnable barrier against the Tartar horse; and Europe is secure from any future irruption of Barbarians, since, before they can conquer, they must cease to be barbarous. Their gradual advances in the science of war would always be accompanied, as we may learn from the example of Russia, with a proportionable improvement in the arts of peace and civil policy; and they themselves must deserve a place among the polished nations whom they subdue.[46]

The increasingly decisive elements of modern warfare were increasingly complex and expensive implements like walls, ships, and gunpowder weapons. Naval and mercantile activities were more dependent upon complex and expensive apparatuses than was land warfare. With the development of naval gunpowder weapons, merchants were able to directly invest in the ability to protect themselves (or attack competitors) without depending upon infantry and cavalry. Both piracy and mutiny did occur, but merchants could be far more confident of secure passage at sea than on land.[47]

The weakening link between citizen military *virtù* and military viability had far-reaching consequences for the character of self-governing regimes. The mildness of a citizenry devoted to commerce was no longer a prelude to military destruction and so could remain unchecked.[48] The prevalence of mild manners and the decay of rude warrior virtues among the self-governing middle strata of society in republics suggested that a new era of relative peace and constrained war was dawning. Glory through heroic conquest began to decline as an important part of the civic culture of republican polities. The crucial assumption in these arguments was not that states devoted to commerce were any less self-interested than others.[49] Rather, the eighteenth-century republican argument is that modern technic- and capital-intensive warfare made possible the survival of mild-mannered peoples, and thus the extended viability and influence of states with mild foreign policies. This in turn suggests that the rapacious military imperialism so often characteristic of ancient city-state republics was the product of a citizen warrior polity rather than popular rule.

Empire without Corruption

To the extent that the restraining power of water was a factor in the rise of liberty in Europe, the absence of restraints upon Europeans on the world Ocean was simultaneously creating a far greater realm of acute domination outside of Europe, as the Europeans plundered, enslaved, conquered, and displaced numerous peoples in the Americas, Africa, and Asia. Leading Enlightenment figures objected to aspects of this prodigious global expansion out of concern for the welfare of the great majority of humankind, but the earlier and later overall European assessment ranged from approval to glorification.[50] However, within the republican pockets of Europe where absolutist monarchs had not gained ascendancy, the European imperial enterprise raised profoundly disturbing questions about whether the creation of external empire was compatible with the preservation of internal liberty. With the experience of the Roman Republic's expansion and demise as their historically inherited model, republican theorists presumptively viewed imperial expansion with great unease.[51]

The answer to this puzzle, advanced first by Venetian and then Dutch and British thinkers, is that maritime expansion does not have the same liabilities for domestic liberty as did territorial expansion on the Roman model. Given the perils of interstate rivalry, the growth in power entailed in imperial expansion held intrinsic appeal as a means of achieving greater security from external predation. Venetian theorists, most notably Paruta, had scorned Machiavelli's attempted revival of the Roman imperial model and touted Venice as a pacific and commercial alternative. However, Machiavelli had classified Venice as a 'republic for preservation' rather than a 'republic for expansion,' with the implication that Venice would remain small and hence subject to external predation, a view that seemed consistent with Venice's loss of its possessions on the Italian *terra firma* in a single battle in 1509.

This dilemma was also widely analyzed by English (and then British) theorists reflecting on the brief Cromwellian Protectorate and then the growing commercial, colonial, and imperial activities after the Glorious Revolution. The problem of achieving external growth for security while sustaining domestic political liberty was a central topic of Harrington's baroquely convoluted tome *The Commonwealth of Oceana*. Although among the most inaccessible major works of early modern republican theory, Harrington, building on and paralleling the ideas of other contemporaries, advanced a design for a polity that would combine external expansion and internal liberty. Reflecting on the experience of Roman yeoman dispossession, Harrington advanced an elaborate scheme to constitutionally preserve small agricultural proprietors as the basis for a militia strong enough to counterbalance political and military centralization.[52] But the viability of this arrangement was directly linked to his maritime argument. The key notion was that expansion which occurred overseas would not present a threat to domestic liberty because the military assets it assembled would not be capable of threatening the liberties of the insular state. Caesar might be able to cross the Rubicon, but he could not so readily cross the Ocean. Further precluding the recurrence of the Roman pattern, the devotion of Oceana to commerce would permit the aggregation of wealth without military conquest. In an often-quoted passage he observed that "[t]he sea giveth law unto the growth of Venice, but the growth of Oceana giveth law unto the sea."[53] This arresting image seems to suggest that Britain as Oceana should or could achieve a hegemony on the Ocean that would enable it to achieve great security and wealth without substantial overseas territorial possessions. At the heart of these arguments is again the restraining power of water. The same topographic impediments and compositional differentiation at work in the preservation of Britain from foreign invasion and from monarchic usurpation would also permit a corruption-free path to imperial enlargement and thus enhanced security. The restraining power of water makes possible the reconciliation of internal *libertas* with external *imperium*.

Size, Interior Balancing, and Regime Type

Another set of early modern arguments about material contexts and republican 'unit-level' structures address the relationship between size and regime type. They are presented most clearly and synthetically by Montesquieu, Hume, and Millar, who build from ancient and late medieval sources.[54] Not involving the restraining power of water, these arguments serve as a stepping stone to the Europe-wide (system-level) arguments explored in the next chapter. These arguments explain how variations in size and speed rooted in material circumstances exert a powerful influence upon political regime types. They combine into one simple schema the pessimistic conclusions of the ancients and the innovations of the early moderns.

Assuming the primacy of security from external threat, Montesquieu observes that political orders exhibit proportionality between their size, the velocity of military power, and the degree of concentration necessary for military viability:

> To preserve a state in its due force, it must have such an extent and magnitude, as to admit of a proportion between the quickness with which it may be invaded, and that with which it may render the invasion abortive. As an invader may instantly appear on all sides, it is requisite that the state should be able to make on all sides its defense; consequently it should be of a moderate extent, proportioned to the degree of velocity that nature has given to man in order to move from one place to another.[55]

The "velocity that nature has given" varies in different geographic contexts and produces three different size units. The absence of natural hindrances on great plains produces large regimes. Moderate natural hindrances, present in Europe, produce moderately sized units. Great natural hindrances, such as mountainous or insular terrains, produce small units. At the largest size, Europe's fragmented political system is the result of its topographical fragmentation, thus impeding 'universal monarchy' and making possible medium- and small-sized units.

The heart of the argument is the claim that different sized units will have different internal structures due to scale effects (see figure 4.3). As Montesquieu succinctly puts it: "It is, therefore the natural property of *small* states to be governed as a *republic*, of *middling* ones to be subject to a *monarch*, and of *large empires* to be swayed by a *despotic* prince."[56] Specific regime types are appropriate to specific spatial sizes, and if a regime is founded with a mismatch to its size, Montesquieu says it will evolve according to defined paths. A large empire must have despotic authority because "it is necessary that the *quickness* of the prince's resolutions should supply the *distance* of the places they are sent to."[57] Despotism, juridically unrestrained internally, is necessary to compensate for the restraining effects of great distance. By the same logic, a monarchy in a large unit would fall apart (or become despotic) because distance diminishes authority.[58] At the low end of the spectrum, republics occur in "a single town" because the concentrated power of a single ruler in such close quarters would be oppressive, stimulating a revolt that the ruler

	Republic	Limited Monarchy	Despotism
Large			X
Medium		X	
Small	X		

Figure 4.3 Montesquieu on the Relation of Size and Regime Type

would lack additional resources to suppress.[59] If a republic becomes large, it will tend to become a monarchy and ultimately despotic; but if a despotism should shrink to the size of a city, it would tend to become a republic. In sum, each of the three regime types is based on a proportion between size, speed, and concentration of power that is a functional adaptation to a particular material context, and when one variable changes the others will as well.[60]

The final element of the argument relates size-based variations to the difficulty of overcoming the collective action problem entailed in interior balancing. As Millar puts it, the ability of "the people, single and unconnected" to "resist the oppression of their governors" and their "power for combining for this purpose" depends on "their peculiar circumstances."[61] In very large states, Hume observes, despotic oppression is facilitated by the difficulty of collective action for interior balancing as "each act of violence" is "performed upon a part" that is "distant from the majority" and therefore "is not taken notice of" and "each part, ignorant of the resolutions of the rest, is afraid to begin any commotion or insurrection."[62] In "large kingdoms" the people "dispersed over a wide country" and subject to "very imperfect means of communication" have "seldom been capable" of "vigorous exertions," and "a rebellion may be quelled in one quarter before it has time to break out in another."[63] Conversely, in a city-state, Montesquieu observes, the oppressive rule of a single man is subject to greater ease of interior balancing as "the people might every instant unite and rise up against him."[64] Picking up on this pattern, Millar argues that the "spirit of liberty" in commercial countries is enhanced by the increased "facility with which the several members of society are enabled to associate and to act in concert with one another."[65]

Montesquieu's formulation (recall figure 4.3) appears to be an analytically sophisticated version of the pessimistic prognosis for liberty found in ancient and Renaissance thought: republics are necessarily small and therefore are viable only in exceptional geographic contexts. Somewhat oddly, however, Montesquieu's schema does not actually incorporate early modern innovations elsewhere analyzed in the *Spirit of the Laws*, and as such should probably best be read as the benchmark against which these innovations are registered. In his famous treatment of the British Constitution in book 11, Montesquieu characterizes this order as a "republic disguised under the form of monarchy,"[66] thus registering the scale-up of republican forms from the city-state to the nation-state size. The key point, as Hume observed in his famous essay "The Idea of a Perfect Commonwealth," is that the classical equation between republics and small size had been broken with the development of representation.[67] Montesquieu also famously hypothesized the possibility of a "confederation of republican city-states" as a means to overcome their vulnerability, and argues that the historic viability of city-state republics had often depended upon this arrangement.[68] This form also solves the security problems of city-states: "should a popular insurrection happen in one of the confederate states, the others are able to quell it. Should abuses creep into one part, they are reformed by those that remain sound. The state may be destroyed on one side, and not the other; the confederacy may be dissolved, and confederates preserve their sovereignty." In short, "a republic of this kind, able to withstand an external force, may support itself without an internal corruption."[69]

The presence in Europe of small and medium polities exerts a pacifying influence on the overall character of interstate life because of the relatively more pacific disposition of monarchies, and especially republics and confederations of republics, combined with extensive commerce. Yet the presence of such polities and interactions ultimately hinges upon the obstacles to the erection of a systemwide despotic empire, the topic of the next chapter.

IMPERIAL REVIVALISM AND POLIS NOSTALGIA

As the first of two steps in concluding this exegesis of the maritime whigs it is useful to cast a brief glance at the treatment of material contexts and republican forms in the works of Machiavelli and Rousseau, the two towering figures who stand like bookends at the beginning and end of early modern republican thought. Despite their great sophistication and

wide influence (and diverse interpretations), the republicanisms of both
Machiavelli and Rousseau are substantially at odds with the new paradigm of modern republicanism pioneered in Venice, the Netherlands, and
Britain. Both look to ancient martial republics (Rome and Sparta) as models to remedy modern political decay; both are hostile in varying degrees
to the pacifying promise of commerce; both weigh political structures for
their effects on civic personality; both posit the superiority of harshly
parochial pagan religion over more cosmopolitan forms; and both have
been appropriated as founders of Realism. Although the topics of violence
restraint and international security are prominent in their thought, they
are essentially backward looking and arrested outliers in the main trajectory of republican security theory.

Machiavelli is universally regarded as the first modern political theorist
due to his realism and instrumentalism, and his correspondent turn from
the morality-centered natural law view of politics. But in terms of substantive treatment of republicanism, Machiavelli might better be thought of
the last of the ancients, for he provides a distillation of the inner logic of
ancient, particularly Roman, statecraft, unshrouded by natural law idealism.[70] Leaving aside the vexed and probably unsolvable problem of the
relationship between the *Prince* and the *Discourses*, and focusing on the
later work, an extended commentary on Livy's history of the early Roman
Republic, we find Roman expansion offered as a model for modern political renewal. Largely ignoring Venice, deemed a "republic for preservation," Machiavelli looks to Rome as a "republic for expansion."[71] Revis-
iting Polybius's question of the causes of the Roman ascent, Machiavelli
follows him in ascribing central importance to the Roman constitution,
but reverses the central claim of Polybius's argument. Like Polybius,
Machiavelli sees Roman religion as particularly well suited to support
military prowess, but he sees Roman political arrangements as sustaining
tumults that stimulate foreign advance, in contrast to Polybius's view of
Roman checks and balances as forcing compromise and agreement.

The energizing role Machiavelli assigns to the balance of power within
a well-ordered republic does not precede his endorsement of it as a mechanism for ordering interstate life. Unlike his contemporary the Florentine
diplomat Francesco Guiccardini, who described and defended the balance
of power among the Italian city-states, Machiavelli seeks to revive a tumultuous domestic balance of power between the many and the few as a
wellspring of imperial expansion at the expense of the independence of
other states.[72] Beyond this, there is a key ambiguity in Machiavelli's view.
On the one hand, it is possible to read his call to emulate republican
Roman expansion as an endorsement of universal empire over interstate
balance and plurality, in which case the demands of size would eventually
lead to despotism and the enervation of popular liberty. If this is his view

then it is glory, not liberty, that is his animating goal. [73] On the other hand, Machiavelli can be read in his contemporary Italian and European setting as offering a program to consolidate the Italian city-states being dwarfed by the emerging Trans-Alpine monarchies in order for Italy to play a role in the larger emerging European system of plurality and balance.[74] If the latter is his view, then he exemplifies the recurrent pattern in balance-of-power thought: it is sometimes necessary to eliminate (or at least domesticate) plurality and balance in order to preserve it on a larger scale, a pattern to recur on yet a larger scale in twentieth-century Europe.

Machiavelli's disposition toward commerce is largely hostile. Wealth is acknowledged as a sinew of war, but he essentially holds the classical view of its dangers to martial *virtù* and seeks laws to remedy its decay. Material contextual factors are not altogether absent in Machiavelli's work, but their overall role is marginal.[75] In stereotypical Renaissance fashion, Machiavelli focuses upon agency as a force for change rather than material context as a patterned source of restraint. The *virtù* of man is pitted and tested against the vicissitudes of *fortuna*, not channeled by the contours of nature. For Machiavelli, *fortuna* is contingency, circumstance, a turn of events demanding situational cunning and flexibility, and there is no expectation that even an individual of extraordinary *virtù* can do any more than temporarily erect 'dikes' and 'dams' to channel contingency.[76] In this dynamic duel, both the regularities and vagaries of nature recede into the background.

On the overall historical balance sheet, the largely archaic character of Machiavelli's substantive political arguments is vastly overshadowed by the influence of his 'new way of proceeding,' his instrumental rationalism and anticlassical idealism, which clearly stands, for better or worse, as foundational to political modernity in both its republican and absolutist branches.

If Machiavelli, standing at the beginning of modernity, is best seen as the last of the ancient republicans, then Rousseau, standing near the end of the European Enlightenment, provides a powerful, if peculiar, evocation of the most illiberal ancient republics against which to measure the failings of early modern republicanism. Despite his powerful evocations of freedom, Rousseau's animating project and its neo-Spartan program, as we suggested earlier, is fundamentally antiliberal. What had been necessary inconveniences for the ancients are embraced by Rousseau as valuable precisely for their illiberal effects. Rousseau sees models such as the United Provinces and Great Britain as irredeemably corrupted by precisely those elements celebrated as innovations by Enlightenment republicans. The overall result is a pessimism about the prospects for political liberty even more severe than in the ancients: the barriers to liberty in climate, size, and geography identified by the ancients still operate, but are joined by the solutions offered by the moderns.

The impediments to political liberty from nature remain very much in force for Rousseau, and he unflinchingly declares that "freedom, not being the fruit of every Clim, is not within the reach of every people."[77] The level of wealth, still primarily a derivative of 'fertility' best "suit free peoples" in "places where the excess of produce over labor is moderate," while monarchies are appropriate to places where "an abundant and fertile soil yields much produce in return for little labor."[78] Size, schematized by Rousseau straightforwardly from Montesquieu, confines republics to a "very small state" and "the more a state expands, the more freedom is diminished."[79] With government making a "constant effort" to usurp sovereignty, large size impedes popular collective action.[80] Also following Montesquieu, Rousseau attributes the survival of medium- and small-sized polities—and thus any prospect for political liberty—to Europe's geographical fragmentation.

This pessimism is deepened by Rousseau's firm rejection of representation and commerce. Although Rousseau admits the necessity of delegations of executive power, he is adamant in rejecting delegation of legislative power through representation.[81] Instead of seeing England as a new and more secure type of republic (cloaked in monarchic form), Rousseau says the English people "thinks itself free" but is "greatly mistaken" because "it is free only during the election of Members of Parliament" and "as soon as they are elected, it is enslaved."[82] For Rousseau the old problems remain, and the new solutions are themselves problems.

Forgotten Foundations, New Optimism

Looking at the liberal-democratic juggernaut at the turn of the twenty-first century, it is easy to forget that republican polities have only recently risen to prominence in world politics. Within the overall mosaic of early modern political development, republics were exceptional rather than typical. It is also easy to forget the very peculiar circumstances that made possible the birth of political and economic freedom in the modern era. The arguments of the maritime whigs remind us that the first enclaves of very imperfect political and economic freedom were in no small measure a gift of nature. The central insight of the maritime whigs is that the small pockets where absolutism did not hold sway were geographically situated in ways that compensated for their small size. The mundane brute fact that landed hierarchs could not readily project their superior mass across water gave these early modern republics, especially Venice and Britain, a crucial security advantage. This in turn made it possible for early modern republics to dispense with the onerous and debilitating martial civic life that had so constricted political liberty in the ancient world.

The material contextual arguments of the maritime whigs contrast sharply with the picture drawn of early modern republicanism by the recent 'republican revisionist' school of intellectual historians, and recovery of the maritime whigs suggests several deficiencies in the republican revivalist account of early modern republicanism. The revivalists' emphasis upon ideology, language, and discourse does not give adequate recognition to the pervasive practical problem-solving dimensions in republicanism, and particularly security-from-violence. Despite their emphasis upon contextual analysis, the revivalists' analysis of institutions without primary reference to their ability to cope with the daunting security problems in different material circumstances produces a highly idealistic image of politics. Neglecting the security problem, the revivalists miss the really crucial early modern development: free polities devoted to commerce are no longer vulnerable because of their wealth, but instead were increasingly secure and powerful because of it.

Because the revivalists focus upon words rather than institutional forms and functions, they see the eighteenth century as the final act of republicanism. In actuality republicanism in this period innovated new solutions to the problem of securing freedom and new opportunities to transcend the severe strictures that had previously bound free polities. The rise of capitalist and individualistic free societies marks not the end of republicanism, but in significant measure is the result of the new material contexts and institutional innovations that permitted free polities to secure themselves without their citizens being soldiers. The virtues necessary for the security of freedom no longer needed to be primarily imprinted in the characters of the citizens, but were increasingly in the institutional machinery of power restraining constitutions and in the physical machinery of nascent industrial military technology. Missing the progressive character of republican power restraint practices, the revivalists erroneously assume that the particular complex of civic humanist political preoccupations (virtue, anticommerce) are equivalent to republicanism, when they were historically particular forms required to secure freedom in particular material contexts.

Within international theory, the arguments of early modern and Enlightenment republican theorists enjoy a very uneven presence. On the one hand, the arguments of the maritime whigs about the material contextual foundations of republics and commerce have largely sunk without a trace. On the other hand, the arguments from this period about the pacific consequences of democratic and commercial republics are enshrined as canonical in contemporary Liberal international theory, under the rubrics of 'democratic peace' and 'commercial peace.' The basic difference between

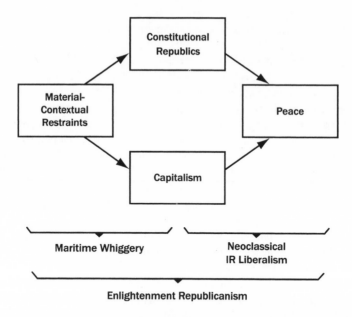

Figure 4.4 Maritime Whiggery and Neoclassical IR Liberalism

the maritime whigs and these thinkers is that the maritime whigs are attempting to explain the *causes* of constitutional republics and commercial capitalism, while the neoclassical Liberals are mainly making arguments about the *consequences* of these political and economic formations [83] (see figure 4.4).

The arguments of the maritime whigs and the neoclassical Liberals are thus complementary rather than competing, and both are necessary to give a complete picture of these formations in international politics. The fact, however, that the first set of arguments has been almost ignored reflects a pervasive amnesia about the role of very specific material contextual restraints in the historical origins of liberal democratic and capitalist polities. It is striking that those Enlightenment figures and arguments that have been preserved and labeled 'early Liberals' are largely the ones who take for granted that democracies and commerce exist in sufficient numbers and magnitude to have consequences to analyze. It seems that what marks the divide between those theorists kept as 'early Liberals' and those consigned to oblivion is not their substantive arguments, but rather the extent to which they take as given what is now taken as given.

The shift from the world of the maritime whigs to the world of the 'Liberals' is also marked by a shift in expectations about the overall prospects for political and economic freedom. The maritime whigs have an only moderately modified version of ancient republican pessimism, while the neoclassical Liberals are modern optimists. Although the maritime whigs offer many reasons to think there have been significant improvements in the security viability of republican polities, they provide no basis for an open-ended optimism. However universal the human desire for political liberty and security might be, early modern republican security theorists believed that nature, and the limits of the arts of politics, condemned most of humanity to live in unfree states. The maritime whigs do not provide any basis for thinking republican political forms could be universally, or even extensively, adopted. In contrast, the turn to the 'Liberal' brings with it a much more expansive view of the potential for free political and economic forms to become universal. No longer bound by the strenuous circumstances of their arduous birthplaces, republican forms can be spread by a process of emulation, competition, and revolution until they become universal.

Turning toward the international system, the arguments of the maritime whigs paint the picture of a complex political order, or Oceana. This sprawling entity was not coincident with the British state, but included important trading enclaves all around Europe. The British core of Oceana was the region's largest 'republican' state, and its limited government constitution was significantly unlike the absolutist monarchies on the continent. Oceana was a dynamo of mercantile activity, but it was always at risk from the continental monarchies with imperial tendencies. This peculiar and revolutionary realm came into being not because of the extraordinary virtue of nautical peoples, nor because of a particularly farsighted acting of founding, but because of the constraints and opportunities offered by geography and technology. To further understand the regionwide material contexts and political structures within which the precocious modern republics emerge takes us to the system-level arguments of Enlightenment republican theory.

Chapter Five

THE NATURAL 'REPUBLIC' OF EUROPE

[T]he political order in this part of the world is, in
certain respects, the work of nature.
—Jean-Jacques Rousseau[1]

THE EUROPEAN STATE SYSTEM AND INTERNATIONAL THEORY

For better or worse, Europe has decisively shaped the last half millennium of world history. Beginning around 1500 and culminating in the early-twentieth century, European imperialism and colonialism influenced or dominated virtually every corner of the planet. Interacting with and fueling this outward expansion, revolutionary developments in science, technology, economy, society, and culture also transformed Europe itself from a relative backwater to the most dynamic civilization in modern times and saw the emergence in Europe of fundamentally novel political forms. Europe's globe-spanning empires almost completely have vanished in the second half of the twentieth century, but the modern world is largely the result of the European vortex and the reactions or emulations of others to it.

The intellectual legacies of the European experience loom equally large in international theory. Despite a few ancient precursors, the modern Europeans largely invented the enterprise of theorizing about international politics, and international theory—and Realism in particular—remains largely a set of generalizations from—and arguments about—European experiences. Enlightenment theorists first employed the expression 'states system,' and the early modern European, or Westphalian, system remains the epitome of state systems. For all Realists the early modern European state system is the paradigmatic model of a multipolar 'balance of power' system. Similarly, contemporary 'society of states' Realists and constructivists direct their attention to the European institutional inventions of mutually recognized sovereignty, permanent diplomacy, and public international law.[2]

Reflecting the continued centrality of European legacies in international theory, diplomatic and intellectual historians, political theorists, and international relations theorists have generated a vast literature critically examining the ideas of particular European theorists (beginning with such titans as Machiavelli, Grotius, Hobbes, Montesquieu, Rousseau, and Kant, and extending to a myriad of lesser figures) and specific topics (most notably the balance of power, sovereignty, diplomacy, international law). This vast outpouring is in turn dwarfed by the immense empirical and narrative literature produced by diplomatic historians of innumerable European battles, wars, armies, navies, statesmen, generals, alliances, diplomatic relations, and peace settlements.

Despite this importance and attention, a central cluster of early modern European international theory is oddly out of focus in contemporary treatments. The key fact, conceptually awkward for contemporary approaches, is that Enlightenment international system theory was cast in the terminologies of physiopolitics and republicanism. A wide array of Enlightenment theorists spoke of Europe as a whole as a 'republic' that was in part 'by nature,' in an effort to comprehend the European political order as structured by a multiplicity of restraints on power, which, as in other republics, prevented the twin perils of full anarchy and full hierarchy. This claim encompasses the now conventional ideas that Europe was a system of multiple interactive parts, that it lacked an overall hierarchical authority (or 'universal monarch'), and that the 'balance of power' was an important mechanism of restraint. But more was meant as well. In calling Europe a 'republic,' the early moderns were offering a more complex view in which topographic divisions, the mixture of land power and sea power creating a special balancer state, practices of division, and societal elements of community and equality operated along with the balance of power to produce restraint.

Some of the ideas of Enlightenment natural republican international theory (most notably the concepts of system, balance of power, and society of states) remain pivotal in contemporary international theory; but others, most notably division and mixture, are almost ignored. In combination, these familiar and unfamiliar concepts add up to a substantially different overall image of Europe than that found in any contemporary theoretical treatment. In addition to gaining a better understanding of the origin of key contemporary international theoretical concepts, there are three main reasons for recovering this overall lost argument.

First, contemporary international theorists see European-wide political patterns—a state system—as the prototypical international or interstate pattern.[3] In contrast, Enlightenment materialist republican theorists saw Europe as novel and anomalous as a persistent state system. Continuing the broad comparative analysis begun by ancient empirical political science, but equipped with the much larger 'data set' produced by the voyages of exploration,[4] Enlightenment theorists perceived that other regions in Eurasia with comparable sizes, populations, and levels of material civilization were tending to consolidate into the regionwide universal monarchies (the Ottomans in the Near East, the Moguls in India, the Manchus in China, and even the Romanovs in Russia). In contrast, they saw similar efforts by the Hapsburgs and Bourbons repeatedly frustrated in Europe, making the European political order an anomalous 'republican' system, paralleling the anomalous situation of republican units within the European system.

Second, a central postulate of contemporary international theory, particularly Realist international theory, is that interstate systems are fundamentally unlike domestic political orders. Virtually every major Realist work emphasizes this point at length, and many critics have argued that international theory is hampered by this assumption of a sharp inside-outside divide, and have sought in a variety of ways to transcend it.[5] In contrast, Enlightenment theorists sought to conceptualize the European interstate system not as the antithesis of the 'domestic,' but rather as a species of a relatively rare domestic regime type—the republic—with which they were long familiar.

Third, contemporary international theory is marked by an increasingly sharp divide between material and ideational/social variables, with Realism condemned (or valued) for its materialism, and various versions of constructivism and Liberalism advanced (or condemned) for their idealism. In contrast, Enlightenment republican theorists employed one conceptual vocabulary to analyze a range of *both* material and ideational/social factors that restrained violent power. While aware of the obvious ontological difference between social practices and natural-material contexts, Enlightenment republican theorists were theorizing about any possible restraints capable of preventing both full anarchy and full hierarchy. In short, international theory begins with a hybrid ontology centered around a common substantive problematic of locating the sources of restraint on violence.

To grasp the main ideas and influence of Enlightenment republican international theory, I begin by examining the widespread Enlightenment characterization of Europe as a 'republic.' Then I examine an extended list of factors, some material and some societal, that together were advanced as causing and constituting Europe as republic. Following Montesquieu's rough hierarchy of importance, I begin with a detailed examination of three natural-material factors (division, balance, and mixture) and then examine more briefly a longer list of societal factors (dividing, balancing, sovereignty, and international law). Finally, I assess the role of contextual material factors in Kant, and relations between the ideas of Enlightenment international republican theory and major contemporary international schools and the republican legacies contained within them.

EUROPE AS A 'REPUBLIC'

The conceptualization of Europe as a 'republic' in part 'by nature' emerged in the early-eighteenth century in order to help describe, explain, and legitimate the actually existing European order. Early modern Europeans were aware that their political order was fundamentally unlike the order of medieval Christendom due to the emergence of territorially integrated political units, the decline of the Holy Roman Empire and the Roman church, the growth in towns and commerce, the progress in science and the practical arts, and the voyages of discovery. In the realm of security politics, Enlightenment observers were aware that they existed in a period of relative order, security, and peace in contrast to the great cataclysms of what recent historians have labeled the 'long sixteenth century' culminating in the Thirty Years' War and the settlements of the Peace of Westphalia.[6]

Despite a wide recognition of Westphalia as a turning point, Enlightenment theorists commonly called it a type of 'republic' rather than the 'Westphalian system.' Calling this new situation a species of 'republic' conveyed that Europe was not an anarchy and it was not a hierarchy. It was not an anarchy because it was more orderly and secure than the frightful turmoil that had characterized all aspects of European life during the period between the beginning of the Renaissance and the early Enlightenment, between roughly 1500 and the late-seventeenth century.[7] It was not a hierarchy because it was unlike the regionwide empire or universal monarchy that some of its leading and ambitious state 'citizens' wished to erect.[8]

In speaking of Europe as a republic partially by nature, and praising this arrangement as superior to universal empire or full anarchy, Enlightenment theorists were explicitly rejecting the dominant inherited intellectual traditions derived from imperial Rome and medieval Christendom, and championed by the Counter-Reformation Roman church, which valued unity and hierarchy over plurality and freedom. The imperial view is captured in Dante Alighieri's *Monarchia*, published in 1310:

> [M]onarchy is necessary to the well-being of the world. . . . Mankind is most a unity when it is drawn together to form a single entity, and this can only come about when it is ruled as one whole by one ruler. . . . Mankind is in its ideal state when it is guided by a single ruler (as by a single source of motion) and in accordance with a single law. . . . Hence it is clear that monarchy (or that undivided rule which is called 'empire') is necessary to the well-being of the world . . . whenever there can be conflict there must be judgment to resolve it. . . . There is always the possibility of conflict between two rulers

where one is not subject to the other's control. . . . [T]herefore there must
be judgment between them. And since neither can judge the other (since neither is under the other's control, and an equal has no power over an equal)
there must be a third party of wider jurisdiction who rules over both of them
by right. . . . [W]e must come to a first and supreme judge, whose judgment
resolves all disputes either directly or indirectly, and this man will be the
monarch or emperor. Thus monarchy is necessary to the world. . . . [T]he
world is ordered in the best possible way when justice is at its strongest in
it. . . . Justice is at its strongest only under a monarch; therefore for the best
ordering of the world there must be a monarchy or empire.[9]

With the rise of consolidated states by the Great Houses, first the Hapsburgs in Austria and Spain and then the Bourbons in France, the project
of universal monarchy appeared to be renewed and found sophisticated
intellectual defenders in Tommaso Campanella and Bishop Bossuet, who
advanced arguments similar to Dante's using the Roman Empire as a
model.[10]

In this political and intellectual context, numerous European writers
began to refer to Europe as a whole as a 'republic.' In the earliest version
of this formulation I have located, the Venetian diplomat Giovanni Botero
spoke of "a republic, composed of other different states," in which peace
is sustained by a "balance of power,"[11] thus beginning the process of describing, explaining, and legitimating the plural state system with the conceptual resources of city-state republicanism. Montesquieu, in a short
essay, "Reflections on Universal Monarchy in Europe," targeted against
the advocates of empire, referred to Europe as a "Nation composed of
many nations," which together constituted a "great Republic."[12] Unlike
the medieval "respublica Christiana"[13] centered upon the 'great chain of
being' of the hierarchical Christian cosmos, the modern republic of Europe was a secular order based in profane nature and human art, defined
by its defiance of hierarchy, and often conceptualized as a self-equilibrat-
ing mechanism analogous to the new Newtonian cosmology.[14]

As the Enlightenment bloomed across the continent, viewing Europe
as a republic became an eighteenth-century "commonplace,"[15] appearing
prominently in the works of diplomats, historians, publicists, and scholars across Europe.[16] Niklas Vogt, historian at the University of Mainz and
teacher of Metternich, entitled his five-volume work *Über die europäische
Republik*.[17] The influential Swiss theorist of public international law Emmerich de Vattel wrote in the *Law of Nations* that current political arrangements and practices "make Europe a sort of Republic."[18] The prolific French commentator Abbé de Pradt observed that "Europe formed a
single social body which one might rightly call the European republic."[19]
The eminent French *philosophe* Voltaire observed in his widely read *The*

Age of Louis XIV that Europe was "a species of great republic, a sort of great commonwealth."[20] Briton Edmund Burke, in his attacks on the expansionist policies of revolutionary France, spoke of a "diplomatic Republik of Europe."[21] Francois de Callieres, author of a widely read diplomatic manual, observed that "we must think of the states of which Europe is composed as being joined together by all kinds of commerce, in such a way that they may be regarded as members of one Republic."[22] Edward Gibbon, in his comparison between contemporary Europe and ancient Rome, provides a particularly florid formulation:

> It is the duty of a patriot to prefer and promote the exclusive interest and glory of his native country: but a philosopher may be permitted to enlarge his views, and to consider Europe as a *great republic*, whose various inhabitants have attained almost the same level of politeness and cultivation. The Balance of Power will continue to fluctuate, and the prosperity of our own or the neighbouring kingdoms may be alternately exalted or depressed; but these partial events cannot essentially injure our general state of happiness, the system of arts, and laws, and manners, which so advantageously distinguish, above the rest of Mankind, the Europeans and their colonies.[23]

Although alien to late modern ears, the basic logic of this usage is easy to discern. By the eighteenth century, Europe was composed of a myriad of units claiming political independence, but interactions among these units, both cooperative and competitive, had also greatly intensified. In this decentralized political association the polities of Europe were like the free citizens of a republican polity, jealously competing for mutual advantage, fearful that one would gain excessive preeminence, but aware that their security rested upon a variety of restraints. Keenly aware that their republic was a middle ground between the Scylla of universal monarchy sought by the leading dynastic houses and the Charybdis of full anarchy experienced in the long sixteenth century, the Europeans sought to locate the sources of their 'liberty' from central rule and the moderation of factional strife.

The analogy between the political patterns of Europe as a whole and republican polities was often explicit. Jonathan Swift in his popular essay "A Discourse of the Contests and Dissentions in Athens and Rome" speaks of "the true meaning of a balance of power, either without, or within a state."[24] Lord Bolingbroke, chief architect of the Treaty of Utrecht and widely read essayist on the balance of power, saw the struggle against intrastate and interstate despotism in common terms.[25] In building on this simple analogy between the whole of Europe and the patterns of domestic politics in smaller republican polities, Enlightenment international theory employed republican categories to both describe and explain European politics, thus creating the first and most fertile international theory.

This deployment of republican terminology, although profoundly influential upon subsequent international theory, rapidly waned in the wake
of the French Revolution. Characterizing Europe as a republic was a move
of the Enlightenment to describe the international system of the *ancien
regime* ascendant between Westphalia and the French Revolution. In the
revolutionary era's political context, characterizing Europe as a republic
had highly charged and confusing ideological associations. As defenders
of the old order, conservatives such as Edmund Burke were placed in the
awkward position of defending the "diplomatic republic of Europe"
against a grave threat posed by the outbreak of excessive "republicanism"
in the radical phase of the French Revolution.[26] The coalitions that defeated the Napoleonic bid for European universal empire were ideologically antirepublican defenders of the restored monarchical *ancien regime*,
and the architects of the early Concert aimed to suppress revolutionary
movements and to prevent great power war in order to avoid unleashing
revolutionary turmoil.[27] Similarly, the swelling ranks of antimonarchical
revolutionists, propagandists, and theorists would not want to legitimate
an international order orchestrated by conservative monarchists by calling it a republic, and increasingly reserved their international use of this
word to characterize the sort of confederation or federal union they believed a system populated by republican units would and should form to
maintain peace and preserve freedom. It was in this context that the more
politically neutral term 'state system' makes its appearance in the writings
of the German scholar A.H.L. Heeren.[28] As the characterization of Europe
as a republic fell into disuse, the many substantive arguments that Enlightenment theorists had advanced about power-restraining contexts and
practices were appropriated and developed by various theorists who came
to call themselves Liberals or Realists rather than republicans.

NATURAL DIVISIONS AND BALANCES

Like earlier republican security theory, Enlightenment international theory had substantial natural and material dimensions, reflected in the pervasive tendency to refer to features of the European political order as 'by
nature,' particularly geography. For example, John Adams argued that
"there is a balance of power in Europe. Nature formed it. Practice and
habit have confirmed it, and it must exist forever."[29] Similarly, Rousseau,
in his short, unfinished and unpublished essays on European international
relations asserts that "the political order in this part of the world is, in
certain respects, the work of nature."[30]

In typical physiopolitical fashion, writers use 'nature' to refer to a variety of geographic factors (topography, climate, and soil fertility) and

18th Century Republican Terminology	Late 20th Century Terminology	Political Consequences
Division	Topographic Fragmentation	Plural State System Favored
Balance	Rough Equality Among Major Units	Plural State System Favored
Mixture	Landpower-Seapower Interaction	Plural State System Favored

Figure 5.1 Natural Material-Contextual Restraints Constituting
Europe as a 'Republic'

classes of artifacts (ships, gunpowder weapons, and fortifications), which
are often clustered under aggregates of 'landpower' and 'seapower.' Early
modern theorists tended to characterize the restraining aspects of these
material contexts in republican terminology, most notably as *division*,
balance, and *mixture* (see figure 5.1). Within the overall system of power
restraints that constituted Europe as a republic, two material variables—
division and balance—stand out as fundamental, particularly in the accounts of Botero, Montesquieu, Hume, Rousseau, and von Bülow. Although dividing and balancing are seen as important republican practices,
the division and balance analyzed here are natural-material, a combination of topographic fragmentation that impedes the aggressive ambitions
of empire builders and roughly equal distribution of arable land that creates a rough equality in overall power potential among the leading states.

Botero, an early pioneer in conceptualizing Europe as a republic, also
attributes the contours of the European plural order in part to nature:
"Europe . . . is full, almost pregnant, of dominions and Kingdoms. That
is the case because from the demise of the Roman Empire onward, she is
divided in many princedoms with such a balance of power [contrapeso di
forze] that there is no power. . . . that is stronger than any other. This is
partly because nature has delimited states' territories with inaccessible
mountains, or with tempestuous seas, or with similar ways."[31] Montesquieu provides a vividly republican account of the material factor of topographical division, a parallel to his widely influential statement on divi-

sion and separation of authority in domestic constitutions.[32] Topographical fragmentation is a 'natural division' that accounts for two of the most distinctive features of European civilization: the plural state system and the presence of numerous 'free' regimes. Topographical fragmentation retards military consolidation, making possible the 'liberty' of Europe. With smaller regimes militarily viable, more units with internal republican government are viable. In his typically empirical and comparative fashion, Montesquieu's clearest statement of this point appears in his analysis of the divergent patterns of European and Asian history:

> In Asia they have always had great empires; in Europe these could never subsist. Asia has larger plains; it is cut out into much more extensive divisions by mountains and sea; and as it lies more to the south, its springs are more easily dried up; the mountains are less covered with snow; and the rivers being not so large, form smaller barriers. Power in Asia ought then to be always despotic: for if their slavery was not severe, they would soon make a division, inconsistent with the nature of the country. In Europe the *natural division* forms many nations of a moderate extent, in which the ruling by laws is not incompatible with the maintenance of the state: on the contrary, it is so favorable to it, that without this the state would fall into decay, and become a prey to its neighbors. It is this which has formed a genius for liberty, that renders every part extremely difficult to be subdued and subjected to a foreign power, otherwise than by the laws and the advantage of commerce. On the contrary there reigns in Asia a servile spirit, which they have never been able to shake off; and it is impossible to find, in all the histories of this country, a single passage which discovers a freedom of spirit; we shall never see anything there but the excess of slavery.[33]

Montesquieu's main analytic categories—"despotic," "moderation," "genius for liberty," "free soul," and "heroism of slavery"—draw upon the general vocabulary of republicanism, as does his pessimism about the potential universalizability of liberty. Unlike later racialist naturalist arguments, however, Montesquieu's concept of the "heroism of slavery" conveys that Asians are not innately servile, but rather are condemned to "slavery" by their material context.[34] In short, the occurrence of both political liberty and subjugation are fruits of nature, produced by different material contexts.

Montesquieu's comparative analysis of the role of division in producing the plural state system in Europe and the absence of division in producing despotic 'universal monarchies' elsewhere nicely summarizes the centerpiece of Enlightenment physiopolitical thinking (see figure 5.2). Division, or topographic fragmentation, a variant of violence interdependence, primarily explains why Europe is a second anarchy rather than a hierarchy. Once division is present, balance can serve to further impede hierarchy.

Coupled with arguments about the relationship between size and regime type analyzed earlier, the system-level plurality underpinned by division provides the necessary precondition for the emergence of smaller—and hence possibly republican or moderate monarchical polities. Restraint at the system-level produces the possibility of restraint at the unit-level.

The role of division and balance by nature is also central to Rousseau's analysis of European political arrangements. Like Montesquieu, Rousseau's image of Europe's "general constitution" incorporates many diverse variables (culture, religion, commerce, domestic regime type, and geography). For Rousseau, Europe's disorderly order exists and persists for three reasons: topographical divisions, rough equality among several of the major units, and balance-of-power practices. In a characteristically compressed passage, Rousseau observes that "the location of the mountains, the seas, and the rivers, which serve as borders to the nations that inhabit Europe, seems to have determined their *number* and *size*."[35] In pointing to Europe's fragmented topography to explain the number of European states, Rousseau holds that Europe, despite its cultural and social unity, is a plural political order because its material context is divided and balanced. The material context is the basic cause of the relatively equal size of the major states. The number of states and their rough balance make it practically impossible for an ambitious prince to subdue the whole of Europe.

An even more elaborate version of this line of argument is provided by the Prussian military analyst Dietrich von Bülow.[36] With military force burdened with new logistical requirements of gunpowder weaponry, topographical barriers loom large in determining outcomes. Mountains "interrupt lines of operation in proportion as they are high, winding, and steep."[37] The sea also "constitutes a very good natural limit"[38] because weather makes military concentration and coordination difficult to plan, because the time spent loading and unloading slows movement, and because of the vulnerability of disembarking forces to a defender's counterattack.[39] Water can connect as well as impede: "what is favorable to social and commercial relations, may impede operations of war, and combinations of politics."[40]

Convinced that these technological-topographical interactions will relentlessly and mechanically shape the European order, von Bülow proceeds to draw a map of Europe in final adjustment to material forces: "The number of European states will sooner or later be reduced to twelve: Spain, France, the Netherlands, (if the latter do not pass into the possession of North Germany), Italy, Switzerland (whose mountainous character is a lasting guarantee of independence), North Germany, the Austrian Danube region including the South German states, Denmark, Sweden, Russia, Greece, and Turkey (with its European possessions reduced to the Aegean

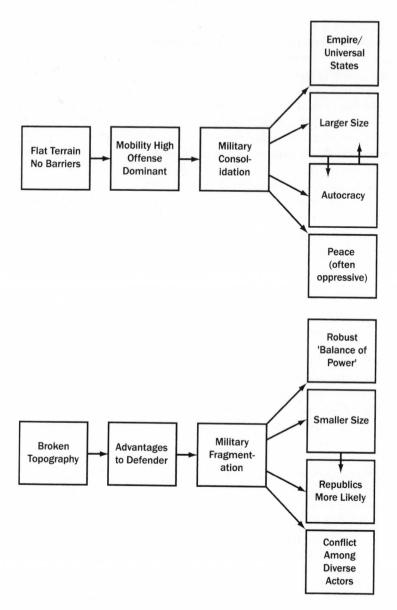

Figure 5.2 Impacts of Topography on Politics

littoral)."[41] Absent from von Bülow's map are the numerous city-states and principalities of Germany, which "will inevitably become the prey"[42] of the larger states as firepower and mass come to dominate war. Language and nationality play no role in his scenario because "[d]ifferent languages and nationalities are this day united in one and the same state."[43] As a prediction of the future map of Europe, von Bülow accurately foresees the union of Northern Germany, the expulsion of Austria from the Po Valley, the unification of the Italian peninsula, the independence of Greece from Turkey, the precarious status of Belgium and the Netherlands, but errs in forecasting the unification of Spain and Portugal. At first glance apparently a prediction of nineteenth-century 'national' unification, von Bülow is actually predicting the logical completion of the process of state-formation shaped by topographical-technological features.

In pointing to the role of 'nature' in shaping the size of the units in the European plural state system, Montesquieu, Rousseau, and von Bülow are capturing the important fact that the quantities of arable land—and hence the size and wealth of the populations of the units demarcated by topographic division—are roughly equal in size. The key fact, discussed by subsequent historians and geographers, is that the process of early modern state-building depended upon clusters of relatively arable land, usefully referred to as European "core areas."[44] The natural republican argument attributing the failure of universal empire in Europe to the fragmented character of Europe's geography has been repeated by a large number of historians and political theorists, who rarely cite Montesquieu's pioneering formulation.[45] This proposition is so widely accepted that it verges on a truism, but is invisible in contemporary Realist international theory. In the natural republican analysis, *division is logically prior to balances and balancing because there must be separate units before the balance of power between them can matter.* As critics have repeatedly pointed out, Realist theories tend to assume the existence of a plural state system. In contrast, the Enlightenment republican analysis of the topographic division of power 'by nature' offers a primitively formulated explanation for why Europe was composed of separate states rather than a single universal state.

The Balancer and the Mixture of Land and Sea Power

A third material contextual factor—the interplay of land and sea power—had implications for the entire system as well as for the unit-level, analyzed in the preceding chapter. Enlightenment republican theorists argue that the mixture of land and sea power provides the basis for a *balancer* state that serves a distinct system-maintaining role. Most republican analyses of mixture concern the differing constitutional roles of social classes, but mixture, like division and balance, also played an important role in the physiopolitical analysis of Europe-wide power restraint.

The special role played by the naval and commercial states Venice and Britain as 'balancers' in their respective state systems was noted by several writers. In his *History of Italy*, Guicciardini argued that Venice's physical separation from Italian *terra firma* allowed the Venetian state to remain aloof from routine or early alliance commitments, and then to cast its weight against aspiring hegemons: "Thus all the other Italian powers were divided: some in favor of the King of France, some opposed. Only the Venetians determined to remain neutral and idly wait the outcome of this affair; either because it was not to their disadvantage that Italy should be in turmoil, in hopes that protracted wars of others would give them an opportunity to expand their empire; or because, being so powerful, they were not afraid of easily falling prey to the conqueror; and that it was therefore unwise, with no evident necessity, to become involved in other people's wars."[46] The idea that Britain played a special role as 'holder of the balance' based on its insular position has been a theme of British political writers since the time of the Tudors.[47] As Francis Bacon, the most philosophically sophisticated of Tudor courtiers, observes, "He that commands the sea is at great liberty, and may take as much and as little of the war as he will."[48]

In these arguments, 'seapower' refers to a cluster of three distinct but related marine physical features of the European region as well as maritime transport and naval warfare. First, the European landscape contains an exceptionally extensive amount of navigable water, a feature emphasized by many historians and geographers. Second is the tendency for one state to specialize in naval force and maritime activity, and for dominance of regional waters to concentrate into the hands of this state.[49] This state on a proximate island was able to specialize in naval and maritime activities, making possible its role as a balancer. Third, naval capability was an asset with a mixture of extreme strengths and weaknesses, both of which greatly influenced the European security order. Naval force was indispensable to protect and deny to an adversary the main transportation system of the region. Naval force was not, however, in itself, capable of defeating land armies in battle, garrisoning territory, or subduing populations.

The *strengths* of naval force enabled the British state to play a leading role in the defeat of a succession of attempts to erect a universal empire in Europe.[50] Seapower's strengths shaped the system in four main ways. First, naval mastery precluded invasion of the British Isles.[51] Second, naval mastery permitted the blockade of continental ports and capture of shipping.[52] Third, the maritime naval state was able to provide subsidies for continental allies with the wealth that was denied continental aggressors.[53] Fourth, sea power mastery permitted military expeditions in peripheral parts of Europe.[54]

Naval force also has important *weaknesses* that prevented the balancer state from becoming the regional hegemon. The key weakness of naval force was recognized by Venetian writers such as Botero, Contarini, and Paruta, who note that the predominantly naval state of Venice was not well equipped to create a regionwide empire.[55] The earliest British writers had emphasized the particular strengths of Britain's position, but as Britain came to dominate European waters, awareness of its weakness grew.

The absence of a 'balance of power' at sea was noted bitterly by continental writers. The French minister Choiseul argued that the English, "while claiming to protect the balance on land which no one threatens. . . . are entirely destroying the balance at sea which no one defends."[56] During the late-nineteenth and early-twentieth centuries the image of Britain as hegemon of the sea and thus on the verge of universal empire fueled the expectations of German strategic writers like Otto Hintze and Friedrich Meinecke that Germany could lead a rebellion against this British hegemony in the same fashion that Britain had led the resistance to earlier continental hegemons.[57] The fallacy of these hopes, as Friedrich von Gentz and later Ludwig Dehio pointed out, is that naval force has limited utility in subjecting territory and that the other states did not experience British naval mastery as a yoke.[58] When confronted with the choice of being part of a territorial empire or allying with the regional naval hegemon, the states of Europe exhibited a strong preference against the aspiring land power hegemon. British dominance over the vital maritime extraterritorial region was much more tolerable than territorial hegemony because of the way the limitations of naval force constrained the ends to which the British could employ their power. These critics of Britain's maritime hegemony failed to realize that the peculiarly hollow character of naval hegemony made Britain's position tolerable to other states.

In short, naval force was highly specialized in its effects: it could do some things extraordinarily well, others hardly at all. Water impeded *military* mobility, but facilitated *commercial* and *naval* mobility. Thus both the intrinsic strengths and weaknesses of naval capabilities shaped the European political order. Britain's ability to play the role of a balancer in the European state system is rooted in material features: its insular position and the strengths and weaknesses of naval force.

The natural republican argument thus provides a theoretical foundation for the concept of a balancer state. This idea has been attacked by several eminent international theorists on the grounds that a state capable of playing so pivotal role in a state system would be unchecked and thus potentially the hegemon of the system, and there is no reason why such a state would be self-restrained.[59] In contrast, the Enlightenment natural republican claim is that the mixture of land and sea powers and the weaknesses and strengths of naval force make a balancer state possible. Balancers do not put the interest of the whole above their own interest, but are so situated and equipped that their pursuit of self-interest coincides more often with the general system interest. The particular strengths of naval power provide the basis for effective antihegemonic leadership, while the weakness of naval power in subjecting territory renders them unable to extinguish the state system and establish a regional empire.

REPUBLICAN INTERNATIONAL SOCIETY AND UNIONS

Enlightenment international theory also drew upon republican concepts to describe and legitimate a variety of important practices and political arrangements that were understood as contributing to the republic of Europe by further restraining violence. Some of these features, most notably balancing, sovereignty, constitutional settlements,[60] international law, and unions have been exhaustively analyzed by recent international theorists, but several have been neglected, and the pervasively republican character of these societal elements has been obscured. An examination of five major societal elements provides a more complete and unified view.

Perhaps most neglected are practices of division and mixture. Unlike topographical fragmentation, which political actors did not create and could not easily change, dividing practices played an important role in the great settlements of Westphalia, Utrecht, and Vienna. Today these settlements are typically seen as making and codifying the preserved or restored balance of power between units, but a prominent feature in all three was the establishment or extension of separation and division between and within the units.

Westphalia, the first great modern political settlement, marks the beginning of the European republic, and its most important accomplishments concerned division, not balance. Westphalia marked the ascendancy of a Europe divided into territorially integrated units at the expense of imperial and religious unity and hierarchy. An element in the restraint of Hapsburg and imperial power was the recognition of the independence of the United Provinces, a move that hobbled the power of the hegemonic aspirant not by aggregating counterweights against it, but by dividing an important asset from it, an event that could be termed *hegemonic secession*. Westphalia also marked the historic turning point for the principle of the separation of church and state.[61]

Practices of dividing power also played a central role in the second great early modern settlement, the Treaty of Utrecht, which ended the War of Spanish Succession. Article II of the Preamble to the Treaty spoke of its measures as aiming to strengthen the peace and stability of Europe by restoring the 'equilibrium' (*equilibro*) of power.[62] The explicit elevation of equilibrium as a central principle of European public order contributed to the widespread sense in the eighteenth century that Europe was appropriately thought of as a republic. This settlement reveals the interplay between dividing and balancing practices that together worked to restrain hierarchy. The key aim of the counterhegemonic coalition victorious against the ambitions of Louis XIV of France was to prevent the union of the crowns of Spain and France. The war did not entail the French invasion of Spain or the imposition of France's will on Spain, but rather the other powers of Europe sought to prevent their union through hereditary succession. A balance of power alliance against France was necessary to frustrate French designs, but this could be realized only through the preservation of a division.

Restraint through mixture was also a central objective of the political order established at the Congress of Vienna after the wars of the French Revolution. Edmund Burke, writing at the time of the Revolution, and Lord Acton, writing in the middle of the nineteenth century, viewed the Revolution as despotic democracy, and attributed its excesses to the loss of restraints. In this view, the French Revolution marked the arrival of a major new power into European politics, the mobilized mass nation, which threatened to undo the Westphalian settlement's fundamental accomplishment of restraint through division.[63] To restore the system of power restraint, Acton advocated the mixture of different nations in one state: "the combination of different nations in one State is as necessary a condition for civilized life as the combination of men in society."[64]

The republican practice of the 'balance of power' is now viewed as the quintessential Realist concept, but is clearly a simple extension of a core republican concept to the interstate realm. Not surprisingly, the earliest recorded uses of the term 'balance' to describe the operations of an interstate system are found in the writings of Renaissance Italians, particularly the diplomats of the Republics of Venice and Florence.[65] As commentators have noted, 'balance' and its cognates are used in a variety of complex ways, to describe and explain as well as to advocate and legitimate the system and the behavior of its actors.[66] Often the phrase is used describe the overall European political system, which risks confusing an important feature of the system with the system itself.[67] More importantly, the phrase describes the various counterhegemonic practices of the actors, what von Gentz called a system of "counterpoise" rather than of "equipoise," what is now called 'balancing' behavior.[68]

Balancing today is widely viewed by Realists as automatic and asocial and by Liberals as archaic. In contrast, Enlightenment international theorists viewed the balance of power as an important *invention* that helped

account for the *progress* of modern over ancient institutions. In his famous discussion of the balance of power in antiquity, Hume observed,
"[T]he maxim of preserving the balance of power is founded so much
on common sense and obvious reasoning, that it is impossible it could
altogether have escaped antiquity," but then concludes that "the ancients
were entirely ignorant of the balance of power" because "the Romans
never met with any such general combination or confederacy against
them."[69] Similarly, the Scottish historian William Robertson declared that
it was "the great secret of modern politics."[70] Although critics objected
to the prevalence of war and the high-handed treatment of weaker states
(like Poland), defenders such as John Witherspoon and Lord Brougham
claimed its advent was an important and new source of order and predict-
ability in interstate affairs.[71]

The early modern conceptualizations of state sovereignty and public
international law also have republican features.[72] Sovereignty and public
international law define the rights and rules of citizenship in the European
republic. As Vattel influentially postulated, sovereign states enjoy equal
status in international law regardless of their unequal power, just as
dwarfs and giants are both men regardless of their relative strength. Unlike the differential rights held by members of medieval corporate polities,
citizens of a republic have formally equal rights, and this central attribute
of equality is republicanism's great legacy to modern sovereignty and international law. Beyond this, the increasingly elaborately codified public
international law can be seen as delineating the responsibilities or duties
of states as citizens in the European republic by specifying the appropriate
standards of behavior "for the maintenance of order and the preservation
of liberty."[73]

Finally, Enlightenment theorists conceptualized states as exercising
their 'foederative' capacities to enter into various alliances, leagues, and
unions.[74] Such unions are understood to be of varied significance and duration, ranging from the ad hoc alliances against common threats entailed
in balancing to perpetual unions with substantial legislative and enforcement capacities. The unions of antihegemonic alliances were an established part of interstate practice, but were temporary and single-purpose
and had the effect of sustaining the state system rather than ending it.
Europe-wide unions of greater weight and duration remained objects of
speculation.

Early modern plans and proposals for more permanent and substantial
unions come in two main types. The first variety, beginning in the sixteenth century, envision very partial unions of states, aiming mainly for
the preservation of general international peace. Their distinguishing feature is an indifference to the domestic regime types of their constitutive
members. Among the more famous such plans are those of Emeric Crucé,

Duke Sully, William Penn, and Abbé Saint Pierre.[75] Such plans commonly include a permanent diplomatic assembly or congress and are often presented as model treaties with accompanying admonitions and rationales. They are commonly European regional in scope, with ocassional gestures toward universal scope. They do not make the case for unions as necessary for security, but rather as beneficial for peace, humanitarian values, and economic improvement. These plans are essentially collective security arrangements in which actually existing states pledge to preserve peace, to submit to arbitration of disputes, and to join together against violators. As such these plans anticipate the two great twentieth-century experiments in universal interstate union to maintain peace, the League of Nations and the United Nations.

The fundamental problem with these schemes is spelled out brilliantly by Rousseau in his commentary on the plan of the Abbé Saint Pierre.[76] Although Rousseau points to anarchy and its dynamics as significant impediments to union, the two really intractable problems lie at the unit-level and in the material context. The first problem is that all European states are based on corrupt social contracts. They are ruled by kings and their ministers, who have no incentive to eliminate war and who value their autonomy and power more than the well-being of their subjects. A Europe-wide union of republican polities is for Rousseau not an object of discussion because he believes that republics are destined to remain extremely rare. Furthermore, his archaic model of publican neo-Spartan republics, marked by economic autarcky, cultural isolation, and fierce patriotism, are unpromising as members of an international union. Second, the topographic fragmentation of the European region, its natural division, ensures that a European-wide union is unnecessary for security. Despite his typically vivid portrayal of the horrors of war, he stops well short of making the claim that the wars endemic to the European anarchic state-of-war jeopardize the survival of the major units. In short, Europe is a second, not a first anarchy. Peace through union would confer benefits, but is not necessary for security.

A second type of interstate union, extensively theorized about in the eighteenth century, is distinguished by an exclusively republican membership. As we saw, Montesquieu argued that republican polities had a particular affinity for unions and that such unions offered republics important security advantages. Yet he also stopped short of envisioning a general European union of republics, probably for some of the same reasons as Rousseau. Montesquieu's model of republics is much more modern than Rousseau's, but he does not seem to have entertained them becoming universal even within Europe. Also, like Rousseau, he saw natural division as constitutive of Europe, thus obviating any imperative need to leave anarchy.

In his Second Article of his perpetual peace plan, Kant argues that the state-of-war anarchy only can be replaced with an established peace through a federative 'league of peace' in which republican states pledge nonaggression and mutual defense. Often hailed (or condemned) as a father of universal federal union with authoritative government over its constitutive nation-state members, Kant actually envisions an institutionally modest arrangement, a sort of 'amity international' rather than government. With such an arrangement, Europe would remain an anarchy albeit a peaceful one. Taken as a whole, such an arrangement would be a modified anarchical state system, and Kant emphasizes that he is not advocating a world state.[77] For Kant, the major restraining work occurs at the unit-level, not the system-level. What is novel in Kant's argument is not that democratic republics are pacific toward one another, or that they have affinities for unions with one another, but that he imagines a system where there are numerous republics.

Looking at the overall Enlightenment conceptualization of republican international society and unions without reference to companion arguments about material contextual factors, it is easy to reach the erroneous conclusion that these societal arrangements and practices were themselves understood to be the primary sources of restraint in making Europe a republic. When the whole panoply of restraint arguments are assembled and their relative weight assessed, it is difficult to escape the conclusion that the 'republic' of Europe was primarily by nature an artifact of its restraining material foundation, and only secondarily social.[78] While republican societal features did not make Europe a second anarchy, they can be reasonably viewed as making it a more peaceful second anarchy. By the same token, the fact that Europe was a second rather than a first anarchy meant that there was an upper limit to the influence of these societal elements. Only after its material contextual divisions had been washed away by the industrial revolution would the European order come to require substantial unions to escape the acute security perils of first anarchy.

NATURE'S SECRET PLAN FOR PERPETUAL PEACE

Given Kant's prominence and the importance of material contextual factors in the arguments of his predecessors and contemporaries, the question of their status in his work naturally arises. Setting Kant in his historical context of Enlightenment republican theory, the ideas of democratic peace and pacific union so widely attributed to him appear largely unoriginal and rather conservative. Given his reputation as a leading 'idealist,' Kant would seem to have little affinity for contextual materialist lines of argument. But upon closer examination, material contextual factors, in princess-and-the-pea fashion, significantly shape his argument. Although these arguments are scattered, underdeveloped, and at times contradictory, they provide an explanation for the limited weight of his 'pacific union' while also pointing toward a much more powerful and dynamic material-contextual approach that would see fruition in the nineteenth century.

Within Kant's large, complex, and influential writings centered on epistemology, ethics, and aesthetics, his treatments on politics are late, short, and scattered, and subject to conflicting interpretations.[79] Kant's turn to politics is driven by a problem emerging from his ethics: having established in his main works that the imperatives of morality are fundamentally grounded in human reason, Kant is driven to ask whether the moral man might find anything in the actual developments of human history that "permits us to hope" for the realization of political arrangements consistent with the dictates of morality.[80]

Kant's sketch of an imagined world of perpetual peace does not solve the problem that gave rise to his turn to politics, but only displaces it onto History and Nature. The imagined world of perpetual peace is not advanced as an *explanation* for the emergence of peace, but rather as a *description* of a peaceful world. Assuming his imagined world would be the one consistent with morality, it still remains to be seen how such a world might actually arise. Kant's attempt to grapple with this problem is much less developed than even his brief sketch of peace, and it is at times contradictory,[81] but it is here that scattered assertions about the influence of the natural-material context come, in princess-and-the-pea fashion, to greatly shape his argument.

Despite Kant's general reputation as a moral idealist and the inspiration moral activists find in his work, he emphasizes that morally motivated action does not produce perpetual peace.[82] The dictates of morality are grounded in man's transcendental reason, but the realization of perpetual peace must occur through a purely secular process undirected by morality. In articulating this historical narrative, Kant begins with a Hobbesian image of man as self-interested and competitively interacting.[83] He then seeks to show how a "race of devils, if only they are intelligent" can be expected to eventually arrive at his ideal world.[84] In this scenario, competition, often violent, between self-regarding individuals and nations is the motor of human progress. Humans are compelled to leave the state-of-nature, establish civil government, and cultivate material civilization driven solely by self-interest. Similarly, violent competition and anticipations of violent competition between nations drive humans to scatter and populate the earth, to cultivate material civilization to enhance competitive position, to establish republican governments, to engage in commerce, and eventually to cease warring altogether.[85] Kant thus arrives at optimistic conclusions from pessimistic assumptions about human nature.

In understanding how a race of devils eventually reaches the near heaven of perpetual peace, material context plays a pivotal but underrecognized role. Kant's evocation of material contextual factors is highly unsystemic and somewhat obscured by being cast as part of a theodicity driven by Providence, understood as a deistic grand designer of Nature. Kant holds that Providence has so created Nature (or at least we would gain hope from so believing) that self-regarding and competitive humanity are driven toward perpetual peace. It is thus "nature's secret plan" that the world is so configured that it provides purely self-regarding individuals with a set of material contextual incentives that eventually, through a lengthy and apparently undirected process, drives men to perpetual peace, the "end of history."[86]

Given this, there must be an intimate relationship between the particular features of divinely planned nature and the political architecture of perpetual peace, between features of the material context and features of political structure. Kant says a league of independent republican nation-states is superior to a world government, which would be "one universal monarchy" and tend to become a "soulless despotism" because "laws always lose in vigor what government gains in extent."[87] This standard Enlightenment claim depends upon an historically specific assumption about *distance*. The buried but pivotal material-contextual factor of violence interdependence pops briefly into view when Kant observes that in order to "be secure against violence from one another" it is necessary for "individual men, peoples, and states" to "leave the state of nature" and "unite itself with all others (*with which it cannot help interacting*)" and "subject itself to a public lawful coercion."[88] "Nature wills" against full cosmopolitanism and federal union by employing "differences of language and religion" to maintain "separate peoples" and to "prevent them from mixing."[89] These differences arise as people spread across all habitable parts of the earth and develop in different material environments. International competition and advancing material civilization produces "devastations, revolutions, and even complete exhaustion," propelling men into a thin "league of nations," but these calamities are not so great as to require more substantive unions.[90] The growth of commerce occurs to an extent that wars become irrational, but not to the extent that the preservation of independent states and distinct nations becomes irrational. In short, key particulars of Kant's imagined world of perpetual peace derive from assumptions he makes about the material world wheeled in on an ad hoc basis, without serious justification. In the end, Kant emerges as a crypto structural-materialist.

Given this, the question arises whether Kant's combination of republican nation-states and light international institutions are the unique 'end of history' consistent with human morality or whether a different Nature as material context could be seen as consistent with a significantly different set of political arrangements. To answer this question requires a more systematic and reflective structural-materialist analysis than Kant provides, but one subsequent contextual materialist theorists will explore at length.

SCATTERED LEGACIES

Enlightenment republican theory was the first international system theory, the Big Bang of international theory, and one is hard-pressed to find a single first-order international theoretical concept that did not appear here. From this compact primordial beginning, subsequent schools and theories have sped off in all directions, and initially primitive and entangled insights have become elaborately articulated and differentiated. Given this, both the distinctive features of Enlightenment republican security theory and the contours of subsequent theoretical orientations can be brought into sharper focus by examining the ways in which these legacies have been appropriated, abandoned, and remembered. Three major contemporary schools—Realism and neorealism, the English school and constructivism, and international Liberalism—can be defined by their relationship to the legacies of European natural republicanism.

Realism is by far the biggest beneficiary of the legacies of Enlightenment republican theory, but this inheritance is curiously underacknowledged and incomplete. The central concept in Realist, and particularly neorealist, international theory is the balance of power. As noted earlier, Waltz, the father of neorealism, observes that "if there is any distinctively political theory of international politics, balance-of-power is it."[91] Yet this theory is clearly and straightforwardly a concept drawn from republicanism.[92] More generally, the natural republican emphasis on the primacy of material over ideational factors has been firmly enshrined in subsequent Realist theory.

Even more important, however, are the contextual-material factors contemporary neorealism neglects. The variable of division, primary in the natural republican architecture of restraint, has tended to be assumed rather than problematized by neorealism, with major consequences for the range of its explanatory power. Montesquieu, Rousseau, and von Bülow were attempting to explain *why* there was a plural state system, but neorealists take its existence for granted and seek to offer insight into its operation. In the language of contemporary theory, natural republicanism had both *system* and *systemic* arguments, while neorealism has only the latter. This lacuna in neorealism is even more surprising since arguments about topographical fragmentation as a major source of Europe's distinctive pattern of political development figure so prominently in the late-twentieth-century historiography of early modern European state and system formation.

The natural republican analysis of mixture of land- and sea-power states (and the resulting possibility of a functionally differentiated balancer state) vanishes in neorealism. But it has recently reappeared in the arguments of 'offensive realism.' In this view, the United States, separated from Eurasia by vast oceans that impede the projection of military power (as opposed to naval and aerial), which alone is held able to conquer territory, has become the 'off-shore balancer,' playing a role in the contemporary global state system analogous to the role played by Britain in the early modern European state system.[93] In Mearsheimer's version of offensive realism, the "stopping power of water" plays a pivotal role in the argument.[94] Aside from the acknowledged historical parallel between America and Britain, these analyses are silent about previous versions of these arguments. The continuing importance of such nondistributional material-contextual factors in international theory reflects their explanatory power, while their ad hoc character reflects the eclipse of the once central compositional variable of violence interdependence.

The importance of the factor of division as a restraint on violence interdependence may not be incorporated in neorealism, but it does continue to play a key role in many analyses of Europe in the industrial era. Indeed, the basic argument of numerous theorists and observers of European politics beginning in the later-nineteenth century is that the industrial revolution either greatly diminishes or effectively eliminates the previously restraining influence of topographic fragmentation. This changes a manageable second anarchy into a perilous first anarchy, and thus requires some form of European unification (whether federal or imperial) to avoid acute insecurity. As the material-contextual restraint diminishes, Europe is left with a possible balance, but diminished division, thus setting the stage for the total wars and system collapse in the early-twentieth century.

Beyond these major but incomplete and underacknowledged materialist inheritances, is the question of political structure. Was the 'republic' of Europe an anarchy or a negarchy? An anarchy and a negarchy are similar in that they are not hierarchies, but an anarchy entails absence of rule and suggests absence of restraint, while a negarchy is a political structure of mutual restraint. Contemporary Realists emphasize the socially permissive implications of anarchy, often characterized as a 'state-of-nature,' while Enlightenment republicans emphasized the ways in which natural restraints made Europe a second rather than a first anarchy. Despite the label of 'republic' it is important to emphasize that the early modern European system *did not* have a political structure of negarchy. Its primary restraints were material-contextual, not political-structural. There is also a sharp difference between Enlightenment natural republicanism and contemporary Realism on the question of whether politics between states is analogous to politics within them. Contemporary Realism draws a sharp divide between these realms, while the starting point of natural republicanism is an analogy between the interstate system and the rare domestic form of the republic.[95]

Aside from their substantive implications for Realist theorizing, these significant gaps in Realism's account of the origins of its core ideas appear particularly surprising given the extensive effort of Realists to construct a tradition. These gaps, however, become intelligible as responses to the political context within which Anglo-American Realism emerged in the 1940s and 1950s. Not only did Realists need to distinguish themselves from the extreme materialism of German *Geopolitik* and Soviet Marxism, but they also sought to position themselves as effective critics of Liberal 'idealistic' internationalism.[96] Thinking of stable state systems as a species of 'republic' implied troubling conceptual similarities between international and domestic politics, and made an international federal republic seem less than fully utopian.

A similar pattern of major but underacknowledged and incomplete inheritances marks the relationship of natural republicanism with the English School and constructivism. The English School's focus on the importance of the societal elements of sovereignty, diplomacy, and international law in constituting European political order and in restraining power closely follows the earlier republican arguments. This clear legacy is oddly unacknowledged, however, despite the English School's close attention to earlier thinkers. The widely used label of 'Grotian' rather than republican for this position is odd and ahistorical, and serves to obscure the unity of the diverse societal features as republican.[97] In contrast, the essentially republican character of these societal elements is prominently discussed by Onuf, but his treatment emphasizes community rather than restraint and justice rather than security as the animating insights of Enlightenment international republicanism.

The legacies of the material variables in natural republicanism have different presences in different English School and constructivist arguments. In Hedley Bull's formulation, the earlier mixed ontology (the combination of material and societal elements) is preserved, although (like other Realists) he neglects division and emphasizes balance.[98] In more recent English School and American constructivist work, this mixed ontology is abandoned in favor of a purely societal emphasis, generating a position that mirror-images the neorealist neglect of society. This tendency is particularly pronounced in Onuf's rich treatment of republican international society, where the material dimensions disappear almost completely.

Finally, what of the relationship between international Liberalism and natural republicanism? Most importantly, Liberals, both domestic and international, have distinguished themselves from Enlightenment republicanism by either neglecting or repudiating the balance of power. The balance of power had been a major concept in ancient and early modern republicanism. But in large measure, early international Liberals of the nineteenth century, most notably Jeremy Bentham, Richard Cobden, and the Manchester School, rejected the balance of power as a source for preserving international security and plurality. This attack on the international balance of power was part of a more general commercial (or bourgeois) Liberal attack on all vestiges of the political order of the *ancien regime*, both domestically and internationally. The balance of power had a particularly diminished role in Bentham's powerful and influential utilitarianism, which (despite its later Liberal associations) Bentham advanced as a program for the Enlightened exercise of unrestrained power.[99]

The material-contextual aspects of Enlightenment republican international theory have a complex presence in subsequent Liberal international theory, as we shall see in the chapters ahead.[100] Many classical Liberals, beginning with Adam Smith and many lesser-known nineteenth-century 'political economists,' gave important emphasis to the industrial revolution as making war too destructive to be a rational security strategy. Many late-nineteenth- and early-twentieth-century theorists who either identified themselves as Liberals or who held broadly (and often advanced) Liberal views placed primary emphasis on the growth of material interdependence, particularly concerning violence, as a factor making greater political unification a security necessity rather than a moral improvement. The strong contextual-materialism of these Liberal theorists, however, has been overlooked, both by the formative figures in twentieth-century Realism who derided them as 'idealists,' and more recent constructivists and theorists of international norms who see this alleged idealism as a virtue and an inspiration. Finally, the material-contextual variable of interdependence has continued to play a major role in various recent Liberal international theories. Unfortunately, while these theorists assign great importance to interdependence, they focus almost exclusively on economic (and increasingly ecological) interdependence and almost completely neglect analysis of violence interdependence, previously so pivotal in republican security theory.

The next chapter in the development of republican security theory occurs in the founding of the United States of America, the climax of early modern republican theory and practice. It is here, not in European international Liberalism of the nineteenth century, that the legacies of Enlightenment republican thought are most completely employed for security purposes. To this story we now turn.

Chapter Six

THE PHILADELPHIAN SYSTEM

What Athens was in miniature, America will
be in magnitude.
—Thomas Paine[1]

BRINGING AMERICA BACK IN

The climax of early modern republican security theory was the founding
of the United States of America.[2] The architects of this political order
boldly referred to it as a *novus ordo saeclorum*, a "new order of the ages,"
distinctive both from the earlier republican city-states and the 'republic'
of Europe. The United States of America between the establishment of the
Union (1781–89) and the War of Southern Secession (1861–65), which I
will refer to as the 'Philadelphian system' in contrast to the Westphalian
system in Europe, has been widely recognized as being 'exceptionalistic'
in several ways.[3] Due to its size and internal diversity, it has been characterized as "what a United States of Europe would be," an alternative to
the European Westphalian system rather than an oddly constituted state
within it.[4] While it had elaborate political structures that went beyond
confederation, European observers such as Tocqueville and Hegel
doubted the American Union was a state.[5] It combined familiar forms of
popular sovereignty, formal state equality, balance of power, and division
of power to create a negarchic political order novel in its overall configuration. For republican security theory the creation of this system marks
the final early modern innovation to overcome the maladies and limitations of the Roman Republic. For international theorists the theory and
practice of the American Union is of enduring interest because its design-
ers had a clear grasp of the dynamics of the European anarchical state
system, but they sought to design and build a political order in North
America that would not fall prey to these patterns of violent competition
and conflict, to avoid the Europeanization of North American politics.[6]

The literature on the founding and antebellum America is vast in quantity and high in quality but almost uniformly presupposes the inside-outside distinction, neatly divides foreign from domestic, and emphasizes
ideological and economic factors more than security.[7] Important exceptions are works on the transition from British colonial status to the Ameri-

can founding focused upon imperial and American interstate dynamics, and explorations by a few political geographers and political scientists.[8] In contemporary international theory, Realist as well as Liberal, the theory and practice of the American founding is almost invisible, in contrast to the attention lavished upon Kant. For Realists the United States is simply a large and particularly powerful nation-state with a somewhat eccentric domestic political system whose expansive claims and unrealistic ambitions are seen as a source of international disorder. For theorists of the democratic peace, the United States is simply another entry on the growing list of democracies whose interaction can be studied. Viewing the American Union as a structural alternative to the European state system and a prototype for new Atlantic or global institutions was once widespread but largely disappeared from international theory in the wake of the postwar debate between Realism and Idealism.[9]

In order to return this climactic episode of early modern security republicanism back into its appropriate place in both republican and international theory, this chapter explores the logic and evolution of the Philadelphian system as a distinctive alternative to the Westphalian system of hierarchies in anarchy. As classically expounded by 'Publius' (Alexander Hamilton, John Jay, and James Madison) in the papers of the *Federalist*, the political theory of the American founding is analyzed as a new solution to the severe security problems that had animated republican security theory from its ancient inception.[10] Widely read in ancient and early modern political thought, the founders developed a new architecture of power restraint structures designed to advance beyond the limits of previous republican orders.[11] Publius advances the argument that these arrangements could simultaneously contribute to addressing all four of the fundamental security problems (revolution, despotism, total war and empire) (recall figure 1.6). They advance federal union, or what Madison termed a 'compound republic,' as the explicit solution to the problems of dwarfdom and vulnerability that had so afflicted previous republics. This union attempted to combine executive capability with mechanisms of popular accountability for a grouping of polities that were not city-states but rather as large and thus potentially powerful as a European nation-state, and that together would be as large as a Montesquieuean continental despotic empire. Their goal was nothing less than to transform the general prospects for free government by breaking the impasses of previous republics.

The argument unfolds in three main steps across twelve sections. In the next three sections the specific political structures of the American Union are analyzed as responses to security problems. Then four sections explore its origins, operation, breakdown, and transformation. The final four sections analyze this order as a system-level negarchy, its similarities and differences with the European Westphalian system, the relative contribu-

Security Threat	Philadelphian Structure
War	Binding union between states State semi-autonomy & arms control
Revolution	Guarantee of republican government in states Application of federal law to individuals
Despotism	Limited central government Separation of powers Popular arms control Extended union
Empire	Union aggregation of power Central government war-making authorities

Figure 6.1 Security Threats and Philadelphian Structures

tions of Publius and Kant to republican security theory, and the republican security logic of twentieth-century American internationalism.

SECURITY AND REPUBLICAN STRUCTURES

The provision of security through restraint on violence was a primary goal of the Framers of the American Constitution. The Declaration of Independence of 1776 lists 'life' before 'liberty and the pursuit of happiness' as the natural animating goals of human beings, and the *Federalist* mentions security 116 times. In contrast to the monarchical sovereignty of the European hier-state, sovereignty in the American system rested with the people, in the arrangement previously discussed as a recessed popular sovereign (recall figure 1.9).[12] Having already drawn heavily upon the arguments of Publius in reconstructing the general arguments of republican security theory (recall figure 1.6), our task here is to relate these general insights to the specific political structural architectures of the Philadelphian system (see figure 6.1).

The Philadelphian solution to the security problem is a fully rounded system of power restraints in which the states, the people, and the central government are mutually bound in what John C. Calhoun called the "Constitution of the negative."[13] Instituting a government to regulate relations between members of the polity is the first and most necessary of political tasks, but it remains incomplete—or too complete—without negatives. Negatives are defined by what they aim to avoid, and their overall arrangement must deal simultaneously with two prime and interrelated threats of anarchy and despotism, of too little and too much order. Absolute opposites, anarchy and despotism are mutually generating. Both anarchy and despotism are threats within and between the states, so that security threats come in four forms: domestic revolution and tyranny and external war and empire.

The arrangements of the Philadelphian system address each of the four perennial threats to security. Ending anarchy between the republican units would address the problem of competitive security conflicts between the units. Civil war and *stasis* within the units would be less likely because militia from surrounding states could be mobilized to maintain order. Anarchy within states, associated with unconstrained democracy and factional strife, was addressed by a union guaranteeing republican government within the units and possessing a union government with the authority and capability to maintain order or repel revolution in the units. Civil war and *stasis* in the overall union would be inhibited by the collective action difficulties of coalition building in an extended and diverse polity.

Interstate anarchy is a hydra-headed source of insecurity, both directly through war and invasion and indirectly as a stimulus to the growth of centralized governmental power within the units. To combat this threat the founders formed a union between the American states that circumscribed the military autonomy of the states, and a union governmental apparatus focused primarily upon counterbalancing threats from other states still in an anarchical relation to the union and its members. Despotism arising from the accumulation of unchecked and oppressive power in the state apparatus was avoided in the union government because the large size of the union would obviate the need to mobilize and concentrate high percentages of the country's population and wealth in military activities. To further impede the coalescence of centralized power, the union government was constituted with an elaborate system of power restraint devices such as popular election of office holders, limited terms of office, and separations, vetoes, and balances of power. But fearing that such measures might ultimately fail, the founders relied upon the armed citizen militia in order to reduce the need for a large standing army in the hands of the union government and to serve as an ultimate external check to its potential for oppression. Finally, the overall size of the union would be sufficient to sustain political independence against foreign threats. Let us examine these threats and the Philadelphian solutions to them in more detail.

Anarchy, Despotism, and Union

The problem of anarchy is central to the architecture of the Philadelphian system. First, the founders feared anarchy, violent disorder, and revolution within the states.[14] They were committed to popular sovereignty, but saw democracy as a source of instability and insecurity. History seemed to show that the small city-states in ancient Greece and early modern Italy were "the wretched nurseries of unceasing discord," in a "perpetual vibration between the extremes of tyranny and anarchy."[15] Direct democracy slid into 'mob rule' and then succumbed to coups and despotism. But a union of such polities with a federal government authorized and equipped to intervene to prevent revolution or coup would preserve democracy in the states by curing it of its excess. Hence, the Constitution (in Article 6) guaranteed the members of the Union 'republican government.' An extended union makes unlikely turmoil in all states at once, and enables the chief federal magistrate to suppress revolutions in one republican state with forces drawn from the others, which is what the Washington Administration did to put down the Whiskey Rebellion.[16]

A second security problem stemming from anarchy was the possibility of violent conflict between the several states. Summarizing the insight now associated with neorealism, Hamilton observed, "To look for a continuation of harmony between a number of independent unconnected sovereignties, situated in the same neighborhood would be to disregard the uniform course of human events."[17] The most probable scenario was that the governors of the larger states would use their militia armies to settle conflicts with their neighbors.[18]

Interstate anarchy is also an indirect security threat because it strengthens internal central power, risking internal despotism. In order to respond to outside threats, more concentrated power is needed, deforming interior balances, thus creating a tragic trade-off for free government. As Publius observed, "Safety from external danger is the most powerful director of national conduct. Even the ardent love of liberty will, after a time, give way to its dictates. To be more safe they at length become willing to run the risk of being less free."[19] Interunit anarchy stimulates preparations for war that entails concentrated government power that eventually itself threatens public security.

The solution to both the direct and indirect threats of anarchy is a union based on the sovereignty of an extended public. Union extends the constitutive principle of the units to the interunit system level and entails the further division of authorities and the relocation of some of them in a new tier of government erected above the existing ones. To say that the people as a whole are sovereign means they can *overthrow* governments that have been usurped or corrupted, and *throw over* existing smaller governments with more extended ones. Recessed popular sovereigns employ union to avoid the threat posed by the expansion of their own governmental authorities. In polities with a recessed popular sovereign, *union preserves sovereignty*, while the strenuous defense of their polities' full autonomy in anarchy risks losing it.

The union to solve the problem of interstate anarchy fell far short of a complete merger. The Constitution did not eliminate the independent military power of the several states but restrained the ends to which the states could employ their militias. The governors of the states could call up the militias in order to maintain order within the borders of their own states but not for activities beyond them.[20] Unrestrained by the Union, state militias were perceived to be an instrument of potential interstate conflict. Within the Union they could play a vital role of counterbalancing power centralized in the union government, a role that would be lost if they were eliminated or their control vested solely in the hands of the central government. The restraint of the states was reinforced by the application of federal law upon *individuals* rather than states. If they sought to exercise violent power outside the parameters set in the Constitution, individual office holders in the states were liable to criminal prosecution in the federal courts.[21]

Sectional rivalries posed a third possible anarchic problem, one upon which the Union ultimately floundered. Sections were understood to be large regions differing in climate and topographically demarcated. Sections had sufficient size and internal homogeneity to be nation-states, and were thus, as Frederick Jackson Turner put it, "the faint image of a European nation."[22] The principal alternative to the Union has never really been dozens of fully independent states, but rather their consolidation into a handful of nation-states based upon sections. Sectional rivalry, whether in or out of a Union, posed a major security threat, and the viability of the Union depended on maintaining a balanced distribution of power between the sections and on channeling their balancing through institutions.[23]

Madison's famous mediation on faction and extension in *Federalist* number 10 contains the Philadelphian strategy toward sectional differences and rivalries.[24] The smaller the number of large groups with intense preferences, the greater the possibility that a majority will oppress a minority, and the greater the possibility that a faction will be big enough to successfully secede from the Union, a particularly acute danger when the factions are territorially segmented as sections. But when numerous sectional factions exist, they serve as an important bulwark against the accumulation and corruption of majority power. In the language of international theory, a Philadelphian type system is strengthened by a multipolar distribution, but threatened by a bipolar one. The great appeal of territorial expansion to continental scope was that the Union would contain a multipolar sectional balance of power system.[25]

EXTERNAL THREATS AND LIMITS ON CONCENTRATED POWER

The union between the American republican states eliminated anarchy between them, but was not so universal as to completely eliminate the threat from foreign powers exercised in interstate anarchy. The newly independent American states feared that European states would attempt to reassert imperial control over them.[26] In order to meet this security threat, the central government was endowed with the authority to raise a standing army and navy, to raise the revenues needed to support them, and to call the state militias into action. The framers also created an office of chief magistrate, the president, whose most important authority was commander-in-chief of the armed forces. Executive command of the armed forces could be an instrument of domestic oppression, but such a concentration of authority was a necessary accommodation to political and military realities.[27]

The Union also sought to secure itself from foreign predation by gaining recognition from the European powers of its independence and rights under international law. Given the greater relative power of the European states in the late-eighteenth century, Americans were forced to interact with the Europeans on terms largely established by the Europeans. Early Americans were strong supporters of the institutions of international society, which afforded them some relief from European predation.[28]

The centralized power of the Union government in turn required carefully designed restraints. The extent of the Union facilitated external defense without a strong state, but the potential relative power of the union government against any one state increased greatly. Furthermore, the union security government entailed the delegation of authorities at even greater distance from the sovereign, thus increasing the chances of usurpation unless accompanied by an increase in negative restraints. The further removed from the people, the more power must be restrained, and therefore the importance of the negative as a principle for structuring governmental organs rises as the people are more extended.

The received wisdom of political theory, the story of the overthrow of the Roman Republic, the memory of the English constitutional struggles in the seventeenth century, and their own recent experience all taught Americans that standing armies were the essential tool for popular oppression and the centralization of political authority.[29] The colonists widely believed that the English constitutional restraints on the monarchical power had been circumvented or corrupted by the Crown's ability to raise a standing army. The Declaration of Independence had condemned George III's effort "to render the Military independent of and superior to the Civil Power." The establishment of a standing army was hotly contested in the debates over ratification, where the Anti-Federalists painted a grave threat to public liberty.[30]

To solve this security threat, the founders went to extraordinary lengths to prevent the central government from initiating war easily or quickly. The election of the officeholders within the central government was an important but incomplete restraint. War-making authority was divided between the legislature and the executive. Although they felt compelled to centralize command of the armed forces, they vested the authority to declare war, raise armies and navies, set military policy, and ratify treaties in Congress.[31] By carefully separating the war-making authority between the executive and the legislature, the founders sought to insure that the decision to make war would involve a process with checks and balances and that the authority to initiate and sustain a war were removed from the hands of the commander-in-chief and vested in the branch of the central government closest to the people.[32]

The founders were not content to rely upon elections and the separation and balance of powers within the central government, but also sought to guarantee that a robust and permanent military counterbalance to the central government continued to exist in the hands of the several states and the citizenry. Fearing the unreliability of 'covenants without the sword,' the founders sought to guarantee that a sword would remain firmly in the hands of the people. Blackstone had insisted that all citizen rights were ultimately dependent upon the possession of arms by the citizen body.[33] The history of state-building in early modern Europe also seemed to demonstrate that an armed people and militia was a vital bulwark against monarchical absolutism.[34] The maintenance of a robust military capacity in the hands of the citizenry served as the ultimate counterweight against a despotic concentration of power in the central government. Should the limitations on the government fail, the people retained the capacity to balance against it, which was enshrined in the Second Amendment's guarantee: "A well-regulated Militia, being necessary to the security of a free State, the right of the people to keep and bear Arms, shall not be infringed."[35] The Constitution did not legalize rebellion, but it did legalize the instruments necessary to do so. Maintaining a significant proportion of the polity's armed force in the militia also helped restrain the ability of the central government to wage unpopular foreign wars. Unfortunately, this diffused military capacity undermined the ability of the government to regulate violent excursions of

American citizens at its borders and periphery, enabling an unregulated populist imperialism to flourish.[36]

THE FORTUNATE FOUNDING

In opening the first *Federalist* paper Hamilton proclaims that the American experiment will answer whether it is possible to establish government by "reflection and choice" rather than "accident and force."[37] Despite its careful design, the formation of the Union was assisted by seven fortuitous favorable circumstances. Because of its rarity and short life span, it is essential to identify the factors facilitating the establishment of the American Union to assess whether they were rare or common.

The geographic position of the American states relative to the rest of the international system, and particularly the great powers of Europe, was one of relative isolation. This fact, combined with the relative weakness of the AmerIndians, meant that security threats were small enough that the military capacities of the polity, and hence the strength of the executive, could be kept small enough for its internal limits and militia counterbalance to work.[38] Although the American Union was militarily separated from Europe, it was not fully isolated because of the extensive economic linkages of Atlantic maritime activity. Therefore a major impetus for union was to put these commercial and maritime relations with Europe on a firmer basis.[39]

At the western frontier a fortuitous institutional legacy from the British colonial period helped catalyze the Union. The lands stretching from the Appalachians to the Mississippi had been ceded by Britain in the Peace of Paris of 1783, but state claims to them overlapped on the basis of original colonial land grants. Some states had claims to enormous areas, while others had none. These conflicting claims could lead to war, resulting in even greater inequality in state size. Because of these overlapping claims, no one state could capture the frontier spaces without significant conflict. The fact that these lands were becoming increasingly populated meant either that new and fully independent states, with uncontrollable characters and foreign attachments, would arise, or else the confederate union had to be expanded and strengthened.[40] In order to deal with these problems the states under the Articles of Confederation agreed to abandon their claims, and negotiated the Northwest Ordinance to govern the creation of additional states in these territories. Once ceded to the Continental Congress, the western lands were joint property. In managing this frontier commons the several states found their fates intertwined. The Union was thus built on two tracks, one that culminated in the Convention, the other in the Northwest Ordinance.[41]

The internal constitutions of the founding states also facilitated the formation of the Union. On the eve of the War of Independence, the internal regime types of the thirteen British colonies exhibited considerable variety.[42] Within their diversity were many of the class and religious differences (most notably Puritan and Cavalier) that had clashed in the English civil wars of the seventeenth century. But between 1776 and 1787 the constitutions of all the states were rewritten, producing political orders quite similar to one another.[43] The delegates that met in Philadelphia all represented republican governments resting ultimately on the people. The Philadelphian system was thus a federal union of republican states.

The states that formed the Union were all relatively weak, and their sizes and shapes varied greatly. The tiny states like Rhode Island and Delaware were unlikely to survive long in a competitive military environment, while the giants, most notably New York, Pennsylvania, Virginia, and Georgia, each possessed claims for even larger areas in the West. Colonial era efforts to consolidate colonies and rationalize administration had been halfhearted and notably unsuccessful.[44] In this juridical jumble, state borders had little relationship to the patterns of economic life or military viability, and the establishment of viable states along Westphalian lines would have entailed a massive redrawing of borders, a process that would have been difficult to accomplish without war.

Hegemony played only an indirect role in the formation of the Union. Among the states, power was widely distributed, and the largest states were at most potential hegemons within their regions. However, hegemony did play an indirect role in the founding. Under British rule the colonies had enjoyed the benefits of hegemonic power, but had suffered few adverse consequences from it. Despite heated polemics about royal despotism, British rule in North America was episodic, incoherent, and distant.[45] Even in the colonies where the Crown's authority was most extensive (the Crown had more legal authority in some colonies than in Britain), the effective distance from London meant that the actual exercise of British rule was quite lax. Due to its effective distance Britain was a *separated hegemon*. Like the God of the Deists, London set the American world in motion, provided basic services at low cost, but lightly directed it. This separated hegemon cast the mold within which the colonies grew, and when they had broken from it, they were eager to provide a functional equivalent to it. The Union was a self-generated replacement for this fortuitous combination of order without strong central direction.

Finally, because the Philadelphian system rested upon popular sovereignty, the identity of the people played an important role. Social class and republican civic identity played a much more central role than either ethnic or national identity. Americans first and foremost thought of themselves as 'free' and 'virtuous.'[46] At a time when individual freedom, political democracy, and social egalitarianism were rare and widely perceived to be precarious, this fundamental liberalism of the American people was both a potent and distinguishing basis of political identity.[47] Liberty was understood to be sustained by virtue, a mixture of self-restraint and compromise norms, and a skilled knowledge of procedures and mechanisms.[48] This republican civic identity was inculcated and reproduced through education, ceremonies, architecture, and iconography.[49] American republican political identity was intimately connected to a pervasive early capitalist class system. Feudal vestiges were few and steadily shrinking, particularly after the flight of many Royalists.[50] The dominant social class in America was property owners without feudal titles, and the cities were dominated by an interstate network of commercial elites. The land tenure and criminal justice systems were served by a large number of lawyers, and as Tocqueville observed, the "American aristocracy" was the "bench and the bar."[51] Lawyers are the organic intellectuals of commercial society, and their commitment to conflict resolution by independent courts applying tort law made recourse to interstate violence less appealing than contracts and arbitration.[52]

The least important feature of early American identity was ethnic and national. Such identity groupings do not match North American political patterns. The British colonies that claimed independence in 1776 were populated by people whose language, 'race,' and religion were not very different from those of Britain.[53] As D. W. Meinig observes, "the rebellion of the 1770s did not arise as an ethnic protest against a foreign ruler, as in the most common imperial disintegrations, but as a civil war over the treatment of overseas 'Englishmen.' "[54] Sectional identities were strong, and the Southern states that sought to achieve independence in the war of 1861–65 claimed to constitute a separate nation and met many of the criteria normally associated with a nation.[55] This war was more an international war within a states-union than a war of national unification.[56] Finally, the differences of national identity between Canada and the United States appear to be no greater than the differences among Americans. Either the United States was part of a multistate nation or the United States was a multinational union.

External Imbalance, Expansion, and Internal Imbalance

Despite its auspicious beginnings, the Union did eventually fall into a great sectional war that ended with the complete conquest of one section by another, and a recast Constitution. Did this breakdown reflect flaws in its structure or the influence of contingent circumstances? The early-nineteenth-century United States is a case study in the effects of rapid expansion upon the balance of power dynamics of a states-union and in the nonformation of a state system. Union expansion was facilitated by the absence of effective external balancing against the Union, and expansion disturbed the interior balance of power between the sections within the Union.

The background of American expansion and the nonemergence of a state system was the fact that Britain, and then the British colonies, were able to frustrate other European great powers from establishing viable colonies in North America. Had a substantial colony of Europeans from another nation-state taken root in the vast interior valley of the continent drained by the Mississippi and the St. Lawrence Rivers, then North America might contain several roughly equal states. It is notable that France twice (in the Seven Years' War and then in Napoleon's sale of his nominal possession of the vast Louisiana region) lost a territorial base in North America that could have sustained a major nation-state. The success of the British colonies in part stems from Britain's maritime superiority, suggesting that the absence of a balanced state system in North America may be partially a side effect of the European maritime balancer's domination of the waters around the European peninsula.

Another factor was that the rate and extent of American expansion in the early-nineteenth century has few precedents. In 1787 the thirteen American states were located only upon the Atlantic coast, but by 1861 Union territory stretched to the Pacific, covering an area nearly five times as large, and the number of states in the Union had nearly tripled. At the founding it was widely assumed that there was a 'Manifest Destiny' that European settlers would expand into the vast interior regions of North America.[57] But the extension facilitated by the union architecture was still limited by the distance representatives had to cover between the electorate and the capital, and many thought effective distance to the interior of North America meant there eventually would be independent states outside the Union.[58] Then the invention and rapid construction of railroad and telegraph systems dramatically shrunk effective distance across the great Western mountains to the Pacific coast.[59]

An anarchic balance-of-power state system did not emerge in North America in part due to the failure of other states to coalesce and then balance either among themselves or with outsiders. The speed and volume of settler expansion into the power vacuum at the frontier also helped foreclose the emergence of independent states. Three sets of actors might have resisted American expansion: European or Asian states, other European settler colonies in North America, and the indigenous population.[60] The failure of an anarchic state system to form in North America was also partially the result of the gravitational attraction and assimilative capacity of the Philadelphian system. In the annals of realpolitik, it is often forgotten that the Philadelphian union peacefully absorbed two quasi-independent states (Vermont and Utah), and Texas which was briefly independent and recognized as such by both the United States and the European powers.[61] These states did not seek to preserve their independence by balancing against the United States, but instead sought and achieved admission to the Union. Texas had good reason to fear attack by Mexico or European states, and could have employed classic Westphalian strategies of balancing and alliance formation, particularly with Britain, in order to sustain its independence. In part their vigorous flight from independence can be attributed to the fact that they were not fully extinguished as states by joining the Union, but rather were preserved as semiautonomous units within it and shared in union government in proportion to their population.

The expansion of the Union redistributed power between the sections, triggering an extremely violent war of secession. Admission of new states in the West had important ramifications for the balance of power between slaveholding and free states in the Senate and Electoral College. In 1820, 1833, and 1850, the Union was preserved by intersectional 'Great Compromises,' which were "something like the diplomatic treaties of European nations, defining spheres of influence, and awarding mandates."[62] Had there been deadlock over new state admissions, the aspirants to admission would have gradually coalesced as an interstate system. The Great Compromises depended upon the ability to roughly pair new entries to the Union, but during the 1850s, new slave states fell behind the establishment of 'free soil' states, portending eventual elimination of the South's veto power.[63] The open civil war that raged between settlers from the North and South on the frontier in 'bleeding Kansas' rehearsed and helped spark the great conflict that was to engulf the core regions of the Union.[64]

The persistence and intensity of the division between free and slave states meant that expansion had failed to achieve the dilution of interest groups that Madison had envisioned. Despite the great importance that the founders had attached to the balance of power, they had not included a constitutional mechanism to provide sections with an ultimate veto against changes that they saw as fundamentally threatening.[65]

The deeper cause of the war, of course, was the 'peculiar institution' of slavery, which fueled these system-structural dynamics and impasses. The American Civil War was a social revolutionary conflict over the status of slavery within market capitalism refracted through the structures of a states-union. Slavery was not simply a regional variation within the liberal social order, but a radically antiliberal relic of preliberal society, and thus the intersectional war as civil war completed the social revolution that had begun in England and deepened in the struggle for American independence. Even without the conflicts at the frontier, a day of reckoning was probably inevitable. With the increased national economic integration brought by the nascent industrial revolution, the working classes in the North, while often quite racist, came to actively oppose African slavery as a competitive threat to their economic prospects.[66]

Overall, the two causes of the Civil War—very rapid expansion and preliberal remnants—suggest that the outbreak of this conflict is not indicative of some flaw integral to its architecture, but rather to the particular geopolitical context and social inheritance of the Union. The universal elimination of slavery and the unlikelihood that any polity will expand so rapidly suggests the two main causes of the Union's crisis are unlikely to be widely occurring obstacles to the stability of states-unions.

Publius versus National and State Sovereignty

Long before the bloodletting of the war of 1861–65 a river of ink was expended defending different interpretations of the Constitution of 1787, particularly concerning the location of sovereignty.[67] The first U.S. Constitution as interpreted by Publius rests on popular sovereignty, but *which people* were sovereign became fundamentally contested. During this period there emerged two alternatives, both claiming to be forms of popular sovereignty, but both subversive of the original design.

One alternative, stated most powerfully by Calhoun, was the proposition that sovereignty resided in the *peoples of the states* and that the Union Constitution was in effect a confederative one that could be ended if the peoples of the several states decided to do so. Calhoun sought to demonstrate that the right of secession was implicit in the Constitution of 1787, but more important, that it was an inherent attribute of sovereignty situated in the hands of the peoples of the several states.[68] The other challenger did not have the philosophical sophistication of Calhoun but ultimately was the victor in the bloodbath of the 1860s. This interpretation, stated most powerfully by Senators Daniel Webster of New Hampshire and Robert Livingston of Louisiana, argued that sovereignty was situated in the people of the American *nation as a whole*, and was exercised by *democratic majorities* operating through the structures of the central government created by the Constitution of 1787.[69]

The views of Webster and Calhoun had radically different implications for the political viability of the American Union, but also have notable similarities. The powers that Webster attributes to the people of the United States, Calhoun attributes to the people of the states. As the Union entered its great crisis in the middle of the nineteenth century, few people still held the Publius understanding of sovereignty in the American Union. The views of sovereignty became polarized, with Southerners adhering to the Calhoun view and Northerners tending toward Webster's.[70] The fate of this clash over the nature of sovereignty in the American system was resolved in favor of Webster's position during the extraordinary presidency of Abraham Lincoln, who subscribed to Webster's view and was able to exercise the extraconstitutional powers that helped preserve—and change—the Constitution.

From States-Union to Federal State

The impact of the War of Southern Secession on the American political order was both revolutionary and restorative.[71] In some ways, the United States entered the war a states-union in crisis and emerged from it a federal state and with a strengthened liberal-democratic national identity.[72] In saving the Union, Lincoln also changed it. The relationship between the parts and the whole was redefined by establishing definitively that the parts could not secede.[73] The federal government grew in size and powers, and the executive branch was strengthened at the expense of the legislative.[74] But much of the earlier architecture remained, and so after military demobilization and the end of the quasi-martial law of Reconstruction, the United States reverted to the federal polity of 'parties and courts,' marked by the atrophy of central capacities.[75] Yet in a more important way, the changes wrought by the war marked the fulfillment and modernization of the principles of the founding. The absolute domination of slavery was abolished, and a major step was taken toward guaranteeing that the state members of the Union did in fact have republican governments.

By the turn of the century, further reconfigurations in the arrangement of governmental authorities became necessary to make the mutual-restraint and power-accountability principles of the founders relevant to the new industrial conditions. Industrial communication and transportation capabilities unimagined at the founding created extensive integration and mobility, contributing to the growth of a strong American national identity. The burgeoning industrial economy created demands for a more substantial government role to balance and check unprecedented concentrations of 'private' power. But this republican modernization was often frustrated by the Constitution's elaborate power machinery designed for preindustrial conditions. The American system seemed to exhibit, as the British Lord Bryce put it, "excessive friction" causing a waste of force in the strife of various bodies.[76] Progressive and New Deal reformers sought to reconfigure these restraining features and increase capabilities for solving new problems while preserving and expanding public accountability.[77] Through constitutional amendments and an elastic interpretation of the Commerce Clause, the central government gradually came to have a role more comparable to preindustrial state or municipal government than to the original federal arrangement.

In the twentieth century, the international effects of the industrial revolution created new demands for enlarged central state security capacities. As the violence interdependence between the United States and the European great powers shifted from weak to strong, the United States was forced to abandon its isolationist posture and develop the capabilities to balance against the predatory states in the international second anarchy. Meeting these new external threats required the further weakening of the state-restraint features of the American political system. In the three great world struggles in the twentieth century (World War I, World War II, and the Cold War) the central government's powers were substantially enhanced. The state militias were gradually transformed into the National Guard and subject almost completely to federal government control.[78] Direct conscription and a large, technically sophisticated standing military force also altered the security order.[79] As war became total in intensity and global in scope, restraints on the central state were weakened in order to mobilize and coordinate the economy and populace.[80] The need for grand strategic and civil-military integration conflicted with the elaborate system of restraints upon executive war making. Although elections and Congress continued to restrain the president, the demands of speed, secrecy, and complexity militated toward vesting extensive powers in the executive and the security apparatus. With the permanent mobilization of the Cold War and the nuclear era, the original republican order regulating violence capability had been altered significantly, and the United States came to increasingly resemble a European hier-state. But, as we shall see, fear of such deformations also gave rise to a new type of internationalist agenda that sought to reduce state-building at home by abridging anarchy abroad.

STATES-UNION AS SYSTEM-LEVEL NEGARCHY

As a first of four concluding steps, it is appropriate to assess the structure of the Philadelphian system as a system-level negarchy. Building on the earlier triad-triangular formulation (recall figure 1.8), it is possible to construct a simple typology of six systems to visualize the system structure of state-unions, and its relationship with the familiar hierarchical and anarchical systems, and three mixed systems of imperial federation, confederation, and hegemony[81] (see figure 6.2). More than a confederation of states in anarchy and less than a state with extensive devolution, the overall structure of the Philadelphian system is negarchical because these

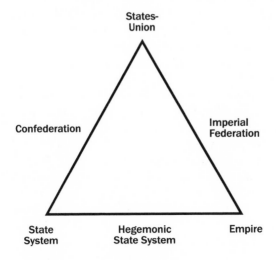

States-
Union

Confederation   Imperial
                                                 Federation

State   Hegemonic   Empire
System   State System

Figure 6.2 Typology of System Structures

structures were configured to prevent simultaneously the emergence of
hierarchy and anarchy. Having already seen how this system differs from
the federal state, we here examine the role of the states in it and its similarities and differences with the confederal (anarchical-negarchical mixture)
system type.

What role remained for the states in this states-union? The Union preserved states from elimination, a fate that surely would have befallen
many of them without it. The Union also incorporated an important element of state equality, and it was customary to speak of the states re-
taining sovereignty in certain spheres.[82] The Senate was designed to be a
body representing the states, a role reflected in the election of senators by
state legislators rather than the peoples of the states directly.[83] In addition
to the militia, the Philadelphian system left policing and criminal law enforcement almost entirely in the hands of the states, where it remained
until the establishment of the Federal Bureau of Investigation in the twentieth century.

The Philadelphian system also contained many features commonly associated with a confederation, and the relations of the units to one another retained similarities with interstate diplomacy. The relationship between the several states and the union government was a hybrid mix of
diplomatic practices carried out between sovereign states and representation between constituencies within a federal state. The representative system was more an evolutionary than a revolutionary departure from the

patterns of British colonial and inter-American interaction during the colonial period.[84] The relations between the several states resembled an interstate anarchy with regard to policing. State law enforcement agencies
rarely coordinated their activities, and until well into the twentieth century they generally did not arrest or extradite suspects accused of crimes
in other states.[85]

The Philadelphian system was certainly federal, but it was as much an
antistate as a state. It had a *government*, but was not a *state*. The state-
restraint features of the American Union were more important and more
articulated than in any previous political order of its size and diversity,
but statist features were not completely absent. This government could
do some tasks of states, most notably to secure its territory from outside
military predation. Internally, however, the United States was clearly not
a European hierarchical state. With the armed citizenry institutionalized,
the central government of the Union explicitly lacked a monopoly of violence capability and of legitimate violence authority.

Conversely, it was not a confederation because the central government
was too organizationally elaborate and the states were too circumscribed.
In advocating ratification of the Constitution of 1787 as a replacement
for the Articles of Confederation, Publius discusses at length the limitations and records of earlier confederations. Alliances and confederations
were seen as prone either to suffer severe collective action and authority
problems or to slide into hegemonic and imperial forms when led by an
energetic and more powerful member (Athens and the Delian League;
Rome and its many allies).[86] Union between the units ended anarchy, but
the ultimate sovereign, the people, is so extended, diverse, and divided
that it cannot rule. Also unlike a confederation, a states-union has organs
invested with substantial authorities and capacities.[87] The authority of
federal organs penetrates into the states and applies to individuals, producing an overall arrangement in which the units, the union organs, and
the people are coordinated and mutually restrained.

This triadic typology of system types also helps frame comparative security system analysis. A state system can be seen as a particular combination of institutional forms (such as sovereignty, the balance of power, the
separation of power, and arms control) that can be combined in different
ways to constitute different systems. This typology is also useful for mapping the evolution of the American political order. In the century between
the French and Indian Wars (1763) and the end of Reconstruction (1877)
political order evolved from a loose empire (British colonial period) to a
modified anarchy (Independence and the Articles of Confederation) to a
states-union (the Philadelphian System), to a weak federal state (after the
Civil War).

	Westphalian System	Philadelphian System
Technical Description	Anarchic State System	States-Union (compound republic/negarchy)
Unit Level	Hier-State	Semi-autonomous republics
System Level	Anarchy and society of states	Federal government
Instrument of System-Level Institution	Treaty and alliance	Constitution
Sovereignty	Located in state and engaged	Located in extended public and recessed
Disposition of Violence	Popular disarmament and concentration in real-state apparatus and minimum regulation between units	Regulated popular armament and limited central concentration with extensive separation
Role of Separation	Minimized within units and maximized between units	Extensive within states and federal government and weak between states
Units Extinguished?	Yes	No
Mechanism for Change	War and compensation	Elections, reapportionment, and amendment
Dominant Social Strata	Feudal aristocracy	Lawyers, merchants, and property owners

Figure 6.3 Westphalian and Philadelphian Systems Compared

PHILADELPHIAN AND WESTPHALIAN SYSTEMS COMPARED

A brief glance at the similarities and differences with the Westphalian system of hierarchies in anarchy completes the comparative analysis (see figure 6.3) and highlights the key differences between a system-level anarchy and a system-level negarchy. Most importantly, these systems differ with regard to the roles of sovereignty and union, separation and union, conflict and balance, and classes and norms.

First, the disposition of sovereignty in the two systems had very different implications for their ability to form unions. European political order in the eighteenth and early-nineteenth centuries had aspects both federal (antihegemonic alliances) and constitutional (the great settlements). Like them, the Philadelphian system was created in the wake of war and revolution that had created both new opportunities and needs for the creation of political order. But the European pattern of sovereignty in the hierarchical state put severe limits on the formation of an organized union. The only unions consistent with hierarchical states are fleeting and contingent alliances that bound the state sovereigns only so long as convenience dictates. In contrast, recessed popular sovereigns harness the interplay between closer and more distant authorities. For states, unions are acts between sovereigns, while for recessed sovereigns they are delegations of government-forming authorities.

Second, both orders depended heavily upon a division or separation of powers. In Europe the decisive division was in the material context of topography, augmented by dividing practices. Division and separation of powers also pervade the Philadelphian system. Violence capabilities and authorities are divided between the people, the states, and the federal government. Within the central government, war making, military command, and foreign affairs are divided between the Congress and the president, and even the legislature is divided. The legislative, judicial, and executive branches of government are divided. The Constitution is separated from government law making, and the church from the state. But these divisions do not produce autonomous authoritative organs, because their authorities are partially shared as well, in effect giving one body veto over acts of the other, thus paralyzing action without concurrent approval.[88] Thus paradoxically, separation and division were much more precarious in Europe because of the weakness of union, while division and separation were more secure in the Philadelphian system because of the strength of the union.

Third, the balance of power plays central but very different roles in both systems. In the Westphalian model, hierarchies within units suppress balance, while anarchy between the units gives it wide reign. The American Union sought to prevent homogenization and consensus by territorial extension, and then to channel and harness conflict by setting power against power. Tottering between full anarchy and universal monarchy, the European plural system persisted only through periodic wars. The American Union had an embedded balance-of-power system.[89] The ultimate balancer, the armed people, remained recessed and never employed, unlike in Europe where cycles of class hegemony within the hier-state evoked periodic armed popular revolution.

Fourth, the social ethos and political identity of the American people was republican and capitalist. In contrast, in Europe the most significant continentwide social formation was the 'aristocracy international,' the interlocking network of feudal houses and dynasties. European capitalist institutions were spliced on to a feudal social structure, and the ethos of the functionally archaic 'aristocracy of the sword,' the economically parasitic descendants of the feudal warrior classes, imbued European politics with a concern for honor, prestige, hierarchy, and violent competition that heavily influenced international politics.[90]

FEDERAL REPUBLICAN SECURITY BEFORE DEMOCRATIC PEACE

Among the legacies of Enlightenment republican security theory, Publius and federal union are nearly invisible in contemporary Liberal international theory, in contrast to Kant and the democratic peace. With a clearer understanding of Publius's contribution to republican security theory in hand, a revision of the positions of Publius and Kant is warranted, for two reasons. First, Publius employs and extends the main arguments of republican security theory much more fully than does Kant. Second, federal union is much more important than democratic peace in the actual historical development of republican polities over the last two centuries. Taken together, these arguments make the case for seeing Publius and federal union, not Kant and democratic peace, as the crowning achievement of Enlightenment republicanism.

Publius and Kant differ in seven important ways (see figure 6.4). Regarding sources and cases there is a striking difference between them. The ideas of numerous ancient and early modern theorists (Polybius, Plutarch, Blackstone, Hume, and Montesquieu) are referenced directly by Publius. The security experience of numerous historical republics and leagues are discussed by Publius, with the Roman Republic being mentioned eleven different times.[91] In contrast, Kant never mentions most of the ancient Greek or Latin authors, nor any of the ancient or early modern polities. This silence is particularly notable, given that Kant was fluent in Latin and drew heavily upon Roman Stoic cosmopolitan ethical theorists (most notably Cicero, Seneca, and Marcus).[92] Of modern theorists, Kant's extensive engagement with Hobbes and Rousseau is accompanied by a nearly complete silence on Machiavelli, British constitutionalism, Montesquieu, and the American founders. In contrast to Kant's abstract and deductive argument, Publius draws heavily upon historical experience for practical lessons, and self-consciously situates itself as a better solution to the problems animating prior republican political theorists.

The next three differences relate to the security problems of republican polities. Republican security theory culminating in Publius dealt with the related security problems of internal *stasis*, the lethal symbiosis of internal Caesarism and external competitive militarism, and external vulnerability rooted in size constraints. In contrast, Kant simply drops or ignores many of these lines of argument. He is silent on the perils of factional *stasis* and says little about the perils of Caesarist coups. Kant says little about how

	Publius	Kant
Sources	Numerous Ancient & Early Modern	Early Republican Security Theory Largely Absent
Cases	Greece, Rome, Venice, Holland, Britain, etc.	None
Stasis	Driving Concern	Barely Mentioned
Vulnerability to Conquest	Driving Concern	Noted
Relations among Republics	Potentially Violently Competitive	Pacific
System-Level Structures	Federal Union (negarchic)	Anarchic (with alliances & amity treaties)
Role of Material Factors	Detailed Analysis	'Nature's Secret Plan'

Figure 6.4 Publius and Kant Compared

democratic republics come into existence, reach sufficient size to be viable, and become numerous enough to substantially populate a state system.[93] Publius, starting from the historical reality of acute republican vulnerability, advances federal union as a means for republics to achieve the size, and thus security, previously available only to monarchic states and despotic empires.

Publius and Kant also differ markedly on the international system. Where Publius held that republics would tend toward violent conflict with each other because of the competitive dynamics of anarchy, Kant held that unit-level constraints in democratic republics would pacify relations among republics. From these different understandings of interstate anarchy, they proposed different system-level authority structures. Kant's thin 'pacific union' composed of treaties of friendship is enough for a world already filled with stable democratic republics, while for Publius a states-union is necessary to take them out of anarchy. Finally, material contextual factors play very different roles in their arguments. Publius builds from earlier claims about material factors such as topography and land-sea interactions. In contrast, Kant is largely silent on the material-contextual dimensions of the mainstream of republican security theory, although, in princess-and-the-pea fashion, material-context actually has a powerful if underspecified and subterranean role, in 'nature's secret plan.'

Overall, it is as if Publius and Kant live in different worlds, or at least radically different historical periods. For Publius, republics are rare, fragile, and vulnerable. Kant seems to leap over these problems, and his argument largely begins with a world where the problems animating Publius have disappeared or been solved.

The second reason for revising the positions of Publius and federal union and Kant and democratic peace emerges from a consideration of the historical record over the last two centuries. Which phenomenon—republican security through federal union or peace among democracies—is more significant in the historical development of liberal democratic republics? To answer this question, it is necessary to look across the industrial divide into the global century and its total conflicts, a very different world from the eighteenth century. On the basis of this substantial historical record Publius and federal union, not Kant and democratic peace, should be seen as primary in the development of republican security theory.[94]

The American founding occurred on the eve of the industrial revolution, whose main external security consequence was to increase sharply the scope of the state system and the size of viable units within it. As the 'age of contending states' unfolded in the century between 1890 and 1990, a handful of continental-sized units and plausible aspirants to world great-power status were locked into a series of mortal combats of worldwide scope. In this brutally competitive interstate environment, the only reason that republican polities could plausibly survive, let alone prevail, was that the United States of America had combined republican government with empirelike size via federal union. All other democratic republics were implausible candidates for survival in the global-industrial era, except as allies of the United States.

In the World War II phase of the struggle, democratic republics at the Western core, already shrunk to a handful in northwestern Europe, were either overrun by Nazi German armies (Holland, Belgium, Norway, Denmark, and France), were neutrals vulnerable to assured eventual conquest by Germany (Switzerland and Sweden), or were snatched from conquest by massive American aid and Hitler's quixotic grand strategy (Britain).[95] Outside the European core, democracies were few, scattered, and weak. They were spared immediate Axis conquest only by their remoteness and American assistance (Australia and New Zealand) or their proximity to the United States (Canada).

After the defeat of Axis imperialism, liberal democracies faced another mortal peril from communist Russia and China, and the survival, reconstruction, and expansion of democracy in the second half of the twentieth century vitally depended upon American military and economic power.[96] American arms shielded the shattered democracies at the western core, American occupation forces and assistance reconstructed western Germany and Japan as liberal democracies, and the American-led NATO alliance thwarted Soviet domination of Western Europe.[97] As Tony Smith observes, "[I]t is difficult to escape the conclusion that since World War I, the fortunes of democracy worldwide have largely depended on American power."[98] Looking at the overall pattern of world politics during the era of contending states, it is difficult to imagine how any liberal democracy would have survived had it not been for the fact that the American Union was large and strong enough to prevail against aggressive anti-democracies and to protect and nurture smaller national democratic states.

Kant's democratic peace argument has been subject to extensive empirical examination, but opinion is sharply divided over whether the evidence is supportive, with questions of when which states qualify as democracies accounting for much of the disagreement. There is, however, agreement that the number of states appropriately viewed as democracies is relatively small, with the number increasing greatly over the last half century. Only recently, mainly in western Europe and the North Atlantic area, has a state system been sufficiently populated by republican democracies to constitute an appropriate case to test Kant's hypothesis.[99] Prior to the second half of the twentieth century, the absence of war between democratic states is easily explained by other factors: democracies have been rare, distant from one another, generally precarious, and subject to predation by nondemocracies.[100] Confining the cases to democratic states that had the minimum security enjoyed by great powers, the American-British dyad is most interesting, but these two states were both essentially status quo powers, driven into alliance by aggressive revisionist states. Furthermore, Great Britain systematically appeased American demands in the late-nineteenth century, not primarily out of democratic solidarity, but rather from a combination of general overextension, fear of rising American power, and hope that the United States would become Britain's ally against the greater threat of rising German power.[101] Over the last half century, power among democratic states has been so concentrated in American hands as to make interdemocratic war unlikely, and other democracies have looked to the United States for protection from predatory communist states in both Europe and East Asia.[102] Not only has the United States been the senior partner in a defensive alliance protecting vulnerable democracies, but American-led institutions have systematically dampened conflictual tendencies among democracies and encouraged a wide range of cooperative activities that have further diminished bellicist encounters. In sum, pre–World War II democracies were too rare, precarious, and noncontiguous to provide much evidence for Kant's claim, while post–World War II democracies have had their relations determined by the twin structural forces of American hegemony and bipolar competition with the Soviet Union, suggesting that Kant's argument remains untested in a compelling way.

Looking at the overall picture, two facts stand out. First, without American power, there would probably not be any democracies at the end of the twentieth century. Second, the democracies that have behaved so impressively pacifically toward one another have largely been junior allies of the United States in a very hostile and competitive interstate environment. Given these patterns, Publius and federal republican security, rather than Kant and democratic peace, have greater claim to being the foundational figures and arguments of Liberal international theory.

REPUBLICAN SECURITY AND AMERICAN INTERNATIONALISM

The first fully global century of the 'age of contending states,' stretching with unusual historical neatness from 1890 to 1990, also has been the first 'American Century.' At its end the United States stands in a position of ascendency unparalleled in modern times.[103] A distinctive or 'exceptional' feature of American foreign policy during this century has been its Liberal internationalist support for international law, organizations, and regimes. Increasingly in disarray and under assault at the turn of the twenty-first century, the Liberal internationalist project has been subject to a number of interpretations and assessments from different schools of thought, none of which adequately acknowledges or captures important parts of its republican security logic and its relationship to the principles of the American founding.

For most Realists, American Liberal internationalism is exceptional as a deviation, the product of happy circumstances and domestic liberalism. It is viewed as utopian in its premises and trivial in its accomplishments. A persistent theme of Realist advice has been for the United States to 'grow up' and behave like a fully 'socialized' great power, and to accept that its support for international organization is as quixotic as its earlier isolationism became.[104] Another group of Realists emphasizes the international ordering role of hegemonic concentrations of power and sees international institutions as useful for providing legitimacy, conserving power, and sharing costs.[105] On the Liberal side, strong support for economic internationalism comes from 'Hamiltonians' who emphasize the economic benefits of open markets and the need for the United States to support international economic institutions for the expansion and stability of the international capitalist order. The other main contemporary Liberal school supporting internationalism, the 'Wilsonians,' emphasizes the humanitarian, religious, and normative impulse to improve and transform the world by exporting American values and institutions. Finally, contemporary American 'neoconservativism' emphasizes its 'Wilsonian' devotion to the spread of democracy as a fundamental goal of American foreign policy, but vigorously opposes international organizations as restraints on American power and threats to American sovereignty. In dropping Wilson's agenda for international law and organization, neoconservatism becomes a curiously 'one-legged Wilsonianism.'

None of these schools and interpretations adequately grasps the republican security logic behind the American Liberal internationalist project and the central role violence interdependence plays in it. Building from the logic of the Philadelphian system as articulated in the *Federalist, the republican security agenda of Liberal internationalism seeks to populate the international system with republics and to abridge international anarchy in order to avoid the transformation of the American limited government constitutional order into a hierarchical state* (recall figure 1.12). In a situation of strong or intense violence interdependence, recurrent major war and perpetual preparation for war deform interior balances and generate a hierarchical state inimical to political liberty, popular sovereignty, and limited government. The essential meaning of President Woodrow Wilson's well-known call 'to make the world safe for democracy' is that the only way for nonhierarchical polities to survive in a world of rising violence interdependence is through the transformation of both system-level anarchy and unit-level hierarchy.[106] The fundamental reality is that rising violence interdependence has shifted the 'possibility frontier' of trade-offs between the extent of domestic hierarchy and the extent to which the external environment is populated by republics and unions (see figure 6.5). Security through hegemonic preponderance risks slipping into imperial dominance, which also severely corrupts republican forms. To replace international anarchy with negarchy, some form of interstate union, configured to reflect scale effects, is necessary for the preservation of free government. This core part of Wilsonian Liberal internationalism is Madisonianism in the context of global interdependence.

Prior to the industrialization of the European great powers, the United States was sufficiently isolated from Europe militarily that a policy of hemispheric isolationism was viable. But during the first global century

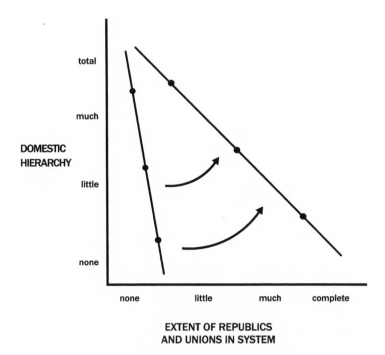

Figure 6.5 Shift in Trade-Off between Domestic Hierarchy and
International Institutional Environment

this material contextual restraint on power diminished, forcing the United
States to either transform the system or be transformed by it. During the
global-industrial era, the level of violence interdependence with Europe
rose to a level that necessitated balancing for the survival of the United
States and cobinding for the survival of the U.S. Constitution. In the
global-industrial material context, American internationalism, while not
always feasible in practice, has always been necessary in principle. In this
view, the success of American foreign policy is ultimately measured not
by the magnitude of American power relative to other states, but by the
extent to which the United States is situated in a nonanarchical international system populated by republican states. Thus what separates the old
isolationist republicans and the new internationalist Liberals is a change
of circumstances that requires a change of strategy rather than a change
of goals. Liberal internationalism is the continuation of isolationist republicanism in interdependent circumstances.[107]

Important articulations of this argument occur at each juncture in the
unfolding of the American century with varying degrees of clarity, consis-
tency, and impact. First were the arguments made by advocates of
strengthening international law and establishing the Permanent Interna-

tional Court at the Hague.[108] During the brief episode of American great-power imperialism culminating in the Spanish-American War and annexation of extracontinental possessions, critics argued that the American acquisition of imperial provinces and colonial dependencies would lead to a corruption of the U.S. Constitution along the lines of the Roman Republic.[109] During the lengthy and complex debate over American entry into World War I, many Progressives articulated the argument that participation in the war would deform American domestic institutions.[110]

This first wave of American internationalist analysis and activity culminated in the effort by Wilson to establish a League of Nations as an international organization for collective security as part of the settlement of World War I. The actual Versailles settlement was a mixture of atavistic as well as progressive elements, the capacities of the League were quite limited, and Wilson's stubbornness and illness undermined the ratification of the League treaty by the U.S. Senate. But what is particularly notable is that the case he made for the League in numerous speeches was essentially that the moderation of international anarchy was necessary not simply to insure peace, but to preserve democracy from corruption produced by periodic major wars and perpetual war preparation.[111]

These arguments gained even wider currency and influence during and after World War II. The republican security logic of the Liberal internationalist program was articulated by Edward Corwin, a leading scholar of the Constitution: "the cause of peace abroad and the cause of constitutional democracy at home are allied causes."[112] Backed by the widespread realization that the flawed settlement of the First World War had contributed to the outbreak of the second, the Roosevelt Administration spearheaded the international effort to create the United Nations, which many saw as a first step toward more substantive international organization.[113] A similar agenda motivated the Truman Administration to advance various proposals for international control and regulation of atomic weapons. The impact of these efforts was greatly reduced by the exigencies of the growing conflict with the Soviet Union, which required another round of international balancing and domestic state-building. Throughout the decades of the Cold War, the United States continued to promote various efforts at international institution-building, particularly in nuclear arms control, at the same time that it sustained a vigorous multidimensional competition with the communist bloc states. This mobilization was haunted by fears that the United States would become what the political scientist Harold Lasswell termed a "garrison state" and that domestic institutions would become corrupted by the influence of the 'military industrial complex' described by President Dwight Eisenhower in his Farewell Address.[114]

With the end of the Cold War and the collapse of the Soviet Union, it seemed that the moment had finally arrived when the United States had the power and influence to realize its long deferred agenda for the substantial replacement of interstate anarchy. But instead of moving toward realization, the United States, particularly after the new Republican Party gained control of Congress, increasingly opposed or rejected major republican security initiatives such as the International Criminal Court, the expansion of international peacekeeping capabilities, and a comprehensive nuclear test ban.[115] Perhaps the reason for this 'great retreat' is that nearly a half century of mobilization for global total war, stretching from the late 1930s until the fall of the Berlin Wall, has profoundly altered the American polity by creating precisely what republican theorists had predicted—a vast national security state increasingly autonomous and ideologically supported by a highly self-conscious elite.[116] Thus emerges the growing *tragedy of American global diplomacy.* In amassing enough power to transform its international context, the United States has been transformed into a polity much less interested in changing its international context.

At the end of the twentieth century, the struggle over the Liberal internationalist program for global republican security has only passed through its opening phases. Throughout the first American Century, this program had been ahead of its time. Its advocates could point to the inexorable tide of global interdependence and extrapolate eventual consequences, but speculative anticipations of future disasters are rarely enough to mobilize support for costly and psychologically difficult ventures. Furthermore, the exigencies of interstate competition in combination with American preponderance made it easy to postpone the day of reckoning until some indefinite future date.

To better understand the implications of the inexorably rising tide of global interdependence for republican security, we turn in the next three chapters to a closer examination of diverse bodies of nineteenth- and twentieth-century thought about the new material context created by the industrial and nuclear revolutions.

PART III

Toward the Global Village

Chapter Seven

LIBERAL HISTORICAL MATERIALISM

It has become a platitude to say that the whole world
is now interdependent.
—Ramsey Muir[1]

ACROSS THE INDUSTRIAL DIVIDE

In the standard narrative of Western history, the decades surrounding 1800 are widely seen as a major turning point, dividing the five centuries of the modern era into early and late modernity. In the narrative of material civilization this period marks the beginning of the industrial revolution.[2] In the realm of intellectual history, the break is marked by the growing centrality of historical change. In the annals of liberal history, this period witnesses the substantial growth of liberal democracy, and for international politics the beginning of a marked intensification of globalization.

The intellectual legacies of the long nineteenth century loom large on our horizon, providing the canonical works of late modernity. The rise in literacy and educations fuels a great increase in the volume and sophistication of writing about politics and an explosion of new 'isms.' The diverse conceptual languages and literatures of this period are commonly grouped into schools of thought such as the Scottish Enlightenment, Political Economy, Marxism, German Idealism, Social Darwinism, Liberal Progressivism, American Pragmatism, Idealist (or Liberal) Internationalism, Global Geopolitics, and German *Geopolitik*, to name some of the most prominent.

Interpreting the thought of this period in terms of such relatively distinct schools has had the unfortunate effect of obscuring the fact that these theorists are grappling with a common set of problems associated with the industrial revolution and globalization. It has also obscured the full range of arguments about Liberal political forms in this new material context. By putting the topics of industrialism and globalization at center stage, we are able to see that different schools and theories are actually offering competing answers to the common question of what social arrangements are appropriate for the global-industrial era (see figure 7.1). Thus unified, much of the intellectual striving and strife of the last two centuries is part of one great sprawling and diverse debate cutting across the domestic-international divide and encompassing a spectrum of Liberal and nonlib-

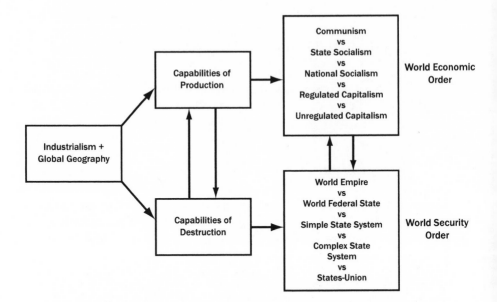

Figure 7.1 Problematics of Global Industrial Historical Materialism

eral economic and political forms. To provide a simple label to capture what these diverse schools have in common, it is appropriate to refer to *industrial historical materialism* for the overall debate and *industrial globalism* for the subset of issues concerned with security globalization.

With the sprawling thought of this period brought together and characterized in this way, this and the next chapters survey arguments about Liberal and republican forms and their interaction with contextual- material factors. Obscured by their explosively diverse conceptual vocabularies, we find arguments advancing the claims of the two main problematiques of republican security theory.

These chapters do not attempt a comprehensive survey of thought in this period. Rather the goals are more specific: first to show that Liberal thinkers deployed a range of sophisticated material-contextual arguments and second to show that recognized bodies of contextual-materialist theorizing that are generally perceived to be mainly or strongly antiliberal actually contain substantial lines of argument about Liberal forms.

This chapter unfolds through six sections. The first explores some of the general issues associated with the turn to history. The following section examines the pivotal role of material-contextual change, partially concerning violence, in the foundational arguments of Scottish Enlightenment stage theory and notes the partial persistence and partial narrowing of these arguments in subsequent political economic thought. Then a brief overview of Social Darwinist thinking reveals that virtually every substantive political orientation of the era was advanced as consistent with Darwinian insights. The final three sections look in greater depth at the arguments about technological interdependence developed by progressives and Liberal internationalists, most prominently Wells and Dewey. The following chapter then systematically examines arguments about the relationship between the industrial-material context and the full range of hierarchical, anarchical, and republican political arrangements.

HISTORICISM, NATURALISM, AND TECHNOLOGY

If Montesquieu's opus culminates ancient and early modern naturalist political science, then the owl of Minerva does indeed fly at dusk, for it was in the few years immediately following its appearance that the problem of historical change, and the corollary issues of progress and the end of history, were first articulated.[3] The basic impulse of this epochal shift is vividly conveyed in a lecture delivered by Turgot, Louis XV's precocious reform minister at the Sorbonne in 1750:

> The phenomena of nature, subject to constant laws, are enclosed in a circle of revolutions which are always the same. Everything is reborn, everything perishes, and through successive generations in which vegetation and animal life reproduce themselves time merely restores at each instant the image which it has caused to disappear. The succession of men, however, presents a changing spectacle from century to century. Reason, the passions, liberty, produce new events without end. The conventional signs of language and writing, affording men the means of assuring the possession of their ideas and communicating them with others, have fashioned of all detailed forms of knowledge a common treasury, which one generation transmits to another like a legacy that is ever being augmented with the discoveries of each century, and thus the human race, considered from its beginnings, appears to the eyes of the philosopher to be one immense whole which, like every individual, has its infancy and its progress.[4]

From such seeds in the late eighteenth and accelerating in the nineteenth century, evolutionary and revolutionary historical change becomes the central topic of investigation in natural and social science, occupying the attention of virtually every school and discipline.[5]

The turn to history had many origins, among them a growing crisis in naturalist theory stemming from its inability to explain differences across time. As we have seen, physiopolitics, the ancient and early modern phase of contextual-materialist theorizing, had an essentially static conception of the material context, and sought to understand how variations in material contexts across space shaped political outcomes. Because nature seemed to change only rarely and slowly, naturalist theories were unable to explain differences across time in polities located in the same place. The problem, to paraphrase Hegel, is that 'nature gives us the Greeks, but history gives us the Turks.'[6] If nature and geography stayed the same, why did society exhibit change? Theorists of historical change differed in many major ways, especially the role assigned to ideational and material factors. Among 'idealists,' Kant, as we have seen, employed material contextual facts in an ad hoc manner in his theory of historical progress. Alternatively, Hegel's model of a complex process of the 'world spirit' unfolding itself through time relegated the influence of natural-material factors to earlier stages and assigned almost no weight to them in its later, modern stages. Many of the major figures of late-nineteenth-century social science, such as Emile Durkheim, Georg Simmel, and Weber, often included geographic and technological material factors in their arguments, but they tended to define their new project of social science as breaking from the naturalistic treatment of human interaction. They sought patterns and laws internal to human interactions as systems, and looked for the source of change in the development of human institutions and culture rather than in the physical environment.[7] Overall, the quest for natural causes of social outcomes gave way to an investigation of the social causes of social outcomes that continues to characterize Western social science.

Some theorists, however, sought to modify and historicize naturalist theory rather than to discard it. One possibility was to conceptualize historical change as the result of improved adaptations to a static material environment, and thus assign to human social development the main motor of change, while recognizing that the content of what constituted a successful adaptation was decisively shaped by the features of the natural-material context. A second approach, present in much of classical Marxism, progressive interdependence theory, and global geopolitics, located the ultimate source of historical change in *changes in the material context* that stimulated or evoked new adaptations from human societies. This approach incorporated changing technology into its conceptualization of the physical environment, thus locating *the driver of change in human arrangements in the nature exogenous to human control that was changing via technological development*. This notion of 'nature changing through technology' underpinned the new historicist materialist project of explaining historically variable political outcomes. Thus is situated the second, late-modern phase of contextual-materialist theorizing, industrial historical materialism, an attempt to explain change across time as well as space.

This focus on technology in the second phase of contextual-materialist theory built upon early modern insights. Early moderns were keenly aware of the wide impacts of specific major new technologies, most notably in gunpowder, printing, and navigation. Early modern scientists, broke with the ancient naturalistic observational passivity in favor of active experimentation. And Francis Bacon outlined a visionary program for technological development in order to radically transform the human estate.[8] But it is only in the late modern era, growing to an all-encompassing scope, self-consciousness, and sophistication in the twentieth century, that both actual and anticipated technologies are analyzed as influential and dynamic factors in human affairs.

A further feature of the new technological materialism's effort to grapple with historical change was a greater conceptual sophistication in understanding *how* material environments shaped political outcomes. Physiopolitical theorists discerned many correlations between different material environments and different security-political arrangements, but their conceptualization of causal mechanisms was often primitive. The idea of natural selection in Darwin's theory of biological evolution offered a conceptually fertile model of how material environments shaped political outcomes. Although Darwin's famous formulations 'the survival of the fittest' and 'competition for survival' implied that natural selection was primarily a violent struggle between competitors, the core idea of natural selection is the functionalist notion that organisms survive by being better fitted to the constraints and opportunities of their environment.[9] Applied to human society and politics, the idea of evolutionary change through natural selection gave new clarity and sophistication to the previously implicit functionalist explanatory logics.[10] Social science functionalism has many variants, but the basic idea is that the persistence of a particular social or political arrangement can be explained by its superior fit with the constraints and opportunities of the context, both natural-material, technological-material, and purely social, within which it operates.[11]

Unfortunately, these advances brought with them a loss of unity in concepts and terminology. The relative conceptual unity in the development of the main trunk of natural contextualist theory from the Greeks to Montesquieu was lost as historical contextual materialist theories branched off in diverse directions and as different schools of theorists emerged, each with increasingly distinct conceptual vocabularies and terminologies. These branching schools also became increasingly specialized, with some focusing on economic and domestic domains while others directed their attention to security and international issues. Perhaps as an inevitable side effect of their divergent courses, the conceptual sophistication of different schools varied greatly. Of these branching schools, global geopolitics was most focused on destructive capabilities and their security implications, but was conceptually inchoate and unsophisticated, laced with loose biological analogies, and prone to extreme reductionism and determinism.[12] In contrast, classical Marxism, building on the initiatives of Scottish Enlightenment historical stage theory, as part of 'political economy,' developed a highly sophisticated conceptual apparatus to theorize changes in productive material contexts that avoided the reductive treatment of social structures and maintained human agency, restrained by contexts, at its center. Among these many schools, progressive interdependence theorists, most notably Dewey and Wells, most straightforwardly extend the main arguments of republican security theory.

STAGE THEORY, POLITICAL ECONOMY, AND HISTORICAL MATERIALISM

The beginning of theorizing about change in material contexts as a political factor occurs in the remarkable burst of late Enlightenment thought in Scotland produced by Adam Smith, Adam Ferguson, and John Millar.[13] Over roughly the second half of the eighteenth century these theorists brought several main Enlightenment ideas to their zenith, while also setting in motion arguments about material change that would develop so luxuriantly in the 'political economy' and 'historical materialism' of the nineteenth and twentieth centuries. Far from being ignored, these theorists and particularly their arguments about commerce are viewed as foundational in contemporary Liberalism's conception of itself as a tradition.

Within Scottish Enlightenment political economy, Adam Smith advances an especially sophisticated set of arguments about material contexts.[14] Smith hypothesizes about the proclivity of different polities to engage in warfare at four different levels of 'material civilization' (see figure 7.2). Employing the general model of human instrumental rationality that plays such a pivotal role in his contributions to contemporary neoclassical economics, Smith looks at whether rational decision making in different stages of material development finds war or other activities more or less appealing as a source of gain. In the first stage, when societies are devoted to hunting, violent intergroup conflict is rational because hunting is arduous and produces uncertain benefits, martial skills are widespread, and the capacity of weapons for destruction is limited. In the second, pastoral stage, violence is still appealing, but less so than with hunting societies. Pastoralists have a great deal of spare time and their martial skill (particularly horsemanship) is high, but the vulnerability of their flocks raises the potential losses from violence. In the third, agricultural stage, the incentive structure begins to shift toward peace because agriculture is a labor-

	Economic Opportunity Cost	Level of Martial Skill	Level of Destruction in War
HUNTING	Low (hunt vs. fight)	High	Low
PASTORAL	Low (abundant spare time)	High	Medium
AGRICULTURAL	High (farm vs. fight)	Medium	Medium
MANUFACTURING	Very High (labor vs. fight)	Low	Very High

Figure 7.2 Smith's Historical Stage Theory

intensive activity leaving little time for conflict. Martial skill remains high, but less so than in either hunting or pastoral stages. Most importantly, the value of crops and various productive infrastructure potentially lost to violence is much greater. In the fourth, nascent stage of manufacturing societies, the incentives for peace greatly exceed those for war. The opportunity costs of fighting over working are high due to the enhanced productivity of technologically augmented manufacturing labor, the waning of martial skill, and the very high costs of the destruction of accumulated property and infrastructure.

This argument has many features, but aside from its highly articulated rational instrumentalism, what is most notable is the claim that manufacturing societies are radically different from their predecessors in the incentives for war and peace emanating from the material context. This argument appears alongside familiar arguments about the negative effects of conflict in situations of economic interdependence, but is different because it concerns the relationship between destructive capacity and the physical vulnerability to destruction. This is a theory about the consequences of differing material contexts rather than their causes. Nor is there any claim that subsequent stages emerge in any tightly logical or necessary way from the previous ones, a view of change that Hegel and to a lesser degree Marx developed.

This line of argument is further developed by many early-nineteenth-century political economists. A particularly clear formulation is provided

by the French political economist Jean-Baptiste Say: "The more industri-
ous a State is, the more destruction and ruinous war is for it. When it
attains a country rich in agricultural, manufacturing, and commercial es-
tablishments, it resembles a fire which reaches places filled with combusti-
bles; its fury increases, and destruction is enormous."[15] As this argument
develops, there is also an increasing recognition that the particular source
of novelty is the growing destructive capacities that industrialism makes
possible. The notion that new weapons technology makes war so destructive that it will be irrational to pursue, or that a catastrophic industrial
war will catalyze major political transformation, becomes a prominent
theme of the vivid technological futurist literature, or what would come
to be known as 'science fiction,' which burgeons in the late-nineteenth
and twentieth centuries.[16] It is also central to early-twentieth-century progressive technological interdependence theory. The main point throughout is, in the words of the Italian political economist Gerolamo Boccardo
that "war will kill war."[17]

The idea of stages defined by material contexts is further developed by
Karl Marx and his followers, where there is a cluster of arguments generally known as 'historical materialism.'[18] Aside from his often problematic
specific claims, Marx developed a theoretical vocabulary that marked a
great increase in the sophistication of materialist theory.

Marx identifies the 'forces of production' as the ultimately decisive material reality of human life.[19] Composed of nature and technology embodied as productive capability (machines and other forms of real capital),
the forces of production were originally very primitive, but have been successively developed as embodiments of human labor and as means to satisfy human wants.[20] Marx relentlessly insisted upon the ultimate primacy
of material conditions, and claimed that his theory of socialism was the
first truly 'scientific' one. Whereas men had dreamed of socialism since
the beginning of history, its realization was a real historical possibility
only in a material context of the developed industrial forces of production.

The second main component of Marx's model is the 'mode of production,' whose viability is conditioned by the material context and whose
operation generates and depends upon distinct social and political arrangements. A productive mode is a cluster of interrelated productive
practices. For Marx capitalism as a mode of production is characterized
by the practices of production for the market and exchange. Marx identifies slave, Asiatic, feudal, capitalist, and socialist modes of production,
and seems to argue that each fits a particular stage in the development of
the forces of production.[21] In one of his most quoted and analyzed (and
criticized) passages, Marx observes that "[t]he hand mill will give you a
society with the feudal lord, the steam mill a society with the industrial
capitalist."[22]

Together the forces and modes of production constitute the 'base' or 'infrastructure,' which he contrasted with the 'superstructure' of political, social, and cultural relations.[23] Different modes of producing generate, and in turn depend upon, different institutional structures and ideologies.[24] In Marx's scheme, the superstructure is ultimately determined by the infrastructure, but not every aspect of a superstructure can be reduced to or is fully determined by the features of the base. What he means by 'determination' is less a claim about strict and tight causality than a claim about how the limits of viability of particular modes and their attendant superstructures are defined, conditioned, and limited by their material context.[25] Agency retains a role but within confining contexts, both material and social structural, or as he famously observed, "Men make their own history, but not in circumstances of their choosing."[26]

Marx is also particularly interested in conceptualizing change between successive forces, modes and superstructures, a process characterized by the emergence of 'contradictions' and their resolution. A contradiction is present when there is a fundamental disjuncture between a particular set of forces and a particular mode, and its attendant superstructure. The core notion here is that change does not occur smoothly and incrementally, but rather that tensions and misfits grow in severity until they are resolved, often violently by a revolutionary change.[27] On the topic of violence and security, the arguments of Marx and his followers are scattered and underdeveloped, with the main line of argument being that violence is a superstructural phenomenon.[28]

Marx's ideas, altered and applied by his many followers, produced horrifically antiliberal polities that murdered tens of millions of people, and the term 'Marxism' has understandably acquired an intensely polarizing character far beyond that associated with any other materialist argument.[29] Given this, it is easy to overlook the fact that Marx himself was a strong democrat, heavily involved in the mobilization of laboring people on behalf of democratic reforms in Britain.[30] Furthermore, his core theoretical apparatus was also developed in the twentieth century by a variety of theorists who make the claim that liberal democratic capitalism, rather than socialism, is actually the economic mode and political superstructure best fitted with the imperatives and constraints of the industrial forces of production in their various phases.[31] These theorists in effect return historical materialist stage theory to its Liberal roots after a long and disastrous detour. A key claim in these writings is that modified capitalism is superior because it has superior abilities to operate in the complex advanced industrial context, in comparison with centralized and bureaucratic socialism. These theorists follow Marx, however, in either not treating violence or in treating it as superstructural and derivative, and thus operate with a much narrower range of argument than their predecessors, the Liberal political economists. Economic centralization not only contributes to unrestrained state power, but also turns out to be economically dysfunctional due to its inability to cope with the extensive complexity and functional differentiation that is characteristic of the advanced industrial era.

SOCIAL AND POLITICAL DARWINISM

Social Darwinism, another vast and influential body of nineteenth-century thought, also contains a bewilderingly varied set of arguments. A brief survey reveals that virtually every political position was advanced as consistent with Darwin's ideas, and that, contrary to appropriations by Realist international theorists, robust variants of Liberal Darwinian thought also exist.

The use of Darwinian ideas to understand society and politics was most visible in the many analysts who explicitly characterized humans as analogous to organisms and species engaged in an evolutionary struggle to survive.[32] Such theories commonly characterized human groups metaphorically as 'organisms' whose viability is determined by their interaction with their material environment and their interactions with other organisms. But which unit of human life—the individual, the social class, the 'race,' the state, or the human species—is analogous to Darwin's organism? And which natural process—intraspecies competition or cooperation, or interspecies competition or cooperation (symbiosis)—is natural? Depending on how one answers these questions, a wide range of different political and social arrangements could be vindicated as natural (see figure 7.3).

By far the most influential answer to the unit-of-analysis question is the human individual. Herbert Spencer, in his influential writings on ethics and politics, began with the human individual and then proceeded to build elaborate justifications for laissez-faire capitalist society.[33] In Spencer's philosophy, so influential it has inappropriately been dubbed 'social Darwinism,' individual human beings are seen as competing fiercely against each other. But exactly the opposite lesson was drawn by the Russian theorist of anarchy Peter Kropotkin in *Mutual Aid*, who argued that the new evolutionary science taught that human cooperation was the key to human evolutionary success.[34] These cooperative interpretations of human social life were then further developed and applied by a variety of critics of Spencerian laissez-faire, notably Leonard Hobhouse and Lester Ward.[35]

The fundamental clash between Spencer and Kropotkin reappeared in many guises. Friedrich Ratzel and Rudolf Kjellén applied a competitive Darwinism to world politics and argued that states were organisms in

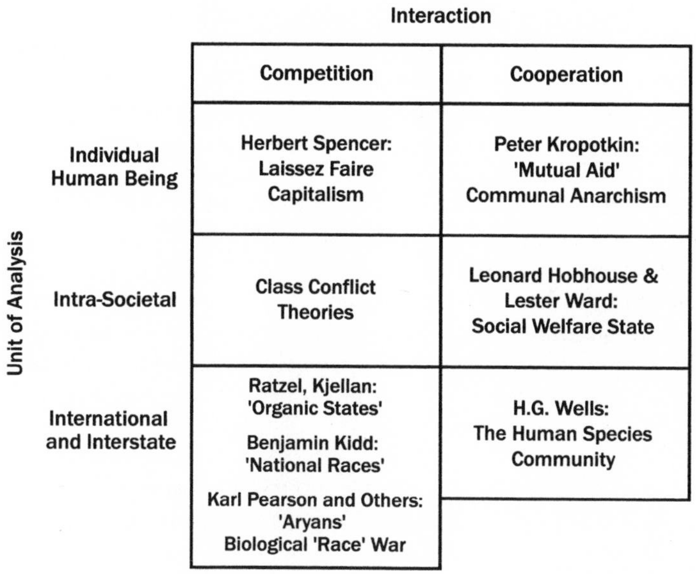

Interaction

	Competition	Cooperation
Individual Human Being	Herbert Spencer: Laissez Faire Capitalism	Peter Kropotkin: 'Mutual Aid' Communal Anarchism
Intra-Societal	Class Conflict Theories	Leonard Hobhouse & Lester Ward: Social Welfare State
International and Interstate	Ratzel, Kjellan: 'Organic States' Benjamin Kidd: 'National Races' Karl Pearson and Others: 'Aryans' Biological 'Race' War	H.G. Wells: The Human Species Community

(left axis label: Unit of Analysis)

Figure 7.3 Darwinian and Organic Analogies for Human Politics

competition for scarce resources, particularly land.[36] Stripped of its bio-logic language, this argument resembles those varieties of Realism that emphasize the competitive and zero-sum nature of interstate life. Another approach was to identify separate human biological 'races' as the main actors. Sometimes, as in the writings of Benjamin Kidd, the term 'race' was a synonym for the 'nation' rather than actual biological groupings. In the writings of Karl Pearson and others, human biological races were understood as being in a primal contest for existence.[37] In the hands of Adolf Hitler these racial Darwinian analogies, inflated into 'theories,' served as a warrant for grotesque genocidal and homicidal policies.

In complete contrast, Wells, building on Kropotkin and Hobhouse, posited the human species itself as the basic unit of analysis and the relationship between the human species and nature as the locus of the evolutionary struggle. For Wells, the human species faced a new material environment and only the rapid evolution of cooperative institutions on a worldwide basis could prevent the human species from regressing.[38]

A notable feature of all these arguments is the way in which they combined cooperation and competition at different levels of their arguments. For example, Spencer supported competition between individual humans, but held a typical nineteenth-century Liberal view that violent interstate competition was obsolete and retrograde: reducing interstate competition would help liberate individual competition, which would in turn further

diminish interstate competition. In contrast, figures such as Ratzel, Kjellén, Haushofer, Kidd, and Pearson generally deplored atomistic individual
competition as dysfunctional and embraced corporatist cooperation of
the members of a state, nation, or 'race' in order to enhance group com-
petitiveness: rampant individualism sapped group strength, and intergroup competition would diminish individualism.

Thus Darwinian analogies were used to justify laissez-faire capitalism,
the welfare state, interstate war, race war and genocide, and cosmopolitan
world government, thus contradicting the widespread view that 'social
Darwinism' is either laissez-faire capitalism domestically or intergroup
rivalry internationally. This extreme diversity leads to the general conclusion that analogic arguments are extremely elastic and can be employed
to support many views, but to demonstrate no view.

Progressive Internationalism and Technological Interdependence

Progressive, pragmatic, and internationalist writers of the early-twentieth
century provide the most explicitly technologically materialist and the
most Liberal analysis of the political implications of the industrial revolution. Liberal progressives and pragmatists directed most of their efforts
toward adjusting and reforming domestic political, economic, and social
arrangements to cope with the many new problems and opportunities
produced by industrialism.[39] Liberal progressives also advanced an international agenda in areas such as cultural internationalism, the movement
for strengthened international law and arbitration, international organizations (most notably the League of Nations), and arms control and disarmament.[40] They served as the 'organic intellectuals' of the popular movements for peace and international organization. These theorists were
mainly British and American, and were given particular impetus by World
War I. Among the better known Liberal internationalists are Norman
Angell, John Dewey, Lord Lothian, Ramsey Muir, James Shotwell, Arnold
Toynbee, H. G. Wells, Leonard Woolf, and Alfred Zimmern.[41] In order to
capture the main ideas of this large body of work, I will focus primarily
on Wells and Dewey, who were extremely prolific, widely influential, and
especially conceptually sophisticated and creative.

As with other episodes in the development of structural-material theory, the legacies of Liberal progressivism have been subject to an extensive, yet oddly fragmented, treatment by subsequent scholars. Most importantly, the strong technological materialism of progressive internationalist arguments has been obscured by the prevalent assumption,
routinely advanced by Realist critics, that the Liberal international

thought of this period is predominantly 'idealistic' in character.[42] The dominance of this interpretation is reflected in the fact that the technological interdependence arguments of Dewey and Wells are completely invisible in accounts of the international thought of this period.[43]

The one Liberal internationalist figure from this period who does still appear in the collective memory of international theory is Norman Angell, whose 1910 book, *The Great Illusion*, has served for generations as a favorite whipping boy of Realists.[44] The author of more than forty books, Angell argued on the eve of the Great War that interdependence, particularly economic, had rendered war between major industrial powers so costly as to be irrational. Since war was so contrary to rational self-interest, it would not occur. Interestingly, in the light of the subsequent close identification of Realism with rational self-interest explanations for war, Angell's book was critically reviewed by the American naval historian Alfred Thayer Mahan, who argued that "the danger of war proceeds mainly from the temper of the people, which, when roused, disregards self-interest" and that "the inciting causes of war in our day are moral" factors such as "self-respect or honor."[45] It is doubly ironic that the 'idealism' label sticks so tightly to Angell's rationalist and materialist arguments about war, since his main foil was the idealist conception of the state popular in Germany and in British Hegelianism.

The primary concept in progressive internationalism is the ubiquitous notion of technologically produced *interdependence*. Many writers expound various arguments about technological change as a source of expanding interdependence and make the case that a major reconfiguration of world political arrangements is necessary. The overall message is stated with particular force and clarity by the British writer Ramsey Muir:

> Since time began, men have lived in more or less isolated communities, severed one from another, and prevented from understanding or influencing one another, by the difficulties of communication. It is impossible that diverse races, ignorant of each other's ideas, resources, ways of life, ignorant even of each other's existence, should grow together into a single social system, until distance was conquered and the transport of goods and the communication of knowledge were made easy. . . . The immense change involved in the establishment of world-interdependence has come very rapidly, without our realizing, at all clearly, what was happening. . . . It has become a platitude to say that the whole world is now interdependent. . . . Yet what a tremendous platitude it is! If all peoples of the earth have been brought within a single social system; if no people can any longer be singly master of its own fate, but must depend for its security and prosperity upon the behavior of the whole human family; and if this state of things is so well established that it is accepted as an obvious commonplace—then surely we have entered upon a new and

thrilling era in human history, an era which for all the long millennia of man's troubled story have been a preparation. If this platitude is unalterably true, its implications must profoundly affect the conditions of human life for the future; it must transform all our thinking about social organization; it must modify all our programmes and policies. Clearly we ought to be thinking seriously about it, and asking ourselves what it involves.[46]

The prolific polymath H. G. Wells was the most inventive and widely read writer on the implications of technological interdependence. A protean intellectual figure and author of more than one hundred books, Wells was an extremely successful publicist, reaching millions through his novels, essays, speaking tours, and radio addresses.[47] As a pioneer of science fiction and futurism, Wells spun out dozens of wondrous scenarios in which the powers of science and technology, or what he refers to as "modern appliances," radically transfigure human life.[48] He also wrote a shelf of quickly written reflections on world events and an extremely popular *Outline of History*, whose culmination is a world federal republic.[49] His most systematic treatments appear in his book *Anticipations of the Reaction of Mechanical and Scientific Progress upon Human Life and Thought* and his essay "The Idea of a League of Nations." He advances several different prognostications on world order to be examined in subsequent sections.

Wells's starting point is starkly simple: an unstoppable growth in science and invention is producing major alterations in the ability of humans to produce, communicate, transport, and destroy. If human attitudes, behavior, and institutions do not also radically change, then widespread misery and disasters will result. Wells characterized historical development in starkly materialist terms: "The whole of history, could, indeed, be written as a drama of human nature reacting to invention."[50] Of the many inventions Wells invokes, no single one has primacy, but the most important fall into two classes: communication and transportation, and destruction. "All political and social institutions, all matters of human relationship, are dependent upon the means by which mind may react upon mind and life upon life" and thus "the intensity, rapidity, and reach of mental and physical communication." All the "great phases" in the history of mankind are "marked by the appearance of some new invention, which facilitates trade or intercourse," which brings about "the enlargement of human intercourse and cooperation from its original limitation within the verbal and traditional range of the family or tribe."[51] Even more important is the intensification of the process of scientific discovery and invention itself, 'the invention of invention.' Wells describes technological progress based on "ideas arising, and of experiments made, and upon laws of political economy, almost as inevitable as natural laws."[52] For Wells technological innovation is as much outside human direction as nature was to earlier geographical materialists.

The political implications of these developments are equally stark. Institutions of less than global scope are being rendered obsolete by scientific and technological progress, particularly in transport and communication, which Wells calls "the distinctive feature of the nineteenth century." Upon inventions of transport "hang the most momentous issues of politics and war."[53] These inventions are producing a "practical revolution in topography" that is undermining "stability within territorial limits" and the "rectification of frontiers means wars."[54] These developments are propelling the world toward unification by "insisting upon a still larger political organization."[55]

Wells's analysis marks a sharp turn in progressive Enlightenment thinking toward a pessimistic image of the future dominated by conflict. As for the early modern prophets of scientific advance and technical invention, history for Wells is moving toward a radically different future. But in Wells dystopias have begun to rival utopias.[56] Like other progressives since the Enlightenment, Wells believed strongly in the power of education as a source of social change, but he insisted that major reforms were no longer *desirable* as a path to improvement, but *necessary* to avoid disaster. The spectrum of possibilities has widened to encompass hitherto inconceivable extremes, realizable utopias of peace and abundance or a secular apocalyptic end of history. Human history had become "a race between education and catastrophe."[57] Wells's images of transition involve titanic violent struggle, of extreme conflict to avoid extreme disaster and achieve extreme progress. Wells sketched many different paths to world integration, often littered with violence, misery, and incompetence of epic proportions.

Wells's hopes for successful transformation rested upon his conception of the emergence of a "new republic" composed of an educated public and a technocratic elite.[58] In some of his formulations the 'new republic' is general modernization, but in others it entails technocratic world governance by a modernized Platonic rule of experts.[59] Wells hoped technocracy would emerge when the 'functional men,' the engineers and professional specialists, organized an 'Open Conspiracy' to replace power politics with practical functional administration.[60] Here Wells jumped from the insight that the services of a great variety of technical specialists would be necessary for society to function in machine civilization to the conclusion, unwarranted in retrospect, that such experts would develop a distinct political consciousness and come to directly rule or replace traditional politics.

Wells was certainly a technological modernist, but to what extent does his vision of politics incorporate political freedom? In *Anticipations* Wells speaks approvingly of "the nation that most resolutely picks over, educates, exports, or poisons its people of the abyss."[61] Wells received extensive indignant criticism of this passage, which he came to regret and renounce. With the rise of fascism in the 1930s, Wells emerged as a strong supporter of liberal democracy and an ardent opponent of Hitler and Nazism.[62]

THE TECHNOLOGICAL PUBLIC AND ITS PROBLEMS

The contextual materialism of late-nineteenth- and early-twentieth-century liberal progressivism finds its most classic and enduring formulation in the political theory of the protean philosopher John Dewey, who is widely regarded as the most theoretically sophisticated and widely influential American Liberal progressive.[63] While recognized as a central figure in progressive political theory, Dewey's simple but far-reaching argument about the effects of the industrial revolution on world politics has been completely ignored by international relations theorists. Like most of his contemporaries, Dewey's political pragmatism and progressivism were profoundly influenced by the Darwinian notion of functional adaptation.[64] In his central work of political theory, *The Public and Its Problems*, he sets forth an abstract but comprehensive analysis of government in the public interest as an adaptation to material circumstances that are changed in fundamental ways by technological development.

Dewey's political theory centers on the relationships among *the public, community, government,* and *material context* (see figure 7.4). The pivotal concept in his model is the public, which "consists of all those who are affected by the indirect consequences of transactions to such an extent that it is deemed necessary to have those consequences systematically cared for."[65] Thus the public is simply a group defined by having a high degree of interdependence, which arises from the indirect consequences of transactions.[66] Conversely, the private is where "the consequences of an action are confined, or are thought to be confined, mainly to the persons directly engaged in it." Acknowledging that borderline phenomena exist, he stipulates that the consequences must be "lasting, extensive and serious" if they are to constitute a public.[67] Given this understanding, it follows that material contexts define the scope of publics, and that their extent depends upon technology: "The consequences of conjoint behavior differ in kind and in range with changes in 'material culture,' especially those involved in exchange of raw materials, finished products and above all in technology, in tools, weapons and utensils. These in turn are immediately affected by inventions in means of transit, transportation and intercommunication."[68] As a result there are potentially many publics, and the size of publics has varied greatly in history.

The relationship of the public to community and government is of decisive political importance. The scope and membership of publics are not

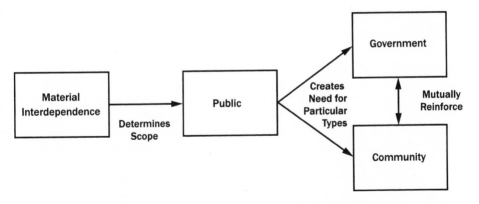

Figure 7.4 The Technological Public and Its Problems

defined by human intentions, feelings of solidarity, or social traits held in common, and so the public is not necessarily equivalent to any political community. Only when the members of a public understand that they are constituted as a public, and develop a shared set of understandings about this relationship, does the public become a political community. The establishment of political community presupposes the existence of a public, but not all publics give rise to communities because "no amount of aggregated collective action of itself constitutes a community."[69] History is replete with publics that fail to develop political communities, and thus whose common interest arising from their "conjoint activity" is never recognized and made the basis of a political identity or a political order.

The final component of Dewey's model is government, which arises when there are "indirect consequences and there is *an effort to regulate them*."[70] The regulatory powers and acts constituted by publics are vast in number and type, corresponding to the "countless forms of joint activity with correspondingly diverse consequences." About these forms "the only statement which can be made is a purely formal one" which is that government is "the organization of the public . . . for the protection of the interests shared by its members."[71] The type of government needed and generated by publics depends upon the character of the interactions that constitute the public, the extent of political community that a public can generate, and its practical inventiveness in generating novel institutions.[72] As publics and their problems evolve, arrangements of government inherited from the past must be restructured, and the public often finds its interests obstructed by inherited governmental arrangements.

With this simple model Dewey analyzes the implications of the industrial revolution: "Steam and electricity have done more to alter the conditions under which men associate together than all the agencies which affected human relationships before our time."[73] The "machine age" has "enormously expanded, multiplied, intensified and complicated the scope of indirect consequences."[74] But forms of community and government appropriate to solving the problems of the new industrial "Great Public" have not emerged. The "existing constitutions of the political state" have "not adjusted" to the "working of non-political forces."[75] This disjuncture is most spectacularly manifested in the Great War of 1914–18, which provided "indubitable proof" that "there is no comprehensive political organization to include various divided but interdependent countries."[76] Given this, "the need" is that "the divided and troubled publics integrate" by establishing appropriate communities and governments.

Beyond providing this simple pragmatic materialist analysis of politics, and its suggestive application to the global interdependence created by the industrial revolution, Dewey is frustratingly vague about the specific forms of community and government needed to solve the problems of the new extended industrial public. However, he is certain that two political forms—laissez-faire and the hierarchical state—are both misfitted to the new problems. As a leading 'new Liberal' Dewey repeatedly criticized the 'old Liberalism' of nineteenth-century laissez-faire and limited government constitutionalism as inadequate for the machine age.[77] At the same time, he was relentlessly critical of the hierarchical state, particularly as developed by German state theory and practiced by Imperial Germany.[78] Beyond this attack, Dewey's positive vision of community and government appropriate for the global-industrial age lacked structural specificity, but emphasized processes of contextual problem solving, pragmatic instrumentalism, and collective education and awareness.[79] Dewey's analysis subsumed the problems of security and violence as an inseparable part of a broader, public governance problematic. As a leader of the 're-volt against formalism' Dewey eschewed structural analysis and at times appears to ignore or sidestep the traditional federal republican emphasis on structural restraints.[80] While Dewey was relentlessly optimistic, there was nothing in this vision that guaranteed that the new extended publics would successfully evolve from an inchoate group of interdependent actors to a community capable of generating appropriate government, and thus avoid unprecedented catastrophe.

TECHNOLOGICAL PROGRESSIVISM AND THE NEW LIBERALS

Before turning in the next chapter to the fuller set of industrial globalist arguments about world order, it is appropriate to sum up the revisionist antiidealistic reading of the technological progressivism of the new Liberals, and reflect upon their relationship to the old Liberals and republicanism. Overall, progressive writers are essentially unintelligible without rec-

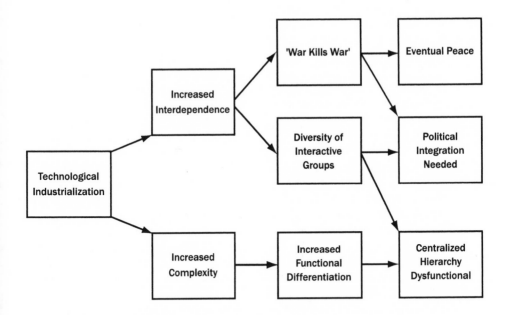

Figure 7.5 Consequences of Technological Industrialism

ognizing that the industrial revolution sits at the center of their thought. Far from seeing ideas as the motor of historical change, these writers are first and most essentially analysts of change in the material context. In contrast to their naturalist physiopolitical predecessors, materialist theorists of industrial society identify the source of change in the dynamism of modern technology. A composite of their arguments (see figure 7.5) captures their main propositions.

Technological change produces rising levels of interdependence across larger spaces. This interdependence is both economic and strategic-military, both productive and destructive. In contrast to their late-twentieth-century successors, these Liberal interdependence theorists operate with the full anarchy-interdependence problematique. The primary expectation regarding security is that 'war will kill war,' although they differed on whether the transition would entail vastly destructive wars before politics adjusted to the new brute facts or could be achieved through enlightened rational self-interest. Eventually, through whatever pathway, they expected that peace would come to define the human political situation. In its essentials this proposition is the projection to a new scale of the core proposition of the anarchy-interdependence problematique that anarchy and intense violence interdependence were incompatible with security and required government. To the extent that contemporary Realists embrace the nuclear peace proposition and discount the prospect of 'irrational' war, they are descendants of the industrial Liberals and have rejected the view of earlier Realists.

The second main overall argument is that broadly liberal-democratic arrangements are also particularly appropriate to the emerging industrial material context. While the new Liberals do hold that such political forms are normatively superior, the main thrust of their argument is that free polities will succeed because they are better fitted to the constraints and opportunities of the industrial material context, not because of their normative superiority. The key assumption is that technological change is producing increased complexity as well as larger scale interdependence. Rising complexity produces increased functional differentiation, which, coupled with the intrinsic rise of diversity accompanying larger political associations, makes centralized hierarchies dysfunctional. The new Liberals are 'optimists from below,' convinced, like the Marxists, that history is on their side.

In assigning such a powerful role for technological change, the new Liberals are swimming in the general current of late modern historicism. Their embrace of historical change, while at times extreme, is never complete and never purely relativistic because of the role played by material context, of nature as articulated technology, in anchoring and channeling the flow of change. This dynamic materialist view of the motor of historical change means that the eventual outcome of peace, unions, and freedom can be conceived as an 'end of history' only to the extent that the industrial material context marks the culmination of science-based technology. If technology drives history, then history can come to an end only when technology comes to rest. Their thought thus contains an unresolved tension between their anticipated outcome of an enduring end or equilibrium and their view that technological change is either unlimited in potential or at least nowhere near exhausted. Their technological historicism also raises the ominous possibility that the trajectory of technological development may take directions subversive rather than supportive of liberal political forms. Such dystopian trajectories, feverishly outlined by Wells and other futurists, become all-too-real historical possibilities in the middle- and late-twentieth century. Ultimately, an optimism rooted in the direction of historical change is a keenly sharpened double-edge sword, for those who rise by history may also fall by history.

Within this essentially materialist conception of history, the posture of the new Liberals toward ideas also becomes intelligible. Change in prevailing ideas is a necessary prerequisite to the adjustment to modern industrial constraints and opportunities, rather than the expression of an idealist theory of history. In part, the keen interest of the technological progressives in public opinion and mass education is driven by their belief that industrial technology has for the first time in history made such mass enlightenment practically feasible. But more basically, their ideational program is aimed at avoiding catastrophe. The haunting image that 'modern man is a monkey in the driver's seat of a speeding automobile' conveys their desperate fear that the education and enlightenment necessary to avoid catastrophe may be out of reach.[81]

Despite these anxieties, the new Liberals hold a much more optimistic view of the prospects for political liberty than do their preindustrial predecessors. The abundance promised by the industrial revolution opened the possibility for the economic improvement and democratic political inclusion of the great masses of the common man. It also held forth the prospect that the previous constricting dependence of free polities on geographic anomalies could be broken. A material context dominated by industrial technology brought the possibility of universalizing republican government in ways foreclosed by the previous dependence of republican polities upon the constricted and uneven geography of nature. No longer would political freedom be confined to minority strata of polities situated in exceptionally favored places.

Finally, the centrality of the industrial revolution in the thought of the new Liberals is also the key to understanding their relationship with the old Liberalism of laissez-faire capitalism and limited government constitutionalism. From the standpoint of the older Liberalism and republicanism climaxing in the American founding, the new Liberal embrace of the administrative state and their criticism of limited government constitutionalism as cumbersome obstacles to social improvement are easily mistaken for a rejection of the power restraint program of security republicanism.[82] Much of the old Liberal hostility reflects a lingering unease with the rolling democratization of liberal republics in the industrial era. Most importantly, however, the old Liberals in the new era fail to grapple with the implications of Dewey's proposition that industrial interdependence had given extended and unrestrained reach to activities that were previously private not just in their formal juridical status, but also in their actual scope of consequence. Viewed in the industrial material context, the progressivism of the new Liberals can be understood as an attempt to modernize rather than to jettison inherited protections and restraints on the abuse of concentrated power. The new Liberals insist that inherited political and economic forms that operate unchanged in the radically new industrial material context either become hollow formalisms or are perverted to serve rather than restrain new forms of concentrated power. The new Liberal program, both domestic and international, is not the rejection of security-restraint republicanism, but rather its modernization. In the face of rising interdependence and complexity, Liberal forms that cease to evolve soon cease to be Liberal.

The new Liberals promoted not only the growth of government, but also new forms of government responsive to the scale shift that technological interdependence created. Within the nation-state, technological development was creating levels of interdependence previously experienced at the municipal level, where intricate penetration of governmental regulatory activities had long been accepted as necessary. Due to the scale effect, a municipal-like government on a nation-state scale could not simply be urban municipal government writ large, but needed to be experimentally reconfigured.

At the same time that municipal-like levels of interdependence were being experienced across nation-state and even continental-sized spaces, levels of interdependence previously experienced within nation-states and continental-sized spaces were increasingly present on a global scale. In seeking to address this new exterior of rising interdependence, the program of Liberal internationalism emerges as the Siamese twin of the new Liberal domestic program (recall figure 6.5). To understand the new globalist phase in the development of security republicanism requires a closer look at the emergent global industrial material context and the industrial globalist theorists who first attempted to map it.

Chapter Eight

FEDERALIST GLOBAL GEOPOLITICS

Today, for the first time, the habitat of each separate
human being is this global earth.
—Halford J. Mackinder[1]

THE FIRST GLOBALISTS

In the broad sweep of five centuries of multidimensional globalization, the first fully global security system emerged as the industrial revolution spread and accelerated in the later-nineteenth century. High levels of material interdependence previously present only in smaller spaces began to be experienced at continental and increasingly global scales, and this primal development transformed the loosely coupled global political and economic systems of the early modern era into much more tightly coupled and increasingly interactive ones (recall figure 1.4). This second phase of globalization was extremely tumultuous, as European imperialism crested and then receded, as the European-centered international system descended into catastrophic world wars, and as the great ideological and military struggle between the Soviet empire and the American-led free world alliance sharply polarized world politics.[2]

Within this context of accelerating globalization and extreme turmoil, the position of republican polities radically changed. During the 'Long Peace' stretching from the Napoleonic Wars to World War I the two leading Liberal states, Great Britain and the United States, enjoyed unprecedented economic and demographic expansion, and together they gave republican polities a salience in international politics unmatched since the late Roman Republic. Over the course of the twentieth century the liberal democracies were embroiled in a series of titanic struggles in which they decisively vanquished their imperial, fascist, and totalitarian adversaries. In the course and wake of these struggles Great Britain experienced steep decline, as the far-flung pieces of its empire gained independence. For the United States, this was the 'American Century,' marked by a shift from hemispheric isolationism to great power balancing and internationalism, the establishment of a large military and national security apparatus, and the assumption of the role of leader of the free world alliance. The number of liberal democratic states also skyrocketed from a handful at the turn of the twentieth century to dozens at the turn of the twenty-first century, and the spatial domain of liberal-democratic government expanded. As their strength and numbers grew, the Liberal states slowly and unevenly created a cumulatively great increase of international organizations, regimes, and transnational activities, moving the core region among Liberal states partially out of anarchy.

The global-industrial period, stretching from roughly the middle of the nineteenth to the middle of the twentieth century, occupies a strikingly uneven position in contemporary international theory. On the one hand, the political *events* of this period have been subject to an unprecedented level of investigation and analysis. Whatever their intellectual pedigree, international theories largely rise or fall on their ability to illuminate the events of twentieth-century international politics. In contrast, most of the actual international *theory* from this period is either ignored or marginalized, and both Realists and Liberals locate their foundational formulations in the eighteenth century or before.[3]

During this period, stretching from the advent of the railroad, steamship, and telegraph in the middle of the nineteenth century through World War II, a sprawling roster of figures wrote with at least some substantial theoretical ambition. In addition to Wells, Angell, Muir, and Dewey, the list includes Alfred Thayer Mahan, Halford Mackinder, John Seeley, Otto Hintze, Karl Haushofer, Friedrich Ratzel, Archibald Coolidge, Henry Adams, Nicholas Spykman, Homer Lea, Frederick Teggart, Frederick Jackson Turner, James Burnham, E. H. Carr, Vidal de la Blanche, and many less-well-known figures.[4]

To the extent these writers are engaged by international theory of the last half century, they are characterized in misleading and easily dismissed ways. On the one hand, some of these figures are cast as theorists of 'global geopolitics' characterized as starkly materialist, hyper-Realist, and thoroughly antiliberal. On the other hand, some are cast as theorists of 'Liberal internationalism' characterized as 'idealist,' 'utopian,' and anti-materialist. Thus grouped and labeled, these theorists are more shunned as embarrassments than hailed as precursors by contemporary Realists and Liberals. American Realists, still seeking to distance themselves from the excesses of Nazi Germany and the 'geopolitial' ideas associated with it, largely ignore this literature. For Liberals, these writings raise the specter of the 'naive' and 'utopian' episode of the League and the interwar years. However well established in the contemporary narratives of the history of international theory, these groupings, labels, and characterizations are substantially misleading. Contextual material factors played, as we have seen, pivotal roles in the arguments of many Liberal internationalists. Strong arguments about liberal-democratic, particularly federal arrangements, are also prominent in 'global geopolitics' and 'German *Geo-*

politik.' And interdependence, far from being a particular Liberal preoccupation, was at the center of the arguments of antiliberal theorists and was explored in relation to nonliberal forms.

When these theorists are looked at as one group, as the *industrial globalists*, we see a sprawling and uneven body of work animated by a common set of general assumptions and approaches, and grappling with a common set of problems, all stemming from the spread of the industrial revolution as it produced unprecedented levels of interaction and interdependence on a global scale. Taken together, these writings are the first in which theories of 'the global' occupy center stage. The common goal of the industrial globalists was to understand the impact on world order of the material capabilities of transportation, communication, and destruction produced by the industrial revolution (most notably railroads, steamships, telegraphy, chemical high explosives, and airplanes) interacting with the largest-scale geographic features of the earth. In approaching these questions, the industrial globalists exhibited great diversity and many disagreements. These writers commonly emphasize, often breathlessly, the novel and revolutionary aspects of the emerging world and the technological forces propelling it, but in their theoretical conceptualizations they are more evolutionary than revolutionary, and they largely employ preindustrial structural-materialist concepts and arguments, particularly about violence interdependence.

The debates among the industrial globalists were highly charged and addressed very basic political issues. They were united in seeing existing world political order as increasingly subject to immense stress, conflict, and change in which the largest-scale political arrangements, ranging from the British Empire, the European state system, and the role of the United States, were likely to be severely altered or challenged. Despite their common assumptions and problems, the industrial globalists were sharply divided about the *character, number,* and *location* of viable security units in the emerging global security system. To answer these questions, these writers analyzed the contours of the emergent industrial material forces, and their relationship to different political arrangements of both systems and units. On the global system level they debated the prospects for the emergence of an imperial world state, a world federal union, and the persistence of anarchy. On a subglobal regional scale, they debated the relative prospects of anarchy, empire, and union in Europe. Given the prominence of the loosely organized liberal British Empire and the continental American federal republic, analysis of the prospects for large-scale republican forms, particularly various species of federal union, was a significant topic for theorists, particularly for Anglo-American theorists (whose company extends from Wells, Dewey, and Muir to include Seeley, Mackinder, Turner, and others). In their analysis of the interplay of global material realities and federal republican forms, they also worked to conceptualize new federal forms for the new large-space governance problems of the era. Liberal forms occupy a central place in these debates, but not all the industrial globalists were sympathetic to broadly Liberal political forms, and the prospects for highly hierarchical empires and what would come to be called 'totalitarian' forms were also assessed.

This examination of industrial globalist thought proceeds in three main steps. In the next three sections I sketch an intellectual group portrait of the industrial global theorists, assessing their globalism and materialism for continuity and novelty, summarizing and evaluating their significant areas of agreement about the emergent globalizing system and then examining their stark disagreement about the relative prospects for anarchic, hierarchic, and republican forms. In the subsequent four sections, the focus narrows to a selective examination of arguments about specific cases of continental-scale negarchical, hierarchical, and anarchical arrangements. These sections evaluate arguments about arresting British decline through federal union, about European order, about the new total hierarchies of unprecedented scale, and about federal unions and new forms of nonhierarchical world government. The concluding section weighs the expectations of the industrial globalists in the light of actual historical developments and reflects on the implications of this revisionist account for international theory.

GLOBALIZATION AND TECHNOLOGICAL MATERIALISM

Today expressions such as 'world politics,' 'world war,' 'whole earth,' 'one world,' 'globalist,' 'think globally,' and 'globalization' are widely used, and the concept of 'the abolition of distance' belabors the obvious. That there are global-scope interactions is now the commonplace background assumption of most people. But in the late-nineteenth and early-twentieth centuries these phenomena were novel and portentous, making this era's platitude that era's revelation: "Today, for the first time, the habitat of each separate human being is this global earth. The tempo of affairs has quickened in a single generation as by a miracle."[5] During the preceding several centuries, many Europeans, whose explosive activities propelled and exploited globalization, voiced frequent recognition of the importance of the 'discovery' of the New World and the circumnavigation of Africa, but it was only in the later decades of the nineteenth century that the emergence of global-scope interactions became the primary topic of observation and analysis.

The shrunken global world may have seemed miraculous, but its causes were certainly not mysterious. The new situation was universally seen as the result of the industrial revolution and its products. New capabilities, particularly of communication, transportation, and destruction, were rapidly altering the human world, leaving nothing untouched. In a lifetime, there was a revolution in the practical experience of time and space that previous generations had experienced as rooted in a timeless or cyclical nature.[6] As the scale and tempo of human affairs changed, a major and tumultuous reordering of large-scale political relationships and institutions seemed imminent and inevitable. A set of simple, but far-reaching, questions demanded answers. Which actors and institutions would survive these upheavals and be most adaptive to the constraints and opportunities of the new era? Would one world empire, state, or federation emerge? And if not, how many actors, of what sort, located where, and interacting how, would survive?

Reflecting their concern with technology, the industrial globalists tended to either be straightforwardly materialist or at least accord substantial significance to material factors.[7] As industrialism revolutionized more and more aspects of life, there was a diverse outpouring of analysis of the emerging 'machine civilization' by Marxists, progressives, sociologists, and economists who were, in the words of Seeley, "alive to the vast results which are flowing in politics from modern mechanism."[8]

Despite their momentous topics, the writings of the industrial globalists were often muddled and undisciplined. They tended to mix analysis with policy advocacy; they were deeply divided in political orientation, ranging from National Socialist to extreme cosmopolitan. They also exhibited many of the most pernicious racial and class prejudices of the era.[9] They brought into their analyses a bewildering range of variables, from political culture and strategic leadership to natural resource endowments and population growth rates, but a very strong contextual materialist line of argument was universally present. Unfortunately for intellectual accumulation and enduring visibility, they spent more energy attempting to influence policy and sway public opinion than attempting to establish a disciplined and institutionalized intellectual or academic enterprise.

The American naval theorist Alfred Thayer Mahan is widely recognized as the first *global* geopolitician because he first theorized about how the interaction between the oceangoing ship and the physical features of the Ocean conditioned the emergence of a system of power relations connecting all littoral peoples as well as features of the European state system. Although subsequent analysis (and Mahan in his later work) generally assigned a diminishing importance of the ocean and maritime capability for world politics, they all recognized its centrality in the 'Columbian Era' stretching from 1500 to 1900.

Technology, implicit in earlier contextual naturalist theories, was explicitly explored as the salient feature of the new material context. Mack-

inder observed that "the relative importance of physical features varies
from age to age according to the state of knowledge and of material civi-
lisation."[10] The later-nineteenth century saw an explosion of interest in
science and technology as a force in human affairs.[11] Communication and
transportation technologies occupied a pivotal position in industrial globalist analysis. Mackinder declared "the marvelous development of human
mobility" to be "the pre-eminent characteristic" of the era.[12] For communication, the arrival of instant transmission of information by the telegraph, the submarine cable, and then radio waves "subjects the whole
surface of the globe to the observation of civilized communities and leaves
no interval of time between widely separated places proportionate to their
distance apart."[13] In short, the world was coming to exhibit levels of interaction and interdependence that had previously existed only on much
smaller spatial scales, thus making possible more centralized, complex,
and extended organizations.[14] For transportation, the railroad seemed to
bring a revolutionary leap in the velocity and volume of movement. After
his first railroad ride, Ralph Waldo Emerson proclaimed "distance annihi-
lated." Seeley declared that distance "is abolished by science," and Marx
wrote of "the annihilation of space by time."[15] The railroad produced a
great reduction in the cost of transporting goods over land and opened
up large areas inaccessible to water to economic and military activities.[16]

The industrial globalists recognized the importance of the uneven acquisition of industrial capabilities in explaining Europe's dominant world
role, but they were mainly interested in analyzing a world in which these
capabilities were widely diffused. Both Mahan and Mackinder observed
that the industrial-technological sources of Western preeminence were
rapidly diffusing to non-Western peoples.[17]

Although often overemphasized by commentators, geography did play
an important role in the global industrialists' analysis of "strategic geography" and the "larger topographical conditions of offense and defense."[18]
Building on earlier naturalist arguments, the pioneering globalists extensively analyzed the interplay between settled territory and extraterritorial
media, such as steppes, the ocean, and the atmosphere, which at various
times had served as conduits or stages for military and economic interactions but which are neither permanently inhabited nor annexed by states
and empires. Because human activity within extraterritorial media is so
dependent upon technology, their implications for security were subject
to the most rapid and extensive change.

A distinguishing feature of the spatial and geographic analysis of this
period is a proliferation of new names for old places, such as the 'pivot
of history,' the 'Heartland,' and the 'Rimland.'[19] These cartographic innovations were an effort to fashion a conceptual framework for global space
to replace the outmoded Euro-centric notions, and to construct this

framework around those aspects of geography most relevant to large-scale human institutions. As the entirety of global geography was revealed by the end of the nineteenth century, the previous continental units of geographical analysis seemed obsolete. The tripartite division of the earth into Europe, Africa, and Asia had been based on the experience of peoples around the Mediterranean basin, but in global perspective Europe was but "a promontory of the World Island," and the Mediterranean was just one of several minor "land bound seas."[20] These new global cartographic nomenclatures provided a conceptual shorthand for the spatial parameters of material constraint and opportunity produced by the interaction of particular geographic and technological factors.[21]

Despite these efforts to formulate a new delineation of global space, the old continental nomenclature continues to provide the 'mental maps' of world politics at the turn of the twenty-first century. In part this failed revision is rooted in the inability of the industrial globalists to reach consensus on the issues they investigated, despite the central role of Mackinder's constructs. The old continental schema also persists because of the political implications of the new nomenclature. Mackinder's original tripartite formulation positions the New World as a 'satellite' of the massive 'World Island' and its 'Heartland' and symbolically relegates maritime states to peripheral status, a formulation unappealing for the 'American Century.' At the same time, the new nomenclature implied an alarmism over Russia that made it an ideological gambit in the Cold War.[22] Whatever its shortcomings, the old nomenclature had the advantage of seeming neutrality because it sidestepped the contentious question of who is at the center and who is relegated to the periphery.

FEATURES OF THE EMERGING GLOBAL SYSTEM

Operating with these common assumptions and questions, the industrial globalists shared a surprisingly large set of substantive assessments about the features of the emerging global scope state system, seven of which deserve closer examination (see figure 8.1).

In the new industrial material context, the world political system would no longer be composed of loosely connected regional systems, nor by a handful of powers located in Europe, but rather by the interaction of the European powers with great powers outside Europe. A strong indicator of the waning of the Euro-centric world political system was the emergence of three extra-European powers (the United States, Russia, and Japan) to great power status. The Europeans had long interacted with non-European states and empires, but these new extra-European world

Industrial Era Outcomes	Source/ Explanations
Global scope	Industrial communication & transportation increases intensity of interaction capability
Closure	End of frontier; all lands appropriated
Increase in size of actors	Industrial communication & transportation favors larger size units
Conflict & change in the short term	System not yet adjusted to new material context
European state system obsolete	Only continental units viable; consolidation via empire or federation
British imperial system obsolete	Scattered possessions connected by vulnerable naval mastery
Declining coincidence of state & nation	Increased identity diversity in larger units

Figure 8.1 Agreed Outcomes in Industrial Globalist Theory

powers were different because they had successfully assimilated modern European forms of technology and organization.

The industrial globalists also attached great importance to the closed character of the emerging political system. Mackinder observed that humanity was "for the first time presented with a closed system" in which "the known does not fade any longer through the half-known into the unknown" and in which "there is no longer elasticity of political expansion in land beyond the Pale." As a result, "every shock, every disaster or superfluity, is now felt even to the antipodes, and may indeed return from the antipodes."[23] With the partition of Africa at the Congress of Berlin in 1885, all lands on the earth had been appropriated (with the exception of Antarctica). The official closure of the frontier in the United States in 1890 stimulated Frederick Jackson Turner's famous reflections on the frontier and American democracy.[24]

The third generally recognized important feature of the new global politics was the *size* of two of the actors on the world political scene. Seeley observed that the ability to "bring together what is remote" was a trend that "favors large political unions."[25] The "political organism" was given a "new circulation" by steam and a "new nervous system" by electricity.[26] Mackinder observed that "the invention of the steam engine and the electric telegraph have rendered possible the great size of modern states."[27] The most salient indicator of this shift in the size of units was the emergence and expansion of United States and Russia, which were approximately an order of magnitude larger than a European great power. Throughout the nineteenth century European figures such as Tocqueville, List, and Ratzel voiced anxious premonitions about the consequences of American and Russian ascent for European preeminence and independence.[28]

Fourth, the industrial globalists generally agreed that the newly heightened abilities to interact in a closed space would increase competition and conflict because the expansion of one group would be increasingly at the expense of another. Haushofer spoke of "waves and repercussions around the world . . . shattering everywhere unnatural coercive structures."[29] Ruminations on a coming 'age of contending states' set the ominous theme of Oswald Spengler's ponderous bestseller, *The Decline of the West*.[30] Similarly, Erich Marcks observed that "the world has become harder and more bellicose," because "everything touches, everything interlocks," and "pushes and bangs together," leaving "few traces of the unprejudiced harmony."[31]

The industrial globalists were keenly aware that the new material factors were exerting their influence unevenly on an existing set of actors and structures, rather than upon a tabula rasa. While America and Russia were favored by the new material possibilities, the European state system, the British Empire, and the nation-state were widely thought to be obsolete.

It was widely feared and predicted that the plural state system in Europe had become obsolete and that Europe would be united in some fashion, even if there was no agreement on the path this unification would and should take. As new industrial technologies produced levels of interaction and interdependence on a global scale previously experienced in the European state system, these same technologies produced within Europe a level of violence and other interdependence previously experienced within the European nation-states. The material patterns of division, balance, and mixture that had made the early modern state system a 'republic' were being eroded as the new industrial technologies of communication, transportation, and destruction diminished topography as a restraint on power. The increased size of Russia and America combined with their increased ability to interact with the Europeans implied that the European great powers had been reduced to relative "dwarfdom."[32] Some, particularly in Germany, saw imperial unification of Europe as both possible and necessary, while many others looked to the American federal system as a model. Due to this shift in material context, the two wars for German hegemony within Europe in the twentieth century were unlike previous struggles over European hegemony because they were about the consolidation of a subsystem rather than a system, and thus resembled a (thwarted) process of absolutist state-building. Similarly, schemes for peaceful federal union were increasingly advanced as vitally necessary for security and survival, unlike earlier schemes animated by the benefits of peace.[33]

The British imperial system also was widely thought to be undermined by the new material constraints and opportunities. The classic analysis of the geographic and technological foundations of Pax Britannica, Mahan's *The Influence of Seapower upon History*, argued that this order was based on the superior mobility of naval over land power, Britain's insular position, and the tendency for naval mastery to consolidate in the hands of one power.[34] The dominant view of Britain in the new era, painfully acknowledged by British writers, most notably Mackinder, and avidly expounded by many Germans, was that the development of the railroad had decisively shifted the balance in favor of 'landpower' over 'seapower.'[35] While the aggregate size of British possessions was great, they were widely scattered and connected by increasingly vulnerable sea lanes. Faced with this new constellation of material possibilities, German *Weltpolitik* writers eagerly anticipated a 'War of English Succession' in which the British Empire would be dismembered with the spoils passing to rising 'landpower' states.[36] In the face of this pessimistic prognosis, Seeley, Mackinder, and others sought to conceptualize ways in which a federal reorganization of the British Empire could exploit the new technologies of communication and technology to incorporate the 'white settler colonies' into a 'Greater Britain' that would be comparable in size, population, and political coherence to the rising continental states of America and Russia.[37]

Finally, the nation-state form of political unit also seemed increasingly obsolete in the emerging global-industrial material context. The industrial globalists recognized that various forms of group solidarity rooted in language, culture, and historical experience were powerful forces in world politics, but commonly assumed that over the longer term identity was shaped by and secondary to military and economic survival. Given the increase in the size of viable units, the industrial globalists generally thought that the European pattern of state-nation coincidence was becoming obsolete, and that transnational units, such as the United States and the Russian empire, were increasingly viable.

Material Context

	Special Place	Scale Effects Alone	
		Continental	Global
Hierarchical-Statist	World domination based on Oceanic, Heartland, Rimland or atmospheric domination	Panregional Superstates	World Imperial State
Federal-Republican	Neutralization of special place	U.S.A. and 'Great Synthesis'	World Federation

Political Structures

Figure 8.2 Contested Outcomes in Industrial Globalist Theory

CONTESTED QUESTIONS

Beyond these areas of rough consensus were two related debates about the relative viability of hierarchical statist and federal republican political forms and about the extent to which the new material context favored centralization. The first debate cut across the divide between domestic and international politics by including arguments about the relative viability of hierarchical and republican forms both within units and between them. In the second debate there are three distinct positions with very different implications for world order and the viability of competing political forms. Was the material context configured with *special places* whose possessors could dominate the entire system? Or was it configured with power potential roughly *divided and balanced*? Or would *scale effects* alone operate to shape the size, number, and character of units in the world security order? Combining the main positions within these two debates produces a matrix of six possible world order outcomes (see figure 8.2).

Some global analysts believed they had identified special places and capabilities in the new global setting that held the potential to dominate the entire world order and that also had proclivities toward consolidation in the hands of one actor. Exemplifying this approach, Mackinder in 1919 asserted that "there are certain strategical positions . . . which must be treated as of world importance, for their possession may facilitate or prevent world domination."[38] Mahan, Mackinder, and Spykman claimed to have identified a different pivotal place around which the rest of human affairs would revolve. For Mahan the Ocean, for Mackinder the 'Heartland' of Eurasia, and for Spykman the 'Rimland' periphery of Eurasia were such *axial regions* or special places, which would determine the structure of the world political system.[39]

With an axial region identified, this line of argument then asked whether the special place would exhibit *integral tendencies* to consolidate into the hands of one actor. The most important reason advanced for such centripetal tendencies was the absence of physical obstacles to strengthen defense and the presence of capacities for mobility. Mahan's theories of sea power, Mackinder's theory of land power in the 'Heartland,' and (less plausibly) Spykman's theory of the 'Rimland' asserted the existence of integral tendencies in an axial asset. The world order implication of this interpretation of the material context was that the world would be consolidated into one unit unless the axial region could be neutralized or somehow separated from the control of any one state. Pursuing this logic, Mackinder's *Democratic Ideals and Realities*, widely viewed as the single most important work of 'global geopolitics,' proposed a 'league of nations' whose main purpose would be to keep Eastern Europe neutralized and separated from the Heartland, in effect sustaining a division through union to preserve the system's plurality after the decline of natural division.[40]

This line of thinking thus took seriously the possibility of a world state or empire. Mackinder claimed that "the grouping of lands and seas, and of fertility and natural pathways, is such as to lend itself to the growth of empires and in the end of a single world-empire."[41] Similarly, Ratzel observed that "there is on this small planet sufficient space for only one great state."[42] Such a complete consolidation also seemed to have pre-global historical precedent since 'universal' states or empires had frequently emerged and persisted for many centuries in large regions such as China, India, and the Mediterranean Basin. The specter of a world state or empire imparted a sense of urgency and paranoia to the grand strategic thinking of the era. Faced with this possibility, states readily viewed their own expansion as defensive and antihegemonic, while viewing the expansive moves of others as steps toward universal empire. Thus many German students of *Weltpolitik* viewed the 'Anglo-Americans' as on the verge of an irreversible world hegemony and therefore thought German efforts to achieve sustainable world status were necessary to ensure a balanced world system.[43] Conversely, many British and American thinkers interpreted German *Weltpolitik* as a drive to achieve world dominion rather than minimum world status. Measured against the assets of a world state or empire, even the greatest states and empires seemed precarious and vulnerable, and thus in urgent need of further expansion. These expectations fueled an eagerness to acquire additional territory, even when there was no current need or benefit from such acquisitions.[44]

A second interpretation of the global-industrial material context, that power potential was clustered into several roughly comparable sections, was advanced by Haushofer and other German theorists of the 'panregion' and by Burnham and Carr.[45] This reading of the constraints and opportunities of the material context suggested that an order composed of more than one unit was likely to endure. Global consolidators, not pluralists, would be running against the grain of material circumstance. Maintaining a plural political system would not require special foresight or strenuous effort because the material context lacked consolidating tendencies. With such a division of power on a global scale, world order would come to resemble a scaled-up version of the early modern European system, and balancing would be largely unnecessary or readily successful.[46]

The third interpretation held that capability was spatially widely distributed, and that the size and character of the units would be shaped solely by the extent of interdependence and complexity and the governance needs they generated. This interpretation, as we have seen, was advanced most compellingly by Wells and other British and American theorists. As interdependence reached critical density on successively larger spatial scales, it would stimulate the formation of nonhierarchical unions, first on a continental and eventually on a global scale.

To further unravel these debates, the next sections examine more closely four potential large-space political orders: British imperial federation, European unification, totalitarian panregions, and republican unions.

BRITISH IMPERIAL FEDERALISM

Events have fully vindicated the widespread industrial globalist view that the British Empire would severely decline in the twentieth century.[47] These events have been intensively studied by diplomatic historians and international theorists, but the alternative of transforming the British Empire into a federation has been largely forgotten by international theorists.[48] This neglected episode is particularly interesting because its main theorists, Seeley and Mackinder, argued that the new global industrial material context created new opportunities for employment of federal republican arrangements to create an intercontinental state. These writers began with the assumption that the British system was an anomaly in world politics that defied simple categorization,[49] and that it faced daunting challenges from continental-scale rivals.

The idea of a 'Greater Britain' is that a slimmer, more efficient, and coherent, and thus less vulnerable, entity could be constructed through a program of 'imperial federation' of those parts of Britain's vast overseas domains settled by colonists from Britain.[50] Seeley gave this vision its most sophisticated and widely influential formulation in his *The Expansion of England,* and Mackinder also wrote extensively on it.[51] These proposals were not implemented, but the general public, leading intellectuals, and government officials discussed and debated them, and organizations dedicated to their realization were established.[52]

Seeley and Mackinder believed new technology was the silver lining in the clouds of doom gathering around the weary British titan. The technologies shrinking the world and bringing Britain into closer proximity with many potentially antagonistic states could also be employed to enhance British viability. The new communication and transportation technologies behind the 'abolition of distance' created two opportunities: large self-governing regimes were possible and the fragments of the British 'nation' scattered across the globe could be integrated into a viable nation-state. Seeley claims these new technologies made the far-flung British settler colonies effectively contiguous with the British Isles, thus permitting a choice of neighbors: "as an island, England is distinctly nearer for practical purposes to the New World, and belongs to it, or at least has the choice of belonging at her pleasure to the New World or to the Old."[53] It was now possible for a Greater Britain to be "a world Venice, with the sea for streets," and even the isolated British settler colonies in New Zealand could now be effectively linked with the British Isles.[54] Mackinder argued that modern technology could overcome climatic constraints, enabling the vast spaces of Canada and Australia to be much more extensively populated and industrialized, enabling Canada to become "the economic centre of the British Empire."[55]

Technology created these possibilities, but political innovations were necessary to realize them. The program of 'imperial federation' had four main parts: separation between the 'settler colonies' and the 'rule of Britain among alien races;'[56] federation between the United Kingdom and the settler colonies;[57] a system of tariff preferences to economically integrate Greater Britain; and a program of social democratization and expanded welfare.[58] Seeley anticipated that such a Greater Britain would be the rough equivalent to the United States, and "far stronger" than Russia because of the ethnically heterogeneous character of the Russian population.[59]

A large number of late-nineteenth- and early-twentieth-century schemes under the general label 'imperial federation' for reorganizing the British Empire were advanced.[60] The phrase 'imperial federation' was something of an oxymoron as Edward Freeman, the Oxford historian of federalism, pointedly observed,[61] but the core idea of 'imperial federation' was that the relationship between the British Isles and the white settler colonies would be equalized. The central political feature of most plans was the creation of a parliament for the British nation in which all citizens would be equally represented, while preserving self-governance for local issues.

The model here was explicitly American federalism, which for Seeley was a pivotal innovation in the development of free government. The combination of industrial technology and representative federalism had enabled the United States to solve "a problem substantially similar" to that which the old British colonial system "could not solve," namely large-scale emigration and expansion without either despotism or fission.[62] Burke, in his defense of American colonial independence, had cited distance as an insuperable barrier to representative government.[63] The independence of British North America in the eighteenth century had been an inevitability, given the state of the mechanical and political arts of the time, but the independence of the English-speaking parts of the British Empire in the twentieth century could be avoided.[64]

The Greater Britain program was never fully attempted, and the white settler colonies increasingly developed their own states, foreign policies, and national identities, leaving only the pale shadow of the British Commonwealth.[65] But formidable barriers rendered it inherently problematic. The key problem, forcefully noted by Wells, was that the Greater Britain schemes were based on a fallacious reading of geographic factors. The assumption that Canada and Australia would become extensively industrialized and populated remains unrealized primarily due to climatic factors (temperature for Canada and aridity for Australia).[66] Enduring climatic realities have not been overcome by technology, and would have precluded Canada and Australia from playing a major role in a Greater Britain.

The expectation that the new space-spanning technologies of steam and electricity would overcome positional liabilities and limits appears even more flawed. Seeley's analogy between Britain and Venice is misleading because it ignores the basic geographic fact that the Ocean bordered on all coastal territories, not just those in British control. The reduction of effective distance between all parts of the world did not make all parts of the world equally distant from each other. Neighbors are still neighbors, and the liabilities and advantages of relative proximity remain. The implications of this simple fact for the viability of the program are numerous and almost entirely negative. The relative positions of the British Isles and the white settler colonies, of the white settler colonies and the United States, of the British Isles and the rest of Europe remained powerful obstacles to the creation of an enlarged British national state. Overall, the vision was critically flawed by an exaggeration of the ability of technology to overcome facts of geography, particularly climate and position. Ironically, the insularity that had privileged Britain in the early modern system proved an insuperable barrier to effective national integration in the global system.

European Anarchy, Empire, and Union

Contemporary Realism views the historical European state system as the exemplar of international politics and is largely bewildered by the emergence of the European Union. In sharp contrast, the near consensus among industrial global theorists was that the European anarchic system was increasingly unstable during the industrial era due to rising levels of violence interdependence. The question for these theorists was not whether, but when and how European anarchy would end. The main novelty of their argument was the claim that replacing European anarchy had become *inevitable* or *necessary.* Preindustrial Europe had been a second anarchy, but industrial Europe had become a first anarchy, intrinsically perilous to security. In the terms of the eighteenth-century image of Europe as a 'republic' 'by nature,' the material division of European space was waning, creating a situation of intense violence interdependence on a continental-regional scale.

In broad terms, two outcomes seemed most likely—either Europe would be consolidated via conquest by one state or else some form of European federal union would emerge, either peacefully or in the ruins of a catastrophic war. The idea of European imperial unification had always been the default alternative to the European anarchic system, which was a 'republic' rather than a 'universal monarchy.' Imperial ideologues had always touted peace as a compelling advantage of consolidation, but antihegemonic wars against leading states, while costly, had never been total in the intensity of their violence, and so had been not only tolerable but preferable to the security uncertainties of universal empire. In the wake of the massive destruction of the Great War of 1914–18, and in the shadow of even more destruction from airplanes, tanks, and poisonous gas, leaving anarchy seemed more compelling. Advocates of imperial European unification in the industrial era, particularly German theorists of the 'panregion,' also warned that Europe would be dominated by Russia and America if it did not consolidate.[67] While the threat of Ottoman encroachments had been evoked earlier with some credibility, the rapid growth of Russia and America in the nineteenth century gave these premonitions a powerful credibility, which Hitler was particularly prominent in voicing and exploiting.

Far more problematic for aspirants of European empire was the rise of national identity among European peoples. Stimulated by reactions to Napoleon's attempt to impose the French revolutionary agenda upon much of Europe and then sustained and amplified by the political mobilization, urbanization, and rising literacy associated with the industrial revolution, Europeans were paradoxically becoming more attached to particularistic nation-states as the military (and economic) viability of such units was waning. This meant not only that resistance to imperial consolidation would be more intense, but also that the ability of any conquering power to legitimate its rule with a unifying ideology would be particularly difficult. In this situation, the Third Reich's volkish German nationalism and its 'Aryan' racial identity agenda also fell short because it consigned large numbers of Europeans to outsider or enemy status.[68]

The alternative scenario for European consolidation through federal union was also not new but was advanced in new ways related to the changing material context. Earlier plans for European federal union had been advanced as a means to avoid war, but advocates of European Union increasingly claimed it was necessary for the survival of European civilization.[69] The United States again served a catalytic role, but as a model rather than a threat.[70] An especially lucid version of these ideas is provided by Wells at the turn of the century, before he expanded his visionary horizons to world union. The overall claim is that "geographical contours, economic forces, the trend of invention and social development, point to a unification of all Western Europe." Wells expects Germany to mount an effort to unify Europe, but predicts that the German Empire and German aggression "will be either shattered or weakened to the pitch of great compromises by a series of wars of land and sea." For Wells, the limitations of Germany's prospects are directly linked to its internal political tradition: "the intensely monarchical and aristocratic organization of the German empire will stand in the way of the synthesis of greater Germany."[71]

The more probable model for European unification is to be found in "Swiss conceptions, a civilized republicanism." Voluntary association, spearheaded by the 'rational middle class' will prevail over the older forms of political association. Wells is unwilling to specify exactly how long the process of integration will take, since the rate of consolidation depends "entirely upon the rise in general intelligence in Europe."[72] But he does predict that a European confederate republic will be "increasingly predominant over the whole European mainland and the Mediterranean basin, as the twentieth century closes."[73]

To finish this discussion, it is instructive to compare these arguments and expectations with the actual patterns of European integration occurring over the second half of the twentieth century. Several broad patterns are salient in this immensely complex and thoroughly studied process. Consistent with Wells's predictions, Germany mounted an unsuccessful attempt at imperial unification, catastrophic war played a catalyzing role, the political interests of the modern middle classes (particularly in economic growth) have propelled union building, and the trajectory of institution building is more confederal than imperial. Outside threats, mainly Russian Soviet but also American, have played a role, as has

America as model. But the actual and the predicted diverge in two important interrelated ways. First, the actual political structures of the European Union, defying traditional classification in important ways, fall significantly short of constituting a federal union, particularly concerning the organization of military capability. Second, a major non-European state, the United States, has played a central role as catalyst and supporter of European unification and has been the dominant military power in Western Europe through its preponderance in the NATO military alliance. This American presence has shaped the pattern of European unification profoundly. Playing a role structurally similar to the British imperial authorities in North America prior to colonial rebellion and independence, the United States' largely benign and Ocean-separated hegemony in Europe has provided a skeletal frame of security stability within which the tissues of economic and social institutions could grow. At the same time American hegemony in Europe has significantly reduced the security imperatives for Europeans to more fully integrate their own military authorities and capabilities. The overall result is that European integration has been simultaneously assisted, retarded, and shaped, producing the oddly lopsided Europe that is 'an economic giant, a political midget, and a military dwarf.'

Panregional Imperialism and Totalitarianism

Each step in the long effort to conceptualize spatial expansions of republican government has been paralleled, haunted, and spurred by innovations in the techniques of domination. Tyranny and despotism have marred political life for millennia, but the material capabilities of the industrial revolution enabled the development of hierarchy into its most ominous and unrestrained form, the totalitarian superstate. Lasswell's specter of the 'garrison state' and its advocates shadowed the free world during the high industrial era of the middle years of the twentieth century. The origins, ideologies, and records of the modernized tyrannies of the twentieth century have been exhaustively scrutinized by scholars, but an important cluster of early-twentieth-century structural-materialist arguments advanced by prominent advocates and critics has been relatively overlooked.

In a famous premonition, the Russian Liberal Alexander Herzon warned in 1857 of a "Genghis Khan with a telegraph, the steamship, the railroad."[74] During the early decades of the twentieth century sophisticated contextual-materialist analysis of the new possibilities for industrial hierarchical rule were developed by the retired German General Karl Haushofer and colleagues associated with the Munich-based *Journal of Geopolitics*, the American polemicist James Burnham, and the renowned

British writer George Orwell. These writers envision a world order shaped by industrial material forces where highly hierarchical states are the exclusive actor, war and imperialism the norm, and economic life tightly subordinated to states. They envision that the leading industrial states, driven to expand to at least continental size to obtain the resource base they need, will clash violently, leaving only a handful of survivors.

The first version of this argument emerges from Haushofer and other German writers and is then adopted, modified, and criticized by Burnham and Orwell. Haushofer's ideas about the scale-up of the autarkic power state build on a long line of German theorists, most notably Fichte, Ranke, List, Trietschke, Kjellén, and Ratzel. Haushofer tutored Adolf Hitler while he was writing *Mein Kampf* and was prominent during the Third Reich, but the specifics of his agenda differed considerably from Hitler's opportunistic and race-obsessed grand strategy.[75] Haushofer's materialist world order analysis centers around the closely related concepts of the great space (*grossraum*), the panregion, autarky, and the panidea. These four phrases capture different aspects of one essential insight: in the twentieth century, military and economic survival requires states to have continent-plus size territories. A panregion is a 'great space' that contains enough and diverse land to enjoy approximate autarky. Being autarkic and large, only panregional states are likely to survive as independent actors in world politics. A 'panidea' is an ideology capable of unifying a panregion.[76]

Another version of this argument is provided by the American James Burnham, whose odyssey from a Trotskyist to an extreme cold warrior produced a stream of works unified only by their political extremism.[77] In *The Managerial Revolution* (1940) Burnham combines a Marxian model of forces and modes of production, a dismissal of socialist egalitarianism, and an extreme version of the elite theory of politics borrowed from Machiavelli, Mosca, and Pareto to argue that capitalism is dying and being replaced not by socialism, but by the "managerial elite."[78] He argues that a worldwide revolution is occurring in which the capitalist mode of production is being rendered obsolete by the functional imperatives of the industrial forces of production because economic decision making by individuals and uncoordinated firms is no longer viable in an era of large-scale industrial planning. The Soviet Union, Nazi Germany, and to a lesser extent the American New Deal are examples of the new social formation in which a managerial elite has supplanted traditional capitalist and aristocratic social and political formations.[79]

The main focus of Burnham's analysis is the internal transformation to strong hierarchy, but in "The World Policy of the Managers" he argues that "[e]xperience has shown that the existence of a large number of sovereign nations, especially in Europe . . . is incompatible with contemporary economic and social needs" because the "complex division of labor, the flow of trade and raw materials made possible and demanded by modern technology, were strangulated in the network of diverse tariffs, laws, currencies, passports, boundary restrictions, bureaucracies, and independent armies." This means "[i]t has been clear for some time that these were going to be smashed; the only problem was who was going to do it and how and when," and "now it is being done under the prime impulse of Germany."[80]

Burnham expects this process of German imperial consolidation in Europe to be replicated elsewhere. While "it is likely that wars will be fought which have a monopoly of world power as the aim of the participants," the process will stop short of the creation of a world state, leaving three "super-states."[81] A "look at an economic map" indicates their number and location: "Advanced industry is concentrated in three, and only three, comparatively small areas: the United States . . . Europe . . . and the Japanese islands together with parts of eastern China."[82] These are superstate nuclei because "[i]t is advanced industry, needless to say, which makes the goods with which modern wars are fought and won." The process of consolidation will leave facades as "some of the many nations which are eliminated *in fact* may be preserved in form; they may be kept as administrative subdivisions, but they will be stripped of sovereignty." Despite the universal rule of managerial elites in the dominant superstates, Burnham does not foresee peace, but rather incessant warfare, which will also be "inconclusive, since none of the three central areas can firmly conquer any of the others." The world will be extremely conflictual since "the managers are carrying on a . . . triple battle . . . against the capitalists, . . . against the masses, and against each other," and starkly imperial and hierarchic as "the disposition of the rest of the world will be decided and redecided" by the managerial elites.[83]

A version of this argument also appears in George Orwell's classic dystopian novel *1984*. The world of *1984*, as set out in an "official document" entitled, "The Theory and Practice of Oligarchical Collectivism," is largely borrowed from Burnham, but Orwell is sharply critical of Burnham's overall approach to politics.[84] In Orwell's rendering, the world is also divided into three superstates closely following Burnham: Oceana (made up of the New World and the remnants of the British Empire), Eurasia (made up of a Russia that had absorbed Europe), and Eastasia (located in the China-Japan region). Although these three regions are ruled by similar groups of managers, these states wage continual warfare against each other. But "none of the three superstates could definitely be conquered even by the other two in combination. They are too evenly matched, and their natural defenses are too formidable."[85] Orwell moves beyond Burnham in arguing that the fight between the elites was the *means* to keep the masses suppressed.[86] The origins of rivalry in Burnham are unclear, but they seem

systemic in nature. For Orwell they are rooted in the logic of internal hierarchical rule "to keep the structure of society intact."[87]

Federal Union, the 'Greater Synthesis,' and New World Government

The most important theoretical contribution of nineteenth- and early-
twentieth-century industrial globalist thinkers is an analysis of the extension of republican government to continental and then global scale (recall
figure 8.2). Ideas about republican unions emerge in three steps, beginning
with American federal continental union, then Wells's 'greater synthesis'
of transcontinental nonhierarchical polities, and culminating in the vision
of Wells and others of a world republican government.

The rise of the United States as a new form of large-space republican
political order attracted extensive attention in the middle and late years
of the nineteenth century. Theorists pointed to geography, technology,
and political innovations as factors in its formation. One widespread argument, influentially articulated by Ratzel and repeated by his American
student Ellen Churchill Semple and Harvard professor Archibald Cary
Coolidge, was that the overall topography of North America favored the
emergence of one state. The argument, cast as a comparison with Europe,
is concisely summarized by Coolidge:

> The physical geography of North America has been described as "large, sim-
> ple, and easily comprehensible." There is no such variety and confusion as
> in the configuration of Europe, with its extraordinary fantastic outlines, its
> scattered ranges of mountains, its many divergent river valleys, and its obvi-
> ously separate regions, like Scandinavia, Spain, Italy, and the Balkan penin-
> sula; but on the other hand, America has proportionately much less available
> coastline. . . . Like eastern Europe and northern Asia, North America ap-
> pears as the setting for a few large states rather than for a mosaic of small
> ones. Within the United States itself, the great physical lines of division are
> few and simple. They run north and south, cutting the parallels of latitude
> and the zones of climate at right angles instead of coinciding with them. This
> fact has been of far-reaching political importance; for it has worked against
> sectionalism, and has produced cross currents of interests. Had the chain of
> the Alleghenies intervened between the free states and the slave states, we
> may doubt whether the Union would have been preserved, or even have been
> formed.[88]

Reinforcing geographic proclivity are the new technologies of transport
and communication. As Wells observed, "[T]he great republic of the
United States would have been impossible before the printing press and
the railway."[89] In the late-eighteenth and early-nineteenth centuries, the

formation and preservation of the union was reinforced by physical geography. As the union spread into the great interior valley the railroad helped preserve it, and then the great transcontinental railroads helped overcome the separating tendencies of the topography of western North America.

Geography and technology may have created favorable conditions for American expansion and union, but there also was widespread recognition that political innovations, most notably federalism, had been necessary as well. Seeley observed that the representative system had made possible the extension of liberty to regimes the size of England from their previous milieu of the city-state, and then the United States added federalism, permitting further spatial extension. Echoing Montesquieu and recalling the Roman and Spanish empires, Seeley notes that "large political organisms were only stable when they were of a low type," in which "the individual is crushed, so that he enjoys no happiness, makes no progress and produces nothing memorable."[90] The Northwest Ordinance of 1787 was also seen as a vital new innovation.[91]

Spatial enlargement provides republican polities a vital degree of military viability in the perilous new global industrial setting. Coolidge observes that smaller regimes like "Athens in antiquity, Venice in the Middle Ages, and the Dutch Republic in the seventeenth century . . . were able to cope with gigantic adversaries—Persia, the Ottoman Empire, Spain," but that in the industrial era "no state that lacks a broad territorial foundation can hope to enjoy permanently a position of the first rank," because "mere mass counts in a way it never did before," because "the latest improvements of mechanical industry and military science may be equally the property of all who can pay for them," and "railways and telegraphs enable even the most unwieldy organizations to bring their full strength to bear." In this new situation the United States has a degree of protection from destruction that Britain lacks because "the United States could not be brought to its knees by one fierce blow at the heart, as England might conceivably be."[92]

At the turn of the century, Wells pushes the argument forward and projects the formation of what he terms 'greater syntheses' of regional and continental scale. There is, he says, "the need for some synthesis ampler than existing national organizations."[93] Wells anticipates that "a great synthesis of the English-speaking peoples" will occur, and that the "head and centre of the new unity" will be in the "great urban region that is developing between Chicago and the Atlantic." This union will have a powerful fleet, and "the transfer of the present mercantile and naval ascendancy of Great Britain to the United States during the next two or three decades [is] a very probable thing." Wells also expects this 'greater synthesis' to administer the territories of the British Empire, and possibly to include Scandinavia. The greatest obstacle to this union is the "want of stimulus," but the "renascence of Eastern Asia," and the German fleet will push the North American and British parts of the Anglo-Saxons together. Once these 'larger syntheses' form, Wells observes that "if these [higher syntheses] do not contrive to establish a rational social unity by sanely negotiated unions, they will be forced to fight for physical predominance in the world."[94]

The 'greater synthesis' is the departure point for Wells's most important and distinctive world order theoretical innovation, a world government of a qualitatively new type. Even in *Anticipations*, in casting his glance at the longer term, Wells sets forth the claim that much of his subsequent work would explore: "The suggestion is powerful, the conclusion is hard to resist, that whatever disorders of danger and conflict, whatever *centuries* of misunderstanding and bloodshed men may still have to pass, this process nevertheless aims finally, and will attain to the establishment of one world-state at peace within itself."[95] In the first decades of the twentieth century Wells's thinking rapidly moves beyond this distant and vague anticipation of world government, and by the time of the Great War he had become convinced that the imperatives pushing toward a world state were rapidly growing in strength. In 1914 in his fictional work *The World Set Free*, Wells envisions the creation of a fantastically destructive 'atomic bomb,' the devastation of civilization in an atomic war, and the subsequent establishment of a world state that permanently abolishes war.[96] It was also during these years that Wells outlined his vision of a global technocratic 'new republic' in *A Modern Utopia*.

The new case for world government is most systematically developed in Wells's essay on the League of Nations, written in collaboration with several well-known British academics and public figures.[97] Although the essay's title suggests a defense of the League of Nations as conceived by the Versailles settlement, it surprisingly contains little discussion of the specifics of the League. Instead, Wells makes a more general case for a more powerful organization—a world government with the power to keep the peace. The specific institutional features of this world government are left largely undefined. The essay thus amounts to a case for a worldwide transnational, transstate governance structure designed to end war. The actual League is only a small first step toward this goal. Wells's essay is an important landmark in both materialist world order thinking and Liberal internationalism, for it is here that the argument for the *necessity* of a world state first appears most clearly:

> Upon them [advances in science and invention] rests the whole case for the League of Nations as it is here presented. It is a new case. It is argued here that these forces give us powers novel in history, and bring mankind face to face with dangers such as it has never confronted before. It is maintained that, on the one hand they render possible such a reasoned coordination of human affairs as has never hitherto been conceivable, and that on the other,

they so enlarge and intensify the scope and evil of war and of international
hostility as to give what was formerly a generous aspiration more and more
the aspect of an *imperative necessity*.[98]

A world state is inevitable if civilization is to survive, but it is not inevitable that a world state will emerge peacefully or quickly.

Wells addresses several objections to the feasibility and desirability of
a world government. He responds to the argument that world government
is contrary to nationalism, and therefore infeasible and undesirable, by
noting that "national governments are the exception rather than the rule"
and that "there are very few nationalities in the world now which are
embodied in a sovereign government." He also points to "the numerous
nations in the British Empire" and "the dissolving nationalities in the
American melting pot" and concludes that "participation in a great synthesis is compatible with intense national peculiarity and self-respect."
He also considers the objections of Realists, who "think of international
relations in terms of 'Powers,' mysterious entities of value entirely romantic and diplomatic," and who see international politics "only thinkable
as a competition of those Powers; they see the lives of states as primarily
systems in conflict." This conception of politics, derived from Machiavelli
and "brought to perfection in Europe in the eighteenth century," is an
"almost entirely European idea of international politics." The primary
limitation of this view is also that it does not correspond to most actual
human political organization because "the great majority of men in the
world live out of relation to any such government with astonishing
ease."[99] The British Empire and the United States exemplify nonstatist
political organizations, and they demonstrate that the nation-state is alien
to the world outside Europe.

In addition to the new case for world government, Wells also makes
the case that such a government would take qualitatively novel forms.
Rejecting the "analogies that people so readily draw from national
states," he suggests that "the governing of the world may turn out to be
not a magnified version of governing part of the world, but a different
sort of job altogether."[100] The most important reason for this difference,
Wells seems to suggest, has to do with the absence of foreign security
threats. He doubts "the world as a whole will need a constitution on the
pattern of the combative sovereign governments of the past" because
there will be "little need for president or king to lead the marshaled hosts
of humanity" in a situation where "there is no need for any leader to lead
hosts anywhere."[101]

Without interstate competition and war to stimulate the erection of a
centralized hierarchical state, "there will never be a World State as we
apprehend a State."[102] Instead, world government can and should be fed-

eral and functional. Wells's image of world government is federal because it is composed of tiers of government and because it arises through voluntary unification. He insists that "every sort of district that has a character of its own must have its own rule" and that the purpose of "the great republic of the United States of the World" would be to "keep the federal peace between them all."[103]

Wells's concept of world government is not, however, simply the projection of nation-state federal government to a world scale, for he rejects the need for a world parliament. Instead he envisions "a system of federally cooperative world authorities with powers delegated to them by existing governments."[104] His vision of the scope of these functional authorities is extensive, and, like many in this period, he was especially fascinated by proposals for an international aviation authority. This concept of sectoral functional authorities extrapolates from the limited experience with such arrangements during the nineteenth century and extends beyond subsequent Functionalist approaches by encompassing rather than circumventing security.[105] Always ahead of his time, Wells's anticipation of nuclear explosives animates his understanding of violence interdependence on a global scale and thus invites a closer examination of theorists of the nuclear revolution and world nuclear government.

IMPERFECT PROPHETS, INCOMPLETE REALITIES

Before following Wells across the divide from the global-industrial to the planetary-nuclear era it is appropriate to venture an overall assessment of the industrial global theorists as prophets of world order and as theorists of technological materialism and republican unions.

Most straightforward to assess are industrial globalist predictions about the number of world great powers that would prove viable in the twentieth century, which ranged from one to four. At one extreme Mackinder in 1919 feared that a world state or empire would emerge, and Wells thought it inevitable that a world state would eventually arise from the ashes of a general collapse or war. At the other extreme, Haushofer and other panregional theorists anticipated four viable world great powers. In between are those, beginning with List and Tocqueville, who expected two or three. Counting the number and determining the location of the world great powers through the era of World War II is a relatively simple task. Two states, the United States and the Soviet Union, distinguished with the appellation 'superpower,' endured, while three 'also ran' states (the British Empire, Germany, and Japan) failed to sustain or achieve world great power status.[106] How inevitable was this outcome? Could three or four world great powers have emerged? Why did two

world great powers *emerge*? And why did three or four world great powers or one world state *not emerge*?

A convergence of positional, topographic, and technological factors
aided the formation of the first two world great powers. Both Russia and
America were classic 'marcher' states situated at the edges of the European core and able to expand relatively freely into the interiors of Asia
and North America, and these positional advantages were amplified by
the ability of the railroad to span the continental interiors. Given the vol-
umes and velocities of violence possible in the industrial era, moving from
a world of these two continental states to a world state by way of military
conquest would have been quite difficult, although not impossible. With
the consolidation of the World Island by a Heartland state, the global
balance of power would have shifted decisively toward unipolarity, but
even with this imbalance, the division provided by the world Ocean might
have tipped the outcome toward a stalemate and thus the persistence of
two superpowers.

Subsequent aspirants to world great power status faced daunting obstacles. Haushofer's vision of a world order organized along panregional
lines contains four units, the already consolidated 'Pan America' and 'Pan
Russia,' but also 'EurAfrica' on the western third of the World Island and
one centered around Japan and encompassing East Asia. The efforts of
Germany and Japan to achieve world great power status by consolidating
panregions through military conquest enjoyed initial success, but were
ultimately defeated by the Grand Alliance of the Soviet Union, the United
States, and British Empire. Did this outcome reflect contingent factors or
deeper forces? The idiosyncratic and disintegrated character of German
and Japanese grand strategies suggests that nonmaterial factors played
significant roles in their defeats.[107] But these outcomes also stem from a
deeper logic, the *paradox of the late panregional consolidators:* late aspirants had to engage the already consolidated panregional states in order
to achieve panregional status due to topographical and positional factors.
The fragmented and mixed topographies of both the European and East
Asian regions were unfavorably configured for consolidation because
proximate islands introduced a formidable logistical barrier and because
the richly articulated maritime frontage of both regions meant that a naval
war as well as a land war had to be waged successfully. This terrain also
meant that outsiders were readily entangled in both regions.[108] And in
contrast to the neolithic tribes encountered in the Russian and American
versions of continental 'Manifest Destiny,' the European and East Asian
regions were occupied by a dense patchwork of peoples with developed
states who were unlikely to fall too far behind technologically due to the
extensive maritime communications of these regions.

Wells's anticipation of the emergence of a 'greater synthesis' sits significantly outside the framework of great powers in anarchy. But it plainly is one of his most important and roughly accurate forecasts, and it clearly sits along the main axis of republican security theory. In broad terms, Wells accurately predicted the emergence of a major feature of world order in the second half of the twentieth century, the partial union of the Western liberal democracies under American auspices.[109] As he expected, this union has drawn liberal democratic states somewhat out of anarchy toward negarchy through the construction of a panoply of problem-solving and mutually restraining institutions and organizations. It is facets of this order that contemporary Liberal theories most compellingly address.

Beyond this big successful republican anticipation, Wells also is surprisingly prescient about important specific features of the actual Western order. Wells's terminology of 'synthesis' and his unwillingness to characterize this order as a state clearly indicate that this system is decentralized and confederal. And unlike the formal federal constitutional union proposed by Clarence Streit and the Atlantic Union Movement, Wells seems to have grasped that the Western union would not be one regime or institution, but a patchwork of them.[110] He also sees that a European Union on a 'Swiss confederal' model would emerge partially within the larger synthesis. Always looking to America as the pioneer of new modern republican forms, Wells correctly foresaw the ways in which the new industrial union of republics would be America writ large, and American led.[111] Wells also gets the essentials correct in locating the main factors driving union-building in a combination of external military threats, common domestic systems, and interdependence produced by industrialism.[112] And he grasped that a massive security and economic breakdown would be required to catalyze political institutional movement. Finally, in the overall sweep of Wells's work, greater synthesis serves as the nucleus and prototype of an eventual world republican union, and it remains the case that the most plausible (and certainly most appealing) prospective world government would be an acephalous republican union rather than a world hierarchical state.

Wells did have blind spots. He did not anticipate the extent to which the members of the Western union would be robustly capitalist or how much union activity would be geared to the needs and interests of market capitalist economics. Wells, understandably, was unable to foresee much detail about the relationship between the actual architectures of the Western system and the contingent and complex features of the wars of breakdown and their settlements.[113] Finally, Wells would probably be justifiably surprised by the fact that such a new model republican union would be so underappreciated by international theorists. And he would surely be shocked at the ignorance, indifference, and hostility of so many of the union's citizens regarding its contribution to security, prosperity, and freedom, and its continuing needs and further potential.

A major problem with all the industrial globalist predictions concerns *timing*. This problem is most acute for Burnham, who several times predicted immediate and drastic change, only to abandon his predictions a few years later in favor of another equally sweeping set of them. The problem of timing is partially rooted in the rapid rate of technological change over the last century. Industrial globalist theorists typically predict the world order consequences of a particular combination of technics and geographies, only to have that combination superseded by another set. If the rate of technological change over the last century had been slower and marked by extended plateaus rather than relentless transitions, much better tests of the predictions might be possible. For example, if technological capabilities had stabilized for many decades or even centuries with the 1890 capabilities of the railroad, steamship, wire-bound speed-of-light communication, and chemical explosives, then the distinctive world order consequences of these capabilities would be much more clear. As it happened, these technics were rapidly superseded and supplemented by the airplane, automotive vehicles, communications carried by radio waves, and then ballistic missiles and nuclear explosives. Unless the adjustment of political arrangements to material constraints and opportunities is nearly instantaneous, a particular geography-technology combination may not stimulate much institutional change. The rapidity of technological succession also reduces the number of discrete cases of adjustment, making it difficult to determine whether contingent factors or material variables account for outcomes.

This rapid technological succession may be the bane of theory, but it was probably a boon for liberty. If technology had plateaued at the late-nineteenth- or early-twentieth-century level, then violence interdependence on a global scale would have persisted as strong, thus creating a global scale second anarchy. In this situation, two (or three or four) states would have probably endured, but the impact of perpetual global industrial total war on the interior balances of a republican state would have been highly unfavorable for the survival of limited government and political liberty. In such a world, republican survival would have hinged upon the strength of the countervailing demands produced by complexity and functional differentiation as forces for the liberalization of industrial totalitarian regimes.

The industrial globalists also had divergent understandings of which aspects of technology were most important. Some theorists concentrated on assessing how a *specific set of technics* would impact world order, while others assigned greatest weight to a more generic *capability to pro-*

duce and use certain classes of technics, or the *ability to discover and invent new technics.*

In the first group, Mackinder sees a specific set of technologies and geographies as permanently and decisively fixed, and thus he speaks about "the lasting realities of our Earthly home."[114] After a series of adjustments, the system would attain a general equilibrium, or at least be bound by a small set of possible outcomes. With such an implicit image of technological stability, he could speak about the Heartland problem as a permanent problem and then seriously propose permanent institutional outcomes. The second view, emphasizing the industrial capability to produce specific technics, is most pronounced in Haushofer, Burnham, and the panregionalists. These factors surely registered as a major influence on the outcome of the World Wars. Since then, however, the military-industrial capacities and the natural resources necessary to acquire nuclear weapons have become widespread and thus a waning limitation. The third view, emphasizing the ability to discover and invent, finds its great champion in Wells, who expounds a vision of permanent scientific-technological revolution. As this process advances, geographical distinctions decline and seem to lose importance. What Toynbee referred to as 'the freakish configurations of the globe's surface' cease to matter much for world order. The dream of effective alchemy dispels the restraint of natural resource inputs as relatively small amounts of nearly ubiquitous materials can saturate resource needs for fabricating weapons of absolute speed, range, and destructiveness. Yet nature, far from disappearing as an influence, reappears through the expansion of scientific knowledge of nature. Scientific advance does not leave nature behind, but rather exposes new facets of nature. An extreme technologism is actually an extreme naturalism.

Finally, these issues of technology also have subversive implications for the proposition of closure that the industrial globalists took to be an established fact. If closure means that there is no more habitable territory on the earth's surface to be discovered and annexed, then the world certainly has been closed in the twentieth century. From this fact of territorial closure the industrial globalists inferred that the existing natural resource base was fixed, and therefore that conflicts over its distribution would grow. In retrospect this conclusion seems flawed, because other types of frontiers have emerged as territorial frontiers closed. 'Frontier' is widely deployed to describe areas of innovative scientific and engineering research.[115] States act as if penetrating these 'frontiers' is a matter of far-reaching importance for military and economic gain. The magnitude of organized state efforts to push back scientific and technological frontiers rivals earlier state efforts to explore and settle earlier territorial frontiers. So long as the material frontier of the state system is composed of science and technology, then the interaction between nature and politics is still open and subject to major change.

Chapter Nine

ANTICIPATIONS OF WORLD
NUCLEAR GOVERNMENT

Atomic weapons are a new control by man over
the forces of nature too revolutionary and dangerous
to fit into the old concepts.
—Henry L. Stimson[1]

GOVERNMENT IN THE GLOBAL VILLAGE

The last half of the twentieth century has been marked by accelerating intensification in all four dimensions of the five-century process of globalization. These multiple accelerations of historical change confront observers living in their midst with a bewildering kaleidoscope of seemingly revolutionary developments, the implications of which are difficult to discern. In this tumult, Marshall McLuhan's concept of the 'global village' and the associated 'whole earth' image of the blue-green earth set against the black void of space have something approximating an archetypal status.[2] Among their many contested implications, they vividly capture the fact that the material context of humanity now imposes a villagelike proximity previously experienced on much smaller scales. To the extent that Western political theory began with analysis of the city-state polis, we have accelerated and expanded back to a situation partly resembling where we began.

The simplicity and unity implied in these emergent planetary archetypes belies, however, a reality that is vastly more complex and as much pulling apart as coming together. In the second half of the twentieth century, world government is more an actual practical possibility than in any previous period in history, and has been more seriously conceptualized, advocated, and predicted than ever before.[3] Yet anticipations of this possibility also seem as much frightening as necessary, and every step toward it seems countered by a movement away from it. The convergence of all regional systems into one global system, the collapse of multipolarity into bipolarity and then into unipolarity, suggests a trend toward world government. To the extent there is an American hegemony or empire of global scope, then the United States, however ambivalently, incompletely, incompe-

US

tently, and temporarily, is a (de facto world government) of some sort.[4] Similarly, the explosion of international organizations and regimes coordinating and governing a diverse and growing set of domains of human activity suggests the emergence of a disaggregated nascent world government of some sort. Yet these halting and incomplete moves toward political integration coexist and interact with powerful centrifugal tendencies, most notably the explosion in the number of sovereign states over the last half century, a development fueled by the rising number of ethnic and national groups who demand greater autonomy and who are increasingly able to obtain and maintain it.[5]

Continuing our narrow focus on the security-from-violence problem viewed through the lenses of the two problematiques of republican security theory, this chapter examines arguments, often cast in diverse conceptual vocabularies, about the implications of nuclear explosives for the contemporary world order composed of islands of hierarchy in a sea of anarchy. Of particular interest are lines of argument that view the (state-centric world order as a first anarchy in need of government for security) and that acknowledge the interplay of domestic and international structures of all three ordering principles. The next section summarizes the main ideas of the five main schools of thought on the implications of nuclear weapons for world order. The following three sections examine in greater depth the arguments of the three schools who anticipate the movement of the international system away from pure anarchy. Then a section casts a brief glance at the emergent security issues of weapons-of-mass-destruction terrorism. A final section reflects on architectural principles for a federal-republican world nuclear government.

FIVE ANSWERS TO THE NUCLEAR POLITICAL QUESTION

Since arriving on the world scene in the final days of World War II, nuclear explosive technology has raised the stakes of politics and political science to now encompass the (fate of civilization,) and perhaps the human species. One awesome fact about the new nuclear world is beyond controversy: science and technology has empowered human beings to wreak violence of unprecedented scale and speed.[6] For the foreseeable future, and perhaps forever, the physical survival of vast numbers of human beings, and much of the nonhuman life on earth, rests upon the (adequacy of the system to restrain the large-scale use of nuclear weapons.)

Beyond these stark certainties there reigns great controversy and conjecture. A thicket of thorny questions about nuclear weapons have been the focus of the 'great debate' of the era, in which the magnitude of the stakes has matched the scope of the disagreements.[7] Do these capabilities

pose a revolutionary challenge to the state and its role as provider of
security? Or can these new realities be accommodated with relatively in-
significant institutional adjustment? If world politics has not yet adjusted
to the nuclear reality, what form might an appropriate adjustment take?
Arguments about the relationship between nuclear weapons and the state
system fall into five broad groups, which I label *classical nuclear one
worldism, nuclear strategism, automatic deterrence statism, institutional
deterrence statism,* and *federal-republican nuclear one worldism.*

The first view, *classical nuclear one worldism,* holds that nuclear explosives pose a radical challenge to the core security-providing function of
the state and that a world state is necessary to provide security. The core
of nuclear one worldism is the simple argument that the size of state viability has shifted: nuclear weapons have pushed states from the moderate
and tolerable vulnerability of second anarchy into the intolerable vulnerability of first anarchy, and in this situation security can only be obtained
through the erection of a larger, all-encompassing world government. Although the emergence of a world state would obviously mark the end of
the systemic anarchy characteristic of the multistate system, a state would
persist, greatly enlarged in size.

During the early years of the nuclear age, nuclear one worldism was a
widely held interpretation of the nuclear situation. Nuclear one worldism
reached its theoretical apogee around 1960 in the works of John Herz
and Kenneth Boulding.[8] At several junctures, most notably the Baruch
Plan,[9] the McCloy-Zorin talks on 'General and Complete Disarmament,'[10] the public declarations of the late Reagan Administration, and
Gorbachev's 'New Thinking,'[11] nuclear one worldist arguments became
the basis of official initiatives. But among international theorists the rise
in deterrence statism has been paralleled by the near disappearance of
nuclear one world theory from the security studies field. Such ideas have
continued to enjoy a strong but indistinct presence in the field of peace
studies and in the citizen peace movement, where typically they are mixed
and linked with ethical criticisms of war, militarism, and oppression that
go far beyond the simple nuclear one world argument.

The second position, *nuclear strategism,* holds that the advent of nuclear weapons marks no decisive break in world politics and observes the
behavior of states to be largely the same before and after their arrival.
This view takes states as given, conflict as endemic, and holds that the
quintessential state activity of preparing for and making war defines
world politics regardless of the type of weaponry prevalent. Nuclear strategism postulates that states seeking security in a nuclear world will—and
should—prepare themselves to exercise a full range of nuclear use options
and seek to gain political advantage from relatively small differences in
nuclear force levels. Not surprisingly, nuclear strategists view interstate
arms control as useless and possibly harmful, seeing such measures as

either impossible when valuable or unnecessary when possible.[12] Nuclear strategists believe public fears of nuclear destruction are hysterical and public involvement in nuclear policy is dangerous. The nuclear strategist view has been most extensively articulated by Herman Kahn and Colin Gray.[13] Although this view has been attacked for a variety of important limitations,[14] the actual force structures and military doctrines of the United States and the Soviet Union during much of the Cold War corresponded to its expectations to a first approximation, but with significant anomalies.

The third and fourth answers to the nuclear-political question are the two varieties of *deterrence statism,* and they emphasize the stabilizing effects of deterrence. The basic argument of deterrence statism is that nuclear weapons have significantly altered the behavior of states by making war between nuclear-armed states prohibitively costly. Deterrence statists take the state as a given, but hold that states can solve the nuclear security problem by changing their behavior and avoiding war. In effect, deterrence statists hold that nuclear weapons demand revolutionary changes in the behavior of states, but not in the hierarchical structure of states or in the anarchical structure of the state system.

Deterrence statism has experienced considerable growth and evolution, from its first formulation by Bernard Brodie in the late 1940s through the debate with nuclear strategists over the usability of nuclear weapons short of full-scale war.[15] At the beginning of the nuclear era, deterrence statism was not widely held but is now the dominant position among international theorists, although publics and militaries have resisted this view. Early proponents emphasized the tentative, second-best, and temporary character of this solution, but many of its contemporary proponents are confident that this solution is highly enduring and close to the best of all solutions.[16]

Deterrence statists divide into two groups. Some, most notably Kenneth Waltz, are *automatic deterrence statists* because they see deterrence as an effectively automatic process, so inescapable and obvious that institutions, either within or between states, are largely irrelevant to it. In this view the states have created a strongly stable—perhaps the best possible—nuclear order by maintaining extensive nuclear forces in order to deter nuclear use.[17] Like nuclear strategism, automatic deterrence statism assigns little value to interstate arms control and little significance to public fear and activism. It has developed a modest academic following, and its main political effect has been to diminish concern about nuclear proliferation.[18]

The second version of deterrence statism, *institutional deterrence statism,* emphasizes that nuclear deterrence has institutional prerequisites. Institutional deterrence statism is an augmented version of deterrence statism, paralleling the way the international society of states is an augmented version of simple structural Realism. This position attaches great importance to the societal aspects of the state system's adjustment to the nuclear era. It emphasizes the importance of internal state institutions and organizations in perfecting deterrence, and views interstate arms control as an important process through which states communicate to one another their recognition of the nuclear facts of life and adjust their political relations and force structures in order to reduce the possibilities of inadvertent nuclear war or use. The core ideas of institutional deterrence statism emerged in the late 1950s and early 1960s in response to fears of surprise attack, inadvertent escalation, and loss of civilian control in crises.[19] Beginning in the 1960s the ideas of the institutional deterrence statists came to play an increasingly prominent role as first the United States and then the Soviet Union at least partially pursued interstate arms control.

The fifth position, *federal-republican nuclear one worldism*, is much less developed and recognized. It holds that nuclear weapons have rendered the statist approach to security nonviable, and that security in the nuclear era requires the establishment of an institutionalized division between territorial units and nuclear capability. Instead of either the continuation of an interstate anarchy or the establishment of a world state, a federal-republican union of strong mutual restraint is needed to provide security. This view holds that a world hierarchical government would entail an uncheckable concentration of power, and is unnecessary in the absence of an interplanetary threat. This position has remained inchoate and underdeveloped, but parts of this answer to the nuclear-political question were implicit in the Baruch Plan and have been articulated by Leonard Beaton, Jonathan Schell, American critics of the extraconstitutional concentration of presidential nuclear authority, and this author.[20]

These five positions vary in their prominence, degree of development, and conceptual vocabulary. To frame them so that the core issues of the debate among them are clear, they can be schematized (see figure 9.1) using the triad-triangle model of ordering principles (recall figure 1.8 and figure 6.2). Two of the positions, nuclear strategism and automatic deterrence statism, maintain the system remains appropriately anarchical after the nuclear revolution, but they differ on the effort needed to achieve deterrence. For nuclear strategism, sustaining deterrence is complex and difficult, leaving open the possibility of nuclear war or usable nuclear supremacy, in which case the position collapses into imperial nuclear one world statism. For automatic deterrence statism, the system remains anarchic, and its overthrow is a remote possibility. But this is a very novel anarchy, marked by diminished concern for relative gains, and curiously resembles a Kantian pacific anarchy.

The other three positions envision much more substantial system structural change. All varieties of classical nuclear one worldism anticipate a shift from anarchy to world government, but, troubled by the peril of

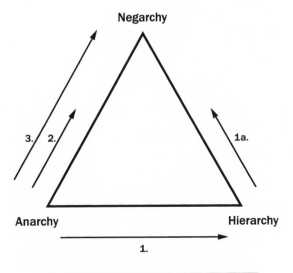

Figure 9.1 System Structural Change in Nuclear-Political Arguments

hierarchical world government, they are attracted to a combination of hierarchy and negarchy. Institutional deterrence statism and federal-republican one worldism hold that the simple anarchic state system is not viable as a security arrangement, but neither argue for a world hierarchical government, and they anticipate change from anarchy toward negarchy. Both hold deterrence to be an ultimate source of restraint, but insist that deterrence must be augmented with institutions. They differ on the extent of change: institutional deterrence statism envisions only a partial movement from pure anarchy toward negarchy, while federal-republican nuclear one worldism holds that anarchy needs to be replaced with more substantive mutually restraining government.

CLASSICAL NUCLEAR ONE WORLDISM

The first two decades of the nuclear era were the golden age of nuclear one world theorizing. For a few years unequivocal nuclear one world testimonials and declarations poured forth from many quarters. A large and vocal segment of informed opinion held that nuclear weapons posed a radical challenge to the core function of the interstate system and only a fundamental change in world order could meet the nuclear challenge.[21] This apocalyptic conviction was typically accompanied by the optimistic belief that far-reaching institutional changes could be achieved in the near term. Seeking 'fundamentally new ways of thinking,' a wide range of fundamental alternatives for reordering the world were debated.[22] Classical nuclear one worldism has two distinct parts: a *diagnosis* of the misfit between the state system and nuclear explosives and a *remedy*, an image of a world order in adjustment to this new reality, typically a world state of some sort. Related ideas about the timing and character of the transition to a world state were also debated.

John Herz makes the most theoretically sophisticated nuclear one world diagnosis, but his ideas about alternative institutional remedies are undeveloped.[23] He argues that the most basic function of states is providing security through military control of territory, which requires territorial "impermeability." It is not enough for a state apparatus to aspire to, claim, or even be recognized as having statehood. The state apparatus must be capable of making good its claim, and states are driven to consolidate as the technological bases of military viability show increasing scale effects. With the advent of nuclear weapons, no state can maintain a protective "shell." Every state has become "permeable," and therefore another consolidation can be expected. When "not even half the globe remains defensible against the all-out onslaught of the new weapons," the "power of protection, on which political authority was based in the past, seems to be in jeopardy for any imaginable entity." Humans inhabit a "planet of limited size" but "the effect of the means of destruction has become absolute."[24] Nuclear explosives have produced "the most radical change in the nature of power and the characteristics of power units since the beginning of the modern state system," or perhaps "since the beginnings of mankind." This development "presages the end of the territorial protective function of state power and territorial sovereignty," and the "chief external function of the modern state therefore seems to have vanished."[25]

The arguments of the early nuclear one worlders are easily and often confused with types of idealism, due to their optimism and because world government had long been advocated by self-consciously idealist writers. However, with nuclear weapons, political universalism was no longer idealistic, but had become intimately connected with the survival concerns that once motivated the critics of idealistic and universalistic thinking.[26] The nuclear one world argument is essentially the main argument of the anarchy-interdependence problematique applied to the nuclear era.

The second main feature of nuclear one worldism was the claim that the problem posed by nuclear weapons required the creation of a world government. Convinced that this invention had rendered the nation-state militarily obsolete, the nuclear one worlders thought only a world *state* with a monopoly of the means of destruction could solve permanently the problem of nuclear explosives. With the *multistate system* no longer able to provide security, they looked for security in an *omnistate*. Although they disagreed about other attributes of a world state, they agreed that a world government required at least the deep disarmament of the existing states and the establishment of a worldwide centralized military apparatus capable of coercing all other actors.

Beyond these points of general agreement, nuclear one world theorists disagreed about the appropriate character of a world state and about whether conditions were or would soon be ripe for the creation of a nonrepressive world state. One of the first nuclear one worldists, James Burnham argued that nuclear weapons made a world state inevitable in the near future and therefore the United States should take the lead in establishing one by whatever means necessary and available.[27] But fearing resistance to American world domination, he insisted that the United States had to govern with "methods of conciliation and concession" or else face worldwide revolt.[28] Alternatively, a group of world federalists associated with the Chicago Committee to Frame a World Constitution argued that in the absence of a sense of world community, the effort to create a world government was either utopian or indistinguishable from a war of aggression for world domination, and a world monopoly of force without world community would produce repressive tyranny. They proposed a world federal state complete with legislative, judicial, executive, and social welfare capacities. They argued that there already was enough world community to start building such a state and that community would grow as the world state grew, and they looked to the American founding as a model.[29] In response, the leading American Realist of the era, Hans Morgenthau, accepted the diagnosis of state-system obsolescence, but argued that world community was largely absent and that the American founding presupposed an American nation, thus leaving a tragic impasse.[30] In further response, yet another group of world federalists argued that it was not necessary to create a full-fledged world state, and instead argued for the creation of a 'minimalist' state with a world military force with a monopoly of heavy weapons for 'peacekeeping' or 'police' functions. They argued it was a major conceptual error to simply project a variant of a national federal state to a world scale.[31] Aware of the dangers of praetorianism among the world state guardians, they suggested the use of special training and psychological screening.[32]

Overall, these classical nuclear one-worldist images of a world government as the remedy to the nuclear security problem reach something of a conceptual impasse. Recognizing that the move from world anarchy to world hierarchy entails grave security risks, they attempt to envision a variety of internal restraints on hierarchy, from concessions stimulated by fear of revolt to world community. Convinced there is a major problem, they try and conceptualize a practicable solution that is not as potentially grave a threat as nuclear anarchy, but they propose only modifications to hierarchy. This impasse ultimately stems from their implicit understanding of government as statist and hierarchical. To move beyond this impasse, it is necessary to conceptualize a path not from anarchy to hierarchy or modified hierarchy, but rather directly toward negarchy. For an initial understanding of this path, the theory and practice of arms control provides a beginning.

Arms Control, External Anarchy, and Internal Hierarchy

Aside from the primacy attached to deterrence, the most novel political feature of the nuclear era is the significance accorded to interstate arms control.[33] Arms control initially was advanced as an alternative to disarmament generally and 'general and complete disarmament' in particular.[34] In contrast to the radical diagnoses and sweeping remedies offered by nuclear one worlders, arms controllers are reformers offering pragmatic incremental steps to improve security, and they generally do not formulate their claims in ways that directly address the nuclear-political question. Nevertheless, nuclear arms control theory does offer an implicit answer, *institutional deterrence statism*. This view holds that arms control both *within* and *between* states is vital to the stability of deterrence. Arms controllers proceed from the basic deterrence statist assumption that nuclear war is always fundamentally irrational due to its great destructiveness, but argue that changes in institutions and force structures are necessary in order to guarantee that this irrationality is always obvious. This is to say that "arms control is really 'deterrence' in a more sophisticated form."[35] For arms controllers, deterrence is potentially fragile rather than robust and automatic: just because nuclear war is irrational does not mean it will not occur. To address these security problems, arms controllers advance an interrelated two-part program: internally structuring nuclear forces in order to minimize the chances of unintentional use and externally dampening antagonistic interstate relations, both of which are facilitated by a process of learning.

Contrary to the widespread notion that arms control primarily involves interstate agreements, arms control theorists have also emphasized the importance of unilateral and internal measures of restraint, and interstate agreements are valuable because they facilitate internal measures. A central objective of arms control has been to assure that military organizations remain tightly responsive to the direction of central state leaders.[36]

Within states there is a perennial struggle between the central authorities seeking perfect subordination and military organizations seeking autonomy. The arms control goal of translating the antistrategic implications of deterrence into an actual military force posture runs against deeply ingrained military interests and assumptions. One of the most important forms of internal arms control has been the employment of electronic locks and codes on nuclear weapons, known as Permissive Action Links (PALS).[37] These technologies made possible for the first time a division between the physical possession of weapons and their direct control, greatly tightening the subordination of military instrumentalities to the command of central state decision makers.

The argument that stable nuclear deterrence depends upon a particular set of internal state arrangements also plays a central role in the arms control argument against nuclear proliferation. For example, responding to Waltz's argument that proliferation may actually contribute to international peace by extending nuclear deterrent relationships among more states, Scott Sagan argues that many countries that might acquire nuclear weapons lack state apparatuses with sufficient organizational and technological capacities to sustain stable deterrence.[38] Thus stable deterrence is not something that springs automatically from the mere possession of nuclear weapons, but rather depends upon complex and difficult-to-acquire technological and organizational measures. These concerns stop short of challenging the central assumptions of deterrence statism. The danger is not state possession of nuclear weapons, but rather the possession of nuclear weapons by imperfect states: nuclear deterrence is stable only for perfected states, leaving a great many states unqualified for nuclear possession.

The second part of the arms control agenda is the alteration of political relations between nuclear-armed states through the establishment of a regime, or international institution, composed of explicit treaties and implicit understandings. Arms controllers often characterize their agenda in apolitical terms, but achieving their program required the alteration of the political relationship between the United States and the Soviet Union. So long as the political relationship remained antagonistic, it would be impossible to internally restrain and restructure nuclear forces. Although the overall Soviet-American relationship was not a regime, there was arguably "a patchwork quilt or mosaic of subissues in the security area, some characterized by rules and institutions," most prominently a "regime for avoiding accidental nuclear war."[39]

Both the internal and external arms control agendas are viewed as part of a process of learning. Although cast in the language of contemporary American social science, nuclear learning continues a core part of the early statist program of enlightened statecraft. Nuclear learning is important because state interests cannot be taken as given, but rather change and evolve over time. Many of the realities of nuclear weapons are complex, emerged gradually, and did not spontaneously spring forth from their mere existence.[40] By drawing the political leaders of states to focus upon the specifics of their inescapable nuclear vulnerability, the arms control process educates leaders about deterrence.[41]

The interstate agenda of arms control extends the society of states to the nuclear era. Like diplomacy, sovereignty, and public international law, arms control moderates rather than replaces anarchy. A fundamental affinity also exists between the intrastate nuclear arms control agenda and the early modern statist program to enlighten and rationalize statecraft. While automatic deterrence statism presupposes an automatically enlightened hierarchy and the rationalization of the hierarch's subordinate instrumentalities, arms controllers seek to realize in practice what ideal statism posits in principle. Arms controllers assume that humans are prone to lapses in rationality and failures of judgment and that large complex organizations are unresponsive to central political control and prone to pursue their own corporate agendas. Arms control thus aims to close the gap between true and apparent interests, to educate power holders about the consequences of actions, and to guarantee that the instrumentalities of state remain fully and uniquely responsive to central authority.

Despite their accomplishments and unrealized potentials, the arms control measures of institutional deterrence statism have major limitations as a general response to the nuclear-political question. Most simply, nuclear arms control is a reformist response to a revolutionary situation.[42] The limits of nuclear arms control are the limits of enlightened statecraft and the society of states: they seek to perfect hierarchy and moderate anarchy rather than replace either. As a program for perfecting deterrence, the arms control program has focused almost entirely on the nuclear *command* structure, but has stopped short of reconfiguring nuclear *authority* structures. Arms control leaves unquestioned the hierarchical structure of nuclear authority. Similar limits also exist in interstate arms control as a program to moderate anarchy. The society of states model assumes that the international system is a second anarchy, which needs to be moderated, rather than a first anarchy, which needs to be fundamentally transcended. When states are 'billiard balls,' the 'cobwebs' of international societal institutions add moderation, but when the units have been transformed into vulnerable and fragile 'eggs,' more substantial structures of restraint are necessary.

FEDERAL-REPUBLICAN NUCLEAR ONE WORLDISM

The fifth school of nuclear thought, modified or *federal-republican nuclear one worldism*, is much less developed than the others, so I will assemble scattered ideas into a composite framed by the main arguments of the two problematiques. The federal republican variant of nuclear one worldism contains modifications of the classical diagnoses and remedies. Three concepts capture the modified diagnosis: *unconquerability, nuclear despotism,* and *nuclear totalitarainism.* Three concepts also capture its modified remedies: *strategic neutralization, recessed deterrence,* and *concurrent authority.*

Unconquerability is the notion that it has become very difficult to conquer, occupy, and govern territories occupied by hostile populations. This feature of contemporary world politics has been widely observed.[43] The important development is that weapons capability has been steadily diffusing to more and more actors. Diffusion is nearly universal with regard to small arms, and as a result conquest and occupation have become very costly. Great powers, especially those with nuclear weapons, still have much more relative power than other actors. But the violence capability in the hands of weaker groups has passed over a crucial threshold beyond which the weak can inflict substantial costs on any state seeking to conquer and occupy their territory. The most powerful states have the ability to destroy, but they cannot bring their surfeit of violence capacity to bear in order to subdue, as the United States discovered in Vietnam and the Soviet Union discovered in Afghanistan. At the heart of this change is what might be called the 'Kalashnakov Revolution' after the hardy and lethal Soviet bloc assault rifle, some 300 million of which are in circulation.[44] The implications of this development for the overall nuclear one world argument is that the problem of interstate aggression has declined, thus obviating the main reason for centralizing violence capacity in a world government.

Nuclear despotism is the notion that temporally compressed decision making must be concentrated by necessity into the hands of one individual. This development has also been widely observed. Whatever their formal constitutional principles, all nuclear-armed states have become 'monarchical' because decision making about nuclear use has devolved into the hands of one individual, creating what has been termed a "nuclear monarchy" or an "absolute monarch."[45] Nuclear explosives are intrinsically despotic for three related reasons: the *speed* of nuclear use decisions; the *concentration* of the nuclear use decision into the hands of one individual; and the *lack of accountability* stemming from the inability of affected groups to have their interests represented at the moment of nuclear use. Nuclear despotism increases the possibilities of nuclear use because of the inherent fallibility and corruptibility of the lone individual.[46]

The tendency toward nuclear despotism is amplified by the temporal compression of decision making stemming from the speed of delivery systems. With large numbers of ready-to-use nuclear weapons deployed on rapid delivery vehicles, the time frame for decision making about nuclear use is compressed into minutes and hours. The pressure for rapid nuclear use decisions is further enhanced by the vulnerability of nuclear command, control, and communication systems.[47] As a result nuclear decision making is dominated by the "dogma of speed," the idea that "response time to a nuclear attack must be prompt, even instant, launching the nearly entire nuclear force."[48] Speed also makes accidental use more likely. Although great efforts have been made to insure that nuclear weapons will not be fired accidentally, systems of nuclear weapons poised for nearly instant use inevitably involve a compromise between the goals of maintaining control and insuring quick response.[49] Temporally compressed decision making is more mechanical than political because rapid decisions cannot be deliberative and because multiple institutional actors cannot be represented.

Nuclear totalitarianism is the notion that fissionable nuclear materials, which make possible both nuclear weapons and nuclear civilian electric energy, are so dangerous that they require regulation and control by highly hierarchical 'total' institutions. This image is developed by various visionaries and prophets of large-scale nuclear civil energy.[50] The underlying material fact here is that large-scale civil nuclear energy systems require the routine commercial and industrial use of staggeringly large quantities of fissile material, particularly plutonium. The nuclear totalitarian prospect is essentially an extrapolation of existing internal hierarchical arms control in proportion to the magnitude of nuclear material usage. Quite explicit in these arguments is that the threat of nonstate actors acquiring nuclear capability is so dangerous that severe diminutions of civil liberties are required. In terms of the two problematiques, the violence intensity of a world heavily reliant on nuclear materials is so great that an anarchic absence of authority is severely threatening.

The alarmist connotations of referring to these hierarchical patterns as 'despotic' and 'totalitarian' are partially subverted by the circumscribed range of their presence to date and by compensating antihierarchical effects of nuclear weapons. The concentration of nuclear command authority in executives has certainly not produced full spectrum political despotism, as leaders of nuclear-armed states remain subject to powerful electoral, judicial, and legislative restraints. Also, the domain of nuclear total institutional control remains concentrated in an archipelago of highly specialized nuclear facilities, and only weakly reaches out to the broader civilian population. At the same time, nuclear weapons during the last half century have reduced the need to strengthen state hierarchies by obviating the need for full industrial mobilization for industrial era warfare, helping to account for the absence of the grim 'garrison state' demise of democracy.[51]

Moving from diagnosis to remedy, the first concept is strategic neutralization, which is the notion that states, when faced with a master asset with highly distinctive capabilities, can achieve security by collectively containing or neutralizing this asset. This notion animates the first and in many ways still most significant proposal for nonhierarchical world nuclear governance, the Baruch Plan. Offered by the United States to the United Nations Atomic Energy Commission in 1946, the Plan was subject to several years of public negotiation before falling victim to rising Cold War tensions.[52] The politics of the proposal have been extensively studied by diplomatic historians, but international theorists have largely ignored it. The proposal evolved in important details, but its central idea was that all nuclear activities would be placed into the hands of an Atomic Development Authority (ADA) controlled by representatives of the major powers and run along the lines of the Tennessee Valley Authority as a public corporation. The ADA would control either directly or indirectly through licensing and inspection all nuclear mining, materials, research, development, and utilization. The ADA was to undertake an extensive research and development effort, including on nuclear weapons.[53] The ADA would be equipped with broad inspection authority, and it was assumed that the mingling of scientific personnel would add to the difficulty of undetected diversion or violation by any state. In the event of a violation, the ADA would *not have enforcement capabilities*, and states would be able to withdraw and pursue unilateral measures. Another feature of the plan, added by Baruch, was that ADA facilities be so situated and configured that no signatory state would be disadvantaged if the arrangement collapsed.

Recessed deterrence (also known as 'weaponless deterrence' or 'virtual arsenals') refers to an arrangement in which deterrence continues without nuclear weapons through the ability to re-create nuclear weapons.[54] This ability is inescapable given the knowledge of modern science and the natural existence of fissile material. This idea has been most associated with Jonathan Schell, whose powerful evocation of the perils of nuclear destruction contributed to popular concern about Reagan nuclear policies in the early 1980s.[55] The heart of Schell's proposal is that states eliminate all nuclear weapons, but also create a "smooth and assured path back to nuclear armament." Acknowledging many technical complexities, Schell argues that the "best way of providing such a path" would be to "establish controls on fissionable materials," possibly "ban nuclear reactors in general," or place them "under the control of an international body."[56] In order to insure that rearmament capability would be secure if one state secretly violated the agreement, antimissile defenses, ineffective against a large attack but effective against a small clandestine arsenal, could also be constructed. The agreement would not be enforced by a "world police force or other organ of a global state," but rather by "every state's knowledge that a breakdown in the agreement would be to no one's advantage" and the threat of "returning the world to something like the balance of terror." This arrangement would be a "logical, evolutionary outgrowth of present-day deterrence," but with "less extreme risk attached."[57] The "modest but invaluable" advantage of such an arrangement would be a "lengthening of the world's nuclear fuse," from the current "seven minutes to weeks or months." In this situation, nuclear war "could begin only as the result of long premeditation and long preparation," thus eliminating the dangers of miscalculation, panic, and accident, producing a "revolution in stability."[58]

Fourth and finally, concurrent authority refers to a republican 'check and balance' authority arrangement made possible by a recessed deterrent. In a concurrent arrangement two or more individuals or corporate entities must both concur to authorize nuclear use, in contrast to highly centralized and rapid-response hierarchies, where nuclear use authority must be vested in the hands of one individual. By employing a form of separation of power, concurrency achieves a republican restraint on power. Concurrency proposals are the political 'software' to complement the recessed deterrent 'hardware' agenda. Concurrency exploits the possibilities created by 'lengthening the fuse' to change nuclear authority structures. An internal version of nuclear concurrency thinking is found in the American debate over the constitutionality of presidential 'first use' of nuclear weapons.[59] An international version of nuclear concurrency was advanced by the Canadian defense analyst Leonard Beaton, who proposed an evolutionary 'reform of power' to be achieved by having all states configure their forces in such a way that time-consuming procedures would be required to launch weapons, and then vesting part of each launch code in an international security agency, thus requiring concurrent authorization for use.[60] In contrast to the existing United Nations security system bound by the great power veto, this approach extends a veto power over nuclear states, completely inverting the world federalist agenda to eliminate the veto and arm the organization.

Taken together, these six scattered and inchoate ideas at the outer edges of conventional arms control thinking can be seen as comprising a distinctive federal-republican contextual-materialist answer to the nuclear political question. Overall, federal-republican nuclear one worldism is substantially different from classical nuclear one worldism in both its diagnosis and remedy. Classical one worldism assumed that nuclear weapons had shifted the scale of state formation processes. In contrast, the modified diagnosis is that nuclear weapons, combined with the general increase and diffusion of violence capability, have greatly reduced the problem of interstate aggression, while creating a new threat of general annihilation. Classical nuclear one world theorists tended to assume that a nuclear-armed anarchy would be highly insecure and did not seriously explore deterrence, while the modified version specifies that the probable failure points for nuclear deterrence stem from excessive concentrations of authority. Classical theorists grappled unconvincingly with the problem of hierarchy in possible world states, while the modified version holds that nuclear-armed states in anarchy are driven toward internal despotic and totalitarian remedies.

The classical and modified remedies are even more divergent than their diagnoses. Classical nuclear one worlders proposed to solve the security crisis of the state system by creating an omnistate in which nuclear capability was to be *concentrated* and then *employed* to maintain peace between the disarmed or dismantled states. In contrast, the modified approach envisions an arrangement in which the territorial state system is not replaced, but rather is complemented with a nuclear containment and restraint system. In this image of adjustment, nuclear capability is separated from state control and paralyzed. The classical remedies are essentially the application of prenuclear images of a world state to the nuclear problem, while the modified remedies are an extrapolation from the theory and practice of nuclear era arms control. The classical diagnosis saw states as perilously vulnerable in anarchy and the classical remedy saw the states as obstacles and wanted to weaken them. In contrast the modified diagnosis identifies acute security problems arising from the interplay of external anarchy and internal hierarchy, and its remedy aims to reconfigure states with mutual restraints, both internally and externally.

The Shadow of 9/11 and WMD Terrorism

The five-sided debate on the nuclear-political question is very much bound by the realities and assumptions of the Cold War. During the 1990s the intellectual ascendancy of the optimistic deterrence statist view produced widespread complacency about nuclear issues, amplified by the unexpected (and unexpectedly peaceful) end of the Cold War and the collapse of the Soviet Union, and the completion of several landmark arms control and disarmament treaties. Augmented by a triumphalist 'end of history' narrative centered on the political economic superiority of liberal capitalist democracy, the 1990s was the first decade since the 1920s in which major war or its imminent outbreak did not dominate world security politics.

This widespread sense of security and complacency came crashing down on September 11, 2001. Killing over three thousand people and destroying $20 billion in infrastructure, these attacks, coupled with mailings of small quantities of highly lethal anthrax biological weapons to a handful of public figures, deeply traumatized the American people, much of world opinion, and the American national security establishment. As shocking as these attacks were, they served even more profoundly as a warning that small groups of malevolent nonstate actors (MANGOs) the size of criminal gangs had the intent and were seeking the means to launch far more devastating attacks with nuclear or biological weapons.[61] The threat of terrorist attack with weapons of mass destruction had long been discussed by security analysts, but the shadow of 9/11 suddenly transformed these speculative scenarios into primary security threats.[62] In the wake of these developments, the decade between the fall of the Berlin Wall and the fall of the Twin Towers now appears to be a halcyon interregnum between the end of the Cold War and the beginning of the era of terrorism and counterterrorism.

Backed by virtually unlimited American public support and the substantial support from both traditional allies and previous great power rivals, the Bush Administration quickly set upon the most far-reaching transformation of American national security policy since the beginning of the Cold War and launched an essentially open-ended 'global war on terrorism.' On the foreign policy front, the Bush Administration, despite its unilateralist predilections, embarked upon a wide range of multilateral efforts with other governments to monitor and interdict potential terrorists. It also announced a far-reaching postdeterrence doctrine of preemptive attack and preventive war against potential threats, with far-reaching implications for state sovereignty and international law.[63] On the domestic front, the administration, despite its ideological antipathy to large government, set in motion the creation of a giant new Department of Homeland Security, and embarked upon unprecedented surveillance programs with troubling implications for civil liberties.[64] In many of the conflict-riven and illiberal polities at the periphery of the international system, the liberty fallout from the war on terrorism also promises to be severe, as repressive states gain new motives and new support for further repression.

As substantial and far-reaching as these efforts are, there is no guarantee that they will forestall an even more devastating attack upon a major city. In a world awash in the materials and knowledge to fashion weapons of mass destruction, and rife with conflicts and grievances increasingly focused upon the United States, the vastness of American power cannot fully guarantee American security. The relative power of the United States and its allies is vastly greater than that of their shadowy adversaries, but MANGOs have or could plausibly acquire the ability to wreak high absolute levels of damage. Indeed, the very vastness of American power, to the extent it generates grievances and serves as the guarantor of repressive states against which grievances fester, may actually motivate more of the relatively powerless to severely damage American security.

A full treatment of this complex and unfolding topic is beyond the scope of this investigation, but a brief outline of its implications in terms of the two problematiques of republican security theory suggests that the main thrust of modified nuclear one worldism has been greatly strengthened. In broad terms, the prospect of MANGOs equipped with weapons of mass destruction undermines deterrence because retaliation is largely infeasible. To the extent that deterrence was a way to reconcile the anarchic state system with intense violence interdependence, and thus push aside the more radical diagnosis of nuclear one worldism, the new threat reverses the balance of argument, returning the nuclear-political debate to its beginnings.

This threat also casts the number of nuclear states and the quantity of nuclear material in their possession in an ominous new light. Because such small quantities of fissile material are sufficient to make a nuclear explosive device, any leakage of this material from any state's nuclear complex must be viewed as a major threat by all states.[65] The prospects for comprehensive interdiction by any state, particularly capitalist states enmeshed in the global transportation networks, are limited by the sheer volume of transborder flows and the sheer smallness of a nuclear device.[66] Progressively leaving interstate anarchy by establishing a comprehensive global nuclear materials control system takes on the character of a security imperative, however many difficulties stand in its way.[67]

Absent the ability to comprehensively shrink and totally contain all nuclear material everywhere, even the most Liberal governments will inevitably be drawn to impose progressively greater restrictions on individuals and groups and to exploit the growing array of monitoring and surveillance technologies produced by the rapid advance of computing and other information technologies. In some rough proportion to the extent of nuclear leakage, there will be strong tendencies to expand the previously sectoral totalitarian order of the nuclear archipelago to civil society. If, as many experts believe, it is a matter of 'not whether but when' more devastating attacks occur, and if this 'terror war' is to last decades, the prospects for political liberty appear bleak.[68] These ominous anarchy-hierarchy trade-offs posed by the mix of weapons of mass destruction and MANGOs may be even more severe in the long term with regard to biological weapons.[69]

These preliminary evaluations of the implications of the newest phase of the nuclear revolution suggest that the security question increasingly hinges on a trade-off between the extent of comprehensive nuclear materials control and the extent of the penetration of domestic hierarchy. If global nuclear material controls are weak, states will be compelled to increasingly penetrate civil society with controls. If global nuclear material containment is strong, then Liberal states will be able to stay Liberal. This reading of the security choices produced by the emergent material context also suggests that the underlying assumption of the global era international republican security project (recall figure 6.5) has moved from the anticipated to the fully actual. The midcentury specter of the 'garrison state' was in part avoided due to the ability of nuclear weapons to substitute for permanent large-scale conventional mobilization, but this breathing space for domestic liberty now appears to be closing, leaving in its wake a potentially even more draconian trade-off. To an unprecedented extent, the preservation of domestic liberty comes to hinge upon the success in abridging international anarchy. Upon the success of the global arms control agenda increasingly hinge the prospects for the survival of political liberty.

Conceptualizing Federal-Republican World Nuclear Government

The prospects for world government have been profoundly haunted by the widespread view, well founded in the overall history of government, that governments tend to be hierarchical and repressive. Unlike previous governments, which could be escaped through emigration, or checked by other states, or ultimately overturned through revolt, a world government looms as a horrific totalitarian end of history. The notion that a world government would be hierarchical is also rooted in the image of the modern state as a monopolizer of all legitimate violence within its territorial domain. Applied to the world as a whole, this image suggests that it could be extremely difficult to restrain such a centralized monopoly in the event it could be assembled. It was on this problem of creating and then restraining a centralized violence monopoly that the classical nuclear one world program floundered.

By assembling the scattered ideas of recent modified nuclear one world thought and conceptualizing them in terms of the two problematiques of republican security theory, a different image has emerged. The specter of a hierarchical world government, while never to be fully discounted as a possibility, emerges as something of an illusion, because of the unlikelihood that states would ever surrender possession of nuclear weapons to a world authority and because of the general difficulty in conquering and controlling territories occupied by resisting populations. Not needing to centralize and monopolize violence capacity in order to address either outside or inside threats, and centripetally anchored by recessed deterrence and unconquerability, a federal-republican image of world government looks fundamentally different from either the starkly hierarchical or the federal state model. The stumbling blocks to a world hierarchy become building blocks for the federal-republican model.

This republican nuclear arrangement would be the last terrestrial step in the scale-up of negarchic structures that has repeatedly occurred in response to changes in violence interdependence. As in previous shifts in the scale of republican government, a world nuclear restraint order would be similar to previous republican unions in its ordering principle, but dissimilar in the arrangements of its parts due to the scale effect (recall figure 1.10) Unlike the governing arrangements of all previous republics, it could be completely lacking in the hierarchical admixtures that free polities have been compelled to adopt to navigate the treacherous realm of external anarchy, and could therefore approach pure negarchy. In broad outlines, such a republican nuclear union would realize Wells's anticipation that a world government would be unlike the governments of states in anarchy and would be a union composed of specialized organs with a highly technological domain of activity. Wells's vision of world government is, however, more comprehensive than the sectorially specific organs appropriate to realizing a nuclear security union, and his technocratic vision of postpolitical administration could easily evolve into an ideology for a mandarin class of planetary overseers.

Surprisingly, Calhoun may be the theorist who offers the best starting point for conceptualizing the principles and architectures of purely negarchical world government. Although his interpretation of the U.S. Constitution of 1787 was fundamentally flawed, and although his powerful defense of states' rights was ultimately conceived to protect the radically antiliberal institution of chattel slavery, he nevertheless provides the most developed theory of a union firmly anchored in a multiplicity of sovereigns. For any world government to be built firmly on negarchical principles, the clear starting point must be union as an expression of sovereignties rather than as their abridgment, and the organs of the union must be unambiguously circumscribed by a constitution of the negative.

The existing rudimentary world Constitution of the United Nations Charter and the existing rudimentary world government of the United Nations Organization provide a seriously compromised starting point for a union of nuclear restraint. On the one hand, the UN Charter and Organization provides states and peoples with a panoply of valuable services, and they embody a valuable thickening and modernizing of the institutions of the society of states into a community of states with obligations as well as rights. On the other hand, the shadow statelike configuration of the General Assembly as parliament, the Security Council as senate, the Secretary-General as president, and the specialized agencies as ministries or departments is more like a nascent or virtual federal democratic state than a union of mutual restraint. Overall, given the specter of a hierarchical world state, and the statelike architectures of the United Nations, the path to a nuclear union of restraint is around, not through, the United Nations.

Given the stakes involved and the fact that the image of world government is so thoroughly imagined as hierarchical, the first step toward a nuclear restraint union is to conduct a global constitutional conversation about first principles. The lines of argument developed here suggest that a world Constitution based on purely negarchical principles would begin and end with unambiguous statements of what was not being constituted or authorized by the union of the sovereign constituting parties. Its preamble should begin with an expression of the shared understandings that its primary purpose is to avoid world hierarchy as well as world anarchy. It should also specify clearly an irrevocable procedure for succession and explicitly stipulate that no organ of the union had authorization to possess or employ instruments of violent coercion. It would also specify that enforcement would take place only through the application of criminal law to individuals.

Of course, the reality of how governments, even constitutional ones, are created is rarely if ever so neat and principled. The main impetus to create a world government comes not from a desire to embody consensual principles of mutual restraint, but rather from the brute facts of rising interdependence in anarchy and the acute insecurity it produces. It is possible that the emergence of such an arrangement will be through incremental steps based on enlightened consensus. More likely, however, is the scenario of 'after the deluge, the covenant.' It took World War I to catalyze the formation of the League of Nations and World War II to do so for the United Nations. But the formation of these international organizations also presupposed a network of activists, theorists, and advocates, which has sadly atrophied over the decades of deterrence complacency.

All things considered, it may well be that the most likely outcome of the current and emergent constraints and opportunities is not a nuclear union of restraint, but rather the incremental extinction of political liberty. It is often said, perhaps accurately, that a frog, if dropped in a pot of very hot water will quickly leap to safety, but that a frog dropped in a pot of warm water which is gradually brought to a boil will allow itself to be cooked to death. Despite some occasional spasmodic twitches, the frog appears to be sleeping peacefully.

CONCLUSION

Who controls the past . . .
controls the future.
—George Orwell[1]

TRADITIONS AS CONSTELLATIONS AND MAPS

Despite the proliferation of advanced social science approaches in international theory, the grouping of arguments into competing traditions still delineates much of the map of international theorizing. In part, this stubborn traditional persistence reflects the fact that the major ideas of international theory were first formulated by political theorists. These ideas, whether relabeled or rediscovered, continue to constitute almost all of the quite limited set of major insights about security politics produced by Western political science. This traditional persistence also reflects the fact that arguments gain authority and plausibility from association with distinguished and antique genealogical lineages. Centered on enduring problematics and cast in long established theoretical vocabularies, traditions also provide a modicum of conceptual continuity and unity for an otherwise highly contested and fragmented intellectual enterprise. Traditions provide scholars with a rich reservoir of claims and concepts and an indispensable baseline against which to measure intellectual progress. Traditions also provide an invaluable basis for bridging the worlds of theory and practice by providing enduring and accessible narratives embodying simple and basic insights about the political world from which actors can draw for problem solving. As authoritative summations of long reflection, the narratives and arguments of traditions provide a set of powerful presumptions about what the world is basically like, what the future is likely to resemble, and what results actions will produce. In short, traditions are mental maps of where we have been, where we are, and where we are going.

In thinking about the role of traditions and about how this reconstruction of Western structural-material republican security theory might be of value, the metaphors of constellations and maps are useful. Traditions are composed of distant luminaries, great intellectual figures of the past whose works are perennially burning lights that can be observed but never changed. Acts of reading and interpreting assemble illuminating texts into various constellations by 'connecting the dots' into a simple pictorial constellation. Often these connections can seem arbitrary, and they can be

redrawn. Through rereadings and reinterpretations subsequent generations sometimes find it useful and necessary to connect different points
into different constellations. These redrawings are undertaken as positions and vantage points move, and as shifting clouds of historical meaning make some distant points of light dimmer and others brighter. We
draw these pictures both to make our world more intelligible and, like
mariners at sea or shepherds in the wilderness, to help tell us where we
are and how we might travel safely to where we want to be.

Like constellations, maps are practical and situational, telling important inescapable brute facts about where we are. Mapping, the encod-
ing in symbols of positions in space, is irreducibly about the natural-material contextual world, and much of the practical value of Western
structural-materialist republican security derives from how it maps the
practical human material context. The major epochs of this theoretical
mapping have been responses to technological alterations in nature as it
presents itself for human practices. Successive waves of technological
change have progressively widened the scope of consequential interactions. With each such expansion in the scope of the political, and especially the security political, Western theorists have had to rescale and reor-
ient their application of enduring basic concerns and needs, to do again
what had been done before, but in a different place.

This reconstruction of our theoretical past is intended, like its predecessors, to be practically useful in servicing present and future needs. It has
sought a tradition of theorizing, a set of arguments and a conceptual vocabulary, useful for grappling with the paramount practical and theoretical development of this time, intensifying globalization (particularly concerning security) and the Liberal ascent. By digging deep into the silted
foundations of our intellectual house, this reconstruction has sought to
uncover sturdier foundations for building higher.

The Main Axis of Western Structural-Materialist Security Theory

Unfortunately, the main line of Western theorizing about the relations
among security-from-violence, types of government, and material contexts has been seriously misread by mainstream and particularly Realist-
centered international theory. This reading, an artifact of the middle years
of the twentieth century, severely limits an appropriate understanding of
security globalization and the Liberal ascent. An alternative reading has
recovered a partially lost and partially fragmented line of thinking centered around republicanism and natural-materialist 'geopolitics.' This tradition of structural-materialist security theory emerged in the ancient and

modern European Enlightenments. Its main successors, Realism and Liberalism, are incomplete fragments of it.

In simple terms, the main axis of intellectual development in Western structural-materialist security theory is republican security theory. It has sought to understand the interplay between material interdependence, security-from-violence, and anarchical, hierarchical, and republican arrangements of political authority. It is composed of two problematiques, the anarchy-interdependence and the hierarchy-restraint. The most essential claim of the anarchy-interdependence problematique is that anarchy is security intolerable in situations with intense levels of violence interdependence. The interaction of geography and technology shapes the level of violence interdependence, which has varied across both space and time in intelligible patterns. The main claim of the hierarchy-restraint problematique is that the extremes of both hierarchy and anarchy are intrinsically security intolerable due to the absence of restraint. Republican forms essentially entail the simultaneous negation of both anarchy and hierarchy, and republics and republican unions have evolved over time to encompass larger spaces. Achieving security in a world of leaping violence possibilities requires changes in the scope of socially constructed practices and structures of restraint. As power potentials bound upward, security comes from new configurations of power bounding.

If the two-hundred-year-old categories of Realism and Liberalism are no longer projected onto the original republican formulations of Western structural-materialist security theory, it becomes clear that this tradition was doing in the past precisely what needs to be done in the present and future, namely, conceptualizing extensions in the scale of republican government in response to changes in material contexts. For contemporary international theory, this reconstructed argument diminishes the appeal of Realism, while expanding, deepening, and recentering international Liberalism, thus pointing toward a unified and expanded structural-material security theory.

Before and After Realism

This reconstruction demonstrates that the current hegemony of Realism, particularly regarding security, is unwarranted. Contemporary Realism is many-sided, but some of its most powerful ideas, about anarchy, balance of power, and international society, were first formulated by republican security theorists. Realism as a recently constructed tradition has benefited heavily from its republican precursors in a variety of unacknowledged ways. Realism claims to be the most structural and materialist approach to international theory. In reality, Realism is deponent or incomplete because it has neglected or rejected important material-contextual and political-structural parts of republican security theory. These important theoretical gaps in Realism limit its ability to apprehend both security globalization and the Liberal ascent.

First and most importantly, Realism has largely dropped or truncated violence interdependence, the single most important material-contextual variable in republican security theory. In contrast to the immense Realist attention to the republican idea of the 'balance' of material power as a factor in security politics, Realists have neglected the even more pivotal material-contextual variable of violence interdependence, except in circumscribed ways. This variable, which has appeared in numerous conceptual languages, sits at the center of the anarchy-inderdependence problematique. It provides the basis for distinguishing between the two anarchies, between the first anarchy marked by intense violence interdependence and the second anarchy marked by lesser degrees of violence interdependence.

When this pivotal piece of the anarchy-interdependence problematique is recovered, Realism's catechism of vital practical insights is amended. As Realists have long insisted, the security perils of a state-of-nature anarchy are always lurking as a possibility that can never be eradicated. No political order, however well established and imposing, is ever more than a few steps from falling back into perilous disorder. To this vital and timeless insight can now be added an equally vital insight, which is sometimes very timely, about historical change in material contexts. State systems, no matter how long established, well balanced, or moderated by societal elements, can be, have been, and may again be thrown back into a first anarchy as a result of changes in technology that produce situations of intense violence interaction capacity over greatly larger spaces. The security viability of both the civil state and a second anarchy compatible with the survival of the civil state are shaped decisively by features of nature as revealed through technology. Therefore the security viability of such arrangements remains in potential jeopardy as long as nature continues to be tortured by scientific and technological knowledge seekers in order to reveal new violence potentials.

The second major narrowing that has made contemporary Realism deficient as an incomplete security theory stems from the Realist rejection of much of the hierarchy-restraint problematique. The Realist image of state systems as antihierarchical arrangements, an unacknowledged legacy of Enlightenment republican international theory, is the only part of the second problematique that has persisted in Realism. Realists seem strongly committed to a dyadic-spectrum model of political structure that encompasses only anarchy, hierarchy, and gradations between them. This model entails a bold rejection of the proposition that republics and republican unions are simultaneously neither hierarchies nor anarchies, but rather are the simultaneous negations of both anarchy and hierarchy. When all nonanarchical arrangements are viewed as hierarchical, the internal security-from-violence difference between modern liberal democracies, such as the United States, and modern totalitarian states, such as the Soviet Union, simply vanishes from the domain of security theory and practice. This Realist narrowing effectively marginalizes hierarchy as a threat to security, and renders invisible the long painful progress of republican polities in solving this problem. By reincorporating negarchy as a third ordering principle into a triad-triangular conceptualization of political structure, the project of structural-materialist theorizing can proceed with a better and more complete typology of political structures.

Republican First Liberal Security Theory and Liberal International Theory

This reconstruction also sheds new light on the origins and limits of contemporary Liberal international theory. It sets forth a view of Liberalism's main predecessor as the locus for a much more powerful Liberal international approach. As a challenger to Realism, Liberalism has lacked a sufficiently compelling approach to security, tended toward idealism over contextual materialism, and been more concerned with process and norms than political structures. Republican security theory as first Liberalism is primarily focused on the security-from-violence problem because avoidance of the ultimate individual evil of violent death is the first and foremost negative freedom that power restraining structures must preserve. First Liberal republican security theory advances an understanding of the security problem that is significantly superior to Realism because it is more complete. It addresses the full insecurity quadrangle of revolution, tyranny, war, and empire, and it clearly registers that the statist solution to security threats is itself a potential threat. It also contains a robustly sophisticated line of arguments about material-contextual differences across space and changes across time and their interplay with political structures.

Republican security theory is greatly older than Liberal international theory and focused on much more elemental problems. The tradition of republican security theory begins in classical antiquity, not the modern Enlightenment, and its Enlightenment culminations are in Montesquieu and the American founding, not Kant. Three of the most powerful ideas in contemporary international Liberalism, democratic peace, commercial peace, and international unions, are the legacies of Enlightenment republican security theory. Early republican security practice and theory is focused on eking out physical security in harshly precarious contexts and is largely pessimistic. In the currently dominant formulation of the neoclassical Liberal tradition, Enlightenment theorists posit a world where commerce is extensive and democratic republics are numerous enough to populate state systems, and then make optimistic predictions about their potential to pacify interstate relations. In contrast, early republican security theorists begin at the beginning, with a much more realistic state-of-nature in which republican polities are rare, precarious, and subject to debilitating internal maladies, and then draw pessimistic prognoses for republics. They seek to explain why republics are rare and precarious and to identify the exceptional circumstances that underpin their tenuous viability.

The naturalist phase of republican security theory was primarily focused on the problem of extent, of breaking the size barriers that seemed to condemn republics to a precarious marginality in security politics. The experience of the Roman Republic's successful expansion but loss of political liberty defined the problem early modern republicans sought to solve. The Enlightenment culmination of this theoretical and practical project was the American founding, which is almost invisible in contemporary Liberal international theory. The innovation of federal union permitted republics to attain the size and thus security previously only available to despotic empires, while at the same time preserving internal political liberty, popular sovereignty, and limited government. In the wake of this innovation, the tenor of republican thought shifts from pessimism to conditional optimism.

This scale-up of republican political association improved the fortunes of political liberty in ways not anticipated at the time of the American founding. As the industrial revolution reduced the isolating value of oceanic separation from the European great powers, it also facilitated the erection of imperial hierarchies of unprecedented power. Had it not been for the ability of the United States to protect smaller liberal democracies and prevail in the total world conflicts of the twentieth century, it is doubtful that republican government would exist at the close of the twentieth century. Security through federal union, not peace among democracies, has been the most important security fact for free polities over the last two centuries.

Republican security theory is closer in its concerns and tenor to traditional Realism than to the postsecurity agendas and relentless optimism of late modern Liberalism. Republican security theory is the foundational, and all-too-readily forgotten, part of the more general tradition of international Liberalism that deals directly with the concerns of Realism, but does so without succumbing to the Realist embrace of a tragic worldview. Security problems are real and difficult to solve, but they sometimes can be effectively mastered with the appropriate set of political practices and structures. Optimism can be warranted, so long as optimism does not blind us to inescapably real problems that must be confronted.

Rethinking security in republican theory also casts into a new light the 'republican revival' that has occurred in political theory and history over the last several decades. This large and sophisticated movement has largely respected, if not reinforced, the inside-outside distinction. It has paid far more attention to the rise of capitalism than the restraint of state and violent power as the crucial move in the shift from 'republicanism' to 'Liberalism' in the early-nineteenth century. When security practice is returned to the center of republicanism, the emergence of Liberalism is seen to depend upon the success of republican state restraint practice to carve out an expansive domain where life and property were safe from state appropriation. The revivalists have emphasized ideological context, but analysis of the interplay between geopolitical context and institutional practices suggests that some institutional forms now taken to be quintessentially republican may in fact be only adaptations to long-lasting, but eventually changed, material circumstances.

REPUBLICAN INTERNATIONALISM AND THE FREE WORLD PROSPECT

This reconstruction of republican security theory also has significant implications for understanding the origins and prospects of the 'free world.' The last two centuries have witnessed the rise of a complex global subsystem composed of the United States of America and its democratic allies to a position of historically unprecedented preeminence in world politics. Liberal democratic constitutional capitalist polities now constitute a zone of peace, freedom and prosperity far greater than any other in history. Breaking their city-state and then nations-state limits over the last two centuries, republics have expanded to continental size through federal union, and successfully competed in the total world conflicts of the twentieth century. The American-led 'free world' overcame the great turmoil and trauma of the middle years of the twentieth century, expanded with the liberal democratic reconstruction of Western Europe and parts of East Asia, and has constructed a thick array of international institutions. This complex of constitutional and federal states, confederal alliances, transnational relations, and international regimes is less like the prototypical Realist state system of hierarchies in anarchy and more like the domestic spheres of earlier republics.

By viewing the republican security project in its entirety and from its beginnings, contemporary Liberals can gain a much-needed sense of sobriety and caution. In contrast to the Realist emphasis on recurrence and pessimism, contemporary Liberalism has tended toward overoptimism, verging on triumphalism and complacency. It thus tends to forget the arduous circumstances and severe problems faced by early republican polities. In contrast to the casual 'end of history' triumphalism prevalent in contemporary Liberal thinking, the long and strenuous history of republics grappling with the security problem reminds us that the current ascendancy of free states was not the result of some inevitable historical process, but depended on fortuitous geographic restraints and was often a 'close run thing.'

A return to the heavily conditioned optimism of republican security theory also may provide useful guidance in managing the emerging issues of sustaining the pacific zone of peace after the Cold War. It is widely recognized that the transcontinental Liberal core of the international system now enjoys higher and more extensive levels of peace, prosperity, and freedom than any before in history, but there is a wide divergence of expectations about the sustainability of this situation. For some Liberals, this order seems so deeply rooted that nothing needs to be done, while for Realists it is so fragile and so the product of the fleeting historical post–World War circumstances that nothing can be done.[2] This combination of Liberal complacency and Realist pessimism produces a vacuum of serious policy initiatives to sustain and deepen the free world complex. A return to the problematics and approaches of republican theory can help fill this gap, providing both a set of strong, historically based reasons for thinking more needs to be done and a set of historically tested approaches for actually doing something.

This reconstruction also helps recover the republican security logic of American internationalism. The internationalist project of 'making the world safe for democracy' seeks to transform other units in the international system from hierarchies into republics and to transform the anarchic system through cobinding mutual restraints. The animating impulse of this project is neither humanitarian idealism nor enlightened imperialism. Rather it is a realism about the preconditions for the survival of constitutionally limited government. The essential assumption of the American internationalist project is that rising levels of interdependence, especially of violence, produced by the industrial and nuclear revolutions have made isolationism impossible and internationalism necessary for the survival of limited government. Appropriately configured authoritative international organs are not threats to republican sovereignty, but rather serve its security needs. As the material context has produced rising levels of interdependence, the United States and other free states face a shifting possibility frontier of trade-offs between the degree of domestic hierarchy and the extent to which the system is populated by republics and unions. With the continuing advance of the nuclear revolution and the emerging threat of nonstate actors equipped with weapons of mass destruction, this frontier of trade-offs now makes the pursuit of increasingly robust international nuclear control vital for the survival of constitutional liberal democracy.

Despite its accomplishments, Liberal internationalism, particularly in the United States, is in retreat. The increasingly swaggering American national security elites have largely adopted the worldview of Realism, with its contempt for international institutions and its obsession with sovereignty as Westphalian autonomy. American internationalist leadership has declined, and the diverse internationalist practical agenda, encompassing arms control, international law, peacekeeping and functional problem-solving regimes, is increasingly under assault. The parts of this agenda are not well connected to one another or to a larger conceptualization of world governance.

Remembering republican security theory casts this turn of events in a light both ironic and potentially tragic, while offering a narrative to recall the United States to its neglected and decaying heritage. American global diplomacy has a tragic dimension. Standing on federal and republican legacies, America ascendant has appropriated an increasingly Prussian strand of Realism, the Realism of the old European Wesphalian system, which the United States was founded to avoid. Having sought to abridge anarchy in inauspicious times and circumstances in order to save the republic from the centralizing and state-expanding consequences of existence in a competitive anarchic state system, the United States was instead forced to build a vast national security state apparatus to survive. This vastly capable American security Leviathan now impedes the strengthening of international cobinding mutual restraints just as the times and circumstances have become unprecedentedly auspicious. In the process of prevailing in the total conflicts of the twentieth century, America has become lost, increasingly transformed into a polity incapable of realizing the full fruits of its costly victory. Just as America finally is able to give its primary attention to realizing its conservative constitutional program of creating an international system no longer requiring a vast national security apparatus, this Leviathan has asserted its own hier-state interest in autonomy from all external institutionalized restraints. Just as American power has become broad and unchallenged, America has increasingly adopted a narrow and power-focused agenda.

The Global Village and (World) Government (Again)

Alongside the Liberal ascent, the other salient fact about the contemporary human situation is multisided and accelerating globalization. Its relation to world government can now be looked at in a new way. In this revised perspective of where we have been, where we are, and where our best-inherited insights say we must go, the image of the 'global village' is fully appropriate. The widespread presumption, particularly prevalent among Realists, is that this image is a utopian vision of naive reformers. In fact, this image, while imperfect in its connotations of stability, provides a good first-cut mapping of where we most fundamentally are. It is a simple summation of the single most important fact about the actual situation of the human species: intense interdependence and particularly intense violence interdependence is occurring on a global scale. Humanity is in something roughly resembling a global village situation, not because it wants to be and not because domesticated neighborly relations have been established among the members of this village. Rather, to acknowledge the existence of this global village situation is to recognize first and foremost that nature as it presents itself for human activity has changed profoundly. To acknowledge this as the primary political fact is simply to recognize that the natural-material context of all practical human security activity has been altered radically and irreversibly (barring some very deep and universal civilizational collapse) by modern science and technology. Viewed over five centuries, a relentless torrent of scientific knowledge and technological invention has altered the actual human place in diverse fundamental ways. Most simply, global technological interdependence has altered the scope of interaction and hence number of humans and human groups among whom restraint of violence is necessary for security. While it is possible to choose and alter how we and our neighbors interact, we cannot alter the fact that the neighborhood of all humans now encompasses the entire planet.

Various expressions of this insight have been a feature of the intellectual landscape for at least a century. They have commonly been accompanied by the assertion that some form of substantive world government is needed in this situation in order to realize basic security needs. Some versions of this argument have features in common with the long lineage of utopian and idealistic internationalism. Recent calls for global-scale government are, however, decisively different from their precursors. They are advanced as necessary to meet basic security (and other) needs, rather than as desirable in order to improve or ameliorate the human condition. Some versions of these arguments have been crude and wishful conclusions have been drawn from them. At the same time, a great many otherwise well-informed and theoretically sophisticated observers have been in various states of denial about this situation and particularly about the need for substantive world government.

What unites the discourse of both globalists and skeptics is a deep sense that this situation and the demands it seems to be making are in some major and conceptually profound manner novel, and that inherited traditions of theorizing about security and political order are ill suited or misfitted to this situation. For globalists and skeptics alike, the global village is bewilderingly novel and world government is breathtakingly unprecedented. Operating within this assumption of novelty, conservative skeptics insist that the establishment of effective world government flies in the face of millennia of inherited experience and theory, and so cannot be seriously entertained. Also operating within this presumption, global reformers are eager to jettison these inherited insights as impediments to doing what never has been done, but now must be done.

The reconstructed problematiques of republican security theory provide strong basis for reversing this presumption of novelty. They reveal inherited insights, lessons, and concepts that provide a rich repository of precedents and categories for both understanding the global village and establishing government appropriate to it. If the centerpiece of the Western tradition of security theorizing is a long argument about the interaction of varied and changing material-contexts, political structures of mutual restraint, and security-from-violence, then it is profoundly well suited to current situations and needs. Viewing the evolution of this tradition as it has grappled with variations and changes in the spatial scope of different degrees of violence interdependence reveals a rich heritage of having repeatedly done what we are again being compelled to do. If the most basic insight of this tradition, the core of the anarchy-interdependence problematique, is that situations of intense violence interdependence combined with anarchy are intrinsically incompatible with security-from-violence and that government is needed for security in such contexts, then the establishment of world government, of government scaled to the spatial scope of contemporary intense violence interdependence, is not in this most important sense novel. Rather it simply stipulates that we again must do what we have done so many times before.

Viewed from the perspective of this reconstructed tradition, what would be unprecedented is the persistence of anarchy with security in the global village situation, not the abridgment of anarchy. The actual presumption of the reconstructed tradition is that there will be either the establishment of world government or the experience of acute insecurity accompanying the continuation of anarchy. If this presumption is vindicated in the course of this century, this would not be something fundamentally novel, but simply the continuation of a long familiar pattern. Conversely, should world government not arise and anarchy persist without great insecurity, then we would indeed be in a radically novel situation, and thus in need of reversing this presumption and calling into question a deeply embedded insight of our inherited tradition.

This reversal of presumption about world government also casts the contemporary relevance of the mainstream of Western political thought in a more favorable light. A major line of contemporary theorizing has cast doubt on the value of Western political thought on the grounds that it presupposes the 'inside-outside' distinction, has been primarily about domestic rather than international order, and therefore is of limited value in thinking about 'international government.' However, in the global village situation this putative focus on the domestic now becomes of primary relevance, since conflict in the global village is de facto civil rather than international war.

One powerful reason for viewing the prospect of world government with skepticism, and indeed dread, is the possibility that such a government would be a repressive hierarchy from which there would be no escape. This specter of an end of history in global totalitarian government looms particularly large within the historical republican mindset due to the association between the large, the distant, and the despotic. Also, the conceptual world of Realism, with its assumption that all government is hierarchical, makes it hard to conceive of a world government that is not hierarchical. If, however, what is large and what is distant are more elastic than the naturalist framework of early republican security thought could imagine, then obsolete assumptions about material context inflate the totalitarian specter. If, however, an essential assumption of republican security theory is that negarchical structures of mutual restraint constitute a distinctive ordering principle with a long and distinguished record of practical success, then it is the narrow conceptual vocabulary of Realism, not the actual range of real possibilities, that darkens the shadow of hierarchical threat.

The global village situation is, however, novel in one important way. While the establishment of world government is in a basic sense quite precedented, and while the main tradition of security theorizing is well equipped conceptually for this eventuality and this project, the tasks of a world government are novel. Unlike virtually every previous government in human experience, a world government would be novel because, barring extensive colonization of outer space or alien visitation, it would not require a foreign policy. A world government would entail only the elimination of first anarchy, without the perennial problem of then coping with the often-strenuous demands of second anarchy within a larger external space.

This fact has great, and largely favorable, implications for the type of world government appropriate to the global village situation, and for the renewed relevance of republicanism. Coping with second anarchies has been deeply problematic for republics, and hierarchical arrangements have shown great practical security utility in second anarchies. Given, however, that a world government would not require a foreign policy and would not face the competitive pressures of an interstate anarchy, then it follows that an important set of pressures for hierarchical centralization would be absent. Therefore a world government, unlike all previous governments, could be a purely republican mutual restraint arrangement. In the global village situation, republican forms become more appropriate than ever before in historical experience. What is unprecedented is not the establishment of substantive world government, but the particular appropriateness of federal-republican arrangements in its establishment.

NOTES

INTRODUCTION
BEFORE REALISM AND LIBERALISM

1. Stanley Hoffmann, "A Retrospective on World Politics," in *Ideas and Ideals*, ed. Linda B. Miller and Michael Joseph Smith (Boulder, CO: Westview, 1993), p. 9.

2. "Capitalization is used to indicate that Realism is a specific school, and that it would be possible to be a realist—in the sense of examining reality as it really is—without subscribing to Realist assumptions." Robert O. Keohane, *International Institutions and State Power* (Boulder, CO: Westview, 1989), p. 68 n. 17.

3. For the recent spread of democracy, see Samuel P. Huntington, *The Third Wave: Democratization in the Late Twentieth Century* (Norman: University of Oklahoma Press, 1991).

4. Samuel P. Huntington, "The West Unique, Not Universal," *Foreign Affairs* 75, no. 6 (November–December 1996), p. 43. For a brief overview, see Daniel H. Deudney and G. John Ikenberry, "The Nature and Sources of Postwar Western Political Order," *Review of International Studies* 25, no. 4 (fall 1999), pp. 179–96.

5. For the 'dangerously naive' argument, see George Kennan, *American Diplomacy* (Chicago: University of Chicago Press, 1951). For the 'disingenuously self-serving' argument, see John J. Mearsheimer, *The Tragedy of Great Power Politics* (New York: Norton, 2001). As a result of the intellectual hegemony of "Continental Realism," United States foreign policy has a "hayseed image," producing "the fascinating paradox that the foreign policy traditions, practices, and institutions of the world's most successful country encounter a near-universal yet strangely incoherent contempt." Walter Russell Mead, *Special Providence: American Foreign Policy and How It Changed the World* (New York: Routledge, 2002), pp. 27 and 34.

6. Leading statements of Liberal triumphalism, emphasizing ideas and economics, are Francis Fukuyama, *The End of History and the Last Man* (New York: Free Press, 1992); and Michael Mandelbaum, *The Ideas That Conquered the World: Peace, Democracy, and Free Markets in the Twenty-First Century* (New York: Public Affairs, 2002). Among Realist skeptics are Fareed Zakana, *The Future of Freedom: Illiberal Democracy at Home and Abroad* (New York: Norton, 2003); and Jack Snyder, *From Voting to Violence: Democratization and Nationalist Conflict* (New York: Norton, 2000).

7. The major intellectual assault on the American Liberal international program of abridging anarchy has come not from Realists (who mainly believe that international organizations, regimes, and law do not have much real consequence), but rather from 'neoconservatives' (whose ideas and commitments are clearly contained within modern Liberalism), who believe such international arrangements do have real consequence and systematically oppose them because

they restrain American power and autonomy. For the most systematic assault on Liberal internationalism, based on a reading of early modern political thought sharply at odds with the one offered here, see Jeremy A. Rabkin, *Law without Nations? Why Constitutional Government Requires Sovereign States* (Princeton: Princeton University Press, 2004). For a trenchant critique, see Andrew Moravcsik, "Conservative Idealism and International Institutions," *Chicago Journal of International Law* 1, no. 2 (autumn 2000). For a spirited statement by an American neoconservative on the growing transatlantic divisions, see Robert Kagan, *Of Paradise and Power: America and Europe in the New World Order* (New York: Random House, 2003).

8. Arms control receives no mention in Robert Jervis, *The Meaning of the Nuclear Revolution: Statecraft and the Prospect of Armageddon* (Ithaca: Cornell University Press, 1989). For a full assault, see Colin S. Gray, *House of Cards: Why Arms Control Must Fail* (Ithaca: Cornell University Press, 1992).

9. Jonathan Haslam characterizes his recent history of modern Realist thought as "the study of power" in contrast to "the study of liberty" provided by Quentin Skinner in his magisterial history of early modern political thought. My aim here is to provide a study of liberty dealing with power. *No Virtue Like Necessity: Realist Thought in International Relations since Machiavelli* (New Haven: Yale University Press, 2002), pp. 1–2; and *The Foundations of Modern Political Thought* (Cambridge: Cambridge University Press, 1978).

10. For short, I shall refer to this set of arguments as 'structural-materialist security theory,' the project of understanding the relationships between different authoritative political arrangements (structure), different material contexts composed of geography and technology (material), and security-from-violence (security). Both material contexts and political arrangements are 'structural' in the broad social science sense of the term, but to avoid conflation of the material with the political, I shall speak of 'structure' as short for 'authoritative political arrangements' (or lack thereof).

11. In part, this may be a consequence of the fact that such regimes were much more hospitable to the free expression of ideas. For the pervasiveness of censorship and some of its consequences, see Leo Strauss, *Persecution and the Art of Writing* (Glencoe, IL: Free Press, 1952).

12. The fullest interpretation employing this scheme is Michael Doyle, *Ways of War and Peace* (New York: Norton, 1997). A recent survey of the field identified twelve different schema but ranked this one first in influence. Steve Smith, "The Self-Images of a Discipline: A Genealogy of International Relations Theory," in *International Relations Today*, ed. Ken Booth and Steve Smith (College Park: Pennsylvania State University Press, 1995), pp. 1–37.

13. An extensive survey of studies in international relations finds the overwhelming majority to be about Realist-inspired topics. John Vasquez, *The Power of Power Politics: A Critique* (Cambridge: Cambridge University Press, 1983), chap. 5.

14. For discussions of the range and varieties of Realist theorizing, see Jack Donnelly, *Realism and International Relations* (Cambridge: Cambridge University Press, 2000); Robert G. Gilpin, "The Richness of the Tradition of Political

Realism," *International Organization* 38, no. 2 (spring 1984), pp. 287–304; Doyle, *Ways of War and Peace*, pp. 41–201.

15. Examining the neglected literature of academic political science emerging from the first such university departments in the late-nineteenth and early-twentieth centuries, Brian C. Schmidt pushes this Realist dominance even further back. *The Political Discourse of Anarchy: A Disciplinary History of International Relations* (Albany: State University of New York Press, 1998).

16. Two particularly canonical statements of this narrative are: Stanley Hoffmann, "An American Social Science: International Relations," *Daedalus* 106, no. 3 (summer 1977); and Ole Waever, "The Sociology of a Not So International Discipline: American and European Developments in International Relations," *International Organization* 52, no. 4 (autumn 1998), pp. 687–727.

17. For a recent sampling of the range and sophistication of Realist readings of earlier figures, see Benjamin Frankel, ed., *Roots of Realism* (London: Frank Cass, 1996).

18. 'International' first appears in the writings of Jeremy Bentham. Hidemi Suganami, "A Note on the Origin of the Word 'International,' " *British Journal of International Studies* 4, no. 3 (1978), pp. 226–32. The German term 'realpolitik' first appears in 1853 in the publicist Ludwig von Rochau's polemics against Liberals who resisted Bismarck and Prussian leadership. Ludwig August von Rochau, *Grundsaetze der Realpolitik: Angewendet auf die staatlichen Zustaende Deutschlands* ([1853] Frankfurt: Ullstein, 1972). 'Liberal' as a political term first appeared in the wake of the French Revolution, probably in Spain, and quickly found wide employment. de Bertier de Sauvigny, "Liberalism, Nationalism and Socialism: The Birth of Three Words," *Review of Politics* 32, no. 2 (April 1970), pp. 147–66. Marxism, obviously, is named after a nineteenth-century figure.

19. R.B.J.Walker, *Inside/Outside: International Relations as Political Theory* (Cambridge: Cambridge University Press, 1993). However, such violence is an inevitable part of any appropriation of any complex figure as part of a tradition.

20. For Thucydides' politics and role in the war, see W. Robert Conner, *Thucydides* (Princeton: Princeton University Press, 1984); and Richard Ned Lebow, *The Tragic Vision of Politics: Ethics, Interests and Orders* (Cambridge: Cambridge University Press, 2003).

21. Machiavelli's republican allegiances are documented at length in virtually every major treatment. For a brilliant meditation on the irony of *The Prince*'s use in absolutist state-building, see Sebastian de Grazia, *Machiavelli in Hell* (Princeton: Princeton University Press, 1989). Mary Dietze goes so far as to argue that *The Prince* was filled with bad advice intended to weaken the Medici usurpers of the Florentine Republic. "Trapping the Prince: Machiavelli and the Politics of Deception," *American Political Science Review* 80, no. 3 (September 1986), pp. 777–99.

22. Within the broader tradition of political theory, Hobbes is now firmly established as an early and strong Liberal and was viewed with suspicion by contemporary monarchists. In his history of 'reason of state' Friedrich Meinecke viewed Hobbes as an odd and alien figure. *Machiavellism*, trans. Douglas Scott (New Haven: Yale University Press, 1957). As Doyle observes, "Hobbes is one of the first of the radical individualists, one of the first and most extreme of the true

moderns." *Ways of War and Peace*, p. 114. For the ways in which Hobbes has been increasingly interpreted as an 'early liberal,' see Charles D. Tarlton, "The Despotical Doctrine of Hobbes, Part I: The Liberalization of *Leviathan*," *History of Political Thought* 22, no. 4 (winter 2001), pp. 587–618. For Hobbes's early reception as nonliberal, see Charles D. Tarlton, "The Despotical Doctrine of Hobbes, Part II: Aspects of the Textual Substructure of Tyranny in *Leviathan*," *History of Political Thought* 23, no. 1 (spring 2002), pp. 61–89.

23. "From Hegel to Weber extends an unbroken etymological tradition in which the master concept of *Herrshaft* [domination] lends coherence to German social thought for a century." Nicholas Onuf and Frank Klink, "Anarchy, Authority, Rule," *International Studies Quarterly* 33, no. 2 (June 1989), pp.149–73, at 154.

24. Of these German figures, Waltz in *Man the State and War* makes one passing reference to Trietschke and Weber, and in *Theory of International Politics* makes one passing reference to Meinecke. Morgenthau makes passing reference once in *Politics among Nations* to Haushofer, Ratzel, and Weber. None of these figures are mentioned in Martin Wight's *State Systems;* Hedley Bull's *The Anarchical Society;* or Hinsley's *Power and the Pursuit of Peace.*

25. For extensive data and discussion, see Rudolph J. Rummel, *Statistics of Democide: Genocide and Mass Murder since 1900* (New Brunswick, NJ: Transaction, 1999); and R. J. Rummel, *Death by Government* (New Brunswick, NJ: Transaction, 1994).

26. These three polar ideas derived from republicanism are particularly prominent in contemporary Realism, but they are not by any means all the main ideas in Realism. They coexist, not always easily, with other distinctly antirepublican or nonrepublican ideas, most notably the *nation* as the primary political association, the *hierarchical state*, and *international hegemony* as a necessary source of international order.

27. Kenneth N. Waltz, *Theory of International Politics* (New York: Random House, 1979), p. 117.

28. Among the major works are Hedley Bull, *The Anarchical Society* (New York: Columbia University Press, 1977); Adam Watson, *The Evolution of International Society* (London: Routledge, 1992); Martin Wight, *Systems of States* (Leicester: Leicester University Press, 1977); Martin Wight, *Power Politics* (London: Holmes and Meier, 1978); Martin Wight, *International Theory: The Three Traditions* (London: Holmes and Meier, 1992); and Barry Buzan, *From International to World Society? English School Theory and the Social Structure of Globalization* (Cambridge: Cambridge University Press, 2004).

29. Kenneth Waltz, *Man, the State and War: A Theoretical Analysis* (New York: Columbia University Press, 1959).

30. Nicholas Greenwood Onuf, *The Repubican Legacy in International Thought* (Cambridge: Cambridge University Press, 1998), p. 15.

31. Strong forms of the behavioral revolution program are vigorously antitraditionalist, making a virtue of not reading earlier 'prescientific' theorists and aspiring to begin investigations de novo, with the result that many theorists making substantively Liberal arguments eschew the label altogether. For diverse statements in the so-called 'second great debate' of (post–World War II American)

international theory between the 'classical' and the 'scientific' approaches, see Klaus Knorr and James N. Rosenau, ed., *Contending Approaches to International Politics* (Princeton: Princeton University Press, 1969).

32. Symptomatic of this proliferation, there is no one generally agreed upon major work of contemporary social science Liberalism. The best general survey and assessment to date is Bruce Russett and John Oneal, *Triangulating Peace: Democracy, Interdependence, and International Organizations* (New York: Norton, 2001).

33. Haslam claims that "the classical liberal viewpoint" accords "the pre-eminence of ideas over material circumstance." *No Virtue Like Necessity*, p. 4. Robert Keohane observes, "In contrast to Marxism and realism [*sic*] Liberalism is not committed to ambitious and parsimonious structural theory." "International Liberalism Reconsidered," in *The Economic Limits to Modern Politics*, ed. John Dunn (Cambridge: Cambridge University Press, 1991), pp. 172–73. The result, as Onuf puts it, is that "weaker, more ambivalent liberal thinkers, like Keohane, offer additional hypotheses, which, if substantiated, enrich rather than replace realist theory." *Republican Legacies*, p. 229.

34. One of the most prominent social scientific liberal international arguments of the last two decades, the neoliberal institutionalism developed by Robert Keohane and his students, is cast as 'modified structural realism.' Alternatively, Andrew Moravscik claims that arguments about differences arising from unit-level variations are distinctively Liberal, a formulation that reassigns a large variety of arguments advanced by theorists who characterize themselves as 'neoclassical realists.' The logic of the view seems to be that Realism (as neorealism and offensive Realism) are purely system-level arguments, and therefore Liberalism, defined by what Realism is not, encompasses all unit-level arguments. "Taking Preferences Seriously: A Liberal Theory of International Politics," *International Organization* 51, no. 4 (autumn 1997), pp. 513–53.

35. Russett and Oneal characterize democracy, interdependence, and international organizations as together making a "virtuous circle" in contrast to the "vicious circle" of Realist practices. *Triangulating Peace*, pp. 15–42.

36. Jack Levy, "Domestic Politics and War," in *The Origin and Prevention of Major War*, ed. Robert I. Rotberg and Theodore Rabb (Cambridge: Cambridge University Press, 1989), p. 88. Similarly, Robert Jervis declares it to be "arguably the most important challenge to one of realism's central precepts." "Realism and the Study of World Politics," *International Organization*, 52, no. 4 (autumn 1998), p. 980. A partial listing of recent book-length treatments favorable to the democratic peace argument includes Rudolph J. Rummel, *Conflict and War* (Beverly Hills, CA: Sage, 1975); Bruce Russett, *Grasping the Democratic Peace* (Princeton: Princeton University Press, 1993); James Lee Ray, *Democracy and International Conflict: An Evaluation of the Democratic Peace Proposition* (Columbia: University of South Carolina Press, 1995); Rudolph J. Rummel, *Power Kills: Democracy as a Method of Nonviolence* (New Brunswick, NJ: Transaction, 1997); John M. Owen, *Liberal Peace, Liberal War: American Politics and International Security* (Ithaca: Cornell University Press, 1997); and Spencer R. Weart, *Never at War: Why Democracies Will Not Fight One Another* (New Haven: Yale University Press, 1998).

37. Thomas Paine's "prophecy of democratic peace preceded Kant" and "Paine's worldview included the most enduring strands of cosmopolitan thought in international relations: democratic governance, free trade, high degrees of interdependence, nonprovocative defense policies, a recognition that conquest cannot be profitable, and a universal respect for human rights." Thomas C. Walker, "The Forgotten Prophet: Tom Paine's Cosmopolitanism and International Relations," *International Studies Quarterly* 44, no. 1 (March 2000), pp. 51–72, at 55 and 52. Michael Howard claims that "virtually every liberal or socialist who has written about foreign policy since then has been able to provide little more than an echo of Paine's original philippic." *War and the Liberal Conscience* (New Brunswick, NJ: Rutgers University Press, 1986), p. 29. Michael Kistler points out that Paine's work was translated into German and was widely read aloud in public, suggesting that Kant may have known but not cited Paine's arguments. "German-American Liberalism and Thomas Paine," *American Quarterly* 14, no. 1 (summer 1962), pp. 81–91.

Regarding the origins of the idea of 'commercial peace' Pocock observes "[A] rhetoric of Dutch and English origin accepted progressively throughout western Europe affirmed that an age of conquest 'in due course to be identified with antiquity as well as recent modernity' was being superseded by an age of commerce, and that consequently universal monarchy had lost what historical justification [for producing peace] it might have possessed." *Barbarism and Religion*, vol. 1, *The Early Enlightenment of Edward Gibbon, 1737–1764* (Cambridge: Cambridge University Press, 1999), pp. 108–9.

38. The fullest statement is Doyle, *Ways of War and Peace*, pp. 205–311. In another major recent reading, David Boucher identifies three traditions—*empirical realism, universal moral order,* and *historical reason.* Within this schema, the arguments of republican security theory are situated mainly in the first and third. *Political Theories of International Relations* (Oxford: Oxford University Press, 1998).

39. For overviews, see Robert Shalhope, "Toward a Republican Synthesis: The Emergence of an Understanding of Republicanism in American Historiography," *William and Mary Quarterly* 29, no. 1 (January 1972), pp. 49–80; Robert Shalhope, "Republicanism and Early American Historiography," *William and Mary Quarterly,* 3rd series, 39, no. 2 (April 1982), pp. 334–56. Isaac Kramnick, "Republican Revisionism Revisited," *American Historical Review* 87, no. 3 (June 1982); pp. 71–104; and J.G.A. Pocock, "*The Machiavellian Moment* Revisited: A Study in History and Ideology," *Journal of Modern History* 53, no. 1 (March 1981).

40. The overall situation is that "the recent discussion of republicanism has proceeded almost entirely as if law and relations among national states, as states, hardly mattered." Onuf, *Republican Legacy,* p. 20.

41. The neglect of Montesquieu in international theory is oddly mirrored by the neglect of his contextual-materialist and international arguments by political theorists and intellectual historians. Note this omission in the most recent (and otherwise outstanding) ten essays in David W. Carrithurs, Michael A. Mosher, and Paul A. Rahe, eds., *Montesquieu's Science of Politics: Essays on "The Spirit of the Laws"* (Lanham, MD: Rowman and Littlefield, 2001).

42. A wide-ranging overview is provided in Fergus Millar, *The Roman Republic in Political Thought* (Hanover, NH: University Press of New England, 2002). Somewhat unexpectedly, the third volume of J.G.A. Pocock's work on Gibbon provides what is probably the most detailed treatment of ancient and early modern explanations for the fall of the republic. *Barbarism and Religion*, vol. 3, *The First Decline and Fall* (Cambridge: Cambridge University Press, 2003).

43. American federal republicanism is almost invisible in several major recent reconstructions of the history of international theory. Knutson's lengthy author and topic index contains no reference to Madison or the *Federalist*, and references to federalism are only to proposals for European federations. Torbjorn L. Knutsen, *A History of International Relations Theory* (Manchester: Manchester University Press, 1992). Boucher's index contains no reference to Madison, the *Federalist*, or the topic of federalism. *The Political Theory of International Relations*. Doyle cites Madison several times for minor points and quotes him once at length on the need for a distinct American identity to sustain American independence, a point neatly fitting in the Liberal nation-state model.

44. Dewey's vast corpus occupies a virtual cottage industry of scholars, but the material contextual argument at the center of his major political treatise, *The Public and Its Problems*, has been widely ignored.

45. Much confusion arises because both 'state' and 'republic' are used in a generic and synonymous sense, and in more specific and opposing senses. For a useful sorting, see Nicholas Onuf, "Civitas Maxima: Wolff, Vattel and the Fate of Republicanism," *American Journal of International Law* 86, no. 2 (April 1994), pp. 288–89.

46. John Adams "Defense of the Constitutions of the Governments of the United States," in Charles Francis Adams, ed., *The Works of John Adams* (Boston: Little, Brown, 1850–56), 10:378.

47. Ian Shapiro notes that of 170 countries existing in 1987, 113 contain the term 'republic' or one of its cognates in their formal names. "History as a Source of Republican Alternatives," in *Political Criticism* (Berkeley and Los Angeles: University of California Press, 1990), pp. 184 n. 17.

48. In one of the few recent attempts to develop a distinctively 'republican' position distinct from communitarianism and historical exegesis of earlier thinking, Philip Pettit emphasizes republican opposition to 'domination' as opposed to Liberal opposition to 'interference,' but does not discuss anarchy, within which domination and coercion occur unchecked, or any aspect of international security. *Republicanism: A Theory of Freedom and Government* (New York: Oxford University Press, 1997).

49. Pocock's magisterial work on the problem of change in early modern republicanism does not emphasize the security-from-violence, international, and material-geopolitical aspects of theory in this period and employs a conception of republicanism essentially civic humanist in character. J.G.A. Pocock, *The Machiavellian Moment: Florentine Political Theory and the Atlantic Republican Tradition* (Princeton: Princeton University Press, 1975).

50. The single most important and substantial treatment of the relationship between republicanism and international theory conceives of republicanism in

civic humanist and communitarian terms, and does not address security, structural or material arguments. Onuf, *Republican Legacy.*

51. Interpretations of democratic Athens and republican Rome through the eyes of critical natural law theorists, most notably Plato and Aristotle, have produced the widespread modern misperception that there was a *difference of kind* rather than a context-necessitated *degree of difference* between the public and virtue-centered republicanism of the ancients and the individual and interest-centered liberalism, between Constant's "ancient and modern liberty." For correctives, see Eric A. Havelock, *The Liberal Temper of Greek Politics* (New Haven: Yale University Press, 1957).

52. Montesquieu defined "political liberty" as "a tranquillity of mind arising from the opinion each person has of his own safety." Montesquieu, *Spirit of the Laws*, trans. Thomas Nugent ([1748] New York: Hafner, 1948), p. 15. Judith N. Sklar, "The Liberalism of Fear," in Nancy Rosenblum, ed., *Liberalism and the Moral Life* (Cambridge: Harvard University Press, 1989). Among recent treatments of early modern Liberalism these issues are extensively discussed in Stephen Holmes, *Passions and Constraint: On the Theory of Liberal Democracy* (Chicago: University of Chicago Press, 1995).

53. Notable exceptions are: Hobbes, who associated 'republicanism' with domestic factionalism; Locke, whose 'constitutionalism' and 'limited government' arguments deferred to the confusing British convention of seeing all monarchies as nonrepublican; Calhoun, whose basic project of limited federal or confederal government was seen as compatible with highly hierarchical member communities of slaveholders; and Hayek and Friedman, whose liberalism is largely antagonistic to democratic elements.

54. Thus the highly influential formulation by Isaiah Berlin of "negative freedom" and "positive freedom" (understood as the fulfillment or realization of some other human good through politics) has the effect of curiously obscuring this central line of first Liberal theory and practice. "Two Concepts of Liberty," in *Four Essays on Liberty* (Oxford: Oxford University Press, 1969). For an astute treatment of the philosophical difficulties entailed in relating political authority and discipline to political freedom, see Richard E. Flathman, *Freedom and Its Conditions: Discipline, Autonomy, and Resistance* (London: Routledge, 2003).

55. Against the general tide of 'republican revivalism' in which he has played a key role, Quentin Skinner argues that an important part of the republican tradition in both ancient Rome and Renaissance Italy was about how government consistent with a maximum of individual liberty could "in practice be established and kept in existence." It was thus concerned with citizen virtue as a means to protect liberty from its own excesses and to enable free political orders to cope with collective threats, rather than as a desirable end in its own right. "The Republican Ideal of Political Liberty," in *Machiavelli and Republicanism*, ed. G. Bock, Q. Skinner, and M. Viroli (Cambridge: Cambridge University Press, 1990), pp. 293–309, at 303; Quenton Skinner, *Liberty before Liberalism* (Cambridge: Cambridge University Press, 1998). A particularly lucid formulation of this position is provided in Maurizio Viroli, *Republicanism* (New York: Hill and Wang, 1999). Stephen Holmes, in one of the best recent treatments of early constitutional Liber-

alism observes, "Liberalism and republicanism are not opposites." *Passions and Constraints*, p. 5.

56. Among the pivotal works of Liberal political theory in the second half of the twentieth century, the topics of security-from-violence and international relations are almost completely absent in Jürgen Habermas, *Knowledge and Human Interests* (Boston: Beacon Press, 1971); and in John Rawls, *A Theory of Justice* (Cambridge: Harvard University Press, 1971). Robert Nozick, *Anarchy, State and Utopia* (New York: Basic Books, 1974) deals extensively with the perils of internal state predation in his defense of a minimalist state, but does not address the question of how such a political order might survive in a competitive interstate system.

57. From the beginning of Western political theory, the image of 'oriental despotism' (most notably the Persian Empire in antiquity, the Ottoman and Chinese Empires in the early modern era, and Russian-Soviet totalitarianism in the twentieth century) has served as the defining 'other' in the republican worldview. For a lively critique of the ethnocentricism of these images, see Patricia Springborg, *Western Republicanism and the Oriental Prince* (Austin: University of Texas Press, 1992). Compare also Plato's image of Atlantis in the *Timaeus* with Wittfogel's 'hydraulic society.' Karl Wittfogel, *Oriental Despotism: A Study in Total Power* (New Haven: Yale University Press, 1957). For detailed analyses of how parts of early modern republicanism were shaped by their opposition to hierarchical and imperial projects, see William J. Bouwsma, *Venice and the Defense of Republican Liberty: Renaissance Values in the Age of the Counter-Reformation* (Berkeley and Los Angeles: University of California Press, 1966); and Mark Hulliung, *Montesquieu and the Old Regime* (Berkeley and Los Angeles: University of California Press, 1976).

58. J.G.A. Pocock, "States, Republics, and Empire: The American Founding in early Modern Perspective," *Social Science Quarterly* 68, no. 4 (summer 1987), pp. 203–23.

59. As Gerald Stourzh observed, "Both the Wilsonian approach to foreign affairs and the reaction to it—the 'pure power politics' school of international relations—have obscured the great subtlety of an empirical science of international politics that flourished between Machiavelli and the French Revolution." *Alexander Hamilton and the Idea of Republican Government* (Stanford, CA: Stanford University Press, 1970), p. 135.

60. The term 'materialism' is also employed in discussions of ethics and politics to describe the view that bodily desires, wants for objects, and crasser interests either are or should be more important than spiritual or ideal values in the lives of human beings and human societies. Ontological materialism asserts that nothing exists except matter, the movement of matter, and the modifications and extensions of matter. Epistemological materialism is the view that sensations are the sole or main source of knowledge, and that the brain and the mind are identical.

61. Clarence Glacken, *Traces on the Rhodian Shore: Nature and Culture in Western Thought from Ancient Times to the End of the Eighteenth Century* (Berkeley and Los Angeles: University of California Press, 1967).

62. The term '*Geopolitik*' was coined by the Germanophile Swedish professor Rudolf Kjellén in 1911, to refer to the dimension of statecraft concerned with geography, but was quickly widely adopted to refer to material-political relation-

ships more generally. The now widespread tendency to use 'geopolitics' to refer to international relations generally seems to have originated with Henry Kissinger. L. W. Hepple, "The Revival of Geopolitics," *Political Geography Quarterly* 5, no. 4 (October 1986), pp. 621–36.

63. Such theories are not exclusively about political outcomes, but encompass sociological, economic, and cultural outcomes as well. Thus understood, physio-political claims are not solely about security and violence, but attempt to shed light on a wide variety of human arrangements.

64. Much of the apparent 'materialism' of contemporary theory is actually an assertion or assumption about actor preferences rather than about the influences of material contexts. Most prominently, various 'rational choice' theories, see actors rationally (i.e., self-interestedly) seeking to achieve 'material' gains in a context of penalties and incentives presented by their 'environment' composed of other actors and a material context. Constructivist theorists cast themselves as useful because they promise either to overthrow or balance this pervasive materialism. In the most sustained constructivist treatment Alexander Wendt characterizes the mainstreams of both contemporary Realist and Liberal theory as being dominated by a "materialist consensus." *Social Theory of International Politics* (Cambridge: Cambridge University Press, 2000), p. 92. However, as many critics have observed, this entails an exaggeration verging on misrepresentation. In particular, see Robert O. Keohane, "Ideas Part-Way Down," *Review of International Studies* 26, no. 1 (January 2000), pp. 125–30.

65. In contrast to their neglect in international theory, many of these arguments, often explicitly derived from Montesquieu, are reappearing and advancing in the burgeoning contemporary literature of 'global history,' or 'macrohistory.' For examples, see Eric Jones, *The European Miracle: Environments, Economics and Geopolitics in the History of Europe and Asia*, 2nd ed. (Cambridge: Cambridge University Press, 1987); and Jared Diamond, *Guns, Germs and Steel: The Fates of Human Societies* (New York: Norton, 1997). Over two decades ago Geoffrey Barraclough observed that "the dominant tendency [in world historical writing] is to adopt a broadly materialist position, in the sense that their central theme is man's conflict with his environment." *Main Trends in History* (New York: Holmes and Meier, 1978 and 1991), p. 158. An important and ambitious recent attempt to integrate world historical narratives with the construct of the anarchical state system is provided by Barry Buzan and Richard Little, *International Systems in World History: Remaking the Study of World History* (Oxford University Press, 2000).

66. For succinct overviews, see Ladis Kristof, "The Origin and Evolution of Geopolitics," *Journal of Conflict Resolution* 4, no. 1 (March 1960), pp. 15–51; Geoffrey Parker, *Western Geopolitical Thought in the Twentieth Century* (New York: St. Martin's, 1985); Haslam, "Geopolitics," in *No Virtue Like Necessity*, pp. 162–82. Neither Kristof, Parker, nor Haslam treat Liberal global materialist world order theories from this period.

67. The extent to which the putatively 'value neutral' enterprise of twentieth-century American social science has been shaped by political and ideological agendas is powerfully documented in Ido Oren, *Our Enemies and US: America's Rivalries and the Making of Political Science* (Ithaca: Cornell University Press,

2003). It remains the case that, as Derwent Whittlesley observed in 1944, "Most people look upon it [German Geopolitics] as a Frankenstein." "Haushofer: The Geopoliticans," in *Makers of Modern Strategy*, ed. Edward Meade Earle (Princeton: Princeton University Press, 1944), p. 410.

68. The complexities of characterizing a body of thought as a tradition are explored in Quentin Skinner, "Meaning and Understanding in the Hitory of Ideas," *History and Theory* 8 (1969), pp. 3–53; and Renée Jeffery, "Tradition as Invention: The 'Traditions Tradition' and the History of Ideas in International Relations," *Millennium* 34, no. 1 (2005), pp. 57–84. Eric Hobsbawn and Terence Ranger, ed. *The Invention of Tradition* (Cambridge: Cambridge University Press, 1983).

Chapter One
Republican Security Theory

1. Theodor W. Adorno, *Negative Dialectics*, trans. E. B. Ashton (New York: Continuum, 1973), p. 320.

2. With a few exceptions, such theories have largely disappeared from political science and particularly international relations but not from social science more generally, as evidenced by the continued vitality of sociobiology, physical anthropology, and biological psychology. All theories of politics entail assumptions about human nature, but vary in their explicitness, complexity, and plausibility. For recent treatments, see Roger Spegele, *Political Realism in International Relations* (Cambridge: Cambridge University Press, 1996); and Joshua S. Goldstein, *War and Gender: How Gender Shapes the War System and Vice Versa* (Cambridge: Cambridge University Press, 2001). Jack Donnelly provides an excellent overview of the role such arguments play in Realism. "Human Nature and State Motivation," in *Realism and International Relations*. Of particular note for its innovative integration of ancient and modern insights is Roger Masters, *The Nature of Politics* (New Haven: Yale University Press, 1989).

3. John Stuart Mill, *Utilitarianism,* ed. George Sher ([1834] Indianapolis, IN: Hackett, 1979), p. 53.

4. For powerful recent treatments, see Melvin Konner, *The Tangled Web: Biological Constraints on the Human Spirit* (New York: Harper and Row, 1982); and Mary Midgley, *Beast and Man: The Roots of Human Nature* (Ithaca: Cornell University Press, 1978).

5. For insightful recent treatments on fear in political theory, see Peter J. Ahrensdorf, "The Fear of Death and the Longing for Immortality: Hobbes and Thucydides on Human Nature and the Problem of Anarchy," *American Political Science Review* 94, no. 3 (September 2000), pp. 579–93; and Corey Rosen, *Fear: The History of a Political Idea* (Oxford: Oxford University Press, 2004).

6. Arguments attributing variations in human behavior to 'race' entail a biological naturalization of second nature and are intermingled with contextual material arguments in late-nineteenth- and early-twentieth-century thought, but entail a biological reductionism inconsistent with the approach developed here and in most of Western security theory.

7. Richard Tuck claims that Hobbes first employed the expression 'state-of-nature' but observes the frequent presence of the basic concept in ancient theorists. *The Rights of War and Peace: Political Thought and International Order from Grotius to Kant* (Oxford: Oxford University Press, 1999). Particularly good on the ancients is Arthur Lovejoy and George Boas, *Primitivism and Related Ideas in Antiquity* (Baltimore: Johns Hopkins University Press, 1935). For recent analyses of early modern uses, see Richard Tuck, *Natural Rights Theories: Their Origin and Development* (Cambridge: Cambridge University Press, 1979); Anthony Pagden, ed., *The Languages of Political Theory in Early-Modern Europe* (Cambridge: Cambridge University Press, 1987); and Asher Horowitz, *Rousseau, Nature and History* (Toronto: University of Toronto Press, 1992).

8. For more detailed treatment of the arguments of Hobbes and Rousseau, see "The Princess and the Pea: Nature and the State-of-Nature" in chapter 2.

9. Thomas Hobbes, *Leviathan*, pt. 1, chap. 13, ed. Michael Oakeshott (Oxford: Blackwell, 1960), p. 82.

10. For 'loss-of-strength gradient,' see Kenneth Boulding, *Conflict and Defense* (New York: Harper and Row, 1963); George Quester, *Offense and Defense in the International System* (New York: John Wiley, 1977); and Patrick O'Sullivan, *Geopolitics* (New York: St. Martin's Press, 1986). For 'offense-defense theory,' see Stephen van Evera, *Causes of War: Power and the Roots of Conflict* (Ithaca: Cornell University Press, 1999). For 'interaction capacity,' see Barry Buzan, Richard Little, and Charles Jones, *The Logic of Anarchy* (New York: Columbia University Press, 1993); and Buzan and Little, *International Systems in World History: Remaking the Study of International Relations* (Oxford: Oxford University Press, 2000). For 'violence interaction capacity,' see Daniel Deudney, "Regrounding Realism: Anarchy, Security and Changing Material Contexts," *Security Studies* 10, no. 1 (fall 2000), pp. 1–45.

11. For discussions of technology interacting with geography in industrial era theories, see Harold H. Sprout, "Geopolitical Hypotheses in Technological Perspective," *World Politics* 15, no. 2 (January 1963), pp. 187–212; and James Dougherty and Robert Pfaltzgraff, "Environmental Theories," in *Contending Theories of International Relations* (New York: Harper and Row, 1981), pp. 54–84.

12. For major surveys of technological development consistent with this periodization, see Bernard Brodie and Fawn M. Brodie, *From the Crossbow to the H-Bomb*, rev. ed. (Bloomington: Indiana University Press, 1973); Trevor N. Dupuy, *The Evolution of Weapons and Warfare* (New York: Hero Books, 1984); and Arnold Pacey, *Technology and World Civilization: A Thousand Year History* (Cambridge: MIT Press, 1990). For an account emphasizing nonlinear processes, see Manuel De Landa, *A Thousand Years of Nonlinear History* (New York: Zone Books, 1997).

13. Despite the later influence of Thucydides' account of Greek interstate war, Greek political theory and practice was much more concerned with the problem of avoiding stasis or internal violent discord. Peter T. Manicas, "War, Stasis, and Greek Political Thought," *Comparative Studies in Society and History* 24, no. 4 (October 1982), pp. 673–88.

14. While largely ignored by recent international theorists, these arguments, combined with analysis of numerous other contextual-material factors, most no-

tably climate, disease, and ecology, play a prominent role in major recent macro-historical analyses. For example, see Jones, *The European Miracle*; and Diamond, *Guns, Germs and Steel*.

15. In contrast to the widespread assumption in international theory that the modern European state system is prototypical, world historians commonly view it as anomalous. Robert Wesson, *State Systems* (New York: Free Press, 1978); William McNeill, *The Pursuit of Power: Technology, Armed Force, and Society since A.D. 1000* (Chicago: University of Chicago Press, 1982).

16. For recent discussions of fungibility and incommensurability of power assets, see David A. Baldwin, "Money and Power," *Journal of Politics* 33, no. 3 (August 1971), pp. 578–614; and "Interdependence and Power: A Conceptual Analysis," *International Organization*, 34, no. 3 (autumn 1980), pp. 495–504; and *Paradoxes of Power* (Oxford: Blackwell, 1989).

17. The term 'constitution' is used in political science to describe three quite distinct phenomena. First and most broadly, it refers to the basic pattern of order in a polity, regardless of type. Second, 'constitutionalism' is used to describe a system of power control and political orders in which the power of government has been effectively limited. Third, a Constitution (usually capitalized) refers to a written charter or set of primary laws that specify the main principles of governing a political order, regardless of its type. Within the large literature on republican constitutionalism, particularly strong synthetic treatments are Charles Howard McIlwain, *Constitutionalism Ancient and Modern* (Ithaca: Cornell University Press, 1940); and Scott Gordon, *Controlling the State: Constitutionalism from Ancient Athens to Today* (Cambridge: Harvard University Press, 1999).

18. John Locke, *Second Treatise on Government*, ed. Peter Laslett (Cambridge: Cambridge University Press, 1960), p. 405.

19. Of course, actual republics, particularly ancient and early modern ones, fell significantly short of realizing this ideal model in a variety of important ways. Marred by slavery and oppression of women, early republics contained a strata of roughly reciprocal restraints combined with hierarchical domination of other strata. Roughly paralleling their expansion in size, republics have gradually expanded reciprocal citizen rights to all their members, a process of great importance and complexity, but beyond the scope of this treatment.

20. Republics are now commonly viewed as one of many possible internal organizations of a state, but originally *stato* and *res publica* were sharp antitheticals. As the historian J. H. Hexter observes, "*lo stato* is not a matrix of values, a body politic: it is an instrument of exploitation, the instrument the prince uses to get what he wants." *The Vision of Politics on the Eve of the Reformation* (New York: Basic Books, 1973), pp. 171–72. For a particularly lucid formulation, see Vincent Ostrom, "Two Different Approaches to the Design of Public Order," in *The Political Theory of a Compound Republic*, 2nd ed. (Lincoln: University Press of Nebraska, 1987), pp. 1–30.

21. In speaking of governments as political structures, it is important to note that such political arrangements are not themselves in any sense natural or contextual-material entities. Political structures are socially created arrangements, and they exist alongside and in continuous interaction with 'ideational' factors such as knowledge, norms, and identities. The emergence and persistence of governments

NOTES TO CHAPTER ONE

depends upon sustained practices of particular sorts. Given this, republican theorists have devoted considerable energies to understanding which knowledges,
norms, communities, identities, and practices are compatible with particular political structures deemed necessary for security. This topic, although beyond the
scope of this treatment, is never cleanly separable from it, and therefore cannot
be altogether avoided. But what distinguishes the structural forms of republican
theory from nonstructural approaches is the view that these ideational factors are
not themselves independently sufficient sources of restraint on violence and that
authoritative political arrangements are, given human nature, necessary.

22. Max Weber, *Economy and Society*, 3 vols., ed. G. Roth and C. Wittich
(New York: Bedminster Press, 1968), p. 219. This exclusive focus on domination
is even more extensive when we are reminded that Weber's term *herrschaft*, widely
translated as "authority," actually means "lordship." Onuf and Klink, "Anarchy,
Authority, Rule," pp. 149–73.

23. Waltz, *Theory of International Politics*, pp. 88–89; and Avery Goldstein,
From Bandwagon to Balance-of-Power Politics (Stanford, CA.: Stanford University Press, 1991), pp. 29–30, 45–49. Waltz emphasizes that anarchy-hierarchy
mixes are widespread, a point ignored by many of his critics. For a useful sorting
of different anarchy-hierarchy mixtures, see David A. Lake, "Anarchy, Hierarchy
and the Variety of International Relations," *International Organization* 50, no. 1
(winter 1996), pp. 1–33. Also see Robert Lieshout, *Between Anarchy and Hierarchy* (Brookfield, VT: Brookfield Press, 1995).

24. In response to my earlier formulation of this concept, Barry Buzan and
Richard Little defend the Realist dyad-spectrum on the grounds that there is no
historical example of a pure negarchy, but the same is true for hierarchies and
anarchies. "Reconceptualizing Anarchy: Structural Realism Meets World History," *European Journal of International Relations* 2, no. 4 (December 1996), pp.
403–38. Regarding the proliferation of terminology for system-level arrangements, Murray Forsyth observes "a wide variety of names, of which confederacy,
confederation, union, Federal union, federal government, system of states, community, perpetual league, *republique federative*, *Staatenbund*, *Bund*, and *Eidge-
nossenchaft* have been the most prominent." *Unions of States: The Theory and
Practice of Confederation* (Leicester: Leicester University Press, 1981), p. 1. Parts
of the large literature on federalism address mutual restraint unions among republican states rather than the more common focus on devolutions within a state. Of
particular note are Daniel J. Elazar, *Exploring Federalism* (Tuscaloosa: University
of Alabama Press, 1987); and Leslie Friedman Goldstein, *Constituting Federal
Sovereignty* (Baltimore: Johns Hopkins University Press, 2001).

25. For rare recent treatments of unit-level balancing patterns, see Steven David's concept of 'omnibalancing' against both internal and external rivals. "Explaining Third World Alignment," *World Politics* 43, no. 2 (January 1991), pp.
233–56. Also see Helen Milner, "The Assumption of Anarchy in International
Relations Theory: A Critique," *Review of International Studies* 17, no. 1 (January
1991), pp. 67–85; and Nelson Kasfir, "Domestic Anarchy, Security Dilemmas, and
Violent Predation," in *When States Fail: Causes and Consequences*, ed. Robert I.
Rotberg (Princeton: Princeton University Press, 2004), pp. 53–76.

26. As Aristotle puts it, "the members of the class which possess arms must necessarily be appointed generals and police magistrates, and must thus hold, in the main, the highest offices." *Politics*, trans. and ed. Ernest Barker (London: Oxford University Press, 1946), bk. 2, viii, p. 70.

27. For an analysis of Plato's vision of the monopoly of violence in the hands of the elite, contrasted with Aristotle's support for wider arms possession as the basis for less oppressive regimes, see Stephen P. Halbrook, "Elementary Books of Public Right," in *That Every Man Be Armed* (Albuquerque: University of New Mexico Press, 1984).

28. Nicholas Onuf provides a useful treatment cutting across international and domestic domains. "Sovereignty: Outline of a Conceptual History," *Alternatives* 16, no. 4 (fall 1991), pp. 425–46. Stephen Krasner usefully distinguishes four different types or meanings of sovereignty, but does not include the notion of sovereign as a source of authority. *Sovereignty: Organized Hypocrisy* (Princeton: Princeton University Press, 1999).

29. For example, Hannah Arendt claims that "the great and, in the long run, perhaps the greatest American innovation in politics as such was the consistent abolition of sovereignty within the body politic of the republic, the insight that in the realm of human affairs sovereignty and tyranny are the same." *On Revolution* (New York: Viking, 1965), p. 152. Similarly, Sanford Lakoff claims the framers of the U.S. Constitution avoided "establishing any locus of sovereignty" and "sought to put it nowhere definitively." "Between Either/Or and More or Less: Sovereignty versus Autonomy under Federalism," *Publius* 24 (winter 1994), p. 70.

30. William Blackstone, *Commentaries on the Laws of England*, 4 vols., 1st edition (Oxford: Clarendon Press, 1765–69) 1:156–57. The usefulness of this concept of sovereignty does not entail a commitment to the view that all political orders have a sovereign, as Bodin and Blackstone claim. Jean Bodin went to considerable lengths to show that apparently mixed regimes actually had an ultimate source of authority, arguing that in the Roman Republic that *maiestatem* (usually rendered as "majesty") was *in populo* making the Roman Republic a democracy. *On Sovereignty*, ed. and trans. Julian H. Franklin ([1576] Cambridge: Cambridge University Press, 1992), p. 53.

31. For simplicity I here exclude 'aristocratic' (i.e., oligarchic) sovereignty, a form much analyzed by republican theorists. It was within such polities that important power restraint practices were developed to deal with factionalism and power abuse, measures that were preserved and strengthened as practical assertions of popular sovereignty were made.

32. Captured vividly in Louis XV of France's assertion: "Sovereign lies in me alone. The legislative power is mine unconditionally. The public order emanates from me, and I am its supreme guardian. My people is one with me." Cited in Russell Kirk, "Introduction," in James Monroe, *The People, the Sovereigns* (Cumberland, VA: James River Press, 1987), p. xi.

33. Alexander Hamilton, James Madison, and John Jay *The Federalist Papers*, ed. Clinton Rossiter (New York: New American Library, 1961), no. 46, p. 294.

34. In the modern era Rousseau provides the most complete and profound analysis of such political orders. In Rousseau's view representation and delegation had to be avoided at all costs, and since the people as a whole were envisioned as

sovereigns directly exercising political authority, the division of the people into various factions or interest groups had to be strenuously avoided through a variety of antiliberal measures. "Sovereignty cannot be represented for the same reason that it cannot be alienated." Jean-Jacques Rousseau, *The Social Contract* in *The Social Contract and Other Later Political Writings*, ed. and trans. Victor Gourevitch (Cambridge: Cambridge University Press, 1997), p. 114.

35. The reigning assumption about popular sovereignty in civic humanist and city-state republican theory was that anything that either introduced division among the people (particularly large, extended, and, therefore, diverse populations) and commerce (which would introduce socioeconomic class stratifications) or undermined virtue (most notably extensive private accumulation and consumption) were mortal enemies of republican government.

36. One of the few recent treatments on the topic concludes that size does not matter, but participatory, representative, and federal forms are all treated as "democracies," effectively assigning this previously core problematic to invisibility. Robert Dahl and Edward Tufte, *Size and Democracy* (Stanford, CA: Stanford University Press, 1973). For a recent exception containing extensive empirical information, see Rein Taagepera, "Expansion and Contraction Patterns of Large Polities: Context for Russia," *International Studies Quarterly*. 41, no. 3 (September 1997), pp. 473–504.

37. The physicist Milič Čapek refers to the absence of scale effects in modern thought as "the theme of Gulliver" "The 'Theme of Gulliver' and the Relativity of Magnitude," in *The Philosophical Impact of Modern Physics* (New York: Van Nostrand, 1961).

38. Galileo Galilei, *Dialogues Concerning Two New Sciences,* trans. H. Crew and A. DeDalvia (Chicago: University of Chicago Press, 1939), p. 230. One of the most important applications of scale effects is that the ratio between the volume and surface area of an object or body changes when the size of the object or body changes in size. For example, insects, whose cells exchange gases with the atmosphere (i.e., breathe) without the intermediation of a functionally differentiated breathing organ (i.e., a lung) are bound to remain small because if they were large the ratio of their volume to surface area would no longer permit direct respiration. Thus larger organisms must have specialized organs of respiration and thus exhibit qualitatively different organs and structures. Knut Schmidt-Nielsen, *Scaling: Why Is Animal Size So Important?* (Cambridge: Cambridge University Press, 1984); and Stephen Jay Gould, "Size and Shape," *Ever since Darwin: Reflections in Natural History* (New York: Norton, 1977). In economics, 'economies of scale in production,' refers to the fact that the relationship of inputs to output has a nonlinear relationship.

39. David Hume, "Of the Rise and Progress of the Arts and Sciences," in *Political Essays*, ed. Knud Haakonssen ([1752] Cambridge: Cambridge University Press, 1994); Montesquieu, *Spirit of Laws*.

40. Recent political science has developed a very sophisticated understanding of collective action: Mancur Olson, Jr., *The Logic of Collective Action: Public Goods and the Theory of Groups* (Cambridge: Harvard University Press, 1965); and Russell Hardin, *One for All: The Logic of Group Conflict* (Princeton: Princeton University Press, 1995).

41. For a more finely parsed list of foreign policy orientations, see Randall L. Schweller, *Deadly Imbalances: Tripolarity and Hitler's Strategy of World Conquest* (New York: Columbia University Press, 1998), pp. 65–91.

42. This proposition is clearly related to the recent 'democratic advantage' arguments which hold that democracies have a competitive advantage in interstate conflict because they are able to sustain greater levels of popular support, and thus mobilize more power. To the extent such a pattern exists, it increases the puzzle of why such regimes have been so rare and generally vulnerable. In combination with the greater size afforded by federal union, the democratic mobilization advantage helps explain the particular success of the United States over the last century. For analysis, see Dan Reiter and Allan C. Stamm, *Democracies at War* (Princeton: Princeton University Press, 2002).

43. For further analysis, see chapters 3, 4, and 8.

44. These arguments, explored at length in chapter 4, are nicely over viewed as central to the 'Anglo-American tradition' of international theorizing in the introductory essay "Political Theory and International Relations," by Arnold Wolfers and Laurence W. Martin, in *The Anglo-American Tradition in Foreign Affairs: Readings from Thomas More to Woodrow Wilson* (New Haven: Yale University Press, 1956), pp. ix–xxvii.

45. 'Alliances of restraint' (*pactum de trahendo*) were part of classic European diplomatic practice according to Paul Schroeder, "Alliances, 1815–1945: Weapons of Power and Tools of Management," in *Historical Dimensions of National Security*, ed. Klaus Knorr (Lawrence: University Press of Kansas, 1976). Borrowing from the language of international law ('binding agreements') European monetary union has been attributed by Joseph Greico to French efforts to "bind" Germany. "The Maastricht Treaty, Economic and Monetary Union and the Neo-Realist Research Programme," *Review of International Studies* 21, no. 1 (1995), pp. 21–40. Numerous authors have recently explored the ways in which the domestic structures of liberal democracies favor international institutional commitments. A good overview of the historical record is provided by Weart, "Leagues of Republics" in *Never At War.* For the role of this practice in the American construction of post–World War II international institutions, see G. John Ikenberry, *After Victory: Institutions, Strategic Restraint, and the Rebuilding of Order after Major Wars* (Princeton: Princeton University Press, 2001). For special capacities of democratic states to cobind, see Charles Lipson, *Reliable Partners: How Democracies Have Made a Separate Peace* (Princeton: Princeton University Press, 2003). Formulations about 'binding' fail to distinguish between asymmetrical binding, which constitutes hierarchical structures, and the reciprocal or 'cobinding,' which constitutes republics and state-unions, thus glossing over the most important of political distinctions.

46. This view of technology as a contextual factor, alongside geography shaping the security viability of political arrangements, entails an understanding of technology at odds with many contemporary approaches. Despite the prevalent rhetoric of 'technological determinism' most recent serious analysts of technology have emphasized its socially constructed character. For example, see Eugene Skolnokoff, *The Elusive Transformation: Science and Technology and the Evolution of International Politics* (Princeton: Princeton University Press, 1993); and Wiebe

E. Bijker, Thomas P. Hughes, and Trevor Pinch, eds., *The Social Construction of Technological Systems* (Cambridge: MIT Press, 1987). The older view gains plausibility by distinguishing between technology (knowledge of how to manipulate nature) and technics (tangible artifacts). Major technological inventions, such as nuclear weapons, rest upon technological discoveries of possibilities given by nature and revealed by science. As such they are similar to geographical discoveries, such as the (European) discovery of the 'New World.' While the timing and location of such discoveries is obviously shaped by a myriad of social factors, what is discovered (while subject to diverse interpretation) is not socially constructed, but is rather a mapping of natural possibilities. The cumulative growth of destructive technology can be conceived as altering the 'destruction possibility frontier' (analogous to the 'production possibility frontier' in neoclassical economics). Whether these destructive possibilities are realized as technics depends upon which configuration of socially constructed restraints (or lack thereof) are present. Thus, once nuclear fission has been discovered, we live in a nuclear material context whether or not any nuclear weapons (technics) actually exist. The domain of choice concerns the extent to which these possibilities are restrained, not whether there are such possibilities. For further description and defense of this view of technology, see Daniel Deudney, "Geopolitics and Change," in *New Thinking in International Relations Theory*, ed. Michael Doyle and G. John Ikenberry (Boulder, CO: Westview, 1997), pp. 91–123. For general discussion of technological determinism, see Leo Marx and Merritt Roe Smith, eds., *Does Technology Drive History? The Dilemma of Technological Determinism* (Cambridge: MIT Press, 1994).

47. Waltz's influential version of balance-of-power theory is also a functionality argument: balancing is held to be necessary for security in systemic anarchies, but states are not held to inevitably balance, or balance effectively, when faced with threats. *Theory of International Politics*, pp. 101–2; and Fred Halliday and Justin Rosenberg, "Interview with Ken Waltz," *Review of International Studies*, 24, no. 3 (July 1998), pp. 371–86. For further discussion of functionality arguments, see Deudney, "Geopolitics and Change," pp. 91–123.

48. For the medical model, see Blair Campbell, "Poliatrics: Physicians and the Physician Analogy in Fourth-Century Athens," *American Political Science Review* 76, no. 4 (December 1982), pp. 810–24. For a powerful recent statement of the logic of a practically based political science, see Hayward Alker, "Aristotelian Political Methodologies" and "The Return of Practical Reason to International Theory," in *Rediscoveries and Reformulations* (Cambridge: Cambridge University Press, 1996), pp. 64–103 and 395–421.

CHAPTER TWO
RELATIVES AND DESCENDANTS

1. Friedrich Nietzsche, *On the Genealogy of Morality*, trans. Carol Diethe (Cambridge: Cambridge University Press, 1994), p. 57.

2. For classic overviews, see Otto Gierke, *Natural Law and the Theory of Society*, trans. Ernest Barker (Cambridge: Cambridge University Press, 1934); Leo Strauss,

Natural Right and History (Chicago: University of Chicago Press, 1950). For a powerful treatment of international topics from this perspective, see Thomas L. Pangle and Peter J. Ahrensdorf, *Justice among Nations: On the Moral Basis of Power and Peace* (Lawrence: University Press of Kansas, 1999).

3. However, the original title of Plato's work was probably "On Justice." Plato's term for the political order, *politeia*, can more accurately be translated "the form of the polis," and this word appearing throughout Aristotle's *Politics* is conventionally translated as "the constitution."

4. This is especially salient for Onuf, who calls Aristotle "the central figure in my characterization of ancient republicanism" and the *Politics* "republicanism's foremost text." *Republican Legacies*, p. 23.

5. He observes that "the principle of rule and subjugation pervades all Nature . . . and we infer that the same principle is true of human beings generally." Aristotle, *Physics*, trans. R. P. Hardy and R. K. Gaye, in Jonathan Barnes, ed., *The Complete Works of Aristotle* (Princeton: Princeton University Press, 1984), p. 336. Building from this and similar passages, Onuf concludes that "[b]y necessity, republics are hierarchical and coercive." But "while republicans take hierarchy for granted, hierarchies are republican only when they match a particular ideology to a familiar paradigm of rule. . . . Good republicans make hierarchy palatable." *Republican Legacy*, p. 7.

6. For reconstructions and interpretative debates, see Margaret E. Reesor, *The Political Theory of the Old and Middle Stoa* (New York: Columbia University Press, 1951); H. C. Baldry, *The Unity of Mankind in Greek Thought* (Cambridge: Cambridge University Press, 1963); Anton-Hermann Chroust, "The Ideal Polity of the Early Stoics: Zeno's Republic," *Review of Politics* 27, no. 2 (April 1965), pp. 173–83; Marcia L. Colish, *The Stoic Tradition from Antiquity to the Early Middle Ages* (London: Brill, 1985); and Francis Edward Devine, "Stoicism on the Best Regime," *Journal of the History of Ideas* 31, no. 3 (July 1970), pp. 323–36.

7. For Enlightenment versions, see Thomas Schlereth, *The Cosmopolitan Ideal in Eighteenth Century Thought: Its Form and Function in the Ideas of Franklin, Hume, and Voltaire, 1694–1790* (Notre Dame, IN: University of Notre Dame Press, 1977).

8. Mason Hammond, *City-State and World State in Greek and Roman Political Thought until Augustus* (Cambridge: Harvard University Press, 1951).

9. The phrase 'civic humanism' first appeared in Hans Baron, *The Crisis of the Early Italian Renaissance: Civic Humanism and Republican Liberty in an Age of Classicism and Tyranny* (Princeton: Princeton University Press, 1955). Onuf's suggestion of "civic activism" does somewhat better in simply conveying its essence. *World of Our Making* (Columbia: University of South Carolina Press, 1989), p. 177. For a treatment that emphasizes a far less communitarian view of Aristotle, see Bernard Yack, *The Problems of a Political Animal: Community, Justice, and Conflict in Aristotelian Thought* (Berkeley and Los Angeles: University of California Press, 1993).

10. Because of its antipathy to complex and mediating political structures of power restraint, the ancient revivalist orientation could better be labeled *publican* rather than republican.

11. For this point, see Michael W. Doyle, "Rousseau: Constitutionalism," in *Ways of War and Peace*, p. 75.

12. Rousseau, *The Social Contract*, p. 54.

13. Moving beyond the abstract formulations of his other works, Rousseau provides an imaginative sketch of such a polity in *The Government of Poland* ([1772] Indianapolis, IN: Bobbs-Merrill, 1972).

14. The Spartan constitution had elaborate political structural restraints on power, but what most distinguished it was a comprehensive program of education for military service. As Bernard Yack points out, Sparta was admired in antiquity for its military strength and political stability, while it is "the Spartan's state of mind that most excites Rousseau's admiration and envy." *The Longing for Total Revolution: Philosophic Sources of Social Discontent from Rousseau to Marx and Nietzsche* (Princeton: Princeton University Press, 1992) p. 66. For the institutions, history, and reception of Sparta, see W. G. Forrest, *A History of Sparta, 950–192 B.C.* (New York: Norton, 1969); and Elizabeth Rawson, *The Spartan Tradition in European Thought* (Oxford: Oxford University Press, 1969). A succinct portrayal is found in Paul A. Rahe, "Politics in Classical Sparta," in *Republics Ancient and Modern: Classical Republicanism and American Revolution* (Chapel Hill: University of North Carolina Press, 1992).

15. For different views of the Rousseau and Robiespierre relationship, see Carol Blum, *Rousseau and the Republic of Virtue: The Language of Politics in the French Revolution* (Princeton: Princeton University Press, 1986); and Yack, *Longing for Total Revolution*, pp. 83–84.

16. For a strong statement of this line of influence, see J. L. Talmon, *The Origins of Totalitarian Democracy* (New York: Norton, 1970).

17. Among the most powerful and influential works developing variants of this orientation are Hannah Arendt, *The Human Condition* (Chicago: University of Chicago Press, 1958); Leo Strauss, *The City and Man* (Chicago: Rand McNally, 1964); and Sheldon Wolin, *Politics and Vision* (Boston: Little, Brown, 1960).

18. C. P. MacPherson, *The Political Theory of Possessive Individualism, Hobbes to Locke* (New York: Oxford University Press, 1962). As Louis Hertz put it: "John Locke dominates American political thought, as no thinker anywhere dominates the political thought of a nation." *The Liberal Tradition in America* (New York: Harcourt, Brace and World, 1954), p. 140.

19. Pocock, *Machiavellian Moment*, pp. 401–505.

20. Bernard Bailyn, *The Ideological Origins of the American Revolution* (Cambridge: Harvard University Press, 1967).

21. Isaac Kramnick, *Republicanism and Bourgeois Radicalism: Political Ideology in Late Eighteenth-Century England and America* (Ithaca: Cornell University Press, 1990); and Joyce Appleby, *Liberalism and Republicanism in the Historical Imagination* (Cambridge: Harvard University Press, 1992).

22. Daniel Rodgers, "Republicanism: The Career of a Concept," *Journal of American History* 79, no. 1 (June 1992), p. 19.

23. Gordon S. Wood, *The Creation of the American Republic, 1776–1787* (Chapel Hill: University of North Carolina Press, 1969).

24. A particularly good overview is provided in "Reason of State," in Haslam, *No Virtue Like Necessity*. Also see William F. Church, *Richelieu and Reason of State* (Princeton: Princeton University Press, 1972).

25. Theodore K. Raab, *The Struggle for Stability in Early Modern Europe* (New York: Oxford University Press, 1975).

26. Detailed discussions of these debates are found in Richard Koebner, "Despot and Despotism: Vicissitudes of a Political Term," *Journal of the Warburg and Courtauld Institutes* 14, no. 3/4 (1951); and Melvin Richter, "Despotism," *Dictionary of the History of Ideas* (New York: Scribner's 1973–74), vol. 2. pp. 1–18.

27. "Contempt for one's sovereign prince is contempt toward God, of whom he is the earthly image." Jean Bodin, *On Sovereignty*, p. 46. For discussion, see H. Hopfl, "Orthodoxy and Reason of State," *History of Political Thought* 23, no. 2 (summer 2002), pp. 211–37; and Julian H. Franklin, *Jean Bodin and the Rise of Absolutist Theory* (Cambridge: Cambridge University Press, 1973).

28. Meinecke, *Machiavellianism*, p. 11.

29. Frederick of Prussia, *Anti-Machiavel*, trans. Paul Sonino (Athens: Ohio University Press, 1981). For a sympathetic treatment of this odd autocrat, see Gerhard Ritter, *Frederick the Great: A Historical Profile,* ed. Peter Paret ([1968] Berkeley and Los Angeles: University of California Press, 1974).

30. Richard Tuck analyzes the role of Stoic ideas transmitted through the spread of Humanist scholarship in *Philosophy and Government, 1572–1651* (Cambridge: Cambridge University Press, 1993). These themes are particularly salient in the now largely forgotten works of Justus Lapsius, whose works went through some fifty editions.

31. Richard Ashley concisely captures their function: "These texts provided operatives of the absolutist state with simplifying axioms to guide behavior, historical models to emulate, and normative claims to legitimate and justify their activities." "The Poverty of Neorealism," *International Organization* 38, no. 2 (spring 1984), p. 265.

32. It is a telling oddity that Machiavelli's many imitators and followers almost universally felt compelled to express explicit rejection—if not indignation—at the notorious Florentine.

33. The long history of this enterprise is artfully treated in Mark Lilla, *The Reckless Mind: Intellectuals and Politics* (New York: New York Review of Books, 2001).

34. For enlightened despotism, see Nanneral Keohane, *Philosophy and the State in France* (Princeton: Princeton University Press, 1980); and C.B.A. Behrens, "The Ideology of Absolutism in France and Prussia," in *Society, Government, and the Enlightenment* (New York: Harper and Row, 1981). For discussion of this episode, see Peter Gay, "Prussia: Sparta in a Cold Climate," in *Voltaire's Politics* (Princeton: Princeton University Press, 1959).

35. This project also stands in sharp contrast to the contemporary neorealist (and neoliberal) positing of states as 'unitary and rational actors,' a move that effectively consigns a key problem of the putative precursor to invisibility. Montesquieu, speaking of Richelieu, says he "has recourse to the virtues of the prince . . . but he requires so many things, that indeed there is none but an angel capable of such attention." *Spirit of the Laws*, bk. 5, chap. 11. Thomas Paine puts the repub-

lican criticism even more pointedly: "the state of a king shuts him from the world" and he is "poisoned by importance" so that he is "the most ignorant and unfit of any throughout the dominion." Thomas Paine, *Common Sense*, in *Thomas Paine: Political Writings*, ed. Bruce Kuklick ([1792] Cambridge: Cambridge University Press, 1989), p. 49.

36. Johann Gottfried Herder, "Yet Another Philosophy of History for the Enlightenment of Mankind," in *J. G. Herder on Social and Political Culture*, trans. F. M. Barnard (Cambridge: Cambridge University Press, 1966). For extended treatment of Herder's thought and influence, see Robert Reinhold Ergang, *Herder and the Foundations of German Nationalism* (New York: Columbia University Press, 1931); F. M. Barnard, *Herder's Social and Political Thought: From Enlightenment to Nationalism* (Oxford: Clarendon, 1965); and Hans J. Reiss, ed., *The Political Thought of the German Romantics, 1793–1815* (Oxford: Basil Blackwell, 1955). For similar notions in England, see David P. Calleo, *Coleridge and the Idea of the Modern State* (New Haven: Yale University Press, 1966).

37. Herder, "Yet Another Philosophy of History for the Enlightenment of Mankind," p. 187.

38. Johann Gottlieb Fichte, *Addresses to the German Nation*, ed. George Armstrong Kelly (New York: Harper Torchbooks, 1968), p. 119–20.

39. G.W.F. Hegel, *The Phenomenology of Mind*, trans. J. B. Baille (London: George Allen and Unwin, 1971), p. 474. He also observes: "just as the blowing of winds preserves the sea from foulness which would be the result of prolonged calm, so also corruption in nations would be the product of prolonged, let alone 'perpetual' peace." G.W.F. Hegel, *The Philosophy of Right*, trans. T. M. Knox (Oxford: Clarendon Press, 1946), para. 324a. As Steven Smith notes, war for Hegel "is the means whereby state sovereignty is expressed as well as where the 'ethical health' of a people, their sense of community and political solidarity, is put to the test." "Hegel's Views on War, the State, and International Relations," *American Political Science Review* 17, no. 3 (September 1983), p. 631. For a reading emphasizing Hegel's liberal elements, see Sholomo Avineri, *Hegel's Social and Political Thought* (Cambridge: Cambridge University Press, 1974).

40. Hegel, *Philosophy of Right*, para. 324a.

41. Heinrich von Treitschke, *Politics*, ed. Hans Kohn, trans. Blanche Dugdale and Torben de Bille ([1916] New York: Harcourt, Brace and World, 1963), p. 10.

42. Treitschke, *Politics* p. 39. For an overview of the Romantic idealization of war, see P. Savigear, "Philosophical Idealism and International Politics: Bosanquet, Trietschke, and War," *British Journal of International Studies* 2, no. 4 (spring 1975).

43. Trietschke, *Politics*, p. 14.

44. Friedrich Meinecke, *Cosmopolitanism and the National State,* trans. Robert Kimber (Princeton: Princeton University Press, 1970), pp. 14–15. For extended treatments of Meinecke's thought and influence, see Richard Sterling, *Ethics in a World of Power: The Political Ideas of Friedrich Meinecke* (Princeton: Princeton University Press, 1958); and Robert A. Pois, *Friedrich Meinecke and German Politics in the Twentieth Century* (Berkeley and Los Angeles: University of California Press, 1972).

45. Meinecke, *Cosmopolitanism and the National State*, p. 4.

46. Meinecke, *Machiavellism*, p. 211–35.

47. Friedrich Meinecke, *The German Catastrophe: Reflections and Recollections*, trans. Sidney B. Fay (Cambridge: Harvard University Press, 1950) p. 15.

48. Meinecke, *The German Catastrophe*, p. 74. For succinct overviews of the cultural and political visions of German nationalism, see Gordon A. Craig, *The Politics of the Unpolitical: German Writers and the Problem of Power, 1770–1871* (New York: Oxford University Press, 1995); and Felix Gilbert, *History: Politics or Culture? Reflections on Ranke and Burkhardt* (Princeton: Princeton University Press, 1990).

49. Meinecke, *The German Catastrophe*, p. 110.

50. For treatment of Hobbes by recent international theorists, see Robert J. Vincent, "The Hobbesian Tradition in Twentieth Century International Thought," *Millennium* 10, no. 2 (summer 1981); Donald W. Hanson, "Hobbes's 'Highway to Peace,' " *International Organization*, 32, no. 2 (spring 1984), pp. 214–55; Mark Heller, "The Use and Abuse of Hobbes: The State of Nature in International Relations," *Polity* 13, no. 1 (fall 1980), pp. 21–32; Michael C. Williams, "Hobbes and International Relations: A Reconsideration," *International Organization* 50, no. 2 (spring 1996), pp. 213–36; and Doyle, "Structuralism: Hobbes," in *Ways of War and Peace*, pp. 11–136.

51. Hobbes, *Leviathan*, pt. 1, chap.13, p. 82.

52. The key passages are: "The nature of warre, consisteth, not in actual fighting; but in the known disposition thereto, during all the time there is no assurance to the contrary" and "in all times Kings, and Persons of Soveraigne authority, because of their Independency, are in continual jealousies, and in the state and posture of Gladiators; having their weapons pointing, and their eyes fixed on one another; that is, their Forts, Garrisons, and Guns, upon the Frontiers of their Kingdomes; and continual Spyes upon their neighbors; which is a posture of warre." Hobbes, *Leviathan*, pp. 82 and 83.

53. In Hobbes's version, the natural fact that all men must sleep, and therefore are vulnerable no matter what their strength, motivates the departure from the state-of-nature and entry into the civil state: "Nature hath made men so equal, in faculties of body and mind, . . . the weakest has strength enough to kill the strongest." Hobbes, *Leviathan*, p. 80.

54. Robert W. Tucker cites Hobbes and speaks of states living "in the state of nature from which they have never emerged." *The Nuclear Debate: Deterrence and the Loss of Faith* (Holmes and Meier, 1986), p. 20; Martin Wight notes "the identification of international politics with the precontractual state of nature . . . [an] identification apparently first made by Hobbes." "Why Is There No International Theory?" in *Diplomatic Investigations*, ed. Herbert Butterfield and Martin Wight (London: George Allen and Unwin, 1966), p. 30.

55. "An armed attack by one state upon another has not brought with it a prospect comparable to the killing of one individual by another. For one man's death may be brought about suddenly in a single act; and once it has occurred it cannot be undone." Bull, *The Anarchical Society*, p. 49. Tuck in analyzing Grotius, Hobbes, and Rousseau also seems to elide first and second anarchy but in the other direction: "the formation of Hobbesian states cannot protect their citizens from the ravages of the state of nature, since on Hobbes's own account the state

is itself an agent in a state of nature. But he [Rousseau] realized that Hobbes's solution could not work, precisely because of the analogy between the state of nature and the international arena: men who sought to avoid death by creating Leviathan states would find themselves at far greater risk of death than they had faced in nature, as their states confronted each other in the circumstances of modern warfare." *Rights of War and Peace*, pp. 207 and 230.

56. However, Hobbes does say, "It is therefore necessary, to the end security sought for may be obtained, that the number of them who conspire in a mutual assistance be so great, that the accession of some few to the enemy's party may not prove to them a matter of moment sufficient to assure the victory." *De Cive, Man and Citizen,* ed. Bernard Gert, trans. Thomas Hobbes (Garden City, NY: Doubleday, 1972), p. 167.

57. As a result of these restraints, a continental European union of the sort proposed by Saint Pierre, whose plan Rousseau analyzes and criticizes, is not necessary for security, and its great potential benefits are not great enough to overcome the numerous obstacles to its creation.

58. For Carr's influence, see William T. R. Fox, "E. H. Carr and Political Realism: Vision and Revision," *Review of International Studies* 11, no. 1 (January 1985); Michael Joseph Smith, "E. H. Carr: Realism as Relativism," in *Realist Thought from Weber to Kissinger;* and Jonathan Haslam, *The Vices of Integrity: E. H. Carr, 1892–1982* (London: Verso, 1999). For discussion of Herz and Morgenthau, see chapter 9.

59. Whittle Johnston, "E. H. Carr's Theory of International Relations: A Critique," *Journal of Politics* 24, no. 4 (November 1967), p. 861.

60. The neorealism developed in Gilpin's theory of hegemonic instability is explicitly an elaboration of Carr's first argument, also rooted in Thucydides. Robert Gilpin, *War and Change in World Politics* (Cambridge: Cambridge University Press, 1982).

61. Carr's materialist argument is most indebted to Marx's production-centered materialism, but he assigns military technology a role not explicitly or readily reducible to productive forces and relationships. E. H. Carr, *Conditions of Peace* (New York: Macmillan, 1942), p. 57.

62. Carr, *Conditions of Peace,* p. 39.

63. Carr, *Conditions of Peace,* p. 54; Andreas Dorpalan, ed., *The World of General Haushofer: Geopolitics in Action* (New York: Farrar and Rinehart, 1942); and Johannes Mattern, *Geopolitik: Doctrine of National Self-Sufficiency and Empire* (Baltimore: Johns Hopkins University Studies in Historical and Political Science, 1942).

64. Carr, *Conditions of Peace,* p. 37.

65. Carr, *Conditions of Peace,* p. 55. Here Carr's reaction to the German geopoliticans' and Burnham's image of a handful of world powers locked in struggle is similar to George Orwell's.

66. Carr, *Conditions of Peace,* p. 60.

67. Kenneth N. Waltz, "Realist Thought and Neorealist Theory," in *The Evolution of Theory in International Relations,* ed. Robert L. Rothstein (Columbia: University of South Carolina Press, 1991), pp. 21–38. For the range of this debate, see Robert O. Keohane, ed., *Neorealism and Its Critics* (New York: Columbia

University Press, 1986); Kenneth A. Oye, ed., *Cooperation under Anarchy* (Princeton: Princeton University Press, 1986); Alexander Wendt, "Anarchy Is What States Make of It," *International Organization* 46, no. 2 (spring 1992); Buzan, Jones, and Little, *The Logic of Anarchy*; Robert Powell, "Anarchy in International Relations Theory: The Neorealist-Neoliberal Debate," *International Organization* 48, no. 2 (spring 1994), pp. 313–44; Justin Rosenberg, *The Empire of Civil Society* (London: Verso, 1994); Michael Brown, ed., *The Perils of Anarchy* (Cambridge: MIT Press, 1995); and Hayward Alker, "The Presumption of Anarchy in World Politics," in *Rediscoveries and Reformulations*.

68. Waltz, *Man, the State, and War*, pp. 171–85.

69. Using Hobbesian categories, Waltz observes that "states in the world are like individuals in the state of nature," but does not conclude from this fact that states must combine because "individuals, to survive, must combine; states, by their very constitution, are not subject to a similar necessity." He thus builds into his definition of a state the security viability that is, in fact, historically variable. Waltz, *Man, the State, and War*, pp. 163 and 162.

70. This narrowing of material context is in part the product of the narrow scope of his main question (what are the causes of war?) which largely assumes the existence of states in systemic anarchy.

71. Waltz, *Theory of International Politics*, pp. 129–60.

72. Waltz, *Theory of International Politics*, p. 173.

73. Waltz, *Theory of International Politics*, p. 175.

74. Kenneth N. Waltz, *The Spread of Nuclear Weapons: More May Be Better* (London: International Institute for Security Studies, 1981); and Kenneth Waltz, "Nuclear Myths and Political Realities," *American Political Science Review* 84, no. 3 (September 1990).

75. "Within very wide ranges, a nuclear balance is insensitive to variation in numbers and size of warheads." Waltz, "Nuclear Myths and Political Realities," p. 740.

76. For substantive criticisms of Waltz's nuclear argument, see Sagan chapters in Scott D. Sagan and Kenneth N. Waltz *The Spread of Nuclear Weapons: A Debate* (New York: Norton, 1995). For more extended analysis of the disjuncture between Waltz's neorealist and nuclear arguments, see Daniel Deudney, "Dividing Realism: Structural Realism versus Security Materialism on Nuclear Security and Proliferation," *Security Studies* 2, nos. 3 & 4 (spring/summer 1993), pp. 7–37.

77. van Evera, *Causes of War*, pp. 7–11.

78. Unlike Waltz, who deals extensively with political theory texts and arguments, van Evera draws primarily on historical cases and military and diplomatic thinkers. In tracing the lineage of his arguments, van Evera identifies early versions in various literatures in the twentieth century and describes in detail the key role played by topography in a lengthy passage without any citations. *Causes of War*, pp. 118–19, and 163. For an excellent, but largely atheoretical, earlier treatment richly illustrated with historical examples, see Quester, *Offense and Defense in the International System*.

79. Mearsheimer, *The Tragedy of Great Power Politics*, particularly "The Primacy of Landpower" and "The Offshore Balancers," pp. 83–137, 234–66.

80. In his many commentaries on contemporary issues in American foreign policy, Mearsheimer often ends up, along with Waltz and van Evera, as a skeptic of foreign intervention, in large measure due to the power of nationalism in mobilizing resistance to outsiders. Whatever the prudence of this advice, the power accorded nationalism belies Measheimer's boilerplate Realist rejection of the power of ideas and identity and of unit-level factors.

81. Buzan, Little, and Jones, *The Logic of Anarchy*. The later chapters of this work, by Charles Jones, provide a rich analysis of compositional factors in ancient state systems.

82. Buzan and Little, *International Systems in World History*.

83. This term is also sometimes used to refer to the branch of the academic discipline of geography concerned with the spatial distribution of political phenomena without much attention to security. For the range of contemporary political geography, see John Agnew, *Place and Politics: The Geographical Mediation of State and Society* (London: Allen and Unwin, 1987); and Robert David Sack, *Homo Geographicus: A Framework for Action, Awareness, and Moral Concern* (Baltimore: Johns Hopkins University Press, 1997).

84. For Colin Gray on the dangerous strategic blindnesses of American Liberal culture, the winnability of nuclear war, the need for a heavy multiple warhead intercontinental nuclear ballistic missile, the geographic inevitability of American-Soviet competition, the need for accelerated outer-space weaponization, and the follies and dangers of arms control, see *Strategic Studies and Public Policy: The American Experience* (Frankfurt: University Press of Kentucky, 1982); "Nuclear Strategy: The Case for a Theory of Victory," *International Security*, 4, no. 1 (summer 1979), pp. 54–87; *The MX ICBM and American Strategy* (Westport, CT: Praeger, 1981); *Geopolitics of the Nuclear Era: Heartlands, Rimlands, and the Technological Revolution* (New York: Crane, Russak, 1977); *American Military Space Policy* (Cambridge, MA.: Abt Books, 1983); and *House of Cards: Why Arms Control Must Fail* (Ithaca: Cornell University Press, 1992).

85. Gray, *Geopolitics of the Nuclear Era*, p. 11, 32, 12, 14.

86. Gray, *Geopolitics of the Nuclear Era*, p. 6.

87. For example, see Gearoid O Tuathail, *Critical Geopolitics* (Minneapolis: University of Minnesota Press, 1996); and Simon Dalby and G. O Tuathail, eds., *Re-thinking Geopolitics* (London: Routledge, 1998).

88. Notable here as a strongly contextual materialist thinker is Paul Virilio, who offers provocative and at times aphoristic and enigmatic meditations on the political implications of speed. Paul Virilio, *Politics and Speed: An Essay on Dromology*, trans. Mark Polizzotti (New York: Foreign Agents, 1977); and analysis in James der Derian, "The (S)pace of International Relations: Simulation, Surveillance, and Speed," *International Studies Quarterly* 34, no. 3 (September 1990), pp. 295–310.

89. Somewhat oddly, the general turn away from security-from-violence has been increasingly paralleled by a widespread tendency to attempt to label traditionally nonsecurity issues as security issues through a process of 'redefinition.' While capturing the fact that a great many nonsecurity issues matter a great deal, and that virtually every substantial human concern, from religion and language to trade and resources, can cause or contribute to conflicts leading the violence

and actual insecurity, these Liberal efforts to redefine security have created the paradoxical situation in which Liberals are expanding the apparent list of security problems while diluting the attention to direct security threats.

90. David Mitrany, "A Working Peace System," and "The Functional Approach and Federalism," in *A Working Peace System* ([1943] Chicago: Quadrangle, 1966), pp. 25–103, 149–215.

91. This absence is notable in the major works of general regime theory: Stephen D. Krasner ed., *International Regimes* (Ithaca: Cornell University Press, 1982); Oran Young, *International Cooperation* (Ithaca: Cornell University Press, 1989); Volker Rittberger, ed., *Regime Theory and International Relations* (Oxford: Clarendon, 1995); and Andreas Hasenclever, Peter Mayer, and Volker Rittberger, *Theories of International Regimes* (Cambridge: Cambridge University Press, 1997).

92. This literature is widely seen as having been catalyzed by a study by an economist about economic interdependence among advanced industrial democracies. Richard N. Cooper, *The Economics of Interdependence: Economic Policy in the Atlantic Community* (New York: McGraw-Hill, 1968).

93. Robert Keohane and Joseph Nye, *Power and Interdependence* (Boston: Little, Brown, 1977). Although Keohane and Nye deride the analytic weakness and 'globalony' of interdependence formulations from the early-twentieth century, David Baldwin has pointed out that lucid formulations of economic interdependence were developed by late-eighteenth- and early-nineteenth-century political economists. "Interdependence and Power: A Conceptual Analysis," *International Organization* 34, no. 4 (autumn 1980), pp. 471–506. Security interdependence remains for Keohane outside of 'globalization.' "Broadly speaking, globalization means the shrinkage of distance on a world scale through the emergence and thickening of networks of connections—environmental and social as well as economic." Robert O. Keohane, *Power and Governance in a Partially Globalized World* (Boulder, CO: Westview, 2002), p. 11. In an ambitious but neglected work from this period, changes in violence capability are analyzed as part of a cluster of powerful factors contributing to a fundamental change in world politics. Edward Morse, *Modernization and the Transformation of International Relations* (New York: Free Press, 1976), pp. 1–21.

94. Constructivism, itself diverse and divided, emphasizes the importance of various ideational factors (most notably shared understandings and identities) over material factors and of social-holistic over atomistic-individualistic models of politics. For an assessment of different constructivist arguments, see Maja Zehfuss, *Constructivism in International Relations* (Cambridge: Cambridge University Press, 2002).

95. These links are salient in the work of Benjamin R. Barber, who began as a scholar of Swiss city-state democracy, then advanced a general argument for participatory democracy, before emerging as a highly visible critic of economic and cultural globalization. *The Death of Communal Liberty: A History of Freedom in a Swiss Mountain Canton* (Princeton: Princeton University Press, 1974); *Strong Democracy* (Berkeley and Los Angeles: University of California, 1984); *Jihad vs. McWorld: How Globalism and Tribalism Are Reshaping the World* (New York: Ballantine Books, 1995).

96. Onuf argues that constructivism is "the most important legacy of republicanism for contemporary international thought." *Republican Legacy*, p. 26.

97. Onuf, *Republican Legacy*, p. 2.

98. Onuf, *Republican Legacy*, p. 5. This 'liberalism of Realism' is most pronounced for neorealists and classical Realists whom he deems to be "weak theorists" and "confused liberals." This same relationship, with the influence running in the opposite direction, is advanced by Richard Tuck. Protoliberal natural rights theorists "took a view of war between states derived from humanist historians and political writers, and inserted it into their view of domestic politics, presenting civil life as a matter of quasi-military tactics. The natural rights theorists then simply took the *jurisprudence* of war which had developed among humanist lawyers, and derived a theory of individual rights from it." *Rights of War and Peace*, p. 11.

99. The degree of violence interdependence does not determine whether the relationship between states is one of 'enemy,' 'rival,' or 'friend,' but it does powerfully shape the security consequences of these relations. With weak violence interdependence, being 'enemies' holds little peril and being 'friends' offers little benefit, but with intense violence interdependence, being 'enemies' is likely to be ruinous.

100. At the end of his extensive analysis of anarchy, in a section entitled "Beyond the Anarchy Problematique?" Wendt briefly suggests the need to begin conceptualizing decentralized nonanarchical governance. *Social Theory*, pp. 307–8.

101. After seeming to establish that "the most important structures in which states are embedded are made of ideas, not material factors," Wendt argues that two of the "master variables" shaping the crucial formation of "collective identities" are "interdependence" and "common fate," and nuclear weapons are acknowledged as powerful shapers of international political life. *Social Theory*, pp. 344–53.

CHAPTER THREE
THE IRON LAWS OF POLIS REPUBLICANISM

1. Montesquieu, *Spirit of the Laws*, bk. 6, sec. 1, p. 126.

2. For a survey of the diverse and changing ways in which the city-state has been treated in nineteenth- and early-twentieth century social theory, see M. I. Finley, "The Ancient City: From Fustel de Coulanges to Max Weber and Beyond," *Comparative Studies in Society and History* 19, no. 3 (July 1977), pp. 305–27.

3. Benjamin Constant, "The Liberty of the Ancients Compared with that of the Moderns," in *Benjamin Constant: Political Writings,* ed. Biancamaria Fontana ([1819] Cambridge: Cambridge University Press, 1988), p. 311. After making this generalization, Constant notes that Athens "was of all the Greek republics the most closely engaged in trade: thus it allowed to its citizens an infinitely greater individual liberty than Sparta or Rome," p. 315.

4. For Plato and Aristotle as oppositional figures, see Josiah Ober, *Political Dissent in Democratic Athens: Intellectual Critics of Popular Rule* (Princeton: Princeton University Press, 1989). Cynthia Farrar argues for the existence of a implicit democratic theory in *The Origins of Democratic Thinking: The Invention of Politics in Classical Athens* (Cambridge: Cambridge University Press, 1988); and in "Ancient Greek Political Theory as a Response to Democracy," in *Democracy:*

The Unfinished Journey: 508 BC to AD 1993, ed. John Dunn (New York: Oxford University Press, 1992), pp. 17–39. For a magisterial account of the Greek concern for political freedom, see Kurt Raaflaub, *The Discovery of Freedom in Ancient Greece*, trans. Renate Franciscono (Chicago: University of Chicago Press, 2004).

5. Montesquieu, *Spirit of the Laws*, p. 126. Along these lines, Peter Burke posits a "power vacuum theory" of city-states, attributing their viability to situations where they are not exposed to predation by larger states. "City-States," in *States in History*, ed. John A. Hall (Oxford: Blackwell, 1986) p. 152.

6. The extent of the complexity is suggested by Arthur Lovejoy and George Boas's inventory of sixty-six different meanings of the term 'nature.' "Some Meanings of 'Nature,' " Appendix, *Primitivism and Related Ideas in Antiquity* (Baltimore: Johns Hopkins University Press, 1935).

7. The best overall statements remain Strauss, *Natural Right and History*; and *The City and Man*.

8. For an overview, see W.K.C. Gutherie, "The 'Nomos'-'Physis' Antithesis in Morals and Politics," in *The Sophists* (Cambridge: Cambridge University Press, 1971), pp. 55–134.

9. An important corrective to the general neglect of these links is provided by Thomas J. Johnson, "The Idea of Power Politics: The Sophistic Foundations of Realism," *Security Studies* 5, no. 2 (winter 1996).

10. Plato, *Protagoras*, 320c–328d; and Plato, *Gorgias*, 483–86. A vast compilation of such thinking is gathered in Lovejoy and Boas, *Primitivism and Related Ideas*.

11. James H. Nichols, Jr., *Epicurean Political Philosophy: The de rerum natura of Lucretius* (Ithaca: Cornell University Press, 1972), pp. 122–48.

12. Strauss and his followers appear to aim at a second Socratic Revolution against the putative amoral and reductionistic naturalism and materialism of modern thinkers, most notably Machiavelli, Hobbes, Marx, and above all Nietzsche (who offers a powerful restatement and radicalization of pre-Socratic power cosmology), as well as against extreme modern political movements, agendas, ideologies on both the communist left and the fascist right. For a succinct statement, see Leo Strauss, "Three Waves of Modernity," in *Political Philosophy*, ed. Hilail Gilden, (Indianapolis, IN: Pegasus, 1975).

13. Plato, *Laws*, 676b–682e; Plato, *Timaeus*, 23b. Extensive discussion in G. W. Trompf, *The Idea of Historical Recurrence in Western Thought: From Antiquity to the Reformation* (Berkeley and Los Angeles: University of California Press, 1979), pp. 9–15.

14. For function arguments in Aristotle, see Roger Masters, "Gradualism and Discontinuous Change in Evolutionary Biology and Political Philosophy," in The *Dynamics of Evolution*, ed. Albert Somit and Steven A. Peterson (Ithaca: Cornell University Press, 1989), pp. 282–317.

15. For a discussion of how Aristotle's comparative and empirical political science are embedded in a more general system significantly unlike modern social science, see Stephen G. Salkever, "Aristotle's Social Science," in *Essays on the Foundations of Aristotelian Political Science*, ed. Carnes Lord and David O'Conner (Berkeley and Los Angeles: University of California Press, 1991), pp. 11–48.

16. A good survey of views is provided by James H. Nichols, Jr., "Technology in Classical Thought," in *Technology and the Idea of Progress*, ed. Arthur M.

Melzer, Jerry Weinberger, and M. Richard Zinman (Ithaca: Cornell University Press, 1993), pp. 27–45. An overview of actual capabilities is provided in John G. Landels, *Engineering in the Ancient World* (Berkeley and Los Angeles: University of California Press, 1978 and 2003).

17. Aristotle, *Politics*, 1253b, p. 10.

18. The standard explanation for this theoretical indifference and conceptual conflation is the observational and philosophical cast of ancient science, and a class-based aversion to experimentation and the mechanical arts. Derek de Solla Price, *Science since Babylon* (New Haven: Yale University Press, 1975). Recent scholarship has increasingly challenged this view, finding a vigorous transnational engineering community playing a prominent role in Hellenistic siege-craft development. Adrienne Mayor, *Greek Fire, Poison Arrows and Scorpion Bombs* (Woodstock: Overlook Duckworth, 2003); and Serafina Cuomo, "The Sinews of War: Ancient Catapults," *Science* 303 (February 6, 2005).

19. The single best reconstruction of these arguments is the magisterial work of Clarence Glacken, *Traces on the Rhodian Shore*. Glacken focuses mainly on theories about the influence of climate, and says little about early theories of nature emphasizing topography, arable land, and land-sea interactions. After several decades of neglect, analysis of climate as a factor, particularly in economic development, has reemerged as a serious enterprise. Recent substantial works include Andrew M. Kamarck, *The Tropics and Economic Development* (Baltimore: Johns Hopkins University Press, 1976); H. H. Lamb, *Climate, History and the Modern World* (London: Methuen, 1982); Jayantanuja Bandyopadhyaya, *Climate and World Order: An Inquiry into the Natural Causes of Underdevelopment* (Atlantic Highlands, NJ: Humanities Press, 1983); and William Easterly, *The Elusive Quest for Growth: Economists' Adventures and Misadventures in the Tropics* (Cambridge: MIT Press, 2001).

20. Hippocrates, "Airs, Waters and Places," in *Hippocratic Writings*, ed. G.E.R. Lloyd (London: Penguin, 1978). For discussion of influences, see W. D. Smith, *The Hippocratic Tradition* (Ithaca: Cornell University Press, 1979); and J. Longrigg, *Greek Rational Medicine: Philosophy and Medicine from Alcmeon to the Alexandrians* (London: Macmillan, 1993). Rosalind Thomas helps dispel the oddness of many of Herodotus's arguments by placing them in the context of debates among nature philosophers and rhetoricians in *Herodotus in Context: Ethnography, Science and the Art of Persuasion* (Cambridge: Cambridge University Press, 2000).

21. Montesquieu, *Spirit of the Laws*, bk. 19, sec. 14, p. 299.

22. Aristotle, *Politics*, para. 1327, p. 296.

23. For an extensive treatment of the explanations of difference-by-nature and their use as justifications for domination-by-nature, see J. M. Blaut, *The Colonizer's View of the World: Geographical Diffusionism and Eurocentric History* (New York: Guilford Press, 1993).

24. For Thucydides' discussion of Minos's naval-based hegemony, see J. R. Ellis, "The Structure and Argument of Thucydides' Archeology," *Classical Antiquity* 10, no. 2 (October 1991), pp. 344–75. For one of the few recent systematic treatments on this topic, see Chester G. Starr, *The Influence of Seapower on Ancient History* (Oxford: Oxford University Press, 1989).

25. Aristotle, *Politics*, 1321 p. 271–2. For a succinct discussion and other sources, see A. Momigliano, "Sea Power in Greek Thought," *Classical Review* 58, no. 1 (May 1944), pp. 1–7.

26. For recent debates, see Joseph M. Bryant, "Military Technology and Socio-Cultural Change in the Ancient Greek City," *Sociological Review* 38, no. 3 (August 1990); A. M. Snodgrass, "The Hoplite Reform and History," *Journal of Hellenic Studies* 85 (1965), pp. 110–22; and J. Salmon, "Political Hoplites?" *Journal of Hellenic Studies* 97 (1977), pp. 84–101.

27. An earlier version of this section appeared in Daniel Deudney, "Bringing Nature Back In: Geopolitical Theory from the Greeks to the Global Era," in *Contested Grounds*, ed. Daniel Deudney and Richard Matthew (Albany: State University of New York Press, 1998), pp. 25–57, at 36–40.

28. For the anticommerce theme in republicanism, see: J.G.A. Pocock, *Virtue, Commerce, and History: Essays on Political Thought and History, Chiefly in the Eighteenth Century* (Cambridge: Cambridge University Press, 1985).

29. Thucydides, *The Peloponnesian War*, trans. Rex Warner (Baltimore: Pelican, 1974); Edward Gibbon, *The Decline and Fall of the Roman Empire* ([1776] New York: Modern Library, n.d.), chap. 26.

30. Ibn Khaldûn, *The Muqaddimah: An Introduction to History* ([1377] Princeton: Princeton University Press, 1967). For recent discussion, see Michael Adas, ed., *Agricultural and Pastoral Societies in Ancient and Classical History* (Philadelphia: Temple University Press, 2001). Nathaniel Schmidt points out that Khaldûn was a "student of Aristotle" and had been called "an Oriental Montesquieu" by a German Arabist scholar. *Ibn Khaldun: Historian, Socialist, and Philosopher* (New York: Columbia University Press, 1930), pp. 13–14.

31. Khaldûn, *Muqaddimah*, p. 107.

32. Bribes played a particularly important role in the Chinese strategy to regulate the predations of the steppe peoples. Lec Kwanten, *Imperial Nomads: A History of Central Asia, 500–1500* (Philadelphia: University of Pennsylvania Press, 1979).

33. In his commentary on the Roman Republic, Machiavelli says that only "laws imposing that need to work which the situation does not impose" can prevent "idleness caused by the amenities of the land." Such laws could make "better soldiers than those in countries which were rough and sterile by nature," making it possible for peoples in "very fertile places" to defend themselves against attack. A promoter of military expansion, which needed wealth, Machiavelli recommends locating cities in relatively agriculturally fertile places, and then socially restraining the militarily enervating effects of wealth. Niccolo Machiavelli, *The Discourses*, trans. Leslie Walker and Brian Richardson (Baltimore: Penguin, 1970), pp. 102–3.

34. For an eloquent statement of this view, see Gibbon, *Decline and Fall*, pp. 436–44.

35. An excellent summation of this widespread view is in Paul Rahe, "Athens' Illiberal Democracy," in *Republics Ancient and Modern*, pp. 186–218.

36. For a magisterial account of the use of Athens as a paragon of democracy and its shifting valuation, see Jennifer Tolbert Roberts, *Athens on Trial: The Anti-*

democratic Tradition in Western Thought (Princeton: Princeton University Press, 1994).

37. The dominant view is that this detailed and nontheoretical treatise was not written by Aristotle, but by one of his students in the Lyceum, and is apparently one of the 150 studies on different ancient constitutions assembled by this group. For discussion of its recovery, authorship, and features, see Kurt von Fritz and Ernst Kapp, "Introduction," in Aristotle, *The Constitution of Athens* (New York: Hafner, 1950).

38. Among major treatments are Mogens Herman Hansen, *The Athenian Democracy in the Age of the Demosthenes: Structure, Principles, and Ideology* (Oxford: Blackwell, 1991); Josiah Ober, *Mass and Elite in Democratic Athens: Rhetoric, Ideology and the Power of the People* (Princeton: Princeton University Press, 1989); and Jennifer Talbot Roberts, *Accountability in Athenian Government* (Madison: University of Wisconsin Press, 1982).

39. During the fourth century, lawmaking was assigned to a smaller body, also constituted by lot, with the Assembly confined to decrees on policy. Martin Ostwald, *From Popular Sovereignty to the Sovereignty of Law: Law, Society and Politics in Fifth Century Athens* (Berkeley and Los Angeles: University of California Press, 1986).

40. For the importance of tyranny as the background alternative, see James F. McGlew, *Tyranny and Political Culture in Ancient Greece* (Ithaca: Cornell University Press, 1993). For the 'age of tyrants' preceding the emergence of democracy, see A. Andrews, *The Greek Tyrants* (New York: Harper Torchbooks, 1963).

41. Gordon, *Controlling the State*, p. 77.

42. As Josiah Ober puts it, "[T]he Athenians developed the pragmatic analogues of modern rights (i.e., guarantees of liberty, political equality, and personal security) without elaborating or relying upon a theory of rights predicated on doctrines of fundamental inherency or inalienability." *The Athenian Revolution: Essays on Ancient Greek Democracy and Political Theory* (Princeton: Princeton University Press, 1997), p. 11.

43. For example, Donald Kagan, prominent American neoconservative scholar and author of a four-volume history of the Peloponnesian War, has recently sought to rehabilitate Cleon and deploy Thucydides in defense of "a unilateralist policy of preemptive war." Daniel Mendelson, "Theaters of War," *New Yorker*, January 12, 2004, p. 82.

44. This view has long been advanced by classicists, such as F. M. Cornford, *Thucydides Mythistoricus* (London: Arnold, 1907); and John H. Finley, Jr., *Three Essays on Thucydides* (Cambridge: Harvard University Press, 1967). Further developing this approach and relating it to the issues of international theory, Richard Ned Lebow also sees Thucydides as the founder of constructivism and looks to economic modernization as creating tensions and contradictions ripe for tragic analysis. *Tragic Vision of Politics*.

45. Lebow, *Tragic Vision*, p. 131.

46. Lebow, *Tragic Vision*, p. 133.

47. Lebow, *Tragic Vision*, p. 128.

48. For the intricacies of Augustus's statecraft and his preservation of republican forms, see Kurt A. Raaflaub and Mark Toher, ed., *Between Republic and*

Empire: Interpretations of Augustus and His Principate (Berkeley and Los Angeles: University of California Press, 1990).

49. For discussion of the complexities, uncertainties, evolutionary development, and historical debates surrounding the Roman republican constitution, see Wolfgang Kunkel, *An Introduction to Roman Legal and Constitutional History*, trans. J. M. Kelly (Oxford: Clarendon Press, 1973).

50. For Polybius's sources, arguments, and biases, see Kurt von Fritz, *The Theory of the Mixed Constitution in Antiquity* (New York: Columbia University Press, 1954); and F. W. Walbank, *Polybius* (Berkeley and Los Angeles: University of California Press, 1972).

51. A succinct treatment of Cicero's shifting historical reception is provided by Neal Wood, *Cicero's Social and Political Thought* (Berkeley and Los Angeles: University of California Press, 1988).

52. This summary is based on Gordon, *Controlling the State*, pp. 96–107; and Michael Crawford, *The Roman Republic* (Cambridge: Harvard University Press, 1978). For debates and complexities, see Mary Beard and Michael Crawford, *Rome in the Late Republic: Problems and Interpretations* (London: Duckworth, 1985); and Andrew Lintott, *The Constitution of the Roman Republic* (Oxford: Oxford University Press, 1999).

53. There is general agreement that the Roman constitution had oligarchic and democratic elements, but became steadily more oligarchic. The dominant view in late-nineteenth and most twentieth-century Latin classical scholarship is formulated by Ronald Syme: "in all ages, whatever the form and name of government, be it monarchy, republic, or democracy, an oligarchy lurks behind the facade; and Roman history, Republican or Imperial, is the history of the governing class." *The Roman Revolution* (Oxford: Clarendon Press, 1939), p. 7. Recent scholarship has begun to reemphasize the continuing political significance of democratic elements. Fergus Millar, *The Crowd in Rome in the Late Republic* (Ann Arbor: University of Michigan Press, 1999). For critique of Millar, see Henrik Mouritsen, *Plebes and Politics in the Late Roman Republic* (Cambridge: Cambridge University Press, 2001).

54. The primary ancient source on this event is Titus Livy, *Ob Urbe Condita*. For a brief summary, see William Everdell, "From Brutus to Brutus: The Rise and Fall of Rome," in *The End of Kings: A History of Republics and Republicans* (New York: Free Press, 1983), pp. 44–68; Kurt Raaflaub, ed., *Social Struggles in Archaic Rome: New Perspectives on the Conflict of the Orders* (Berkeley and Los Angeles: University of California Press, 1986).

55. A detailed discussion of the complexities of this argument, its similarities with other cycle arguments, and its long influence is provided by Trompf, *Idea of Historical Recurrence*.

56. Polybius, *Histories*, in von Fritz, *Theory of the Mixed Constitution*, bk. 6, sec. 18, p. 372.

57. "Superstition appears to be the very mainstay of the Roman republic." Polybius, *Histories*, bk. 6 sec. 56, p. 383.

58. As the constitutional theorist C. H. McIlwain puts it, "there is a fundamental difference between the checks and balances . . . which to Polybius constitute the greatest merit . . . of the Roman state . . . and the *fusion* of political *principles*

which characterized the government under the supremacy of the middle class" in Aristotle's polity. *The Growth of Political Thought* (New York: Macmillan, 1932), p. 100.

59. Victor Ehrenberg reports that the Athenian polis (the city of Athens and the hinterland of Attica) was approximately the size of contemporary Luxembourg. *The Greek State* (London: Methuen, 1969), pp. 27–28. Aristotle prescribes a citizen population of between ten and a hundred thousand. *Politics*, 1328b. Plato's dictum that "up to the point in its growth at which it's willing to be one, let it grow, but not beyond." Plato, *The Republic*, trans. Allan Bloom (New York: Basic Books, 1968), p. 101.

60. Constant, "The Liberty of the Ancients Compared With That of the Moderns," p. 312.

61. "Like all ancient cities, but perhaps to a greater extent than any other, Rome was a community of warriors. . . . In this system the Roman is first and foremost a warrior, or rather a soldier." Claude Nicolet, *The World of the Citizen in Republican Rome*, trans. P. S. Falla (Berkeley and Los Angeles: University of California Press, 1980), pp. 89 and 91.

62. For powerful corrections of the general neglect of war in the classical experience, see Paul Rahe, "Paideia: Preparation for Battle," in *Republics Ancient and Modern*, pp. 105–35; Victor Davis Hanson, *The Western Way of War: Infantry Battle in Classical Greece* (New York: Knopf, 1989); and M. I. Finley, *Politics in the Ancient World* (Cambridge: Cambridge University Press, 1983), pp. 113–21.

63. For the prevalence of ancient concern for internal conflicts, see Peter T. Manicas, "War, Stasis, and Greek Political Thought,"*Comparative Studies in Society and History* 24, no. 4 (October 1982), pp. 673–88; Andrew W. Lintott, *Violence, Civil Strife and Revolution in the Classical City* (Oxford: Oxford University Press, 1982); and the detailed Marxian treatment of G.E.M. de Ste Croix, *The Class Struggle in the Ancient Greek World: From the Archaic Age to the Arab Conquests* (London: Duckworth, 1981).

64. *Federalist*, no. 9, p. 73.

65. Yack sums up the situation: "The traditional argument for the subordination of the individual to the community stresses the overriding importance of some collective goal. . . . [T]he most common argument has always been the need to increase the military and political power of the state." *Longing for Total Revolution*, p. 63.

66. Polybius, *Histories*, bk. 6, sec. 2, p. 356.

67. Machiavelli, *Discourses*, pp. 17–18.

68. Crawford, *The Roman Republic*, pp. 31–56.

69. Among the numerous accounts of this struggle the work of R. M. Errington is exceptional in incorporating a political science rather than a classicist perspective. *The Dawn of Empire: Rome's Rise to World Power* (Ithaca: Cornell University Press, 1972), pp. 4–5, 62–90.

70. For a brief compilation of ancient and modern views that emphasizes the central role of expansion, see Jürgen Deininger, "Explaining the Change from Republic to Principate in Rome," *Comparative Civilizations Review* 2, no. 4 (spring 1980), pp. 77–99. For a succinct summation, incorporating recent debates, see Nathan Rosenstein, "Republican Rome," in *War and Society in the*

Ancient and Medieval Worlds: Asia, the Mediterranean, Europe, and Mesopotamia, ed. Kurt Raaflaub and Nathan Rosenberg (Cambridge: Harvard University Press, 1999). For an extended treatment of ancient and early modern thinking about the fall of the Republic, see J.G.A. Pocock, *The First Decline and Fall,* vol. 3 of *Barbarism and Religion* (Cambridge: Cambridge University Press, 2003).

71. For detailed treatment of this agricultural displacement, see Keith Hopkins, *Conquerers and Slaves* (Cambridge: Cambridge University Press, 1978).

72. The interactions between agriculture and ancient warfare is analyzed in detail in Victor Davis Hanson, *Warfare and Agriculture in Classical Greece* (Berkeley and Los Angeles: University of California Press, 1998).

73. P. A. Brunt, *The Fall of the Roman Republic and Related Essays* (Oxford: Clarendon, 1988).

74. E. Gabba, "Rome and Italy: The Social War," in *Cambridge Ancient History,* vol. 9 (Cambridge: Cambridge University Press, 1975); and T. J. Cornell, "Rome: The History of an Anachronism," in *City-States in Classical Antiquity and Medieval Italy,* ed. A. Molho, K. Raaflaub, and J. Emlen (Ann Arbor: University of Michigan Press, 1991). Speaking of both the Hellenistic states and the Roman world, Sheldon Wolin observes: "The concept of the political community had been overwhelmed by the sheer number and diversity of the participants." *Politics and Vision* (Boston: Little, Brown, 1960), p. 77.

CHAPTER FOUR
MARITIME WHIGGERY

1. Destutt de Tracy, *A Commentary and Review of Montesquieu's "Spirit of the Laws,"* trans. Thomas Jefferson (Philadelphia: William Duane, 1811), p. 79.

2. The fullest statement is Doyle, "Liberalism," in *Ways of War and Peace,* pt. 2, pp. 205–311.

3. The two seminal works of 'republican revivalism' in European intellectual history are Skinner, *Foundations*; and Pocock, *Machiavellian Moment.* In both accounts, republicanism succumbs, to monarchical state-building for Skinner and to rising commercial liberalism for Pocock.

4. In his extended recent treatment of the distinctive features of modern republicanism, Paul Rahe almost completely ignores the international, security, and material-contextual dimensions. Rahe, "New Modes and Orders," in *Republics Ancient and Modern,* pp. 233–544.

5. For synoptic treatments of these developments, see Perry Anderson, *Lineages of the Absolutist State* (London: New Left Books, 1974); Charles Tilly, ed., *The Formation of National States in Western Europe* (Princeton: Princeton University Press, 1976); and Thomas Ertman, *The Birth of Leviathan: Building States and Regimes in Medieval and Early Modern Europe* (Cambridge: Cambridge University Press, 1997). For an extended comparison with early Chinese state formation, see Victoria Tin-bor Hui, *War and State Formation in Ancient China and Early Modern Europe* (Cambridge: Cambridge University Press, 2005).

6. For the florescence of late medieval municipal self-government, see J. K. Hyde, *Society and Politics in Medieval Italy: The Evolution of the Civil Life,*

1000–1350 (London: Macmillan, 1973); and Wim P. Blockmans, "A Typology of Representative Institutions in Late Medieval Europe," *Journal of Medieval History* 4, no. 2 (June 1978), pp. 189–215. Skinner emphasizes that the emergence of city-state self-governance occurred prior to the revival of republican theory, a development that occurred as part of the defense of self-government increasingly under assault. *Foundations*, p. 139. For detailed analysis, see Maurizio Viroli, *From Politics to Reason of State: The Acquisition and Transformation of the Language of Politics, 1250–1600* (Cambridge: Cambridge University Press, 1992).

7. For Italy as a miniature prototype of the modern state system, see Garrett Mattingly, *Renaissance Diplomacy* (Boston: Little, Brown, 1971); and Julius Kirshner, ed., *The Origins of the State in Italy, 1300–1600* (Chicago: University of Chicago Press, 1995).

8. For a vivid account of these tumults, see John Addington Symonds, "The Age of Despots" and "The Republics," in *The Age of Despots: The Renaissance in Italy* (New York: Putnam/Capricorn, 1960).

9. For narrative histories, see Frederic Lane, *Venice: A Maritime Republic* (Baltimore: Johns Hopkins University Press, 1973); William McNeill, *Venice: The Hinge of Europe, 1081–1797* (Chicago: University of Chicago Press, 1974); and John Julius Norwich, *A History of Venice* (New York: Knopf, 1982).

10. "The enormous majority of the political units that were around to bid for autonomy and strength in 1500 disappeared in the next few centuries, smashed or absorbed by other states-in-the-making." Charles Tilly, "On the History of European State-Making," in *Formation*, pp. 3–38, at 38.

11. For recent histories and analyses of these developments, see Janice Thomson, *Mercenaries, Pirates and Sovereigns: State-Building and Extraterritorial Violence in Early Modern Europe* (Princeton: Princeton University Press, 1994); A. R. Myers, *Parliaments and Estates in Europe to 1789* (New York: Harcourt, Brace, Jovanovich, 1975); Philippe Dollinger, *The German Hansa*, trans. D. Ault and S. Steinberg (Stanford, CA: Stanford University Press, 1970); and Hendrik Spruyt, *The Sovereign State and Its Competitors* (Princeton: Princeton University Press, 1995).

12. For treatment of this neglected chapter in European history, see J. T. Lukowski, *Liberty's Folly: The Polish-Lithuanian Commonwealth, 1697–1795* (London: Routledge, 1990).

13. As Montesquieu observed, "mountaineers preserve a more moderate government, because they are not so liable to be conquered. They defend themselves easily, and are attacked with difficulty." *Spirit of the Laws*, bk. 18, sec. 2, p. 272. Similarly, Otto Hintze: "Switzerland occupies an exceptional position. . . . [T]he nature of the country is such that it can be defended like a huge fortress." "Military Organization and the Organization of the State," in *Historical Essays*, ed. Felix Gilbert (New York: Oxford University Press, 1975), p. 214.

14. These and numerous other testaments to influence are found in Franz Neumann, "Introduction," in *Spirit of the Laws*, pp. ix–lxiv.

15. Louis Althusser captures the standard view: "It is the received truth that Montesquieu is the founder of political science. Auguste Comte said it, Durkheim repeated it and no one has seriously disputed their judgment." "Montesquieu: Politics and History," in *Politics and History* (London: New Left Books, 1972),

p. 17. The best biography remains Robert Shackleton, *Montesquieu: A Critical Biography* (Oxford: Oxford University Press, 1961). Judith Sklar provides a brief, balanced, and accessible overview in *Montesquieu* (New York: Oxford University Press, 1987).

16. As he observes, with critical reference to Machiavelli: "It is not chance that rules the world. There are general causes, moral and physical, which act in every monarchy, elevating it, maintaining it, or hurling it to the ground. All accidents are controlled by these causes. And if the chance of one battle—that is, a particular cause—has brought a state to ruin, some general cause made it necessary for that state to perish from a single battle. In a word, the main trend always draws with it all particular accidents." Montesquieu, *The Greatness of the Romans and Their Decline*, trans. Richard Lowenthal ([1734] Ithaca: Cornell University Press, 1965), p. 169.

17. For a short account of the nature and limits of Montesquieu's empirical material, see David Young, "Montesquieu's View of Despotism and His Own Use of Travel Literature," *Review of Politics* 40, no. 3 (July 1978), pp. 392–405.

18. The only treatment of Montesquieu in recent international theory I have encountered is Robert Wesson, *State Systems* (New York: Free Press, 1978), pp. 207–11. For a particularly good account of natural restraints on the realization of political freedom, see Thomas L. Pangle, *Montesquieu's Philosophy of Liberalism: A Commentary on "The Spirit of the Laws"* (Chicago: University of Chicago Press), pp. 161–99.

19. John Millar, *The Origin of the Distinction of Ranks; or, An Inquiry into the Circumstances which Give Rise to Influence and Authority in the Different Members of Society*, 3rd ed., enl. and corr., (London, 1781), pp. 2–3.

20. For a richly nuanced treatment of Montesquieu's work in its French context, see Nannerl O. Keohane, *Philosophy and the State in France*; and Mark Hulliung, *Montesquieu and the Old Regime* (Berkeley and Los Angeles: University of California Press, 1976). His favorable and influential British and American reception are explored in F.T.L. Fletcher, *Montesquieu and English Politics, 1750–1800* (London: Arnold, 1939); and Paul Spurlin, *Montesquieu in America, 1760–1801* (Baton Rouge: Louisiana State University Press, 1940). In contrast to this favorable reception in the English-speaking world, Montesquieu's defense of the French aristocracy as a restraint on the absolutizing tendencies of the French monarchy made his reception among the increasingly radicalized *philosophes* much less favorable.

21. For a succinct description of the Venice constitution, see Gordon, "Venice," in *Controlling the State*, pp. 78–125. For discussion of Venetian political thought, see Pocock, *The Machiavellian Moment*, pp. 167–250. In a survey of recent historical treatments of Venice James S. Grubb notes that historians have mainly been addressing issues of class, culture, intellectual life, and economics, in contrast to earlier emphasis on political and military topics. "When Myths Lose Power: Four Decades of Venetian Historiography," *Journal of Modern History* 58, no. 1 (March 1986), pp. 43–94. For the decline in Venice's reputation in the eighteenth century, see David W. Carrithurs, "Not So Virtuous Republics: Montesquieu, Venice and the Theory of Aristocratic Republicanism," *Journal of the History of Ideas* 52, no. 2 (April–June 1991).

22. Due to its ambiguity and complexity, and for brevity, I do not treat seventeenth-century Dutch politics or thought. An excellent overview, emphasizing the elaborate, but jerry-rigged, restraints on power in the Dutch constitutions, and contributions to contract theory, is provided in Gordon, "The Dutch Republic," in *Controlling the State*, pp. 166–222. Gordon observes that "terms such as 'cumbersome,' 'sclerotic,' 'designed for deadlock,' and 'unworkable' are common in the modern historiography [describing the Dutch constitution]" (p. 204). Half oriented to the naval and mercantile world, and half defined by the rural feudalism and the ambitions of the House of Orange, the Dutch political order wavered between the Venetian-British model and the continental autocratic. Martin van Gelderen, *The Political Thought of the Dutch Revolt, 1555–1590* (Cambridge: Cambridge University Press, 1992); E. Haitsma Mulier, *The Myth of Venice and Dutch Republican Thought in the Seventeenth Century* (Assem: Van Gercum, 1980).

23. *Magistratibus et De Respublica Venetorum* (Paris, 1543). This work was translated into English by Lewes Lewkenor in 1599 under the title *The Commonwealth and Government of Venice*. Pocock reports this "became a book of European reputation and was many times reprinted." *Machiavellian Moment*, p. 320. For other treatments, see Elizabeth G. Gleason, ed., *Gasparo Contarini: Venice, Rome and Reform* (Berkeley and Los Angeles: University of California Press, 1993).

24. "[O]ne of the main reasons for the peaceful condition of Venice is the canals which so intersect the city that its inhabitants can only meet together with difficulty and after much delay, during which their grievance is remedied." Giovanni Botero, *The Reason of State*, trans. Richard Waley (New Haven: Yale University Press, 1956), p. 109. More recently Brian Pullen has documented the operation of an elaborate social welfare system that helped distribute the city's commercial wealth. *Rich and Poor in Renaissance Venice: The Social Institutions of a Catholic State to 1620* (Cambridge: Cambridge University Press, 1971).

25. Charles Davanent, *The Political and Commercial Works of Dr. Charles Davanent*, ed. Sir Charles Whitworth, 6 vols. (London, 1771), 1:408.

26. John Trenchard and Thomas Gordon, *Cato's Letters; or, Essays on Liberty, Civil and Religious, and Other Important Subjects*, 3rd ed. (London, 1723), 2:272–77.

27. "The inhabitants of islands have a higher relish for liberty than those of the continent. Islands are commonly of small extent; one part of the people cannot so easily be employed to oppress the other; the sea separates them from great empires; tyranny cannot so well support itself within a small compass." Montesquieu, *Spirit of the Laws*, bk. 18, sec. 5, p. 273.

28. Millar's two main works, his four-volume *An Historical View of English Government* (posthumously published in 1804) and his pioneering sociological treatise, *The Origin of the Distinction of Ranks* (1781), employed an explicit and sophisticated contextual materialist framework to explain the origins of political institutions. For discussion of Millar's life, thought and influence, see William C. Lehmann, *John Millar of Glasgow* (Cambridge: Cambridge University Press, 1960), pp. 7–166.

29. John Millar, *An Historical View of the English Government, From the settlement of the Saxons to the Revolution of 1688*, 4 vols. (London: J. G. Barnard, 1812), pp. 118, 119, 119, 122, 125.

30. Millar, *Origin of Ranks*, p. 294.

31. Although this argument appears to be similar to Aristotle's argument connecting naval polises with democracy, the logic of the links is very different. For Aristotle, democracy is strengthened by the ability of citizen rowers to participate in domestic politics, while the maritime whig argument is that naval force cannot be brought to bear in civil conflicts.

32. "The sea, therefore, is, of all natural limits, the best; and has also a property admirable and peculiar to itself, that is, the naval power which defends it, employs few men; those men are useful in promoting the public prosperity; and another advantage, they can never in a body take part in civil disorders, nor alarm interior liberty; consequently the advantages of an island for happiness and liberty are very great." de Tracy, *Commentary*, p. 79.

33. de Tracy, *Commentary*, p. 79.

34. "Land forces are a kind of organization that permeates the whole body of the state and gives it a military cast. Sea power is only a mailed fist, reaching out into the world; it is not suitable for use against some 'enemy within.' . . . England, with her insular security . . . needed no standing army, at least not one of Continental proportions, but only a navy which served commercial interests as much as war aims. In consequence she developed no absolutism. Absolutism and militarism go together on the Continent just as do self-government and militia in England." Hintze, *Historical Essays*, pp. 215 and 199. Mackinder notes that because of her insular position the British were "able to refuse to maintain a standing army which might{{dagger}}become a weapon of royal oppression. There was no similar danger to be feared from a fleet." Halford J. Mackinder, *The Nations of the Modern World* (London: George Phillip and Son, 1911), p. 54.

35. "It is noteworthy that historians such as L. Stone, C. Hill, and P. Anderson, who in other respects hold very diverse views, all agree more or less about the initial cause of the country's [Britain's] originality. Although England,{{dagger}}at the beginning of the modern age, was subjected to a centralizing pressure just as powerful as that which prevailed among the continental states, that pressure did not lead to the establishment of a standing royal army. This omission in the monarchical apparatus subsequently imposed very strict limits on action by the monarchy, regardless of what the political aims of any particular sovereign were to be. And England's position in relation to the international pattern is clearly what made that omission possible." Aristride Zolberg, "Strategic Interaction and the Formation of Modern States: France and England," *International Social Science Journal*, 32, no. 4 (1980), p. 707.

36. For recent arguments about the genesis of capitalism, among the most important and hotly debated issues in economic, social, and political history, see Douglass C. North and Robert Paul Thomas, *The Rise of the Western World: A New Economic History* (Cambridge: Cambridge University Press, 1973); Albert O. Hirschman, *The Passions and the Interests: Political Arguments for Capitalism before Its Triumph* (Princeton: Princeton University Press, 1977); Jones, *The European Miracle*; and John Hall, *Powers and Liberties: the Causes and Consequences*

of the Rise of the West (Berkeley and Los Angeles: University of California Press, 1985). For the superiority of maritime over land transport before the railroad, see James E. Vance, Jr., *Capturing the Horizon: The Historical Geography of Transportation* (New York: Harper and Row, 1986).

37. The connection between the sea and capitalism plays an partial role in Max Weber's classic account. He begins by assigning great importance to geography: "The external conditions for the development of capitalism are rather, first, geographical in character. In China and India the enormous costs of transportation, connected with the decisively inland commerce of the regions, necessarily formed serious obstructions for the classes who were in a position to make profits through trade and to use trading capital in the construction of a capitalistic system, while in the west the position of the Mediterranean as an inland sea, and the abundant interconnections through the rivers, favored the opposite development of international commerce. But this factor in turn must not be overestimated." Max Weber, *General Economic History*, trans. Frank Knight (Glencoe, IL: Free Press, 1927), p. 353. He notes that some of the most important innovations in early capitalism took place in Florence and the cities of the German interior, where the maritime link was less pronounced. He then proceeds with a typically 'Weberian' argument about cultural, intellectual, and religious causal factors.

38. "Sea powers have always been distinguished by much freer and more mobile societies than their territorial neighbors. . . . [T]erritorial powers have always been distinguished by very much more repressive societies." Peter Padfield, *Tides of Empires: Decisive Naval Campaigns in the Rise of the West*, vol. 2, *1654–1763* (London: Routledge and Kegan Paul, 1982), pp. 2–3. For the mercantile and naval aspects of Venetian power, see Frederic C. Lane, *Venice: A Maritime Republic* (Baltimore: Johns Hopkins University Press, 1973).

39. Montesquieu, *Spirit of the Laws*. For extended discussion, see Eric Jones, *European Miracle*; Edward Whiting Fox, *History in Geographic Perspective: The Other France* (New York: Norton, 1971); Eugene D. Genovese and Leonard Hochberg, eds., *Geographic Perspectives in History* (Oxford: Blackwell, 1989); and Michel Mollat du Jourdin, *Europe and the Sea*, trans. T. L. Fagen (Oxford: Blackwell, 1993).

40. Dugald Stewart, "Account of the Life and Writings of Adam Smith, LLD," in *The Glasgow Edition of the Works and Correspondence of Adam Smith* (Oxford: Oxford University Press, 1980), 3:322. For the relationship between widely distributed private property and political freedom, see Richard Pipes, *Property and Freedom* (New York: Random House, 2000).

41. Montesquieu, *Spirit of the Laws*, bk. 21, sec. 5 and 20, pp. 333, 365. For the relationship between capitalism and British power, see John Brewer, *The Sinews of Power: War, Money and the English State, 1688–1783* (New York: Knopf, 1989).

42. Montesquieu, *Spirit of the Laws*, bk. 21, sec. 20, p. 366. Montesquieu's language here bears striking resemblance to that of Thomas Gordon, writing as 'Cato,' when he observes that Trade is "a coy and humorous Dame, who must be won by Flattery and Allurements, and always flies Force and Power, she is not confined to Nations, sects, or Climates, but travels and wanders about the Earth, till she fixes Residence where she finds the best Welcome and Kindest Reception; her Contexture is so nice, that she cannot breathe in a tyrannical Air." Thomas

Gordon, "Trade and Naval Power the Offspring of Civil Liberty only and cannot subsist without it," no. 64, February 3, 1721, in *Cato's Letters; or, Essays on Liberty, Civil and Religious, and Other Important Subjects*, 4th ed., 4 vols. (London, 1737), 2:267.

43. McNeill, *Pursuit of Power*, pp. 106, 113, and 114; Stein Rokkan, "Territories, Centres and Peripheries: Toward a Geoethnic-Geoeconomic-Geopolitical Model of Differentiation within Western Europe," in Jean Gottman, ed., *Centre and Periphery: Spatial Variation in Politics* (Beverly Hills, CA: Sage, 1980). For maritime accessibility in Europe and comparison with other regions, see Roy I. Wolfe, *Transportation and Politics* (Princeton: Van Nostrand, 1963).

44. Felix Gilbert, "Machiavelli and the Art of War," in *Makers of Modern Strategy*, ed. Edward Meade Earle (Princeton: Princeton University Press, 1944), pp. 3–25.

45. Pocock suggests that the complex mechanical arrangements of the Venetian constitution, such as lot and rotation of offices, constituted a "mechanization of *virtú*." In contrast, I argue that the onerous security tasks assigned to martial *virtú* were increasingly replaced by machines, most notably ships. *Machiavellian Moment*, pp. 284–85.

46. Edward Gibbon, "General Considerations on the Decline and Fall of the Roman Empire," in *The Decline and Fall of the Roman Empire*, 1:437 (my emphasis).

47. For discussions of the evolution of naval capability and its impact upon commerce, see Frederic C. Lane, *Profits from Power: Readings in Protection Rent and Violence-Controlling Enterprises* (Albany: State University of New York Press, 1979); and Carlo Cipolla, *Guns, Sails, and Empires: Technological Innovation and the Early Phases of European Expansion, 1400–1700* (New York: Minerva Press, 1965).

48. For discussion of the realization that the militia would no longer be central to republican security, see John Robertson, *The Scottish Enlightenment and the Militia Issue* (Edinburgh: Edinburgh University Press, 1985); and David Wootton, "Ulysses Bound? Venice and the Idea of Liberty from Harrington to Hume," in *Republicanism and Commercial Society*, ed. David Wootton (Stanford, CA: Stanford University Press, 2003).

49. Indeed, as many Marxist critics of liberal-state imperialism point out, a free people devoted to the rapacious and in principle limitless pursuit of property and wealth had its own expansionary foreign policy logic.

50. For eighteenth-century critics of European predation, see Sankar Muthu, *Enlightenment against Empire* (Princeton: Princeton University Press, 2003).

51. In his recent penetrating treatment of this topic, David Armstrong observes that "how to achieve empire while sustaining liberty became a defining concern of British imperial ideology from the late sixteenth century onwards." *The Ideological Origins of the British Empire* (Cambridge: Cambridge University Press, 2000), p. 125.

52. For detailed discussion of these schemes, see Pocock, *Machiavellian Moment*, pp. 383–400.

53. J.G.A. Pocock, ed., *The Political Works of James Harrington* (Cambridge: Cambridge University Press, 1977), p. 160. For the subsequent use of these ideas

in British imperial thought, see Judith Sklar, "Ideology-Hunting: The Case of James Harrington," *American Political Science Review* 53, no. 3 (September 1959).

54. Aristotle argued that a genuine 'political' association required face-to-face interaction and was therefore bound to a city-state, and that very large empires would be despotic. In the late-fourteenth century Bartolus, in a commentary on Roman law, distinguished between three grades of regimes by size and argued that the smallest were appropriate to popular government, the middle to aristocracies, and the largest to one individual. The apparent differences between Bartolus and Montesquieu are less than they appear because Montesquieu emphasizes the key role played by aristocracies in monarchies. For discussion, see Onuf, *Republican Legacies*, pp. 70; Skinner, *Foundations*, pp. 10–12 and 62–65; and Wight, *Systems of States*, pp. 130.

55. Montesquieu, *Spirit of the Laws*, bk. 9, sec. 6, pp. 129–30.

56. Montesquieu, *Spirit of the Laws*, bk. 8, sec. 20, p. 122 (my emphasis).

57. Montesquieu, *Spirit of the Laws*, bk. 8, sec. 19, p. 122 (my emphasis).

58. "[W]ere it [a monarchical state] *very large*, the nobility possessed of great estates, *far* from the inspection of the prince, . . . might throw off their allegiance, having nothing to fear from too *slow* and too *distant* a punishment." Montesquieu, *Spirit of the Laws*, bk. 8, sec. 17, p. 121 (my emphasis).

59. "Excepting particular circumstances, it is difficult for any other than republican government to subsist long in a single town. A prince of so petty a state would naturally endeavor to oppress because his power would be great while the means of enjoying it or causing it to be respected, would be very inconsiderable. . . . [S]uch a prince might be easily crushed by a foreign force or even by a domestic force. . . . Now as soon as a prince of a single town is expelled, the quarrel is over; but if he has many towns, it only begins." Montesquieu, *Spirit of the Laws*, bk. 8, sec. 16, p. 120.

60. "[I]n order to preserve the principles of the established government, the state must be supported in the extent it has required, and with that the spirit of this state will alter in proportion as it contracts or expands its limits." Montesquieu, *Spirit of the Laws*, bk. 8, sec. 20, p. 122.

61. Millar, *An Historical View of the English Government*, p. 135.

62. Hume, "Of the Rise and Progress" p. 64.

63. Hume, "Of the Rise and Progress," p. 64.

64. Montesquieu, *Spirit of the Laws*, bk. 8, sec. 16, p. 121. And Hume observes that "[i]n a small government, any act of oppression is immediately known throughout the whole: The murmurs and discontents, proceeding from it, are easily communicated." "Of the Rise and Progress," p. 64.

65. Millar, *An Historical View of the English Government*, p. 115. In his discussion of Millar, Hirshman notes that this capacity for the 'crowd' to produce urban tumult would in the nineteenth century be central to the anticapitalist revolutionary aspirations of the working classes. *Passions and Interests*, pp. 88–93.

66. Montesquieu, *Spirit of the Laws*, bk. 5, sec. 19, p. 68.

67. David Hume, "The Idea of a Perfect Commonwealth," in *Political Essays*, pp. 221–33. For Hume's influence, see Douglass Adair, "That Politics May Be

Reduced to a Science: David Hume, James Madison, and the Tenth Federalist," in *Fame and the Founding Fathers* (New York: Norton, 1964).

68. In a section entitled "In what manner republics provide for their safety," Montesquieu refers to confederate republics as a "kind of constitution that has all the internal advantage of a republican, together with the external force of a monarchial government." He also claims that this type of association played important roles in ancient Greece, the Roman ascent, among the Germanic tribes, and in Holland, Germany, and Switzerland. *Spirit of the Laws*, bk. 9, sec. 20, p. 126.

69. Montesquieu, *Spirit of the Laws*, bk. 9, sec. 20, p. 127.

70. Like Thucydides, Machiavelli wrote after a forced retirement from an active political career. For succinct and balanced overviews, see Quentin Skinner, *Machiavelli* (New York: Oxford University Press, 1981); and Isaiah Berlin, "The Originality of Machiavelli," in *Against the Current* (New York: Viking, 1980).

71. Machiavelli, *Discourses*, pp. 34–38. For the multiple uses of 'Rome' as an exemplar in Machiaveli, see Vicki Sullivan, *Machiavelli's Three Romes* (Champaign-Urbana: Northern Illinois University Press, 2004).

72. For this relationship and contrasting views, see Felix Gilbert, *Machiavelli and Guicciardini: Politics and History in Sixteenth Century Florence* (Princeton: Princeton University Press, 1965).

73. For an extended discussion, see Harvey C. Mansfield, Jr., *Machiavelli's Virtue* (Chicago: University of Chicago Press, 1996).

74. Doyle's insightful treatment of both Machiavelli and Rousseau treats them as simultaneously 'republicans' and 'Realists.' See Michael W. Doyle, "Machiavelli: Fundamentalism," in *Ways of War and Peace*, p. 78.

75. Concerning technology, Machiavelli's reaction to the emergence of gunpowder weaponry is not as backward looking as his views on commerce, but is largely conservative, as described in his *Art of War*, his only book published in his lifetime. For discussion, see Gilbert, "Machiavelli: The Renaissance Art of War," pp. 3–25.

76. Roger Masters argues that Machiavelli had a much more active technological program to bend nature to human purpose, a view that reads Bacon and subsequent tendencies into his work. *Machiavelli, Leonardo and the Science of Power* (Notre Dame, IN: University of Notre Dame Press, 1996); and Roger D. Masters, *Fortune Is a River: Leonardo da Vinci and Niccolo Machiavelli's Magnificent Dream to Change the Course of Florentine History* (New York: Free Press, 1998).

77. Rousseau, *Social Contract*, p. 100.

78. Rousseau, *Social Contract*, p. 101.

79. Rousseau, *Social Contract*, pp. 91 and 84.

80. Rousseau, *Social Contract*, p. 106. Rousseau's passage on this point reads much like Montesquieu.

81. "Any law which the People has not ratified in person is null; it is not a law." Rousseau, *Social Contract*, p. 114.

82. Rousseau, *Social Contract*, p. 114.

83. The maritime whig contextual-materialist arguments are similarly complementary to 'rational choice' explanations that attribute the rise of capitalism to 'getting the incentives right.' Most importantly, this entails the avoidance of predatory taxation and occurs when property owners control the state. How this hap-

pened to occur where it did is explained by the maritime whig arguments. Douglass C. North and Barry R. Weingast, "Constitutions and Commitment: The Evolution of Institutions Governing Public Choice in Seventeenth-Century England," in Paul W. Drake and Mathew D. McCubbins, eds., *The Origins of Liberty: Political and Economic Liberalization in the Modern World* (Princeton: Princeton University Press, 1998).

CHAPTER FIVE
THE NATURAL 'REPUBLIC' OF EUROPE

1. Jean Jacques Rousseau, "Summary of Saint-Pierre's Project for Perpetual Peace," in *Reading Rousseau in the Nuclear Age*, ed. and trans. Grace Roosevelt (Philadelphia: Temple University Press, 1990), p. 205.

2. Most constructivist analysis has been unconcerned about precursors, with the important exception of Nicholas Onuf's substantial treatment of Enlightenment ideas of Europe as a republic, but his analysis neglects structural and material aspects of these ideas. "City of Sovereigns," in *Republican Legacy*, pp. 58–84.

3. So strong is "the deep-seated assumption in IR that the Westphalian system epitomizes the international system" that Buzan and Little refer to "the Westphalian straitjacket." *International Systems*, pp. 5 and 7.

4. For discussions of growing European knowledge of other regions of the world, see John Larner, *Marco Polo and the Discovery of the World* (New Haven: Yale University Press, 1999); Peter Marshall and Glyndwyr Williams, *The Great Map of Mankind: British Perceptions of the World in the Age of Enlightenment* (London: J. M. Dent, 1982); Anthony Grafton et al., eds., *New Worlds, Ancient Texts: The Power of Tradition and the Shock of Discovery* (Cambridge: Harvard University Press, 1992); Fred Chiappelli, ed., *First Images of America: The Impact of the New World on the Old* (Berkeley and Los Angeles: University of California Press, 1976); and Julia Ching and Willard G. Oxtoby, ed., *Discovering China: European Interpretations in the Enlightenment* (Rochester: University of Rochester Press, 1992).

5. Critical treatments of the 'inside-outside' problem are available from many different perspectives. Hidemi Suganami examines this issue in international law and world order reform proposals in *The Domestic Analogy and World Order Proposals* (Cambridge: Cambridge University Press, 1989). R.B.J. Walker argues the distinction has constitutive roots in modern political thought in *Inside/Outside*. James N. Rosenau argues that the recent explosive growth in interstate flows and nonstate actors has rendered the distinction untenable in *Along the Domestic-Foreign Frontier* (Cambridge: Cambridge University Press, 1997). Helen Milner outlines the 'rational choice' program of viewing domestic and international politics through a unified approach in "Rationalizing Politics: The Emerging Synthesis of American, International, and Comparative Politics," *International Organization* 52, no. 4 (autumn 1998), pp. 759–86.

6. Rousseau summarizes this sentiment with the observation that "the treaty of Westphalia will perhaps forever be the basis of the political system among us."

"Rousseau's 'Summary' of the Abbé De Saint-Pierre's *Project for Perpetual Peace*," in Roosevelt, *Reading Rousseau*, p. 207.

7. For a brilliant overview of the dimensions of this disorder, see Raab, *The Struggle for Stability in Early Modern Europe*; and the classic treatment of H. R Trevor-Roper, "The General Crisis of the Seventeenth Century," in *Crisis in Europe, 1560–1660*, ed. Trevor Aston (Garden City, NY: Anchor Books, 1967), pp. 63–102.

8. This analogy between feuding domestic factions and European great monarchical houses is clearly drawn by Edmund Burke: "The same principles that make it incumbent upon the patriotic member of a republic, to watch with the strictest attention the motions and designs of his powerful fellow-citizens, should equally operate upon the different states in such a community in Europe, who are also the great members of a larger commonwealth." Edmund Burke, *The Annual Register; or, a View of the History, Politics, and Literature, For the Year 1760*, 7th ed. (London, 1789), p. 3. Cited in Haslam, *No Virtue Like Necessity*, p. 107.

9. Dante, *Monarchy*, ed. and trans. Prue Shaw (Cambridge: Cambridge University Press, 1996), pp. 12–15. In this passage I have assembled key sentences over several pages of Dante's text. For discussions of Dante, see Skinner, *Foundations*, 1:16–18; and Anthony Black, *Political Thought in Europe, 1250–1450* (Cambridge: Cambridge University Press, 1992), pp. 96–100. The position of Thomas Aquinas, as I understand it, is much more supportive of plurality.

10. For descriptions and discussions of the theorists and advocates of universal monarchy, see Richard Koebner, "'Imperium': The Roman Heritage," and "From Imperium to Empire," in *Empire* (Cambridge: Cambridge University Press, 1961); Anthony Pagden, "Instruments of Empire: Tommaso Campanella and the Universal Monarchy of Spain," in *Spanish Imperialism and the Political Imagination* (New Haven: Yale University Press, 1990), pp. 37–64; Anthony Pagden, "The Legacy of Rome," and "Monarchia Universalis," in *Lords of All the World: Ideologies of Empire in Spain, Britain and France, c. 1500–c. 1800* (New Haven: Yale University Press, 1994), pp. 11–62; and James Muldoon, "The Golden Age of Empire," in *Empire and Order: The Concept of Empire, 800–1800* (London: Macmillan, 1999), pp. 114–38.

11. Giovanni Botero, *Relatione della Respublica Venetiana* (Venice, 1605), p. 9.

12. This essay, not yet translated into English, is found in *Deux opuscules de Montesquieu, publies par le Baron de Montesquieu* (Paris, 1891), p. 15. For detailed discussions of its contents and importance in Montesquieu's work, see Mark Hulliung, "A World of Leviathans," in *Montesquieu and the Old Regime*, pp. 173–211. Paul A. Rahe argues that fear of censorship inhibited Montesquieu from publishing this work in "The Book That Never Was: Montesquieu's *Consideration of the Romans* in Historical Context," *History of Political Thought*, 26, no. 1 (spring 2005), pp. 43–89.

13. Richard Tuck reports that this expression was not widely used in the medieval period, but rather came into general use as popes and their humanist advisers sought to mobilize Christendom against the Turks. *Rights of War and Peace*, pp. 28–29. For differing assessments, see Walter Ullmann, *Principles of Government and Politics in the Middle Age* (London: Methuen, 1961), p. 224.

14. For the prevalence of such mechanical models, see Otto Mayr, *Authority, Liberty and Automatic Machinery in Early Modern Europe* (Baltimore: Johns Hopkins University Press, 1986); Richard Striner, "Political Newtonianism: The Cosmic Model of Politics in Europe and America," *William and Mary Quarterly* 52, no. 4 (October 1995), pp. 583–608; and Michael Foley, *Laws, Men and Machines: Modern American Government and the Appeal of Newtonian Mechanics* (London: Routledge, 1990).

15. Within treatments of republicanism, the conceptualization of Europe as a 'republic' is almost completely neglected, with the important exception of Onuf, who largely neglects our main interest, the structural and material parts of the argument. In his classic account of diplomatic theory and practice, Edward Vose Gulick cites many uses of 'republic' to refer to Europe, but draws no special attention to the broader implications of such usage beyond a sense of shared historical experience and customs. *Europe's Classical Balance of Power* (New York: Norton, 1967).

16. As usual a dissenter, Rousseau reserves the expression "the European Republic" to refer to proposed confederations to replace the state-of-war anarchy. Roosevelt, *Reading Rousseau*, pp. 209 and 221.

17. Niklas Vogt, *Über die europäische Republik*, 5 vols. (Frankfurt am Main, 1787–92) (cited in Gulick, *Europe's Classical Balance of Power*, p. 11).

18. Emmerich de Vattel, *The Law of Nations* ([1756]Washington, DC: Carnegie Institute, 1916), vol. 3, sec. 251, para. 47.

19. Dominique de Fourt de Pradt, *La Prusse et sa neutralite* (London, 1800), (cited in Gulick, p. 11).

20. Voltaire, *The Age of Louis XIV*, trans. Martyn Pollack ([1751] New York: Dutton, 1961), chap. 2. For discussion, see Merle Perkins, "Voltaire's Concept of International Order," *Studies in Voltaire and the Eighteenth Century* 36 (Geneva: Institutet Musee Voltaire, 1965).

21. Edmund Burke, "France and the 'Diplomatic Republic of Europe'," in Ross Hoffman and Paul Levack eds., *Burke's Politics* (New York: Knopf, 1949), p. 443. For extended discussion emphasizing the conservative and cultural dimensions of Burke's understanding of European public order, see Jennifer M. Welsh, *Edmund Burke and International Relations: The Commonwealth of Europe and the Crusade against the French Revolution* (New York: St. Martin's Press, 1994), p. 250.

22. Francois de Callieres, *On the Manner of Negotiating with Princes*, trans. A. F. Whyte ([1716] Notre Dame, IN: University of Notre Dame Press, 1963), p. 11.

23. Edward Gibbon, "General Observations on the Fall of the Roman Empire in the West," in vol. 2, chap. 38, *The Decline and Fall of the Roman Empire* ([1776] New York: Modern Library, n.d.), pp. 436–44, at 437 (my emphasis). These ten paragraphs of Gibbon's work, added in the second edition, are strikingly different in topic and scope from the rest of his writings. David P. Jordan judges that "Gibbon was the most successful and most brilliant disciple of Montesquieu." *Gibbon and His Roman Empire* (Urbana: University of Illinois Press, 1971), p. 71. For an extended meditation on Gibbon's view of Europe in the light of subsequent European calamities, see Arnold J. Toynbee, "The Prospects for Western Civilization," chap. 12, in "A Critique of Gibbon's General Observations

on the Fall of the Roman Empire in the West," *A Study of History* (New York: Oxford University Press, 1954), 9:424–40 and 741–57.

24. Jonathan Swift, "A Discourse of the Contests and Dissentions in Athens and Rome," in *A Tale of a Tub and Other Early Works*, ed. Herbert Davis ([1701] Oxford: Blackwell, 1957), p. 197. Similarly John Barrington observes: "the constitution of England consists in a balance of parties; as the liberties of Europe do in a balance of powers." *The Interest of England Considered in Respect to Protestants Dissenting from the Established Church* (London, 1702), pp. 29–30; and David Hume's observation on the relationship between the Athenian institution of ostracism and the principle of the balance of power in foreign policies. David Hume, "Of the Balance of Power," in *Political Essays*, ed. Knud Haakonssen ([1752] Cambridge: Cambridge University Press, 1994), pp. 154–65, at 155.

25. Issac Kramnick reports that "Bolingbroke saw both constitutional and international politics in terms that postulated rival independent powers who were still independent enough to check a single power's claim to hegemony." "Introduction," in *Lord Bolingbroke: Historical Writings* (Chicago: University of Chicago Press, 1972), p. xlvi.

26. "France and the 'Diplomatic Republic of Europe'," in *Burke's Politics*, ed. Hoffman and Levack (New York: Knopf, 1949), p. 443. And the Prussian diplomat Friedrick von Gentz speaks of the "new federal system" advanced by Napolean at the expense of the "true federal system" of the old order. *Fragments upon the Balance of Power in Europe* (London, 1806), p. xiii.

27. This shift is registered in the complete absence of any talk about Europe as a republic in Carsten Holbraad's careful history of nineteenth-century theories of the Concert in Britain and Germany. *The Concert of Europe: A Study in German and British International Theory* (London: Longman, 1970).

28. A.H.L. Heeren, *The History of the Political System of Europe and Its Colonies*, trans. Richard Smith ([1834] London: Henry Bohn, 1846).

29. Cited in James Hutson, *John Adams and the Diplomacy of the American Revolution* (Frankfort: The University Press of Kentucky, 1980), p. 29.

30. Rousseau, "Summary," in Roosevelt, *Reading Rousseau*, pp. 205.

31. Giovanni Botero, *Delle Relazioni Universali*, parte seconda, libro primo (Paris, 1605), p. 1. I am indebted to Riccardo Pelizzo for bringing this passage to my attention and translating it.

32. Here Montesquieu stands against the general tendency of the French *philosophes* to criticize the balance and separation of power both within and between the states of Europe, and to support enlightened despotism and administered peace. Helvetius, in his famous letter to Montesquieu, complained that "your combination of balanced powers only tend to separate and complicate individual interests, rather than to separate them." de Tracy, *Commentary*, p. 287. For the general tendency of *philosophes* to attack the balance of power and advocate its elimination, see Felix Gilbert, "The 'New Diplomacy' of the Eighteenth Century," *World Politics* 4, no. 1 (October 1951), particularly pp. 1–16.

33. Montesquieu, *Spirit of the Laws*, bk. 18, chap. 6, pp. 278–79 (my emphasis).

34. Thus Montesquieu's elaborate arguments about the influence of material contexts is not a species of arguments about 'race' (i.e., biological innate differences between groups), which do have a growing presence in Enlightenment thought. In this posture Montesquieu is consistent with the dominant view on this

topic in the classical Greek and Roman, medieval Christian, and early modern European West. Ivan Hanniford argues that Jean Bodin, the early antirepublican theorist of nascent absolutism, was the first prominent Western theorist to advance race variation arguments, that Enlightenment comparative anthropology helped further them, and that twentieth-century mistranslations of classical texts misrepresented ancient perspectives. *Race: the History of an Idea in the West* (Baltimore: Johns Hopkins University Press, 1996). Conversely, Benjamin Isaac finds abundant evidence for racial prejudices (beyond ethnic and cultural) in Greek and Roman writers. *The Invention of Racism in Classical Antiquity* (Princeton: Princeton University Press, 2004).

35. Rousseau, "Summary," in Roosevelt, *Reading Rousseau*, pp. 205 (my emphasis).

36. A. H. Dietrich von Bülow, *The Spirit of the Modern System of War* (London: Mercier, 1806). Von Bülow is best remembered as the target of Clausewitz's theory of war, discussed in Azar Gat, *The Origins of Military Thought: From the Enlightenment to Clausewitz* (Oxford: Oxford University Press, 1989), pp. 79–94. Von Bülow also advanced a complex set of arguments about how the interaction of topographic constraints and gunpowder weapons would contribute to democratization in the units and the gradual cessation of interstate war.

37. von Bülow, *Modern System of War*, p. 202.

38. von Bülow, *Modern System of War*, p. 205.

39. von Bülow, *Modern System of War*, p. 204. For detailed case studies of the impacts of weather on amphibious assaults, see Harold A. Winters et al., *Battling the Elements: Weather and Terrain in the Conduct of War* (Baltimore: Johns Hopkins University Press, 1998).

40. von Bülow, *Modern System of War*, p. 211.

41. von Bülow, *Modern System of War*, p. 283.

42. von Bülow, *Modern System of War*, p. 196.

43. von Bülow, *Modern System of War*, p. 284. In predicting that the German nation (as defined by language) would remain separate in two states, von Bülow points to an important feature of the European political scene often glossed over by descriptions of the nineteenth century as an era of national unification.

44. N.J.G. Pounds and S. S. Ball, "Core-areas and the Development of the European States-System," *Annals of the Association of American Geographers* 54, no. 1 (March 1964), pp. 24–40.

45. Jean Baechler, *The Origins of Capitalism*, trans. Barry Cooper (New York: St. Martin's Press, 1976); Robert Gilpin, "Economic Interdependence and National Security in Historical Perspective," in *Economic Issues and National Security*, ed. Klaus Knorr and Frank N. Trager (Lawrence: University Press of Kansas, 1977), p. 25; Robert G. Wesson, *State Systems: International Pluralism, Politics and Culture* (New York: Free Press, 1978), p. 110; Joshua S. Goldstein, *Long Cycles, Prosperity and War in the Modern Age* (New Haven: Yale University Press, 1988), p. 290; Paul Kennedy, *The Rise and Fall of the Great Powers* (New York: Random House, 1987), p. 17; and Eric Jones, *The European Miracle* (Cambridge: Cambridge University Press, 1981), p. 105.

46. Franceso Guicciardini, *History of Italy*, ed. and trans. Sidney Alexander ([1543] Princeton: Princeton University Press, 1984). For a similar argument, see

Jacob Burkhardt, *The Civilization of the Renaissance in Italy*, trans. Robert Middlemore ([1860] London: Phaidon Books, 1960).

47. Henry VIII is reported to have commissioned a painting of himself holding a scale in whose two trays France and Austria are placed. In another early reference (in a dedication to Queen Elizabeth), England's role as balancer is highlighted: "[God] hath erected your seate upon a high hill or sanctuarie, and put into your hands the ballance of power and justice." Geffray Fenton, *The Historie of Guicciardini . . . Reduced into English* (1579), p. iv, cited in Martin Wight, "The Balance of Power," in *Diplomatic Investigations*, ed. Herbert Butterfield and Martin Wight (Cambridge: Harvard University Press, 1966). Somewhat later William Camden said of Elizabethan England "that France and Spain are as it were the Scales in the Balance of Europe and England the Tongue or the Holder of the Balance." *Annales of the History of the Most Renowned and Victorious Elizabeth, late Queen of England* (London, 1635), p. 196. (cited in Morgenthau, *Politics among Nations*, 2nd ed. (New York: Knopf, 1954) p. 144).

48. Francis Bacon, "True Greatness of Kingdoms and Estates," in *Bacon's Essays*, ed. W. A. Wright (London: Macmillan, 1939), p. 128.

49. In these arguments the existence of substantial and proximate island—the British Isles—is a contingent geographic fact of great significance. Its existence can be easily conflated with the extensive maritime access, but it is possible to have one without the other.

50. Not as immediately decisive as defeat of a field army or occupancy of a stronghold, these factors were 'indirect' in their effects, and together they comprise what Liddell Hart calls 'the British way in war.' For discussion, see Michael Howard, *The British Way of Warfare: A Reappraisal* (London: Jonathan Cape, 1975); and Jeremy Black and Philip Woodfine, eds., *The British Navy and the Use of Naval Power in the Eighteenth Century* (Atlantic Highlands, NJ: Humanities Press International, 1989).

51. The most dramatic examples were the defeat of the Spanish Armada in 1588 by the combined British and Dutch fleets and the victory of the British navy over the combined French-Spanish fleet at Trafalgar in 1805. For a survey of the various invasion attempts that Britain weathered, see Frank McLynn, *Invasion: From the Armada to Hitler, 1588–1945* (London: Routledge and Kegan Paul, 1987).

52. For discussion, see Francois Crouzet, "Wars, Blockade and Economic Change in Europe, 1792–1815," *Journal of Economic History* 24, no. 2 (December 1964), pp. 567–88. Francis Drake's attacks on Spanish commerce in 1585–86 contributed to the paralysis of Philip II's advance in Flanders by keeping from Parma the funds needed to support the army. In 1590 the capture of the annual treasure fleet by Frobisher and Hawkins forced Spain to forgo a planned invasion of France.

53. In the Seven Years' War the British system of subsidies played an important role in sustaining the military presence of Frederick the Great of Prussia. In the Napoleonic Wars, the subsidy system played a major role in sustaining resistance to the French in Southern and Eastern Europe. For discussion, see John M. Sherwig, *Guineas and Gunpowder* (Cambridge: Harvard University Press, 1969); and

Paul Kennedy, *The Rise and Fall of British Naval Mastery* (London: Macmillan, 1983), p. 136.

54. The most famous land campaign based upon sea power was Wellington's 'peninsular war' in Spain and Portugal against Napoleon's occupation forces. For general discussion, see C. E. Callwell, *Military Operations and Maritime Preponderance: Their Relations and Interdependence* (Edinburgh: William Blackwood, 1905); and *The Effect of Maritime Command on Land Campaigns since Waterloo* (Edinburgh: William Blackwood, 1897).

55. Botero observed: "history shows that no empire founded upon maritime power has ever spread far inland." *Reason of State*, p. 216. Paruta argues that Venice escaped one of the two greatest flaws, absence of limitation (the other being imbalance), because the Venetian navy was less capable than the Roman army in conquering and holding territory. *Discorsi Politici*, p. 215.

56. Cited in George Rude, *Europe in the Eighteenth Century: Aristocracy and the Bourgeois Challenge* (New York: Praeger, 1972), p. 214.

57. Otto Hintze, in his essay "Germany and the World War," provides this interpretation of British naval hegemony: "Our aim in this war can only be to force England to abandon her claim to absolute supremacy at sea, and thus to create a state of equilibrium within the world system of states. . . . It is our aim to complement the balance of power on land with a balance of power at sea." Hintze cited in Ludwig Dehio, *Germany and World Politics in the Twentieth Century*, trans. Dieter Pevsner (New York: Knopf, 1959), p. 53. For Friedrich Meinecke's description of Germany's mission in almost identical terms, see Dehio, *Germany and World Politics*, p. 59.

58. Dehio, "Thoughts on Germany's Mission, 1900–1918," in *Germany and World Politics*, pp. 72–109. For a detailed account of Britain's lengthy and unsuccessful attempt to claim sovereignty over the seas around the British Isles, see Thomas Wemyss Fulton, *The Sovereignty of the Sea* (Edinburgh: William Blackwood, 1911).

59. "It also seems the balancer is somehow different from other nations . . . who would make use of a preponderance of power to upset peace and conquer their neighbors. . . . This quest for maximum power is a universal law, but it apparently does not apply to the balancer." A.F.K. Organski, *World Politics*, 2nd ed. (Ann Arbor: University of Michigan Press, 1968), p. 288. See also Quincy Wright, *A Study of War* (Chicago: University of Chicago Press, 1942), 2:757–58.

60. The historiography of major European peace settlements is vast in extent. For recent major theoretical treatments of major diplomatic congresses as producing constitution-like peace settlements, see Kalevi J. Holsti, *Peace and War: Armed Conflicts and International Order, 1648–1989* (Cambridge: Cambridge University Press, 1991); Andreas Osiander, *The States System of Europe, 1640–1990: Peacemaking and the Conditions of International Stability* (Oxford: Clarendon Press, 1994); and Ikenberry, *After Victory*.

61. The religious component of the settlement, recognized by both contemporaries and historians as central, has been downplayed by more recent international theorists, even though it dramatically restrained the power of the most powerful actors in European politics. Viewed through the lenses of a secular age, the separation of church and state would seem to mark the liberation of states rather than

their restraint. But at a time when religious passions were great, and when secular authorities used religions to legitimate their authority and to mobilize their subjects, the separation of church and state constituted a major restraint on state power. The relatively mild character of European conflicts between the Peace of Westphalia and the beginning of the Wars of the French Revolution was understood by many Europeans to be a direct legacy of the depoliticalization of religion. Recent treatments differ sharply on the importance of Westphalia as turning point, with Krasner, *Sovereignty*, expressing doubts, and Daniel Philpott defending the traditional view. *Revolutions in Sovereignty* (Princeton: Princeton University Press, 2001).

62. For detailed discussion, see Osiander, "The Peace of Utrecht," in *States System of Europe*.

63. The nation was not exactly a religion, but was even more problematic because it was so well suited to being directly harnessed by states and because it lacked the modicum of restraint found in the moral dimensions of the Christian religion.

64. Lord Acton, "Nationality," in *Essays in the Liberal Interpretation of History*, ed. William McNeill ([1862] Chicago: University of Chicago Press, 1967), p. 150.

65. These uses are clearly spelled out in Alfred Vagts, "The Balance of Power: Growth of an Idea," *World Politics* 1, no. 1 (October 1948).

66. M. Anderson, "Eighteenth-Century Theories of the Balance of Power," in R. Hatton and Anderson eds., *Studies in Diplomatic History* (London: Longmans, 1970); Herbert Butterfield, "The Balance of Power," and Martin Wight, "The Balance of Power," in *Diplomatic Investigations*; Morgenthau, "The Balance of Power," in *Politics among Nations,* pp. 117–67; Ernst Haas, "The Balance of Power: Prescription, Concept or Propaganda?" *World Politics* 5, no. 4 (July 1953); and Michael Sheehan, *The Balance of Power: History and Theory* (London: Routledge, 1996).

67. Vattel, for example, defined the "balance of power" as "a state of affairs such that no one power is in a position where it is preponderant and can lay down the law to others." J. B. Scott, *The Classics of International Law: Le Droit des Gens* (Washington, DC: Carnegie Institute, 1916), p. 40. And von Gentz holds that "the old magnificent constitution of Europe" helped "the preservation and reciprocal guarantee of the rights of all its members," and had "for centuries protected the liberty of Europe, with all its ornaments and excellencies, its constitutions and laws, its territorial limitations, and its adjudication of rights." *Fragments upon the Balance of Power*, p. 61.

68. "It perhaps could have been with more propriety called a system of *counterpoise*. For perhaps the highest of its results is not so much a perfect *equipoise* as a constant alternate oscillation in the scales of the balance, which, from the application of *counterweights*, is prevented from ever passing certain limits." Von Gentz, *Fragments upon the Balance of Power*, p. 63n. For discussion, see Richard Little, "Friedrich Gentz, Rationalism and the Balance of Power," in *Classical Theories of International Relations*, ed. Ian Clark and Iver B. Neumann (London: Macmillan, 1996), pp. 210–32.

69. David Hume, "Of the Balance of Power." For illuminating discussion, see John Robertson, "Universal Monarchy and the Liberties of Europe: David Hume's Critique of English Whig Doctrine," in *Political Discourses in Early Modern Britain*, ed. Nicholas Phillipson and Quentin Skinner (Cambridge: Cambridge University Press, 1993).

70. William Robertson, *The History of Scotland*, 2nd ed. (London: 1759), 1:73.

71. The Reverend John Witherspoon, president of The College of New Jersey (renamed Princeton University in the late-nineteenth century), a student of David Hume and Adam Smith, and teacher of James Madison, proclaims: "It is but little above two hundred years since that enlarged system called the balance of power took place; and I maintain, that it is a greater step from the former disunited and hostile situation of kingdoms and states, to their present condition, than it would be from their present condition to a state of more perfect and lasting union." Cited in John Hutson, *John Adams and the Diplomacy of the American Revolution* (Lexington: University Press of Kentucky, 1980), p. 71.

72. The extensive literatures on early modern ideas about 'sovereignty' and the even longer development of international law make virtually no mention of these republican associations. The key exception, again, is Onuf, *Republican Legacy*.

73. Vattel, *The Law of Nations* ([1756] Washington, DC: Carnegie Institute, 1916), p. 81.

74. The Latin term *foederus*, meaning "treaty" or "compact," gives rise to a family of not clearly distinguished cognates, most notably 'confederate' and 'federate.' Pocock's formulation captures the fact that eighteenth-century writers use 'anarchy' to mean chaotic: "If the relation between 'states' constituted a 'state of nature,' it was not an anarchy; it was capable of being regulated by sovereigns exercising their 'federative' power." In the terms of republican security theory, Europe was a second, not a first anarchy. In this context it was not necessary to exercise 'federative powers' to leave anarchy, but beneficial to exercise these powers as a restraint in anarchy. Pocock, "States, Republics, and Empire," p. 716.

75. The best treatment remains John Sylvester Hemleben, *Plans for World Government through Six Centuries* (Chicago: University of Chicago Press, 1945). Also see Emeric Crucé, *The New Cyneas*, trans. T. W. Balch ([1623] London: Allen, Lane and Scott, 1909).

76. These ideas are in three short unfinished and unpublished parts of his sprawling and complex corpus that were lost until 1896. Jean-Jacques Rousseau, "The State of War," "Summary of Saint-Pierre's Project for Perpetual Peace," and "Critique of Saint-Pierre's Project for Perpetual Peace," in Roosevelt, *Reading Rousseau*, pp. 185–229. Here Waltz finds the key ideas for his 'third image' and arguments about why the anarchic interstate state-of-war is simultaneously undesirable, difficult to overcome, and an independent cause of conflict among states. Waltz, *Man, the State and War*, pp. 191–210. For other readings of Rousseau's theory of international politics, see Stanley Hoffmann, "Rousseau on War and Peace," in *Rousseau on International Relations*, ed. Stanley Hoffmann and David Fidler (Oxford: Clarendon Press, 1991); Doyle, "Constitutionalism: Rousseau," in *Ways of War and Peace*, pp. 137–60; and Michael C. Williams, "Rousseau, Realism and Realpolitik, *Millennium* 18, no. 2 (summer 1989), pp. 185–203;

Patrick Riley, "Rousseau as a Theorist of National and International Federalism," in *Federalism as Grand Design*, ed. Daniel Elazar (Lanham, MD: University Press of America 1987).

77. In comparing Kant and neorealism, Georg Sorensen suggests that Kant's pacific union is appropriately viewed as what Barry Buzan has termed a "mature anarchy." "Kant and the Processes of Democratization: Consequences for Neorealist Thought," *Journal of Peace Research* 29, no. 4 (November 1992), pp. 410–11.

78. Strong skepticism is voiced by Montesquieu and Rousseau about the restraining ability of international law. For Montesquieu's skepticism, see Mark Hulliung, "A World of Leviathans" in *Montesquieu and the Old Regime*, pp. 173–211. Rousseau: "As for what is called the law of nations, it is clear that without any real sanction these laws are only illusions." "The State of War," in Roosevelt, *Reading Rousseau*, p. 186.

79. For a selection of substantial interpretations by international theorists, see Carl Joachim Friedrich, *Inevitable Peace* (Cambridge: Harvard University Press, 1948); F. H. Hinsley, "Kant," in *Power and the Pursuit of Peace* (Cambridge: Cambridge University Press, 1963), pp. 62–80; Kenneth Waltz, "Kant, Liberalism and War," *American Political Science Review* 56, no. 2 (June 1962); W. B. Gallie, "Kant on Perpetual Peace," in *Philosophers of Peace and War* (Cambridge: Cambridge University Press, 1978), pp. 8–37; Michael W. Doyle, "Kant, Liberal Legacies, and Foreign Affairs," *Philosophy and Public Affairs* 12, no. 3 (summer 1983), pp. 205–35, and pt. 2, 12, no. 4 (fall 1983), pp. 323–53; and Boucher, "International and Cosmopolitan Societies: Locke, Vattel, and Kant," in *Political Theories*, pp. 255–88.

80. Immanuel Kant, "Idea for a Universal History from a Cosmopolitan Point of View" in *On History* ed. and trans. Lewis White Beck (New York: Macmillan, 1963), p. 11. As such, Kant's intricate argument, whatever its merits, is not a theoretical prediction of the future, but rather an elaborate device to hearten the moral man, a philosophical pep talk, and is analogous to his claim that God must exist because his existence is necessary to underpin morality. For discussion of this move, see William A. Galston, *Kant and the Problem of History* (Chicago: University of Chicago Press, 1975).

81. In "Perpetual Peace" Kant says, "The republican constitution . . . gives a favorable prospect for the desired consequence, i.e., perpetual peace." But the Seventh Thesis in "The Idea of a Universal History from a Cosmopolitan Point of View" holds that "[t]he problem of establishing a perfect civic constitution is dependent upon the lawful external relation among states and cannot be solved without a solution of the latter problem." He seems similarly of two minds about the relationship between unit-level despotism and republicanism and competitive strength in the state-of-war. In the "Conjectural Beginning of Human History" he says, "[T]he danger of war is the only factor which mitigates despotism. For a state cannot be powerful unless it is wealthy, but without liberty, wealth-producing activities cannot flourish." But in an appendix to "Perpetual Peace" he says, "[A] state cannot be expected to renounce its constitution [to become a republic] even though it is a despotic one (which has the advantage of being stronger in

relation to foreign enemies) so long as it is exposed to the danger of being swallowed up by other states." *On History*, pp. 94, 12, 65, and 120.

82. "[I]t [the realization of the just social contract] does not require that we know how to attain the moral improvement of men but only that we should know the mechanism of nature in order to use it on men." "Perpetual Peace," in *On History*, p. 112.

83. For an especially penetrating analysis of these links, see Tuck, *Rights of War and Peace*, pp. 207–25.

84. "Perpetual Peace," in *On History*, p. 112. At first glance, Kant's argument would seem a particularly pure version of 'rational choice' assumptions, but Kant simultaneously develops a view of 'enlightenment' as the social cultivation and refinement of human sensibilities (or 'preferences') consonant with contemporary constructivism. "What Is Enlightenment?" in *On History*, pp. 3–10.

85. The importance of competition as system transforming in Kant's argument, and its similarities and differences with Waltz's neorealist argument that competition is system maintaining and reproducing is explored in Wade L. Huntley, "Kant's Third Image: Systemic Sources of the Liberal Peace," *International Studies Quarterly* 40, no. 1 (summer 996), pp. 45–47; and Ewan Harrison, "Waltz, Kant and Systemic Approaches to International Relations," *Review of International Studies* 28, no. 1 (summer 2002), pp. 143–62.

86. "Idea for a Universal History," and "Conjectural Beginning of Human History," in *On History*, pp. 21 and 63.

87. "Perpetual Peace," in *On History*, p. 113.

88. Kant, *Metaphysics of Morals*, ed. Mary Gregor, trans. H. B. Nisbet (Cambridge: Cambridge University Press, 1991), p. 124 (my emphasis).

89. "Perpetual Peace," in *On History*, p. 113.

90. "Idea for a Universal History," in *On History*, p. 18.

91. Waltz, *Theory of International Politics*, p. 117.

92. Realist accounts of the origins of the 'balance of power' go to great lengths to avoid this fact. One major explanation advanced by Realists is that the idea emerged from models of weights and counterweights employed in commerce and early modern mechanical physics. Morgenthau makes this argument in *Politics among Nations*, and Jonathan Haslam provides a strong version: "The Balance of Power thus became an openly acknowledged, popular concept only in early modern Europe. Like so many notions in international relations, it was an analogy drawn from the world of natural sciences, and indeed from everyday life." *No Virtue Like Necessity*, pp. 90–91. The balance of power as a political phenomenon was indeed analogized in this manner, but this is the restatement of a political republican concept in a mechanical form, a move that both added clarity to it and associated it with the prestige and authority of modern science. Ironically, Haslam's frequent lengthy quotations from early modern writers contain numerous references to Europe as a 'republic,' all of which he ignores.

93. Christopher Layne, "From Preponderance to Offshore Balancing: America's Future Grand Strategy," *International Security* 17, no. 4 (spring 1993), pp. 5–51.

94. Mearsheimer, *The Tragedy of Great Power Politics*, pp. 114–19.

95. Waltz draws an extremely sharp dividing line, and Martin Wight argues that the "balance of power" idea had "a distinct and parallel history from Aristotle to Polybius to Harrington, Montesquieu and the pluralists." Martin Wight, "The Balance of Power," in Butterfield and Wight, *Diplomatic Investigations*, p. 151.

96. For discussion of this reformulation, see William T. R. Fox, *The American Study of International Relations* (Columbia, SC: Institute of International Studies, 1968); and Michael Joseph Smith, "Modern Realism in Context," in *Realist Thought from Weber to Kissinger* (Baton Rouge: Louisiana State University Press, 1986). For the role of political and ideological factors in shaping American political science, see Oren, *Our Enemies and US*.

97. Even more telling for this appropriation of Grotius is Richard Tuck's re-evaluation, based on lesser known works, of Grotius as a precursor to Hobbes. *Rights of War and Peace*, pp. 78–108.

98. Bull, *The Anarchical Society*. In contrast to the general tendency of recent English School work toward a historically situated constructivist orientation, Barry Buzan maintains (and extends) the mixed ontology of Bull's formulations in "From International System to International Society: Structural Realism and Regime Theory Meet the English School," *International Organization* 47, no. 3 (summer 1993), pp. 327–52.

99. The legacies of these developments mark the recent formulations of neoliberalism, particularly its emphasis upon information problems as a barrier to international cooperation. For a powerful treatment of the utilitarianism of the 'neo-neo' synthesis, see John Gerard Ruggie, "What Makes the World Hang Together? Neo-Utilitarianism and the Social Constructivist Challenge," *International Organization* 52, no. 4 (autumn 1998), pp. 855–85.

100. Onuf advances a conceptually elegant characterization of the shift from the unified Enlightenment republican international theory to Realism and Liberalism in the nineteenth century. He sees the triumph of a view assigning prior existence to the parts before the whole, in contrast to the "republican" view which asserts that units are intelligible only as members or parts of a prior whole. He characterizes this triumphant view as "liberal" and holds that the state atomism of Realism is the transference of this elemental "liberal" model to international politics, with the seemingly paradoxical result that Realists, particularly neorealists, are "strong liberals." *Republican Legacy*, pp. 35–39. In contrast, I maintain that the different versions of Realist and Liberal international theory have appropriated different parts of a larger and earlier argument cast in republican terminology about restraints on violence in the defense of liberty and that a wide variety of both political structural and material contextual restraints were at play in this argument.

CHAPTER SIX
THE PHILADELPHIAN SYSTEM

1. Thomas Paine, *The Rights of Man* in *Thomas Paine: Political Writings*, ed. Bruce Kuklick ([1792] Cambridge: Cambridge University Press, 1989), p. 185.

2. Earlier versions of this chapter appeared as Daniel Deudney, "The Philadelphian System: Sovereignty, Arms Control, and Balance of Power in the American

States-Union, 1787–1861," *International Organization* 49, no. 2 (spring 1995), pp. 191–228; and "Binding Sovereigns: Authorities, Structures, and Geopolitics in Philadelphian Systems," in *State Sovereignty as Social Construct*, ed. Thomas J. Biersteker and Cynthia Weber (Cambridge: Cambridge University Press, 1996), pp. 190–239.

3. On the American Civil War as a second founding, the historian James McPherson notes: "Before 1861 the two words 'United States' were generally used as a plural noun: 'the United States' *are* a republic.' After 1865 the United States became a singular noun. The loose union of states became a nation." "The Second American Revolution," in *Abraham Lincoln and the Second American Revolution* (New York: Oxford University Press, 1991), p. viii (his emphasis). For recent international comparison, see Seymour Martin Lipset, *American Exceptionalism: A Double-Edged Sword* (New York: Norton, 1996).

4. Frederick Jackson Turner, *The Significance of Sections in American History* (New York: Henry Holt and Company, 1932), p. 316.

5. Tocqueville saw "two governments, completely separate and almost independent. . . . [and] twenty-four small sovereign nations, whose agglomeration constitutes the body of the Union." *Democracy in America*, trans. William Jonson (New York: Knopf, 1945), p. 61; for Hegel's view, see G. A. Kelley, "Hegel's America," *Philosophy and Public Affairs* 2, no. 1 (fall 1972), pp. 3–36.

6. For the sophistication of the founders' understanding of European politics, see Stourzh, *Alexander Hamilton*; and Hutson, *John Adams*.

7. For an overview of recent work on the founding period, see Peter S. Onuf, "Reflections on the Founding: Constitutional Historiography in Bicentennial Perspective," *William and Mary Quarterly*, 3rd series, 46, no. 2 (April 1989).

8. Jack P. Greene, *Peripheries and Center: Constitutional Development in the Extended Polities of the British Empire and the United States, 1607–1788* (Athens: University of Georgia Press, 1986); and Peter S. Onuf, *The Origins of the Federal Republic: Jurisdictional Controversies in the United States, 1775–1787* (Philadelphia: University of Pennsylvania Press, 1983). Of particular value is the monumental work of the geographer D. W. Meinig. *Atlantic America, 1492–1800,* vol. 1 of *Shaping America* (New Haven: Yale University Press, 1986); *Continental America, 1800–1867* vol. 2 of *Shaping America* (New Haven: Yale University Press, 1993); and *Transcontinental America, 1850–1915*, vol. 3 of *Shaping America* (New Haven: Yale University Press, 1998). Two political science works stand out as a balanced treatment of internal and external security issues: Gottfried Dietze, *"The Federalist": A Classic on Federalism and Free Government* (Baltimore: Johns Hopkins University Press, 1960), pp. 177–254; and the magnificent reconstruction by David C. Hendrickson, *Peace Pact: The Lost World of the American Founding* (Lawrence: University Press of Kansas, 2003). Especially useful for federal union in the context of and in comparison with Enlightenment thinking on international law and federation is Peter Onuf and Nicholas Onuf, *Federal Union, Modern World: The Law of Nations in an Age of Revolutions, 1776–1814* (Madison, WI: Madison House, 1993).

9. Among early-twentieth-century works in this vein, see James Brown Scott, *The United States of America: A Study in International Organization* (New York: Oxford University Press, 1920). Later Clarence Streit advanced "Atlantic Union"

modeled on the U.S. founding, sought to dispel the "fog over sovereignty" and attacked the "national sovereignty," of Nazi Germany and Soviet Russia. *Union Now* (New York: Harper and Row, 1940), p. 13; and Clarence Streit, *Freedom's Frontier: Atlantic Union Now* (New York: Harper and Row, 1961). Hans Morgenthau responded to this *structural* alternative with an argument about *identity*: the American founding was essentially an event in *national* history, exceptional in size but not in form. Subsequent idealist work, most notably by Karl Deutsch and associates, followed suit, focusing on identity and treating all American order after 1789 as 'amalgamated' and thus otherwise undistinguished structurally from a federal state or, indeed, a totalitarian one. Morgenthau, *Politics among Nations*, pp. 496–500; Karl Deutsch et al., *Political Order in the North Atlantic Area* (Princeton: Princeton University Press, 1957), p. 29, n. 7.

10. I treat Publius as one voice and as the authoritative understanding of the Constitution of 1787. Subsequent scholarship has emphasized the differences between Hamilton and Madison, but several of the key papers were jointly authored, and their authorship was not established until well into the nineteenth century. For the emergence and components of the Constitution as 'Grand Compromise,' see Thornton Anderson, *Creating the Constitution: The Convention of 1787 and the First Congress* (University Park: Penn State University Press, 1993); and Clinton Rossiter, *1787: The Grand Convention* (New York: Norton, 1987).

11. These influences are described in Carl J. Richard, *The Founders and the Classics: Greece, Rome and the American Enlightenment* (Cambridge: Harvard University Press, 1994).

12. Alexis de Tocqueville, a close reader of the *Federalist*, observed, "The people reign over the American political world as God rules over the universe. It is the cause and end of all things; everything rises out of it and is absorbed back into it." *Democracy in America*, p. 59. For an extended treatment with extensive historical comparisons, see Monroe, *The People, the Sovereigns*.

13. "The power of preventing or arresting the action of the government, be it called by what term it may, veto, interposition, nullification, check, or balance of power. . . . It is, indeed, the negative power which makes the constitution, and the positive which makes the government. The one is the power of acting, and the other the power of preventing or arresting action. The two, combined, make constitutional governments." John C. Calhoun, *A Disquisition on Government* in *Union and Liberty: The Political Philosophy of John C. Calhoun*, ed. Ross M. Lence ([1853] Indianapolis, IN: Liberty Press, 1992), pp. 28–9.

14. The rebellion of debtors in Western Massachusetts led by retired officer Daniel Shays, which the Massachusetts militia refused to suppress, galvanized support for a stronger Union government. For pervasive fears of anarchy, see Peter Onuf, "Anarchy and the Crisis of the Union," in *To Form a More Perfect Union*, ed. Herman Beltz (Charlottesville: University of Virginia Press, 1987); and Max M. Edling, *A Revolution in Favor of Government: Origins of the U.S. Constitution and the Making of the American State* (New York: Oxford University Press, 2003).

15. *Federalist*, no. 9, pp. 73 and 71.

16. Thomas P. Slaughter, *The Whiskey Rebellion: Frontier Epilogue to the American Revolution* (New York: Oxford University Press, 1986).

17. *Federalist*, no. 6, p. 54. For fears of interstate American wars, see Onuf, *Origins*.

18. Jackson Turner Main, "The American States in the Revolutionary Era," in *Arms and Independence: The Military Character of the American Revolution*, ed. Ronald Hoffman and Peter J. Albert (Charlottesville: University Press of Virginia, 1981), pp. 1–30; and Merrill Jensen, *The Articles of Confederation* (Madison: University of Wisconsin Press, 1940).

19. *Federalist*, no. 8, p. 67.

20. For discussion of problems with the militia during the early-nineteenth century, see Lawrence Delbert Cress, *Citizens in Arms: The Army and Militia in American Society to the War of 1812* (Chapel Hill: University of North Carolina Press, 1982), pp. 94–110; Richard H. Kohn, *Eagle and Sword: The Federalists and the Creation of the Military Establishment in America, 1783–1802* (New York: Free Press, 1975), pp. 40–90. For the continuing role of the militia as instruments of the states, see William Riker, *Soldiers of the States: The Role of the National Guard in American Democracy* (Washington, DC: Public Affairs Institute, 1957).

21. Hamilton observes that "the great radical vice" of the Articles of Confederation is "the principle of legislation for states or governments, in their corporate or collective capacities" and praises the new Constitution for extending "the authority of the Union to the persons of citizens—the only proper object of government." *Federalist*, no. 15, pp. 108–9.

22. Turner, *Sections*, p. 50. For discussion, see David M. Potter and Thomas G. Manning eds., *Nationalism and Sectionalism in America, 1775–1877* (New York: Holt, Rinehart and Winston, 1949); Fulmer Mood, "The Origin, Evolution, and Application of the Sectional Concept, 1759–1900," in *Regionalism in America*, ed. Merrill Jensen (Madison: University of Wisconsin Press, 1952), pp. 5–98; and Cathey D. Matson and Peter S. Onuf, *A Union of Interests* (Lawrence: University of Kansas Press, 1990).

23. For the continuing sectional influence, see Joel Garreau, *The Nine Nations of North America* (Boston: Houghton Mifflin, 1981); and Peter Trubowitz, *Defining the National Interest: Conflict and Change in American Foreign Policy* (Chicago: University of Chicago Press, 1998).

24. *Federalist*, no. 10, pp. 77–84. Three of the most influential readings of the American Constitution in the twentieth century, by Charles Beard, Robert Dahl, and William Riker, attack Madison's strategy to check faction as an antidemocratic protection of *economic* interest, thus ignoring the intergroup *security* dynamic that is cumulatively addressed in the *Federalist*, nos. 1–10. Charles Beard, *An Economic Interpretation of the Constitution* (New York: Macmillan, 1913); Robert Dahl, *A Preface to Democratic Theory* (Chicago: University of Chicago Press, 1956), pp. 4–33; William Riker, *Federalism: Origin, Operation, Significance* (Boston: Little, Brown, 1964).

25. This explains the "supreme paradox" of the years before the Civil War observed by David Potter: "northern unionists who believed in American nationalism resisted most proposals for further territorial growth of the nation, while states' rights southerners who denied that the Union was a nation sought to extend the national domain from pole to pole." David M. Potter, *The Impending Crisis*,

1848–1861 (New York: Harper and Row, 1976), p. 197. For the ways in which sectional rivalry in a federal union impeded American expansion, see Scott A. Silverstone, *Divided Union: The Politics of War in the Early American Republic* (Ithaca: Cornell University Press, 2004).

26. For a detailed account of fears of foreign threats as motive for union, see Frederick W. Marks III, *Independence on Trial: Foreign Affairs and the Making of the Constitution* (Baton Rouge: Louisiana State University Press, 1983).

27. The Convention considered emulating the Roman model of a dual executive, the two simultaneously serving consuls, but the necessity of unitary command of the military forces in the field, demonstrated so memorably at Cannae, convinced them to construct a unitary commander-in-chief of the armed forces. *Federalist*, no. 70, pp. 423–31.

28. For early American attitudes toward and uses of Vattelian public international law, see Daniel Lang, *Foreign Policy in the Early Republic: The Law of Nations and the Balance of Power* (Baton Rouge: Louisiana State University Press, 1985); and Onuf and Onuf, *Federal Union, Modern World*. For the problems posed by European decolonization, see James E. Lewis Jr., *The American Union and the Problem of Neighborhood: The United States and the Collapse of the Spanish Empire, 1783–1829* (Chapel Hill: University of North Carolina Press, 1998).

29. *Federalist*, no. 8, pp. 67–69. Lois G. Schwoerer, *"No Standing Armies!" The Antiarmy Ideology in Seventeenth Century England* (Baltimore: Johns Hopkins University Press, 1974); and Trevor Colborn, *The Lamp of Experience: Whig History and the Intellectual Origins of the American Revolution* (Chapel Hill: University of North Carolina Press, 1965).

30. Herbert Storing, *What the Antifederalists Were For* (Chicago: University of Chicago Press, 1981).

31. As Louis Henken observed: "Every grant to the President . . . relating to foreign affairs, was in effect a derogation from Congressional power, eked out slowly, reluctantly, and not without limitations and safeguards." *Foreign Affairs and the Constitution* (New York: Norton, 1975), p. 33.

32. Francis D. Wormuth and Edwin B. Firmage, *To Chain the Dog of War: The War Power of Congress in History and Law* (Dallas: Southern Methodist University Press, 1986).

33. "[T]o protect and maintain inviolate the three great and primary rights of personal security, personal liberty, and private property . . . when actually violated or attacked" required courts, the right of petition and "the right of having and using arms for self-preservation and defense." Blackstone, *Commentaries*, pp. 136–40.

34. For background, see Joyce Lee Malcolm, *To Keep and Bear Arms: The Origins of an Anglo-American Right* (Cambridge: Harvard University Press, 1994); and Halbrook, *That Every Man Be Armed*.

35. The recent debates over the Second Amendment have inadequately distinguished the founders' *original intent* with regard to the question of personal gun control from the question of the *original function* of a well-regulated militia in the Union's security order. Contemporary defenders of an armed public primarily fear the failure of policing to insure personal safety, while the founders primarily

wanted a counterweight against too much government policing capacity. For a particularly balanced treatment, see H. Richard Uviller and William G. Merkel, *The Militia and the Right to Bear Arms; or, How the Second Amendment Fell Silent* (Durham, NC: Duke University Press, 2002). For a critique of the various ends to which the Second Amendment has been put, see David C. Williams, *The Mythic Meanings of the Second Amendment: Taming Political Violence in a Constitutional Republic* (New Haven: Yale University Press, 2003).

36. As American citizens pushed steadily westward into Indian territories, the central government was often unable to compel American citizens to abide by the treaty agreements that it had signed with the Indians. Meinig, *Atlantic America*, pp. 407–9; and *Continental America*, pp. 170–96. In 'filibustering,' Americans (including members of Congress), sought to seize control of Cuba, Nicaragua, and large parts of Mexico and Canada. William O. Scroggs, *Filibusters and Financiers* (New York: Russell and Russell, 1916); Basil Rauch, *American Interest in Cuba, 1848–1855* (New York: Octagon, 1948); and Donald F. Warner, *The Idea of Continental Union: Agitation for the Annexation of Canada to the United States* (Lexington: University of Kentucky Press, 1960).

37. *Federalist*, no. 1, p. 33. For overviews of the period preceding the Constitutional Convention, see Allan Nevins, *The American States during and after the Revolution, 1775–1789* (New York: Macmillan, 1924); and Richard B. Morris, *The Forging of the Union, 1781–1789* (New York: Harper and Row, 1987).

38. For the importance of geographic isolation in the American founding, see the *Federalist*, no. 9, pp. 70–71; Felix Gilbert, *To the Farewell Address: Ideas of Early American Foreign Policy* (Princeton: Princeton University Press, 1961); Arnold Wolfers and Laurence Martin, *The Anglo-American Tradition in Foreign Policy* (New Haven: Yale University Press, 1956), pp. i–xxvii; and Hintze, "The Preconditions of Representative Government in World History," in *Historical Essays*, pp. 302–56.

39. These economic connections produced competing sectional interests. The New England states dependent upon maritime commerce gave serious consideration to secession during the War of 1812, and the interests of the agrarian staple economy of the South and West continually clashed with the Northern desire for tariff protection to promote indigenous manufactures. For treatments of the international political economy of the early United States, see Robert O. Keohane, "Associative American Development, 1776–1860: Economic Growth and Political Disintegration," in *International Institutions and State Power* (Boulder, CO: Westview, 1989); and J. Ann Ticknor, *Self-Reliance versus Power Politics* (New York: Columbia University Press, 1987), pp. 71–132.

40. Maryland, a 'landless state' refused to ratify the Articles of Confederation without cessions of western lands. Virginia, the state with the largest population and land claims, ceded its western claims to the Continental Congress, thus preserving individual property claims in frontier areas while avoiding the corruption of their republican constitution through imperial rule.

41. For accounts of the Northwest Ordinance and its role in the American founding, see Meinig, *Continental America*, pp. 432–47; Peter Onuf, *Statehood and Union: A History of the Northwest Ordinance of 1787* (Bloomington: University of Indiana Press, 1987); and Frederick D. Williams, ed., *The Northwest Ordi-*

nance: Essays on Its Formulation, Provisions, and Legacy (East Lansing: Michigan State University Press, 1989).

42. The colonies had been established over more than a century (1607–1733) without coordination and coherence; they included governors appointed in London (VA, GA, and SC), radical religious groups that had fled Europe (MA), private families granted land charters (PA and MD), and even a facsimile of feudalism (NY).

43. For the extent of these changes in the states, see Gordon S. Wood, *The Radicalism of the American Revolution* (New York: Knopf, 1993).

44. For accounts of these efforts, see Henry M. Ward, *The United Colonies of New England, 1643–1690* (New York: Vantage Press, 1961); and Henry M. Ward, *"Unite or Die": Intercolony Relations, 1690–1763* (Port Washington, NY: Kennikat Press, 1971).

45. For discussion of lax imperial rule, see Greene, *Peripheries and Center*; and Richard Koebner, *Empires* (Cambridge: Cambridge University Press, 1961), pp. 61–193.

46. For an overview of American history as the successive expansion of freedom from white male property owners to near universal enjoyment, see Eric Foner, *The Story of American Freedom* (New York: Norton, 1998).

47. For major statements on American civic identity, see Hans Kohn, *American Nationalism* (New York: Collier Books, 1957); Merle Curti, *The Roots of American Loyalty* (New York: Columbia University Press, 1946); and Liah Greenfeld, *Nationalism: Five Roads to Modernity* (Cambridge: Harvard University Press, 1992), pp. 397–484. For the union itself as object of American political identity, see Rogan Kersh, *Dreams of a More Perfect Union* (Ithaca: Cornell University Press, 2001).

48. For compromise as a constitutive norm, see Peter B. Knupfer, *The Union as It Is: Constitutional Unionism and Sectional Compromise, 1787–1861* (Chapel Hill: University of North Carolina Press, 1991).

49. For republican symbols, see Wilbur Zelinsky, *Nation into State: The Shifting Foundations of American Nationalism* (Chapel Hill: University of North Carolina Press, 1988). For George Washington as exemplar of republican virtue as a founder with self-restraint, immortalized as Cincinnatus rather than Caesar, see Garry Wills, *Cincinnatus: George Washington and the Enlightenment* (Garden City, NY: Doubleday, 1984).

50. Richard Hofstadter, *America at 1750: A Social Portrait* (New York: Vintage, 1973).

51. Tocqueville, *Democracy,* 1:178.

52. The strength of these institutions of common law and private property is visible in the interstate territorial conflict between Connecticut and Pennsylvania over the Wyoming Valley in what is now northeastern Pennsylvania that stemmed from overlapping Charter grants. After several violent skirmishes, both states accepted legal arbitration of the dispute by a special court in Trenton established by the Confederation Congress. A crucial feature of the resolution of conflicts between the states over frontier settlements was that the landowners from the losing side had their property rights guaranteed, even as their statehood changed. For discussion of the Wyoming Valley and other similar conflicts, see Onuf, *Origins,*

pp. 49–73; Meinig, *Atlantic America*, p. 290; and Morris, *Forging the Union*, pp. 222–23.

53. "There was . . . a standard culture throughout the colonies, not strictly American, but one heavily indebted to England. For the most part the institutions of politics and governments on all levels followed English models; the 'official' language, that is the language used by governing bodies and colonial leadership, was English; prevailing social values were also English." Robert Middlekauf, *The Glorious Cause: The American Revolution, 1763–1789* (New York: Oxford University Press, 1982), p. 92.

54. Meinig, *Atlantic America*, p. 385. If ethnic identity had been the impetus for independence, the French Canadians, rather than colonial Englishmen, would have rebelled from British rule.

55. For discussions of sectional of Southern identity, see Drew Gilpin Faust, *The Creation of Confederate Nationalism: Ideology and Identity in the Civil War South* (Baton Rouge: Louisiana State University Press, 1980); Emory M. Thomas, *The Confederate Nation, 1861–1865* (New York: Harper and Row, 1979); John McCardell, *The Idea of a Southern Nation, 1830–1860* (New York, 1979); and Avery Craven, *The Growth of Southern Nationalism, 1848–1861* (Baton Rouge: Louisiana State University Press, 1953).

56. The standard classification of the American war of 1861–65 along with the wars that led to the unification of Germany and Italy in the middle years of the nineteenth century as 'wars of national unification' obscures major differences. The wars in Germany were against other states, most notably France, with interests among the smaller German states rather than against other Germans. In contrast, the Southerners who resisted American 'national unification' had been citizens of the United States who felt their distinct 'national' way of life was under attack by the Northern states. For insightful discussion, see Carl N. Degler, "One among Many: The United States and National Unification," in *Lincoln: The War President*, ed. Gabor S. Boritt (New York: Oxford University Press, 1992).

57. For an analysis of the role expectations of this expansion played in motivating the break with Britain, see Marc Egnal, *A Mighty Empire: The Origins of the American Revolution* (Ithaca: Cornell University Press, 1988).

58. For such speculations, see David M. Potter, *The Impending Crisis, 1848–1861* (New York: Oxford University Press, 1976), p. 10 n. 16.

59. Looking back at the turn of the twentieth century, the Harvard political scientist Archibald Cary Coolidge emphasized the role of the railroad and the telegraph in making possible continental union. Many in the founding generation had thought that "if the country extended its boundaries, it must soon break up into several independent communities." Even California, which "differed materially from the rest of the country, and hence might wish to obtain its autonomy," was maintained and "all danger of a separation of this kind vanished after the completion of the Union Pacific" railroad. *The United States as a World Power* (New York: Macmillan, 1908), p. 37. Also see George Rogers Taylor, *The Transportation Revolution, 1815–1860* (New York: Holt, Rinehart and Winston, 1951); and Albert Fishlow, *American Railroads and the Transformation of the Antebellum Economy* (Cambridge: Harvard University Press, 1965).

60. Demographic, technical, and organizational factors hobbled Amerindian resistance. But had the American expansion not been so rapid, these groups might have been able to defensively modernize. For British attempts to employ AmerIndians as a break to American expansion, see Leitch J. Wright, Jr., *Britain and the American Frontier, 1783–1815* (Athens: University of Georgia Press, 1975); and Malcolm J. Rohrbaugh, *The Trans-Appalachian Frontier* (New York: Oxford University Press, 1978).

61. Before Vermont joined the Union in 1791, "[i]nfluential Vermonters began to discuss special relationships with Britain, some envisioning an imperial protectorate, others a Switzerland-like neutrality." Meinig, *Continental America*, p. 349; Onuf, *Origins*, pp. 127–45; and Chilton Williamson, *Vermont in Quandary, 1763–1825* (Montpelier: Vermont Historical Society, 1949). For Texas, see Andreas V. Reichstein, *Rise of the Lone Star: The Making of Texas*, trans. Jeanne R. Willson (College Station: Texas A&M University Press, 1989); David Pletcher, *The Diplomacy of Annexation: Texas, Mexico, and the Mexican War* (Columbia: University of Missouri Press, 1973); and Meinig, *Continental America*, pp. 128–58.

62. Turner, *Significance of Section*, p. 88. For descriptions, see Potter, *Impending Crisis*; and Knupfer, *Union As It Is*.

63. For pairing of new entrants to the Union, see Meinig, *Continental America*, pp. 449. Four free soil state admissions (California, Oregon, Minnesota, and Kansas) in a row made the Southern position seem irrecoverable without expansion into the Caribbean, schemes for which are discussed in Robert E. May, *The Southern Dream of a Caribbean Empire, 1854–1862* (Baton Rouge: Louisiana State University Press, 1973).

64. Jay Monaghan, *Civil War on the Western Border, 1854–1865* (Boston: Little, Brown, 1955); and James A. Rawley, *Race and Politics: "Bleeding Kansas" and the Coming of the Civil War* (Philadelphia: Lippincott, 1969).

65. As the conflict between the North and the South grew, Southerners developed reinterpretations of the Constitution and proposals such as a dual presidency to preserve sectional veto on major measures of the federal government. For visions of Constitutional modifications to avert secession, see Robert G. Gunderson, *Old Gentleman's Convention: The Washington Peace Conference of 1861* (Madison: University of Wisconsin Press, 1961); and Meinig, "Geopolitical Alternatives," in *Continental America*, pp. 489–502.

66. For this aspect of the struggle, see Barrington Moore, "The American Civil War: The Last Capitalist Revolution," in *Social Origins of Dictatorship and Democracy: Lord and Peasant in the Making of the Modern World* (Boston: Beacon Press, 1966).

67. For antebellum struggles between the states and the federal government, see Forrest McDonald, *States' Rights and the Union: Imperium in Imperio, 1776–1876* (Lawrence: University Press of Kansas, 2000); and Goldstein, *Constituting Federal Sovereignty*, pp. 14–16.

68. John C. Calhoun, *A Discourse on the Constitution of the Government of the United States* in *Union and Liberty*. Richard Hofstadter refers to Calhoun as "the Marx of slave-owning class." *The American Political Tradition* (New York: Random House, 1954), p. 125.

69. For discussion of Webster's position, see Forsyth, *Unions of States*, pp. 112–20.

70. For the role of the great sectional statesmen in articulating competing concepts of sovereignty and their relations to section interests, see Merrill D. Peterson, *The Great Triumvirate: Webster, Clay and Calhoun* (New York: Oxford University Press, 1987).

71. The many labels for this war reflect different interpretations of its origins and character. The War of 1861–65 is known in the South as the 'War between the States,' and in the North as the 'Civil War.' It would be more accurate to call it the 'War of Southern Secession' or the 'War between the Sections.'

72. As James McPherson puts it, "The United States went to war in 1861 to preserve the *Union*; it emerged from war in 1865 having created a *nation*." *Abraham Lincoln and the Second American Revolution* (New York: Oxford University Press, 1990), p. viii (his emphasis).

73. Ironically, the victorious North dared not amend to the Constitution to explicitly outlaw state secession, for doing so would have vindicated the South's interpretation of the terms of the 1787 Constitution.

74. For descriptions and analyses of these changes, see Leonard P. Curry, *Blueprint for Modern America: Non-military Legislation of the First Civil War Congress* (Nashville, TN: Vanderbilt University Press, 1968); Richard Franklin Bensel, *Yankee Leviathan: The Origins of Central State Authority in America, 1859–1877* (Cambridge: Cambridge University Press, 1990); Mark E. Neely, Jr., *The Fate of Liberty: Abraham Lincoln and Civil Liberties* (New York: Oxford University Press, 1991); Harold M. Hyman, *A More Perfect Union: The Impact of the Civil War and Reconstruction on the Constitution* (New York: Knopf, 1973); and Melinda Lawson, *Patriot Fires: Forging a New American Nationalism in the Civil War North* (Lawrence: University Press of Kansas, 2002).

75. Stephen Skrowronek, *Building a New American State: The Expansion of National Administrative Capacities* (New York: Cambridge University Press, 1982).

76. Lord Bryce, *The American Commonwealth* (New York: Macmillan, 1888), p. 78.

77. For classic Progressive indictments, see Herbert Croly, *The Promise of American Life* (New York: Macmillan, 1909); and John Dewey, *The Public and Its Problems* (New York: Henry Holt, 1927).

78. For this evolution, see Louis Smith, *American Democracy and Military Power* (Chicago: University of Chicago Press, 1951); John K. Mahon, *History of the Militia and the National Guard* (New York: Macmillan, 1983); and Uriller and Merkel, *The Militia and the Right to Arms*, pp. 126–33.

79. For a succinct overview, see Harold Koh, "The National Security Constitution We Inherited: From the Founding to the National Security Act," in *The National Security Constitution* (New Haven: Yale University Press, 1990).

80. Edward Corwin, *The Constitution and Total War* (Ann Arbor: University of Michigan Press, 1947).

81. For other system typologies, see Morton A. Kaplan, *System and Process in International Politics* (New York: John Wiley, 1957), pp. 21–53; Richard N. Rosecrance, *Action and Reaction in World Politics* (Boston: Little, Brown, 1963),

pp. 219–75; Richard Falk, *A Study of Future Worlds* (New York: Free Press, 1975), pp. 150–223; Adam Watson, *The Evolution of International Society* (London: Routledge, 1992), pp. 13–18; Forsyth, *Union of States*, pp. 204–9; and Hendrickson, *Peace Pact*, pp. 263–80.

82. Concerning the Senate, Madison writes that "the equal vote allowed to each State is at once a constitutional recognition of the portion of sovereignty remaining in the individual States, and an instrument for preserving that residual sovereignty." *Federalist*, no. 62, p. 378. This language implies that sovereignty is being divided, but is better interpreted as expressing the view that the authorities divided by the Constitution are fundamental within it. Also see Paul C. Nagel, *One Nation Indivisible: The Union in American Thought, 1776–1861* (New York: Oxford University Press, 1961); and James Alexander, "State Sovereignty in the Federal System," *Publius* 16, no. 2 (spring 1986), pp. 1–15.

83. The decisive events in the weakening of the Senate as an assembly of the representatives of the states were the rise of transstate political parties and the failure of the 'doctrine of instruction' stipulating that state legislatures could instruct Senators how to vote and recall them if they failed to obey. For discussion, see William Riker, "The Senate in American Federalism," *American Political Science Review* 49, no. 2 (June 1955), pp. 452–69.

84. During the British colonial era the governments of the several colonies had sent what were known as 'agents' both to London and to one another's capitals. Benjamin Franklin and Edmund Burke served as such agents in behalf of colonial interests before Parliament, the ministries, elite society, and the press. These agents occupied a role somewhere in between that of diplomatic ambassador and parliamentary representative. For the workings of the agency system, see Michael G. Kammen, *A Rope of Sand: The Colonial Agents, British Politics, and the American Revolution* (Ithaca: Cornell University Press, 1968); and James Tapier Lowe, *Our Colonial Heritage: Diplomatic and Military* (Lanham, MD: University Press of America, 1987).

85. The process by which interstate rendition and extradition became widespread was by interstate treaties and compacts remarkably similar to those that sovereign nation-states have employed in recent years to fight criminal activity occurring across international borders. John Bassett Moore, *A Treatise on Interstate Extradition and Rendition* (Boston: Boston Book Company, 1891); and Ethan Nadelmann, *Cops across Borders: The Internationalization of U.S. Criminal Law Enforcement* (University Park: Penn State University Press, 1993).

86. The limitations of confederations are discussed at length in the *Federalist*, nos. 17–20, with detailed discussion of historical cases.

87. These distinctions are explored in a sophisticated late-nineteenth-century German literature. For 'states-union' (*Staatenbund*) versus 'federal state' (*Bundestaat*), see Georg Waitz, *Grundzuege der Politik* (Kiel: Homan, 1862); and attacks by Max von Seydel, *Staatsrechtliche und politische Abhandlungen* (Frieberg: Kail Krozeisen, 1893). For 'union with organs,' see Georg Jellinek, *Lehre von Staatenverbindungen* (Berlin: O. Haering, 1882).

88. For a discussion of this concept's convoluted history and theory, see M.J.C. Vile, *Constitutionalism and the Separation of Powers* (Oxford: Oxford University Press, 1967).

89. Because of the different degrees of embeddedness, the relationship between polarity and system stability was very different. In an anarchy, the complexity of multipolarity leads to destabilizing misperceptions, in contrast to the simplicity and stability of bipolarity. In a states-union, a bipolar distribution means that one faction or section has a majority, while the other has enough power to make armed secession viable.

90. Joseph Schumpeter, *The Sociology of Imperialisms*, trans. Victor Falla ([1919] New York: Meridian, 1972); V. G. Kiernan, *The Duel in European History: Honour and the Reign of the Aristocracy* (New York: Oxford University Press, 1986); and Arno J. Mayer, *The Persistence of the Old Regime: Europe to the Great War* (New York: Pantheon, 1981). The feudal character of the European units was particularly pronounced in the Concert system that emerged from the Congress of Vienna. While marking the most moderated anarchical European security order prior to the post–World War II American reconstruction, the Concert had a strongly reactionary social character.

91. Among those mentioned are the Amphictyonic and Achaean Leagues, the Roman Republic, modern Britain, Scotland, the Netherlands, Poland, Switzerland, and the Holy Roman Empire. This list is derived from the index of Clinton Rossiter's edition of the *Federalist* (New York: New American Library, 1961).

92. For discussion of Kant's knowledge and use of Roman Stoic ethical theory, see Martha C. Nussbaum, "Kant and Cosmopolitanism," in *Perpetual Peace: Essays on Kant's Cosmopolitan Ideal*, ed. James Bohman and Matthias Lutz-Bachman (Cambridge: MIT Press, 1997), pp. 25–57.

93. Kant does briefly note the possibility of a "Great Republic" aiding smaller republican states, but says nothing about how such a great republic could come into being. He also briefly notes the role of the militia in republican states as a deterrent to invasion. Immanuel Kant, "Perpetual Peace," in *On History*, p. 87. Kant also seems to have subscribed to prevalent eighteenth-century views of the degenerating effects of climate in America, discussed in Gilbert Chinard, "Eighteenth Century Theories on America as Human Habitat," *Proceedings of the American Philosophical Society* 91, no. 1 (February 1947), pp. 25–57.

94. These arguments are not logically contradictory, and either may be true or false independently of the other. Assessment is hampered by the very small number of qualifying candidates in the total population of states in the last two centuries. For federal union, only one unit (the United States of America) qualifies as a federal union, with a second possible candidate (Great Britain) being an unwilling and probably infeasible federal union. This fact is partly mitigated by its 'monadic' character (rather than the 'dyadic' democratic peace argument) and by the fact that the number of possible global great powers is inherently limited to a handful.

95. The demise of the Weimar Republic seems a clear case of factional *stasis* leading to dictatorship. There are a great many data sets of 'democracies' differing on the basis of standards for classifying 'democracy,' but the great die-off in the 1930s and near extinction in the early 1940s is clearly evident in Doyle's table. *Ways of War and Peace*, pp. 261–65. For an account of the decline of democracy in Europe during this period, see Michael Mazower, *Dark Continent: Europe's Twentieth Century* (New York: Vintage Books, 1998). Bruce Russett, a prominent advocate of the 'democratic peace' addresses this period in *No Clear and Present*

Danger: A Skeptical View of the United States Entry into World War II (New York: Harper and Row, 1972).

96. In the large literature on these topics, the best overall thematic treatment is provided by Tony Smith, *America's Mission: The United States and the World-wide Struggle for Democracy in the Twentieth Century* (Princeton: Princeton University Press, 1994).

97. For a detailed account, see Peter Duignan and L. H. Gann, *The Rebirth of the West: The Americanization of the Democratic World, 1945–1958* (Oxford: Blackwell, 1992).

98. Smith, *America's Mission*, p. 10.

99. For recent statements of the view that peace contributes to democratization, see William Thompson, "Democracy and Peace: Putting the Cart before the Horse?" *International Organization* 50, no. 1 (winter 1996), pp. 141–74; and Mark E. Pietrzyk, *International Order and Individual Liberty: Effects of War and Peace on the Development of Government* (Lanham, MD: University Press of America, 2002).

100. For criticisms of the 'democratic peace' hypothesis, see Raymond Cohen, "Pacific Unions: A Reappraisal of the Theory that Democracies Do Not Go to War with Each Other," *Review of International Studies* 20, no. 3 (July 1994), pp. 207–23; Henry S. Farber and Joanne Gowa, "Common Interests or Common Polities? Reinterpreting the Democratic Peace," *Journal of Politics* 59, no. 2 (May 1997), pp. 393–417; Nils Petter Gleditsch, "Geography, Democracy and Peace," *International Interactions* 20, no. 4 (1995), pp. 297–323; Christopher Layne, "Kant or Cant: The Myth of Democratic Peace," *International Security* 19, no. 2 (fall 1994), pp. 5–49; Ido Oren, "The Subjectivity of the 'Democratic' Peace: Changing U.S. Perceptions of Imperial Germany," *International Security* 20, no. 2 (fall 1995), pp. 147–87; and David Spiro, "The Insignificance of the Liberal Peace," *International Security* 19, no. 2 (fall 1994), pp. 50–86.

101. For this relationship, see William Archibald Dunning, *The British Empire and the United States: A Review of Their Relations during the Century of Peace following the Treaty of Ghent* (New York: Scribner's Sons, 1914); Bradford Perkins, *The Great Rapprochement: England and the United States, 1895–1914* (New York: Atheneum, 1968). Stephen R. Rock argues that American-British peace was primarily the result of balance of power and threat concerns. "Anglo-U.S. Relations, 1845–1930: Did Shared Liberal Values and Democratic Institutions Keep the Peace?" in *Paths to Peace: Is Democracy the Answer?* ed. Miriam Fendius Elman (Cambridge: MIT Press, 1997), pp. 101–48.

102. Of particular difficulty for democratic peace theorists is the proposition that post–World War II interdemocratic peace is the product of American hegemony, an argument made, among others, by Joanne Gowa, *Ballots and Bullets: The Elusive Democratic Peace* (Princeton: Princeton University Press, 1999). This antiliberal argument does not address the crucial question of how a democracy became large enough to be hegemonic in a state system of such scope.

American foreign policy has not been unambiguously prodemocratic, particularly in relations with smaller states in the Western hemisphere where American economic interests were seen as threatened by popular democratic movements, and during the Cold War, when many populist 'democratic' socialist movements in the Third World were seen as potential Soviet allies. For sustained analysis, see Alan Gilbert, *Must Global Politics Constrain Democracy? Great-Power Realism, Democratic Peace, and Democratic Internationalism* (Princeton: Princeton University Press, 1999); and Walter LaFeber, "The Tension between Democracy and Capitalism during the American Century," *Diplomatic History* 23, no. 2 (spring 1999), pp. 181–205.

103. For a balanced overview of these developments, see Akira Iriye, *The Globalizing of America, 1913–1945;* and Warren I. Cohen, *America in the Era of Soviet Power, 1945–1991,* vols. 3 and 4 of *The Cambridge History of American Foreign Relations* (Cambridge: Cambridge University Press, 1993). For an artful overview of American debates, see H. W. Brands, *What America Owes the World: The Struggle for the Soul of American Foreign Policy* (Cambridge: Cambridge University Press, 1998).

104. The main debates over American foreign policy have been largely intrarepublican, with various schools advancing partial or deponent versions of republican security arguments. American Realists, emphasizing the republican power restraint practice of balance of power, fail to take adequate account of shifting levels of violence interdependence, a reflection of their narrowing of the anarchy-interdependence problematique into the anarchy problematique.

105. For the case that it is rational for a hegemon to 'invest' in institutions to conserve its power and reduce the likelihood of a challenge, see Gilpin, *War and Change;* and especially Ikenberry, *After Victory.*

106. For a concise formulation of this view, see Thomas I. Cook and Malcolm Moos, "Foreign Policy: The Realism of Idealism," *American Political Science Review* 46, no. 2 (spring 1952), pp. 343–56; and Thomas I. Cook and Malcolm Moos, "The American Idea of International Interest," *American Political Science Review* 47, no. 1 (March 1953), pp. 8–44. Moos also served as Eisenhower's speechwriter and wrote his Farewell Address warning of a 'Military-Industrial Complex.'

107. Walter Russell Mead's typology of the four 'traditions' in U.S. foreign policy misses the essential continuity between the Madisonian project of domestic restraint and the later Liberal 'Wilsonian' international project of preserving limited government at home through the abridgment of anarchy abroad. Mead treats limited government as the goal of the largely obsolete 'Jeffersonian' tradition. He locates the wellspring of Wilsonianism in Christian missionary humanitarianism and sees the international institutional agenda as a means to the realization of such values. *Special Providence.*

108. Calvin DeArmond Davis, *The United States and the Second Hague Peace Conference: American Diplomacy and International Organization, 1899–1914* (Durham, NC: Duke University Press, 1975); and Francis Anthony Boyle, *Foundations of World Order: The Legalist Approach to International Relations, 1898–1922* (Durham, NC: Duke University Press, 1999).

109. For an extended analogy between the American and Roman Republics, see Goldwin Smith, *Commonwealth or Empire* (New York: Macmillan, 1902). Robert L. Beisner, *Twelve against Empire: The Anti-Imperialists, 1898–1900* (New York: McGraw Hill, 1968); Sondra R. Herman, *Eleven against War: Studies in American Internationalist Thought, 1889–1921* (Stanford, CA: Hoover Institu-

tion Press, 1969); and E. Berkeley Tompkins, *Anti-imperialism in the United States: The Great Debate, 1890–1929* (Philadelphia: University of Pennsylvania Press, 1970).

110. John A. Thompson, *Reformers and War: American Progressive Publicists and the First World War* (New York: Cambridge University Press, 1987); and Robert David Johnson, *The Peace Progressives and America Foreign Policy* (Cambridge: Harvard University Press, 1995).

111. Wilson's speeches are collected in Hamilton Foley, *Woodrow Wilson's Case for the League of Nations* (Princeton: Princeton University Press, 1923). For Wilson's agenda, see Thomas J. Knock, *To End All Wars: Woodrow Wilson and the Quest for a New World Order* (Oxford: Oxford University Press, 1992). The Republican statesman Elihu Root forcefully articulates the same argument: "The world cannot be half democratic and half autocratic. It must be all democratic or all Prussian. There can be no compromise." "The Effect of Democracy on International Law," in *Miscellaneous Addresses,* ed. Robert Bacon and James Brown Scott (Cambridge: Harvard University Press, 1917), p. 293. The broader American internationalist efforts are described in Warren F. Kuehl, *Seeking World Order: The United States and International Organization to 1920* (Nashville, TN: Vanderbilt University Press, 1969).

112. Edward Corwin, *The Constitution and International Organization* (Princeton: Princeton University Press, 1944), p. 56. Also, see Edward Corwin, *The Constitution and Total War* (Ann Arbor: University of Michigan Press, 1947). For debates on constitutional impacts, see Herman Belz, "Changing Conceptions of Constitutionalism in the Era of World War II and the Cold War," *Journal of American History* 59, no. 3 (December 1972), pp. 640–69. For the domestic impact of World War II, see Bartholomew Sparrow, *From the Outside In: World War II and the American State* (Princeton: Princeton University Press, 1996). For a libertarian view of the role of interstate war in American state-building, see Robert Higgs, *Crisis and Leviathan: Critical Episodes in the Growth of American Government* (New York: Oxford University Press, 1987). For conservative critics, see Ronald Radosh, "Robert Taft and the Emergence of the Cold War," in *Prophets on the Right: Profiles of Conservative Critics of American Globalism* (New York: Simon and Schuster, 1975).

113. For the evolution in American attitudes toward international organization, see Robert A. Divine, *Second Chance: The Triumph of Internationalism in America during World War II* (New York: Atheneum, 1967); and Elizabeth Borgwardt, *A New Deal for the World: America's Vision for Human Rights* (Cambridge: Harvard University Press, 2005). For the role of the United Nations, see Stephen C. Schlesinger, *Act of Creation: The Founding of the United Nations* (Boulder, CO: Westview, 2003). For the wide range of alternatives considered in these debates, see Wesley Wooley, *Alternatives to Anarchy: American Supranationalism since World War II* (Bloomington: University of Indiana Press, 1988).

114. Harold Lasswell, "The Garrison State," *American Journal of Sociology* 46 (January 1941), pp. 455–68. Fears of excessive state strength and its impact on patterns of American mobilization are analyzed in detail by Aaron Friedberg, who makes no mention of the role of these fears in animating the parallel interna-

tionalist project. *In the Shadow of the Garrison State: America's Anti-statism and Its Cold War Grand Strategy* (Princeton: Princeton University Press, 2000).

115. A concise description and analysis of this reversal is provided in Charles William Maynes, "America's Fading Commitment to the World," in *Global Focus: U.S. Foreign Policy at the Turn of the Millennium*, ed. Martha Honey and Tom Barry (New York: St. Martin's, 2000), pp. 85–106. John Bolton, prominent official in the George W. Bush administration, provides a forceful indictment of international institutions as undesirable restraints on American sovereignty in "Should We Take Global Governance Seriously?" *Chicago Journal of International Law* 15, no. 2 (fall 2000), pp. 205–21. The Republican Party that emerged after the realignment of 1968 sustains a (selective) opposition to domestic *government*, but has largely become the party of *state*.

116. Among recent treatments are Chalmers Johnson, *The Sorrows of Empire: Militarism, Secrecy, and the End of the Republic* (New York: Henry Holt, 2004); Andrew J. Bacevich, *The New American Militarism: How Americans Are Seduced by War* (Oxford: Oxford University Press, 2005); and Andrew Rudalevige, *The New Imperial Presidency: Renewing Presidential Power after Watergate* (Ann Arbor: University of Michigan Press, 2005).

CHAPTER SEVEN
LIBERAL HISTORICAL MATERIALISM

1. Ramsey Muir, *The Interdependent World and Its Problems* ([1933] Port Washington, NY: Kennikat Press, 1971), p. 2.

2. For an overview on industrialism, see David S. Landes, *The Unbound Prometheus: Technological Change and Industrial Development in Western Europe from 1750 to the Present* (Cambridge: Cambridge University Press, 1969); and Peter N. Strauss, *The Industrial Revolution in World History* (Boulder, CO: Westview, 1993). For treatments by political theorists, see John P. McCormick, ed., *Confronting Mass Industrial Democracy and Industrial Technology: Political and Social Theory from Nietzsche to Habermas* (Durham, NC: Duke University Press, 2002).

3. For overviews, see Friedrich Meinecke, *Historicism: The Rise of a New Historical Outlook*, trans. Douglas Scott (New York: Herder and Herder, 1972); and Maurice Mandelbaum, *History, Man and Reason: A Study in Nineteenth Century Thought* (Baltimore: Johns Hopkins University Press, 1971).

4. Turgot, *Tableau philosophique des progres successifs de l'espirt humain* (delivered as lectures in the Sorbonne, 1750), in Frank E. Manuel, *The Prophets of Paris* (New York: Harper Torchbook, 1965), p. 21.

5. For overviews, see Peter Bowler, *Evolution: The History of an Idea* (Berkeley and Los Angeles: University of California Press, 1983); and Stephen K. Sanderson, *Social Evolutionism: A Critical History* (Oxford: Blackwell, 1990).

6. G.W.F. Hegel, *Introduction: Reason in History*, in *Lectures on the Philosophy of World History*, trans. H. B. Nisbet (Cambridge: Cambridge University Press, 1975), pp. 152–61. Similarly, Henry Thomas Buckle observes, "the advance of European civilization is characterized by a diminishing influence of physical

laws, and an increasing influence of mental laws." *History of Civilization in England* (London: Longmans, Green, 1883), 1:156.

7. Particularly illustrative on this point is the pioneering French sociologist Emile Durkheim's criticism of Montesquieu, the topic of his doctoral dissertation, for failing to see political science as the study of the human causes of human arrangements. A similar move is found in Talcott Parsons, *The Structure of Social Action* (New York: McGraw-Hill, 1937).

8. For modernity as technological civilization and Bacon as its founder, see Stanley Rosen, *The Ancients and the Moderns: Rethinking Modernity* (New Haven: Yale University Press, 1989); Hiram Caton, *The Politics of Progress: The Origins and Development of the Commercial Republic, 1600–1835* (Gainesville: University of Florida Press, 1988); and Peter Medawar, *Pluto's Republic* (Oxford: Oxford University Press, 1982).

9. An important limitation of Darwin's theory was its lack of an explanation of how different species arise in the first place, a gap in evolutionary theory that was only to be filled with an understanding of genetics. Social scientific functionalist arguments have a similar limitation, in that they do not attempt to explain the sources of a new practice or structure, but only whether they are fitted or unfitted to their context.

10. For an overview of the many varieties of functionalist argument, see Chalmers Johnson, *Revolutionary Change* (Berkeley and Los Angeles: University of California Press, 1968).

11. This kind of thinking is also appropriately referred to as structural-functionalism, to reflect the fact that it is social or political structures whose viability is held to be determined by the extent of their functional fit.

12. For a reformulation of classical global geopolitics with a conceptual apparatus generalized from Marxism, see Daniel H. Deudney, "Geopolitics as Theory: Historical Security Materialism," *European Journal of International Relations,* 6, no. 1 (fall 2000), pp. 77–107.

13. The secondary literature on this group is large and of high quality, and key works are Istvan Hont and Michael Ignatieff, eds., *Wealth and Virtue: The Shaping of Political Economy in the Scottish Enlightenment* (Cambridge Cambridge University Press, 1983); Ronald Meek, *Economics and Ideology and Other Essays* (London: Chapman and Hall, 1967); Albert Hirschman, *Rival Views of Market Society* (Cambridge: Harvard University Press, 1992); and Gladys Bryson, *Man and Society: the Scottish Inquiry of the Eighteenth Century* (Princeton: Princeton University Press, 1945); Q. S. Skinner and T. Wilson, eds., *Essays on Adam Smith* (Oxford: Oxford University Press, 1967).

14. Smith, *Wealth of Nations* ([1776] New York: Modern Library, 1965), bk. 5, chap. 1. Particularly good treatments are found in Michael W. Doyle, "Commercial Pacifism: Smith and Schumpeter," in *Ways of War and Peace*, pp. 230–41; Crauford Goodwin, "National Security in Classical Political Economy," *History of Political Economy* 25, no. 4 (winter 1993), pp. 23–35; and Richard B. Sher, "Adam Ferguson, Adam Smith, and the Problem of National Defense," *Journal of Modern History* 61, no. 2 (June 1989), pp. 240–81.

15. Say, cited in Edmund Silberner, *The Problem of War in Nineteenth Century Thought* (Princeton: Princeton University Press, 1946), p. 71, which provides an extensive treatment of these figures.

16. I. F. Clarke, *The Pattern of Expectation, 1644–2001* (New York: Basic Books, 1979).

17. Gerolamo Boccardo, cited in Silberner, *Problem of War*, p. 117.

18. For his concise summary, see Karl Marx, "Preface," in *A Contribution to the Critique of Political Economy*, trans. S. W. Ryazanskya ([1859] New York: International Publishers, 1970).

19. "In his programmatic proclamations Marx always accents the determination of the relations of production by their forces, and never the reverse. He clearly believed that the relations of production were dependent on the productive forces in a way in which the former were not dependent on the latter." William H. Shaw, "'The Handmill Gives You the Feudal Lord': Marx's Technological Determinism," *History and Theory* 18, no. 2 (May 1979), pp. 155–76 at 163.

20. For force-centric interpretations of Marx, see William Shaw, *Marx's Theory of History* (Stanford, CA: Stanford University Press, 1978); G. A. Cohen, *Karl Marx's Theory of History: A Defense* (Princeton: Princeton University Press, 1978).

21. Marx's most extensive analysis of these earlier economic formations, contained within the unpublished *Grundrisse*, can be found in Eric Hobsbawm, *Precapitalist Economic Formations* (New York: International Publishers, 1964).

22. Karl Marx, *The Poverty of Philosophy* ([1864] London: Lawrence and Wishart, n.d.), p. 92. The accuracy of Marx's understanding of the feudal system has been disputed by Marc Bloch, *Land and Work in Medieval Europe* (London, 1967), pp. 136–68.

23. For general discussions of base-superstructure relations, see Raymond Williams, "Base and Superstructure," in *Marxism and Literature* (New York: Oxford University Press, 1977); and George V. Plekhanov, "Interaction of Base and Superstructure," in *Fundamental Problems of Marxism* (New York: International Publishers, 1969).

24. This idea that practice generates structures has been revived by Anthony Giddens and others as 'structuration theory.' *Central Problems in Social Theory: Action, Structure, and Contradiction in Social Analysis* (Berkeley and Los Angeles: University of California Press, 1979).

25. For a lucid discussion of determinism, see Williams, "Determination" in *Marxism and Literature*, pp. 83–89. For criticisms of force-centric interpretations and defenses of mode-centric interpretations, see Richard W. Miller, *Analyzing Marx* (Princeton: Princeton University Press, 1984); and Jon Elster, *Making Sense of Marx* (Cambridge: Cambridge University Press, 1985).

26. Karl Marx, *The Eighteenth Brumaire of Louis Bonaparte* ([1869] New York: International Publishers, 1969), p. 15.

27. Led by Karl Kautsky and Eduard Bernstein, the mainstream of Western Marxism in the last decades of the nineteenth and first decades of the twentieth century tended to emphasize the possibilities of a slower and less violent transition to socialism.

28. Marx's coauthor and benefactor Frederick Engels wrote extensively about military issues, but he treats developments in violence capability as being fundamentally derivative of developments of the forces of production. Frederick Engels, *Anti-Duhring* (New York: Progress Publishers, 1947). For discussion, see Bernard Semmel, ed., *Marxism and the Science of War* (Oxford: Oxford University Press, 1981). For criticism of deficiencies regarding violence, the state, and interstate relations, see Anthony Giddens, *The Nation-State and Violence,* vol. 2 of *A Contemporary Critique of Historical Materialism* (Berkeley and Los Angeles: University of California Press, 1985).

29. The closest to a full tabulation of the damage is provided by Stephane Courtois et al., *The Black Book of Communism: Crimes, Terror and Repression,* trans. Jonathan Murphy and Mark Kramer (Cambridge: Harvard University Press, 1999).

30. For this story, see August Nimtz, *Karl Marx and the Democratic Breakthrough* (Chicago: University of Chicago Press, 1995).

31. Among such theorists are James Burnham, Clark Kerr, and Daniel Bell, who are discussed in Krishan Kumar, *Prophecy and Progress: The Sociology of Industrial and Post-industrial Society* (London: Penguin Books, 1978).

32. For an early overview, see Robert Mackintosh, *From Comte to Benjamin Kidd: The Appeal of Biology or Evolution for Human Guidance* (New York: Macmillan, 1899). For an especially sophisticated treatment of the ways in which widely different political orientations employed Darwinian ideas, see Paul Crook, *Darwinism, War and History* (Cambridge: Cambridge University Press, 1994). Part of the reason Darwin's thought lent itself to such diverse employment is that he advanced not one but several quite distinct theories. For a masterful synopsis and assessment, see Ernst Mayr, *One Long Argument: Charles Darwin and the Genesis of Modern Evolutionary Thought* (Cambridge: Harvard University Press, 1991). For the classic account of how Darwin was influenced by Malthus, see Barry G. Gale, "Darwin and the Concept of a Struggle for Existence: A Study in the Extrascientific Origins of Scientific Ideas, *Isis* 63, no. 218 (September 1972), pp. 321–44. Also see Gregory Claeys, "The 'Survival of the Fittest' and the Origins of Social Darwinism," *Journal of the History of Ideas* 61, no. 2 (spring 2000), pp. 223–40.

33. Herbert Spencer, *Man versus the State* (London: Watts, 1892). For discussion, see M. W. Taylor, *Men versus the State: Herbert Spencer and Late Victorian Individualism* (Oxford: Clarendon Press, 1978); and M. W. Taylor, ed., *Herbert Spencer: Contemporary Assessments* (London: Routledge, 1996). For a succinct treatment, see Cook, *Darwinism and War,* pp. 29–62.

34. Peter Kropotkin, *Mutual Aid* (London: Macmillan, 1903). For similar efforts and Kropotkin's influence, see D. A. Stack, "The First Darwinian Left: Radical and Socialist Responses to Darwin, 1859–1914," *History of Political Thought* 21, no. 4 (winter 2000), pp. 682–710.

35. Leonard T. Hobhouse, *Social Evolution and Political Theory* (New York: Columbia University Press, 1911); Leonard T. Hobhouse, *Morals in Evolution: A Study in Comparative Ethics* (London: Allen and Unwin, 1904); and Lester Ward, "Social and Biological Struggles," *Lester Ward and the Welfare State,* ed. Henry Steele Commager (Indianapolis, IN: Bobbs-Merrill, 1967).

36. For overviews of German *Geopolitik* in English, see Johannes Mattern, *Geopolitik: Doctrine of National Self-Sufficiency and Empire* (Baltimore: Johns Hopkins University Press, 1942); Robert Strausz-Hupé, *Geopolitics* (New York: Putnam's Sons, 1942); Andreas Dorpalan, *The World of General Haushofer* (New York: Farrar and Reinhardt, 1942); and Geoffrey Parker, "German *Geopolitik* and Its Antecedents," *Western Geopolitical Thought*. For a recent similar use of Darwinian thought, see Bradley A. Thayer, *Darwin and International Relations: On the Evolutionary Origins of War and Ethnic Conflict* (Lexington: The University Press of Kentucky, 2004).

37. Benjamin Kidd, *Individualism and After* (Oxford: Clarendon Press, 1908); Benjamin Kidd, *Social Evolution,* 3rd ed. (London: Macmillan, 1898); Karl Pearson, *National Life from the Standpoint of Science,* 2nd ed. (London: Black, 1905). For analysis of Kidd and Pearson, see Semmel, *Imperialism and Social Reform,* pp. 74–105.

38. H. G. Wells, "Human Evolution, an Artificial Process," *Fortnightly Review* 69 (October 1896), pp. 590–95. For the different ways in which 'struggle' is employed in Darwin, see Peter J. Bowler, "Malthus, Darwin, and the Concept of Struggle," *Journal of the History of Ideas* 37, no. 4, (October–December 1976), pp. 631–50.

39. For British progressivism, see Michael Freeden, *The New Liberalism: An Ideology of Social Reform* (Oxford: Clarendon, 1978). For American progressivism, see Richard Hofstadter, *The Age of Reform: From Bryan to F.D.R.* (New York: Knopf, 1955). For the importance of the industrial revolution, see John M. Jordan, *Machine-Age Ideology: Social Engineering and American Liberalism, 1911–1939* (Chapel Hill: University of North Carolina Press, 1994). For the transnational dimensions, see Daniel T. Rodgers, *Atlantic Crossings: Social Politics in a Progressive Era* (Cambridge: Harvard University Press, 1998).

40. For recent historical treatments of these movements, see Akira Iriye, *Cultural Internationalism and World Order* (Baltimore: Johns Hopkins University Press, 1997); Warren F. Kuehl, *Seeking World Order: The United States and International Organization to 1920* (Nashville: Vanderbilt University Press, 1969); Cecelia Lynch, *Beyond Appeasement: Interpreting Interwar Peace Movements in World Politics* (Ithaca: Cornell University Press, 1999); and Francis Anthony Boyle, *Foundations of World Order: The Legalist Approach to International Relations, 1898–1922* (Durham, NC: Duke University Press, 1999). Among recent treatments of specific theorists are Harold Josephson, *James T. Shotwell and the Rise of Internationalism in America* (Rutherford, NJ: Fairleigh Dickinson University Press, 1975); John Turner, ed., *The Larger Idea: Lord Lothian and the Problem of National Sovereignty* (London, 1988); Jeanne Morefield, *Covenants without Swords: Idealist Liberalism and the Spirit of Empire* (Princeton: Princeton University Press, 2005); and David Long, *Towards a New Liberal Internationalism: The International Theory of J. A. Hobson* (Cambridge: Cambridge University Press, 1996).

41. Among the major texts are Norman Angell, *The Great Illusion: A Study of the Relation of Military Power in Nations to Their Economic and Social Advantage* (London: William Heinemann, 1910); Norman Angell, *Arms and Industry: A Study of the Foundations of International Polity* (New York: Garland Publishers,

1973). G. N. Clark, *Unifying the World* (London: Swarthmore Press, 1920); J. A. Hobson, *Towards International Government* (New York: Macmillan, 1915); Ramsey Muir, *Nationalism and Internationalism: The Culmination of Modern History* (London: Constable, 1917); Leonard S. Woolf, *International Government* (London: Fabian Society, 1915); Sir Alfred Zimmern, *The Prospects of Civilization* (Oxford: Pamphlets on World Affairs, 1939).

42. In an insightful recent treatment, Andreas Osiander argues that Realist interpretations have neglected the key fact that these theorists had a progressive rather than a cyclical view of history, but he also neglects the fundamentally materialist dimension of their arguments. "Rereading Early Twentieth Century IR Theory: Idealism Revisited," *International Studies Quarterly* 42, no. 3 (September 1998), pp. 409–32.

43. A recent insightful collection on early-twentieth-century British liberal internationalists fails to include Wells and makes virtually no mention of these materialist dimensions. David Long and Peter Wilson, eds., *Thinkers of the Twenty Years' Crisis: Interwar Idealism Reassessed* (Oxford: Oxford University Press, 1995). These absences also characterize the otherwise insightful treatment in Casper Sylvest, "Community and Change in British Liberal Internationalism, c. 1900–1930," *Review of International Studies* 31, no. 2 (April 2005).

44. Angel, *The Great Illusion*. For Angell's life, thought, and influence, see J.D.B. Miller, *Norman Angell and the Futility of War: Peace and the Public Mind* (New York: St. Martin's, 1986). For sympathetic treatment of Angell's argument, see John Mueller, *Retreat from Doomsday: The Obsolescence of Major War* (New York: Basic Books, 1989), pp. 27–29.

45. Alfred Thayer Mahan, *Armaments and Arbitration* (Boston: Little, Brown, 1912), p. 122–23.

46. Muir, *The Interdependent World*, pp. 1–2. (I have assembled and reordered this passage from text spread over two pages.) For an important exception to the general neglect of Muir, see Jaap de Wilde, *Saved from Oblivion: Interdependence in the First Half of the Twentieth Century* (Brookfield, VT: Dartmouth, 1991).

47. Wells has been the subject of numerous biographies, but the definitive accounts of Wells's world order thought and influence are W. Warren Wager, *H. G. Wells and the World State* (New Haven: Yale University Press, 1961); and John S. Partington, *Building Cosmopolis: The Political Thought of H. G. Wells* (Aldershot: Ashgate, 2003).

48. H. G. Wells, *The Discovery of the Future* (New York: Huebach, 1913); and Roslynn D. Haynes, *H. G. Wells: Discoverer of the Future* (New York: New York University Press, 1980). For the range of Wells's scientific visions, see W. Warren Wager, *H. G. Wells: Traversing Time* (Middleton, CT: Wesleyan University Press, 2004).

49. H. G. Wells, *An Outline of History, Being a Plain History of Life and Mankind*, 3rd ed. rev. (New York: Macmillan, 1921). Wager reports that Wells's *Outline* sold more copies than any other English language book in the 1920s except the Bible. *H.G. Wells and the World State*, p. 17. George Orwell observed that "thinking people who were born about the beginning of this century are in some sense Wells's own creation. . . . The minds of all of us, and therefore the physical world, would be perceptibly different if Wells never existed." "Wells,

Hitler and the World State," in *Dickens, Dali and Others* (New York: Macmillan, 1946), p. 121.

50. H. G. Wells et al., *The Idea of the League of Nations* (Boston: Atlantic Monthly Press, 1919), p. 7.

51. H. G. Wells, *Anticipations of the Reaction of Mechanical and Scientific Progress upon Human Life and Thought* (New York: Harper and Brothers, 1901), p. 6.

52. Wells, *Anticipations*, p. 5.

53. Wells, *Anticipations*, p. 68.

54. Wells, *Anticipations*, p. 111.

55. Wells, *Outline*, p. 1087.

56. Mark R. Hillegas observes that "many of the central as well as peripheral images in the anti-utopias were first generated in Wells's early scientific romances, chiefly those written in the 1890s" and that "to an extraordinary degree the great anti-utopias are both continuations of the imagination of H. G. Wells and reactions against that imagination." *The Future as Nightmare: H. G. Wells and the Anti-Utopians* (New York: Oxford University Press, 1967), p. 5.

57. Wells, *Outline*, p. 1101.

58. Wells, *Anticipations*, p. 284.

59. "Viewed from at least one angle, he was simply in the Platonist tradition, which is to say in the old historic stream of elitist thought. A grateful admirer of Plato's *Republic*, he remained under its spell all his life." Wager, *Wells and the Idea of the World State*, p. 166.

60. H. G. Wells, *The Open Conspiracy: Blue Prints for a World Revolution* (London: Gollancz, 1928).

61. Wells, *Anticipations*, p. 230.

62. For a sustained defense of Wells's political attitudes and activities as consistent with liberalism, see Partington, *Building Cosmopolis*, pp. 85–101.

63. Dewey's contributions span aesthetics, ethics, epistemology, metaphysics, education, and political theory, and during the first half of the twentieth century he was America's "intellectual voice" and "for a generation no issue was clarified until Dewey had spoken." Alan Ryan, *John Dewey and the High Tide of American Liberalism* (New York: Norton, 1995), p. 19. Also see Robert B. Westbrook, *John Dewey and American Democracy* (Ithaca: Cornell University Press, 1991).

64. John Dewey, "The Influence of Darwinism on Philosophy," in *The Influence of Darwinism on Philosophy and Other Essays in Contemporary Thought* (New York: Henry Holt, 1910).

65. John Dewey, *The Public and Its Problems* ([1927] Chicago: Swallow Press, 1954), pp. 15–16.

66. Dewey, *Public and Its Problems*, pp. 18–19.

67. Dewey, *Public and Its Problems*, p. 67.

68. Dewey, *Public and Its Problems*, p. 44.

69. Dewey, *Public and Its Problems*, pp. 149 and 152.

70. Dewey, *Public and Its Problems*, p. 18 (my emphasis).

71. Dewey, *Public and Its Problems*, pp. 32–33 and 74.

72. The enhancement of social inventiveness through education is central to Dewey's theory of democracy and constituted most of his policy agenda. *Public*

and Its Problems, pp. 46–47; and *Democracy and Education* (New York: Macmillan, 1916).

73. Dewey, *Public and Its Problems*, p. 141.

74. Dewey, *Public and Its Problems*, p. 126.

75. Dewey, *Public and Its Problems*, pp. 128–29.

76. Dewey, *Public and Its Problems*, p. 128.

77. Dewey, *Public and Its Problems*, p. 74; and John Dewey, *Liberalism and Social Action* ([1935] New York: Capricorn, 1963).

78. John Dewey, *German Philosophy and Politics* (New York: Putnam, 1915); and *Public and Its Problems*, pp. 37–73.

79. Dewey's emphasis on process, education, learning and cognition thus has striking similarities to the more recent social scientific theories of Karl Deutsch ('transactions' and 'cybernetics'), Ernst Haas ('social learning'), and Emanuel Adler ('epistemic communities' and 'cognitive evolution').

80. Morton White, *Social Thought in America: The Revolt against Formalism* (Boston: Beacon Press, 1947).

81. H. G. Wells, *A Mind at the End of Its Tether* (London: Macmillan, 1945), p. 17.

82. For a concise overview, see Clyde W. Barrow, "Historical Criticism of the U.S. Constitution in Populist-Progressive Political Theory," *History of Political Thought 9*, no. 1 (spring 1988), pp. 171–205. For a recent restatement of the old Liberal interpretation, see Paul Carrese, "Montesquieu, the Founders and Woodrow Wilson: The Evolution of Rights and the Eclipse of Constitutionalism," in *The Progressive Revolution in Politics and Political Science*, ed. John Marini and Ken Masugi (Lanham, MD: Rowman and Littlefield, 2005).

CHAPTER EIGHT
FEDERALIST GLOBAL GEOPOLITICS

1. H. J. Mackinder, "Geography, an Art and a Philosophy," *Geography 27*, no. 2 (1942), pp. 122–30 at 123.

2. The best succinct treatment remains Geoffrey Barraclough, *An Introduction to Contemporary History* (London: C.A. Watts, 1964). The best synthetic treatment of European imperialism and its demise is David B. Abernethy, *The Dynamics of Global Dominance: European Overseas Empires, 1415–1980* (New Haven: Yale University Press, 2000).

3. A notable recent exception treats 'globalization' as liberal economic openness and 'geopolitics' as a doctrine of autarkic self-sufficiency, and interprets the twentieth century as a struggle between 'geopolitical states' and 'globalization states.' Brain W. Blouet, *Geopolitics and Globalization in the Twentieth Century* (London: Reaktion, 2001). This same pattern is analyzed by Richard Rosecrance as a clash between 'the trading world' and the 'military-political world.' *The Rise of the Trading State: Commerce and Conquest in the Modern World* (New York: Basic: 1985). Buzan and Little also analyze state system globalization at length. *International Systems.*

4. The key texts are Alfred Thayer Mahan, *The Influence of Sea Power upon History, 1660–1783* (Boston: Little, Brown, 1890); Halford J. Mackinder, *Democratic Ideals and Reality* (New York: Henry Holt and Co., 1919); Vidal de la Blache, *Principles of Human Geography* (London: Constable, 1936); Frederick Teggart, *Theory of History* (New Haven: Yale University Press, 1925); Frederick Jackson Turner, *The Frontier in American History* (New York: Holt, Rinehart, and Winston, 1920); James Burnham, *The Managerial Revolution* (New York: Macmillan, 1940); Nicholas J. Spykman, *America's Strategy in World Politics* (New York: Harcourt, Brace and Co., 1942); and J. R. Seeley, *The Expansion of England* ([1883] Chicago: University of Chicago Press, 1971).

5. Mackinder, "Geography," pp. 122–30 at 123. For a nuanced treatment of early-twentieth-century globalization thinking, see Jo-Anne Pemberton, *Global Metaphors: Modernity and the Quest for One World* (London: Pluto Press, 2001).

6. For powerful portrayals of the pervasiveness of these themes in the thought of the era, see Stephen Kern, *The Culture of Time and Space, 1880–1918* (Cambridge: Harvard University Press, 1983); and Wolfgang Schivelbusch, *The Railway Journey: Industrialization of Space and Time in the Nineteenth Century* (Berkeley and Los Angeles: University of California Press, 1987). For a recent sophisticated assessment of political consequences, see William E. Scheuerman, "Liberal Democracy and the Empire of Speed," *Polity*, 34, no. 1 (fall 2001), pp. 41–67.

7. For materialistic thinking, see Carlton J. H. Hayes, *A Generation of Materialism, 1871–1900* (New York: Harper and Row, 1941).

8. Seeley, *Expansion of England*, p. 236.

9. The nature and extent of these political orientations is succinctly portrayed by David N. Livingstone, "Should the History of Geography be X-Rated?" and "A 'Sternly Practical' Pursuit: Geography, Race and Empire," in *The Geographical Tradition: Episodes in the History of a Contested Enterprise* (Oxford: Blackwell, 1992).

10. Halford J. Mackinder, "The Scope and Methods of Geography," *Proceedings of the Royal Geographical Society* 9 (January 1887), p. 27. Also see Spykman, *America's Strategy*, pp. 123; Albert Wohlstetter, "Illusions of Distance," *Foreign Affairs* 46, no. 2 (January 1968), p. 243.

11. An indicator of this turn of thought was the deployment of the novel argument that European ascendency was justified by European technological progress, a line of thinking explored at length in Michael Adas, *Machines as the Measure of Man: Science, Technology, and Ideologies of Western Dominance* (Ithaca: Cornell University Press, 1989).

12. Halford J. Mackinder, "Geographical Considerations affecting the British Empire I: The British Isles," *Geographical Journal* 33, no. 4 (April 1909), p. 474. Several outstanding recent histories explore these developments at length: Carolyn Marvin, *When Old Technologies Were New: Thinking about Communications in the Late Nineteenth Century* (New York: Oxford University Press, 1988); Daniel R. Headrick, *The Invisible Weapon: Telecommunications and International Politics, 1851–1945* (New York: Oxford University Press, 1991); Peter J. Hugill, *Global Communications since 1844: Geopolitics and Technology* (Baltimore: Johns Hopkins University Press, 1999); and David Paull Nickles, *Under the Wire: How the Telegraph Changed Diplomacy* (Cambridge: Cambridge University Press, 2004).

13. Sanford Fleming, "Time Reckoning for the Twentieth Century," *Smithsonian Report* (1886), pp. 345–66. For nineteenth-century views on the impact of the transoceanic cables, see Vary Coates and Bernard Finn, *A Retrospective Technology Assessment: Submarine Telegraphy* (San Francisco: San Francisco Press, 1979); and Paul Kennedy, "Imperial Cable Communication and Strategy, 1870–1914," *English Historical Review* 86, no. 3 (October 1971), pp. 728–52.

14. As G. N. Clark observed: "the quicker and easier the communication between different men and different places, the more unity of all kinds will come to exist among them." *Unifying the World* (London: Swarthmore Press, 1920), pp. 38–39.

15. Emerson also observed that "the very permanence of matter seems compromised" and "hitherto esteemed symbols of stability absolutely dance before you" and notes that "an hourly assimilation goes forward and there is no danger that local peculiarities and hostilities should be preserved." Ralph Waldo Emerson, "The Young American," in *Complete Works* (Boston: Little, Brown, 1903–4), 1:117; Seeley, *Expansion of England*, p. 63; Karl Marx, *Grundrisse*, trans. Martin Nicolaus (New York: Penguin, 1973), p. 524. For a rich account of the prevalence of such thinking, see Duncan S. A. Bell, "Dissolving Distance: Technology, Space, and Empire in British Political Thought, c. 1770–1900," *Journal of Modern History*, 77, no. 3 (September 2005), pp. 523–62.

16. For accounts of the impact of the railroad, see Edwin Pratt, *The Rise of Rail-Power in War and Conquest, 1833–1914* (Philadelphia: Lippincott, 1916); George Rogers Taylor, "Changing Costs and Speed of Transportation and Communication," in *The Transportation Revolution, 1815–1860* (New York: Holt, Rinehart and Winston, 1951); Donald Showalter, *Railroads and Rifles: Soldiers, Technology, and the Unification of Germany* (Hamden, CT: Shoestring Press, 1975); Steven G. Marks, *Road to Power: The Trans-Siberian Railroad and the Colonization of Asian Russia, 1850–1917* (Ithaca: Cornell University Press, 1991); Clarence B. Davis and Kenneth E. Wilburn, Jr., ed., *Railway Imperialism* (New York: Greenwood Press, 1991); and James E. Vance, Jr., *The North American Railroad: Its Origin, Evolution and Geography* (Baltimore: Johns Hopkins University Press, 1995).

17. Mahan observes: "the Eastern world . . . is rapidly appreciating the material advantages and the political traditions which have united to confer power upon the West." *Harper's* 95 (September 1897), pp. 523–33. Halford J. Mackinder, *Nations of the Modern World* (London: Philips, 1911), p. 227. For the extent of such diffusion, see Daniel Headrick, *The Tentacles of Progress: Technology Transfer in the Age of Imperialism, 1850–1940* (New York: Oxford University Press, 1988). The speed with which Japan had incorporated industrial military capability suggested to the Australian writer Charles H. Pearson that "with civilization equally diffused, the most populous country must ultimately be the most powerful" and predicted the eventual "preponderance of China over any rival." *National Life and Character: A Forecast* (London: Macmillan, 1883), pp. 84 and 130.

18. Mackinder, *Britain and the British Seas* (Oxford: Clarendon Press, 1902), p. 194. Although global geopolitical writers often are accused of 'geographic determinism,' their more complex view is well expressed by Coolidge: "the influences of geography are to be reckoned with, though they are not infrequently overborne by what seems like mere historical accident. The strongest frontiers

are not impassable. . . . Since mankind may thus develop in opposition to mere geographical influences, it is dangerous to lay much weight on them, yet, though they may be neutralized, if not altogether overcome, it cannot be denied that they are forces of great magnitude." *The United States as a World Power*, p. 18.

19. Geographers have generated an extensive literature employing and assessing these concepts. For example, see Saul B. Cohen, *Geography and Politics in a Divided World* (New York: Oxford University Press, 1963, 1975).

20. Mackinder, *Democratic Ideals and Reality*, p. 150; Eugene Staley, "The Myth of the Continents," *Foreign Affairs* 19, no. 3 (April 1941).

21. Recent constructivist and postmodern geographers have extensively 'deconstructed' geographic constructs and labels as subjectively generated to serve various imperial and ethnocentric projects. Martin W. Lewis and Karen E. Wigen, *The Myth of Continents: A Critique of Metageography* (Berkeley and Los Angeles: University of California Press, 1997). In contrast, the new cartographic divisions advanced by globalist geographers were intended to represent objective gradients of the material context significant for security.

22. Kjellén coined the word 'geopolitics' while discussing Russian encroachment into the Baltic Sea. The emerging Russian threat to the West was a central theme in the later works of Mahan's and in Mackinder's best-known works. Haushofer and the Germans were also preoccupied with Russia. After the Second World War, the threat of the world communist movement merged with the specter of Heartland domination. And the persistence of the classical geopolitical images has been in large measure due to efforts by various American political figures and scholars to raise public awareness of the Soviet threat to the West.

23. Mackinder, *Democratic Ideals and Reality*, p. 40. For discussion of the prevalence of such thinking, see Gerry Kearns, "Fin-de-Siècle Geopolitics: Mackinder, Hobson, and Theories of Global Closure," in *Political Geography in the Twentieth Century*, ed. Peter J. Taylor (London: Belhaven, 1993), pp. 9–30.

24. For the consequences of frontier closure, see Frederick Jackson Turner, *The Frontier in American History* (New York: Holt, Rinehart and Winston, 1920); and Walter Prescott Webb, *The Great Frontier* (Austin: University of Texas Press, 1951).

25. Seeley, *Expansion of England*, p. 204.

26. Seeley, *Expansion of England*, p. 62.

27. Mackinder, "The Scope and Methods of Geography."

28. Alexis de Tocqueville, *Democracy in America* (New York: Knopf, 1945), p. 452; Friedrich List, *National System of Political Economy* (Philadelphia: Lippincott, 1856), pp. 487–88; and Friedrich Ratzel, *Politische Geographie der Vereinigten Staaten von Amerika*, 2 vols. (Munich: Oldenberg, 1893). For the impact of the American experience upon European, particularly German thinking, see Raymond Betts, "Immense Dimensions: The Impact of the American West on the Late Nineteenth-Century European Thought about Expansion," *Western Historical Quarterly* 10, no. 2 (April 1979) pp. 149–66.

29. Haushofer, quoted in Derwent Whittlesey, *German Strategy of World Conquest* (New York: Farrar and Rinehart, 1944) p. 100.

30. Oswald Spengler, *The Decline of the West*, vol. 2. *Perspectives on World History*, trans. Charles Francis Atkinson ([1922] New York: Knopf, 1928), p. 429.

31. Erich Marcks, "Die imperialistische Idee in der Gegenwart" (1903) (cited in Kern, *Culture of Time and Space*, p. 240).

32. Seeley, *Expansion of England*, p. 35. Global analysts frequently compared the European state system in the global-industrial era with city-state systems of classical Greece and Renaissance Italy, which were unable to unite in order to check the rising power of their larger neighbors. Also on this theme, see A. Demangeon, *America and the Race for World Domination*, trans. Arthur B. Maurice (Garden City, NY: Doubleday, 1921).

33. Ludwig Dehio, *The Precarious Balance* (New York: Knopf, 1960).

34. Mahan, *Influence of Sea Power*. For systematic treatments, see Herbert Rosinski, *The Development of Naval Thought* (Newport: Naval War College Press, 1977); and Colin S. Gray, *The Leverage of Seapower: The Strategic Advantage of Navies in War* (New York: Free Press, 1992).

35. For lucid summary of the debate, see Paul Kennedy, "Mahan versus Mackinder: Two Interpretations of British Seapower," in *Strategy and Diplomacy, 1870–1945* (London: Fontana, 1983), pp. 41–86.

36. For discussion of a 'War of English Succession,' an expression coined by Max Lenz in 1900, see Dehio, "Thoughts on Germany's Mission, 1900–1918," in *Germany and World Politics*, pp. 27–32. In 1902 Friedrich Ratzel observed that "our earth is proving too small for a system of 'imperial connection,' such as Britain is hoping for. . . . [F]aced by continental policies, such as Russia is pursuing in Asia and the United States in America, Britain's sea power policy is doomed to setbacks today." *The Sea as a Source of National Greatness*, cited in Dorpalan, *World of Haushofer*, p. 123.

37. It is telling that one of the prominent early treatments of 'Greater Britain' by Charles Wentworth Dilke, *Greater Britain* (London: Macmillan, 1868) actually used this expression to refer to the United States, viewed as British political forms applied on a larger scale. However, in his later works the expression is used to refer to Britain and its still dependent settler colonies. James Anthony Froude, *Oceana* (New York: Charles Scribner's Sons, 1886); Charles Wentworth Dilke, *Problems of Greater Britain* (London: Macmillan, 1890); and E. A. Freeman, *Imperial Federation* (London: Macmillan, 1885).

38. Mackinder, *Democratic Ideals and Reality*, p. 150.

39. For the Rimland theory, see Nicholas John Spykman, *The Geography of the Peace* (New York: Harcourt, Brace and Co., 1944); and David Wilkinson, "Spykman and Geopolitics," in *On Geopolitics: Classical and Nuclear*, ed. Ciro Zoppo and Charles Zorgbibe (The Hague: Martinus Nijoff, 1985).

40. Mackinder proposes locating the headquarters of this proposed league in Constantinople, making it the "Washington of the League of Nations," and he holds that this arrangement will help penetrate the Heartland with "oceanic freedom." He refers to the approaches of the Heartland as being like the "police in London and Paris," which are "regarded as a national and not merely a municipal concern." Mackinder, *Democratic Ideals and Reality*, pp. 215–16 and 203.

41. Mackinder, *Democratic Ideals and Reality*, p. 5. See also Mark Bassin, "Imperialism and the Nation-State in Friedrich Ratzel's *Political Geography*," *Progress in Human Geography* 11, no. 4 (1987), pp. 473–95.

42. Ratzel cited in Strausz-Hupé, *Geopolitics*, p. 31.

43. "In Germany, Max Goldberger, Wilhelm Polenz, and Otto, Count Moltke, published books in effect declaring that Americans were working day and night to achieve domination over the world." Ernest R. May, *Imperial Democracy: The Emergence of America as a Great Power* (New York: Harcourt, Brace, Jovanovich, 1961), p. 263. For the ways in which the Germans understood British hegemony and ambitions, see Dehio, "Thoughts on Germany's Mission, 1900–1918," in *Germany and World Politics*, pp. 71–88.

44. As the British foreign minister Lord Rosebery observed, "we are engaged at the present moment, in the language of mining, 'in pegging out claims for the future'." cited in William Langer, *The Diplomacy of Imperialism* (New York: Knopf, 1935) 1:78.

45. Derwent Whittlesey, "Haushofer: The Geopoliticans," in E. M. Earle, ed., *The Makers of Modern Strategy* (Princeton: Princeton University Press, 1944), pp. 388–411; Burnham, *The Managerial Revolution*; and Edward Hallett Carr, *Conditions of Peace* (London: Macmillan, 1942).

46. The image of the global system as a scaled-up version of early modern Europe is further completed by bringing in the material factor of the mixture of land and sea power as the basis for a 'balancer' state and then transposing the role of 'offshore balancer' and 'hollow hegemon' from Britain to the United States. This image is most developed in Spykman, *America's Strategy*.

47. For a longer version of this section, see Daniel Deudney, "Greater Britain or Greater Synthesis? Seeley, Mackinder and Wells on Britain in the Global Industrial Era," *Review of International Studies* 27, no. 2 (April 2001), pp. 187–208.

48. Due to haunting similarities with the United States, British decline has been treated at length by, among others, Robert Gilpin, *War and Change in World Politics* (Cambridge: Cambridge University Press, 1982); Paul Kennedy, *The Rise and Fall of the Great Powers* (New York: Random House, 1987); and Aaron Friedberg, *The Weary Titan: Britain and the Experience of Relative Decline, 1895–1905* (Princeton: Princeton University Press, 1988). For a concise assessment of the analogy, see John A. Hall, "Will the United States Decline as Did Britain?" in *The Rise and Decline of the Nation State*, ed. Michael Mann (Oxford: Blackwell, 1990), pp. 114–45.

49. As Seeley puts it, "Our Empire is not an Empire at all in the ordinary sense of the word." *Expansion of England*, p. 44. Similarly, Ramsey Muir observes: "This amazing political structure, which refuses to fall within any of the categories of political science, which is an empire and not yet an empire, a state and yet not a state, a supernation incorporating in itself an incredible variety of peoples and races, is not a structure which has been designed by the ingenuity of man." *The Expansion of Europe: The Culmination of Modern History* (Boston: Houghton Mifflin, 1917), p. 232.

50. This idea seems to have been first advanced by J. A. Froude, who states the British predicament clearly: "When we consider the increasing populousness of other nations, their imperial energy, and their vast political development, when we contrast the enormous area of territory which belongs to Russia, to the United States, or to Germany, with the puny dimensions of our own island home, prejudice itself cannot hide from us that our place as a nation is gone among such rivals

unless we can identify the Colonies with ourselves, and multiply the English soil by spreading the English race over them." "England's War" (1871) in *Short Studies on Great Subjects, 1867–1884* (London: Longman Green, 1894), 2:500.

51. Halford Mackinder, *Our Own Islands: An Elementary Study in Geography* (London: Philip, 1906); Halford Mackinder, *Lands beyond the Channel* (London: Philip, 1908); Halford Mackinder, *Distant Lands* (London: Phillip, 1910); and Halford Mackinder, *Nations of the Modern World*, 2 vols. (London: Philip, 1924).

52. Seeley, professor of Modern History at Cambridge, was described at his death as having altered "the general political thinking of a nation" more than any previous historian. Seeley's influence described in John Gross, "Introduction," in Seeley, *Expansion of England*. Seeley's book served as a catalyst for the founding of the Imperial Federation League in 1884, whose members included Lord Bryce, James Froude, and Lord Rosebery. For the activities of the Imperial Federation League, see C. A. Bodelsen, *Studies in Mid-Victorian Imperialism* (London: Heinemann, 1960), pp. 205–14.

53. Seeley, *Expansion of England*, p. 62.

54. Seeley, *Expansion of England*, p. 227. "[It is] . . . to all intents and purposes, a fragment of the old country lying moored in the antipodean ocean, a portion of that agricultural land which we shall need to add to this country if, with the present scale of our industries, we were to be a balanced and self-contained community." Mackinder cited in Parker, *Mackinder*, p. 68. Also, see Geoffrey Blainey, *The Tyranny of Distance: How Distance Shaped Australia's History* (Melbourne: Sun Books, 1966).

55. Mackinder cited in Parker, *Mackinder*, p. 68. In a letter to the London *Times* Mackinder says: "Canada was essential to the Empire. If all North America were a single Power, Britain would, indeed, be dwarfed. That great North American Power would, of necessity, take from us the command of the ocean." Cited in Parker, *Mackinder*, p. 40.

56. Despite the fact that India was the 'crown jewel' in the British Empire, Seeley and Mackinder both assumed that India would become independent and that British resistance to an Indian independence movement would be doomed to failure. For the diverse meanings of 'race' in this period, see Peter Mandler, " 'Race' and 'Nation' in Mid-Victorian Thought," in *History, Religion, and Culture: British Intellectual History, 1750–1950*, ed. Stefen Collini et al. (Cambridge: Cambridge University Press, 2000).

57. Seeley labeled the relationship between the settler colonies and the British Isles 'organic' and thus enduring, while the rest of the empire was 'mechanical' and thus easily sundered. Seeley, *Expansion of England*, pt. 2, chaps.2–6 concerning India. Similarly, Mackinder distinguished between the "the federation, loose or close, of several British commonwealths, and the maintenance of British rule among alien races." Mackinder, *Britain and the British Seas*, p. 346.

58. For an excellent history and analysis of the social aspects of Liberal Imperialism, see Bernard Semmel, *Imperialism and Social Reform: English Social-Imperial Thought, 1895–1914* (London: Allen and Unwin, 1960).

59. Seeley, *Expansion of England*, p. 62. For Mackinder a Greater Britain would be comparable in strength "with a potential United States of Europe and the actual United States, and with other great agglomerations which are not, perhaps, immediately upon us, but are yet looming on the horizon." Mackinder cited in Parker, *Mackinder*, p. 73.

60. For an extensive catalog of proposals, see Seymour Cheng, *Schemes for the Federation of the British Empire* (New York: Columbia University Press, 1931).

61. For Freeman's views and their impact, see M. D. Burgess, "Imperial Federation: Edward Freeman and the Intellectual Debate on the Consolidation of the British Empire in the Nineteenth Century," *Trivium* 13 (1978), pp. 77–94.

62. In combination, Seeley thinks these inventions made conceivable a different outcome of the American War for Independence which ended the first British Empire. *Expansion of England*, p. 62.

63. Edmund Burke, "Observations on the Late State of the Nation," in vol. 1, *Works* (Boston: Charles Little and James Brown, 1839).

64. Seeley, *Expansion of England*, p. 62.

65. For a discussion of competing views of the nature of the British Commonwealth, see Hedley Bull, "What Is the Commonwealth?" *World Politics* 11, no. 4 (July 1959), pp. 577–87. For discussion of Seeley's influence upon and relation to subsequent ideas for the Commonwealth and Anglo-American unity, see David Calleo and Benjamin Rowland, *America and the World Political Economy: Atlantic Dreams and National Realities* (Bloomington: University of Indiana Press, 1973), pp. 56–57.

66. Mackinder's misreading of the climatic constraints upon Australian and Canadian development parallels his errors concerning the Heartland interior of Eurasia. As several generations of geographers have argued, Mackinder consistently overestimated the power potential and role in world order of the interior of Eurasia because he underestimated the *climatic* constraints on agriculture, urbanization, and industrialization. In particular, see George Cressey, *Soviet Potentials: A Geographic Appraisal* (Syracuse, NY: Syracuse University Press, 1962); and W. H. Parker, *The Superpowers: The United States and the Soviet Union Compared* (London: Macmillan, 1972).

67. For exploration of the long-standing conservative European view of the United States as a cultural threat, see James W. Ceaser, *Reconstructing America: The Symbol of America in Modern Thought* (New Haven: Yale University Press, 1997).

68. For discussion of the tortured efforts of the German theorist Carl Schmitt to conceptualize the nature of a German imperial unification, see Peter Stirk, "Carl Schmitt's *Volkerrechliche Grossraumordnung*," *History of Political Thought* 20, no. 2 (summer 1999), pp. 357–74. David Calleo suggests that the Hapsburg multinational cosmopolitanism scorned by Hitler offered a much more viable model for Europe-wide political order than Hitler's national and racial projects. *The German Problem Reconsidered: Germany and the World Order, 1870 to the Present* (Cambridge: Cambridge University Press, 1978), pp. 116–19.

69. The French writer Gustave Hervé observed that as a result of industrial science and technology "historically determined political frontiers appear anach-

ronistic." *L'Internationalisme* (Paris, 1910) cited in Iriye, *Cultural Internationalism and World Order*, p. 71.

70. After a five-month tour of United States, the Paris journalist Urbain Gohier declared that "[t]he American nation is the living realization of the dream of internationalism" because it had produced the "fusion of European races." *The People of the Twentieth Century in the United States* (Paris, 1903), cited in Iriye, *Cultural Internationalism*, pp. 22–3. The overall view of European Liberal internationalists regarding the United States is captured in the title of Wells's book, *The Future in America* (New York: Macmillan, 1906).

71. Wells, *Anticipations*, pp. 274, 280, 278.

72. Wells, *Anticipations*, pp. 280, 281.

73. Wells, *Anticipations*, p. 280. Wells was also "inclined to believe" that a "great synthesis of the English-speaking peoples" would occur and that the "head and centre of the new unity" would be in the "great urban region that is developing between Chicago and the Atlantic." *Anticipations*, p. 283.

74. Cited in Bertram D. Wolf, *Revolution and Reality* (Chapel Hill: University of North Carolina Press, 1981), p. 330.

75. For a vivid account of how Haushofer was portrayed in the United States as the master strategist of the Third Reich, see Gearoid O Tuathail, " 'It's Smart to Be Geopolitical': Narrating German Geopolitics in U.S. Political Discourse, 1939–1943," in *Critical Geopolitics* (Minneapolis: University of Minnesota Press, 1996), pp. 111–40. For a penetrating exploration of the important differences between Haushofer geographic contextualism and Hitler's racism, see Mark Bassin, "Race contra Space: The Conflict between German *Geopolitik* and National Socialism," *Political Geography* 6, no. 6 (April 1987), pp. 115–34.

76. Noting that "without ideological content imperialism soon dies off," Haushofer defines panideas as "supernational all englobing ideas seeking to manifest themselves in space." Haushofer, cited in Parker, *Western Geopolitical Thought*, p. 73. Haushofer, *Geopolitik der Panideen* (Berlin: Vowinckel, 1931). Panideas are indispensable for panregional states, but their content is otherwise left unspecified, so long as they are ideologies of sufficient breadth or appeal to organize and unify large numbers of people over large space.

77. For an astute account of Burnham's torturous political evolution, see John Patrick Diggens, *Up from Communism: Conservative Odysseys in American Intellectual History* (New York: Harper and Row, 1975). For a full-length biography emphasizing his later anticommunist activities, see Daniel Kelly, *James Burnham and the Struggle for the World: A Life* (Wilmington, DE: ISI Books, 2002).

78. Burnham, *The Managerial Revolution,* p. 200; James Burnham, *The Machiavellians: Defenders of Freedom* (New York: John Day, 1943).

79. "Communism (Leninism-Stalinism), fascism-Nazism, and to a more partial and less developed extent, New Dealism and Technocracy, are all *managerial ideologies.*" Burnham, *Managerial Revolution*, p. 200.

80. Burnham, *Managerial Revolution*, p. 173.

81. "Even if, by a lucky chance, some one power might win what would look like a world victory, it could prove only temporary. The disintegrative forces would be sufficient to pull it rapidly to pieces." Burnham, *Managerial Revolution*, p. 174–75.

82. Burnham's omission of the Soviet Union is striking since the Soviet Union had moved closest to the pure form of a managerial society untainted with capitalist remnants and democratic admixtures. But the Russians lack the critical mass of industrial development necessary to make the demanding grade, and a powerful "infiltration of German managers (into the Soviet Union) is a large step on the road toward the fusion of European Russia with the European centre." Burnham, *Managerial Revolution*, pp. 175–76 and 204.

83. Burnham, *Managerial Revolution* pp. 176, 175, 224, 155 and 224.

84. For discussion of this influence, see Jenni Calder, "Orwell's Post-war Prophecy," in *George Orwell: A Collection of Critical Essays,* ed. Raymond Williams (Englewood Cliffs, NJ: Prentice Hall, 1974), p. 134. Orwell offers a scathing assessment: "Burnham's writings are full of apocalyptic visions. Nations, governments, classes, and social systems are constantly described as expanding, contracting, decaying, dissolving, toppling, crashing, crumbling, crystallising, and in general behaving in an unstable and melodramatic way. The slowness of historical change, the fact that each epoch always contains a great deal of the last epoch, is never sufficiently allowed for. Such a manner of thinking is bound to lead to mistaken prophecies, because, even when it gauges the direction of events rightly, it will miscalculate their tempo." George Orwell, *The Managerial Revolution of James Burnham* (London: Socialist Book Centre, 1947), p. 14.

85. George Orwell, *Nineteen Eighty-four* (New York: Harcourt, Brace and Co., 1949), section entitled "The Theory and Practice of Oligarchic Collectivism," p. 187.

86. "There is no longer, in a material sense, anything to fight about. With the establishment of self-contained economies, in which production and consumption are geared to one another, the scramble for markets that was a main cause of previous wars has come to an end, while the competition for new materials is no longer a matter of life and death." "[T]he primary aim of modern warfare . . . is to use up the products of the machine without raising the general standard of living. . . . The destruction of the products of labor is essential to maintain control of the masses, for they might make the masses too comfortable, and hence, in the long run, too intelligent. . . . The problem was how to keep the wheels of industry turning without increasing the real wealth of the world. Goods must be produced, but they must not be distributed. And in practice the only way of achieving this was by continuous warfare." Orwell, *Nineteen Eighty-four*, pp. 189–92.

87. Or as he puts it, "so long as they remain in conflict they prop one another up like three sheaves of corn." Orwell, *Nineteen Eighty-four*, pp. 198 and 200.

88. Coolidge, *The United States as a World Power*, p. 19. This passage is a synthesis of points made at length in Ellen Churchill Semple, *American History and Its Geographic Conditions* (Boston: Houghton Mifflin, 1903), which is in turn derived from Ratzel, *Politische Geographie der Vereinigten Staaten von Amerika*.

89. Wells, *Outline*, p. 1087.

90. Seeley, *Expansion of England*, pp. 62 and 187.

91. Coolidge calls it "a landmark in the story of government." Prior to this innovation, colonies had tended toward independence because "the territory did not

form an equal part of the parent state," except for despotisms, where "all lands were at the disposal of the sovereign." *The United States as a World Power*, p. 29.

92. Coolidge, *The United States as a World Power*, p. 16, 18.

93. Wells identifies "five movements of coalescence" on the contemporary scene: Anglo-Saxonism, the Pan-German movement, Pan-Slavism, a union of the Latin peoples, and a union of the "Yellow Races." He considers the prospects for these various movements and concludes that only three unions appear likely to succeed: an Anglo-Saxon, a European, and an Asian. The success of the European unification will, in Wells's view, impede both the Slavic and Germanic aspirations. *Anticipations*, p. 269.

94. Wells, *Anticipations*, pp. 283, 287, 269.

95. Wells, *Anticipations*, p. 267 (my emphasis).

96. H. G. Wells, *The World Set Free* (London: Macmillan, 1914). Wells followed scientific developments closely, and this prediction is based on his familiarity with the ideas of the chemist Frederick Soddy, who was speculating on the possibilities of tapping the immense energies of the atomic nucleus. For these links, see Richard E. Sclove, "From Alchemy to Atomic War: Frederick Soddy's 'Technology Assessment' of Atomic Energy, 1900–1915," *Science, Technology and Human Values* 14, no. 2 (spring 1989), pp. 163–94.

97. Wells, *Idea of the League of Nations*, pp. 5–6.

98. Wells, *Idea of the League of Nations*, p. 21 (my emphasis).

99. Wells, *Idea of the League of Nations*, pp. 35, 35, 36, 37, 37.

100. H. G. Wells, *The Salvaging of Civilization* (London: Cassell, 1921), p. 82 (his emphasis).

101. H. G. Wells, *Guide to the New World: A Handbook on Constructive Revolution* (London: Victor Gollancz, 1941), p. 17; H. G. Wells, *What Are We to do with Our Lives?* (London: Watts, 1935), p. 40.

102. H. G. Wells, *Phoenix: A Summary of the Inescapable Conditions of World Reorganization* (London: Secker and Warburg, 1942), p. 182.

103. H. G. Wells, *Mr Britling Sees It Through* ([1916] London: Hogarth, 1985) p. 395. He also says that "governments have to surrender almost as much of their sovereignty as the constituent sovereign States which make up the United States of America have surrendered to the federal Government." *What Is Coming? A Forecast of Things after the War* (London: Cassell, 1916), p. 13.

104. Wells, *Phoenix*, p. 181.

105. For the history of these early efforts, see H.L.S Lyons, *Internationalism in Europe, 1815–1914* (Leiden, Netherlands: Grumbach, 1963). Leonard Woolf emphasized their appeal and novelty in 1915 in his *International Government*, Wells adopted this model in the 1920s, and David Mitrany made them the basis for his influential program for a 'working peace system.' Partington complains that "Wells's ideas were taken on wholesale by the political scientist David Mitrany in his functionalist theory of international relations, without any acknowledgment of Wells's groundwork." *Cosmopolis*, p. 9.

106. For the prenuclear introduction of 'super-power' to designate the top tier of great powers, see William T. R. Fox, *The Super-Powers* (New York: Harcourt, Brace, 1944).

107. Had Hitler stopped his aggressions short of attacking Russia and instead 'rounded out' his conquest of the European peninsula with a closure of the Mediterranean and the conquest of Britain, and then successfully consolidated this domain, a third world great power would have formed. Attacking Russia and declaring war on the United States precipitated a world war before the war of European empire was finished, needlessly lengthening the odds against German success. For an account of World War II emphasizing the possibilities of alternative outcomes and the importance of Hitler's grand strategic mistakes, see Richard Overy, *Why the Allies Won* (New York: Norton, 1995).

108. In retrospect it seems that the prospects for European consolidation were higher than East Asian. Germany was the largest European state, was located in a central position, and surrounded by kindred peoples (the Dutch, Swiss, and Nordic peoples). In East Asia Japanese prospects were dimmer because the vast mass of China could not be fully conquered, let alone consolidated by Japan. As Spykman pointed out, the more probable long-term outcome in East Asia was for the restoration of Chinese hegemony.

109. My earlier characterization along these lines is in Deudney, "Binding Sovereigns," pp. 224–28. Also see Deudney and Ikenberry, "The Nature and Sources of Postwar Western Order"; Ikenberry, *After Victory;* John Gerard Ruggie, *Winning the Peace: America and World Order in the New Era* (New York: Columbia University Press, 1996); and G. John Ikenberry, *Liberal Leviathan* (forthcoming).

110. Clarence Streit, *Union Now: A Proposal for a Federal Union of the Democracies of the North Atlantic* (New York: Harper and Brothers, 1939); and *Freedom's Frontier: Atlantic Union Now* (New York: Harper and Brothers, 1961).

111. For a view of American leadership and its effects in Europe from a European theorist, see Geir Lundestad, *The American "Empire" and Other Studies of U.S. Foreign Policy in Comparative Perspective* (Oxford: Oxford University Press, 1990).

112. For the pre–World War II roots of this institution-building, see Craig N. Murphy, *International Organization and Industrial Change* (New York: Oxford University Press, 1994).

113. For a detailed history of the settlement, see Marc Trachtenberg, *A Constructed Peace: The Making of the European Settlement, 1945–1962* (Princeton: Princeton University Press, 1999); and especially Ikenberry, *After Victory,* pp. 162–214.

114. Mackinder, *Democratic Ideals and Reality,* p. 7.

115. In the United States, one of the most influential policy reports about state science and technology was entitled *Science: The Endless Frontier* (Washington DC: Government Printing Office, 1947).

CHAPTER NINE
ANTICIPATIONS OF WORLD NUCLEAR GOVERNMENT

1. Memorandum to President Truman, in *On Active Service in Peace and War,* by Henty L. Stimson and McGeorge Bundy (New York: Harper and Brothers, 1947), p. 644.

2. Despite its halcyon connotation, McLuhan emphasized the violently unsettled features of the 'global village.' Marshall McLuhan, *War and Peace in the Global Village* (New York: Bantam, 1968). For diverse contestations over 'whole earth' imagery, see Denis Cosgrove, "Contested Global Visions: One-World, Whole-Earth, and the Apollo Space Photographs," *Annals of the Association of American Geographers* 84, no. 2 (summer 1994), pp. 270–94; and Wolfgang Sachs, "The Blue Planet: An Ambiguous Modern Icon," *Ecologist* 24, no. 5 (September/October 1995), pp. 171–98.

3. Among major statements from the middle years of the twentieth century are Ely Culbertson, *Total Peace: What Makes Wars and How to Organize Peace* (Garden City, NY: Doubleday, Doran, 1943); Emery Reves, *The Anatomy of Peace* (New York: Harper, 1946); A. C. Ewing, *The Individual, The State and World Government* (New York: Macmillan, 1947); Cord Meyer, Jr., *Peace or Anarchy* (Boston: Atlantic, 1947); Owen Roberts, John F. Schmidt, and Clarence K. Streit, *The New Federalist* (New York, 1950); Frederick Schuman, *The Commonwealth of Man: An Inquiry into Power Politics and World Government* (New York: Knopf, 1952); Grenville Clark and Louis B. Sohn, *World Peace through World Law* (Cambridge: Harvard University Press, 1960); and W. Warren Wager, *Building the City of Man: Outlines of a World Civilization* (New York: Grossman, 1971). In the flagship publication of the World Order Models Project (the main intellectual descendant of world federalism) Richard Falk conceptualizes a range of plausible future world orders, assesses their compatibility with four world order values, and advances a 'preferred world order' centered around a 'central guidance mechanism.' Richard Falk, *A Study of Future Worlds* (New York: Free Press, 1973). In subsequent works he rejects this approach for 'premature specificity' and embraces diverse 'grass-roots movements' as agents to realize a 'humane world order.' Richard Falk, *The End of World Order* (New York: Holmes and Meier, 1984); and Richard Falk, *On Humane Governance: Toward a New Global Politics* (College Park: Penn State University Press, 1995). More recently, a sophisticated and updated version of much of the world federalist program, as 'cosmopolitan democracy' is developed in Daniele Archibugi and David Held, eds., *Cosmopolitan Democracy: An Agenda for a New World Order* (Cambridge: Polity, 1995); and Daniele Archibugi, David Held, and Martin Kohler, eds., *Reimagining Political Community: Studies in Cosmopolitan Democracy* (Stanford, CA: Stanford University Press, 1998). Most recently, Alexander Wendt, emphasizing ideational processes of recognition, but partly drawing on nuclear one world arguments, discerns a teleology in world history leading to the inevitability of a world state, and identifies two variants ('Weberian' and 'Hegelian'), which correspond very roughly to hierarchical and negarchical alternatives. "The Inevitability of a World State," *European Journal of International Relations* 4, no. 9 (spring 2004), pp. 539–90.

4. For competing assessments, see Andrew J. Bacevich, *American Empire: The Realities and Consequences of American Diplomacy* (Cambridge: Harvard University Press, 2002); and Michael Mandelbaum, *The Case for Goliath: How America Acts as the World's Government in the Twenty-first Century* (New York: Public Affairs, 2005).

5. An early statement of the simultaneous presence of fragmentation and integration is found in Edward L. Morse, *Modernization and the Transformation of International Relations* (New York: Free Press, 1976). For extended analysis of this pattern, which he labels 'fragmagration,' see James Rosenau, *Turbulence in World Politics* (Princeton: Princeton University Press, 1990).

6. For details on the dimensions of nuclear destructive potential, see Jonathan Schell, *The Fate of the Earth* (New York: Knopf, 1982); Paul R. Ehrlich, Carl Sagan, Donald Kennedy, and Walter Orr Roberts, *The Cold and the Dark: The World after Nuclear War* (New York: Norton, 1984); and Office of Technology Assessment, *The Effects of Nuclear War* (Washington DC: Government Printing Office, 1979).

7. Raymond Aron, *The Great Debate: Theories of Nuclear Strategy*, trans. Ernst Pawel (Garden City, NY: Doubleday, 1965).

8. John Herz, *International Politics in the Atomic Era* (New York: Columbia University Press, 1959). Much of Herz's argument is devoted to prenuclear arguments about the security political implications of changes in technological material contexts. Using a very different conceptual vocabulary, Kenneth Boulding makes essentially the same argument in *Conflict and Defense: A General Theory* (New York: Harper and Row, 1962).

9. The range and scope of early proposals is documented in Bernhard G. Bechhofer, *Postwar Negotiations for Arms Control* (Washington, DC: Brookings, 1961).

10. The Arms Control and Disarmament Agency in the U.S. Department of State commissioned a series of studies on complete disarmament that emphasized the need to have an international peacekeeping capability tantamount to a world security state. Arnold Wolfers and Robert Osgood et al., *The United States in a Disarmed World: A Study of the U.S. Outline for General and Complete Disarmament* (Baltimore: Johns Hopkins University Press, 1966); and Charles Burton Marshall, "Character and Mission of a United Nations Peace Force, under Conditions of General and Complete Disarmament," *American Political Science Review* 59, no. 2 (June 1965), pp. 574–98.

11. Stephen Shenfield describes how late-Soviet thinking on nuclear issues arrived at a nuclear one worldist view by employing a version of Marxian historical materialism to include destruction technology and a species interest in survival. *The Nuclear Predicament: Explorations in Soviet Ideology* (London: Routledge and Kegan Paul, 1987). For Reagan's and Gorbachev's nuclear one worldism as factors in the end of the Cold War, see Daniel Deudney and G. John Ikenberry, "The International Sources of Soviet Change," *International Security* 16, no. 3 (winter 1991/92), pp. 74–118. For Reagan's nuclear one worldism, see Paul Lettow, *Ronald Reagan and His Quest to Abolish Nuclear Weapons* (New York: Random House, 2005).

12. For the most forceful indictment, see Gray, *House of Cards*.

13. Herman Kahn, *On Thermonuclear War* (Princeton: Princeton University Press, 1961); Herman Kahn, *Thinking the Unthinkable* (New York: Harper and Row, 1965); and Gray, "Nuclear Strategy," pp. 54–87.

14. For extended critiques, see Louis Rene Beres, *Mimicking Sisyphus: America's Countervailing Nuclear Strategy* (Lexington, MA: Lexington Books, 1982);

and Robert Jervis, *The Illogic of American Nuclear Strategy* (Ithaca: Cornell University Press, 1984).

15. Bernard Brodie, "War in the Atomic Age," and "Implications for Military Strategy," in *The Absolute Weapon* (New York: Harcourt, Brace, 1946). For synthetic and measured statements, see Michael Mandelbaum, *The Nuclear Revolution* (Cambridge: Cambridge University Press, 1977); and Robert Jervis, *The Meaning of the Nuclear Revolution: Statecraft and the Prospect of Armageddon* (Ithaca: Cornell University Press, 1989).

16. For the strong initial ambivalence of Realists toward nuclear deterrence, see Campbell Craig, *Glimmer of a New Leviathan: Total War in the Realism of Niebuhr, Morgenthau, and Waltz* (New York: Columbia University Press, 2004).

17. Kenneth N. Waltz, "Nuclear Myths and Political Realities," *American Political Science Review* 84, no. 3 (September 1990), pp. 731–44; and Waltz, *The Spread of Nuclear Weapons*.

18. For example, see John J. Mearsheimer, "The Case for a Ukranian Nuclear Deterrent," *Foreign Affairs* 72, no. 3 (summer 1993), pp. 50–66.

19. The core ideas of nuclear arms control were developed in the late 1950s and early 1960s by Donald Brennan, Hedley Bull, and Thomas Schelling and Morton Halperin, and further developed by members of the Cambridge Arms Control School. Many of the key early statements are in Donald G. Brennan, ed., *Arms Control, Disarmament and National Security* (New York: Braziller, 1961). The founding work of the Cambridge School is Thomas C. Schelling and Morton H. Halperin, *Strategy and Arms Control* (New York: Twentieth Century Fund, 1961). Also setting out the approach is Hedley Bull, *The Control of the Arms Race* (London: Weidenfeld and Nicolson, 1961).

20. Daniel Deudney, *Whole Earth Security: The Geopolitics of Peace* (Washington, DC: Worldwatch Institute, 1983); Deudney, "Dividing Realism," pp. 7–36; Daniel Deudney, "Political Fission: State Structure, Civil Society and Nuclear Security Politics in the United States," in *On Security*, ed. Ronnie Lipschultz (New York: Columbia University Press, 1995), pp. 87–123; Daniel Deudney, "Nuclear Weapons and the Waning of the Real-State," *Daedalus* 124, no. 2 (spring 1995), pp. 209–31; and Deudney, "Regrounding Realism: Anarchy, Security and Changing Material Contexts," pp. 1–45.

21. For histories of these concerns, see Paul Boyer, *By the Bomb's Early Light: American Culture at the Dawn of the Atomic Age* (New York: Pantheon, 1985), pp. 1–106; Wesley Wooley, *Alternatives to Anarchy: Postwar American Supernationalism* (Bloomington: University of Indiana Press, 1988); Lawrence S. Wittner, *One World or None: A History of the World Nuclear Disarmament Movement through 1953* (Stanford, CA: Stanford University Press, 1993); and Spencer Weart, *Nuclear Fear: A History of Images* (Cambridge: Harvard University Press, 1988).

22. For discussions of world federal government design, see Inis Claude, "World Government and World Order," in *Swords into Plowshares* (New York: Random House, 1971); Wooley, *Alternatives to Anarchy;* Louis Rene Beres, *Peoples, States, and World Order* (Itasca, IL: Peacock Publishers, 1981); and Joseph Preston Baratta, *Strengthening the United Nations: A Bibliography on U.N. Reform and World Federalism* (Westport, CT: Greenwood Press, 1987).

23. Herz viewed world government schemes as "detached from present realities," and "either antedate the nuclear situation or are conceived without much
attention to the newness of the new." He sees the need for "holding action" and
new forms of "collective security" that were not "the extreme opposite of power
politics" but rather "an attempt to maintain, and render more secure, the impermeability of what were still territorial states." Such an approach "appears ques-
tionable not because of its innovating, but because of its conservative nature."
Atomic Era, pp. 303 and 230.

24. Herz, *Atomic Era*, p. 13.

25. Herz, *Atomic Era*, p. 22.

26. Herz, *Atomic Era*, p. 310.

27. James Burnham, *The Struggle for the World* (New York: James Day, 1947).
Emory Reves makes the point even more bluntly: "If we cannot attain to universalism and create union by common consent and democratic methods as a result of
rational thinking—then rather than retard the process, let us precipitate unification by conquest." *The Anatomy of Peace* (New York: Harper and Row, 1946),
p. 269.

28. Burnham, *Struggle*, p. 216.

29. Robert Hutchins et al., *Preliminary Draft of a World Constitution* (Chicago: University of Chicago Press for the Committee to Frame a World Constitution, 1947); and G. A. Borgese, *The Foundations of a World Republic* (Chicago:
University of Chicago Press, 1953).

30. Hans Morgenthau, "The Four Paradoxes of Nuclear Strategy," *American
Political Science Review* 58, no. 1 (March 1964), pp. 25–35. For discussion of
Morgenthau's nuclear one worldism, see James Speer, "Hans Morgenthau and the
World State," *World Politics* 20, no. 2 (January 1968), pp. 206–27; and Richard
Rosecrance, "The One World of Hans Morgenthau," *Social Research* 48, no. 4
(winter 1981), pp. 749–65.

31. For the logic of minimalist world federal statism, see Emile Benoit-Smul-
lyan, "An American Foreign Policy for Survival," *Ethics* 56, no. 4 (July 1946), p.
283.

32. For discussions, see Albert Guerard, "The Peril of Pretorianism," *Common
Cause* (December 1947); Arthur Waskow, *Quis Custodiet? Controlling the Police
in a Disarmed World* (Washington, DC: Peace Research Institute, 1963); and
Richard Barnet and Richard Falk, eds., *Security in Disarmament* (Princeton:
Princeton University Press, 1965).

33. Among major agreements are the Limited Test Ban and the Non-prolifera-
tion Treaties of the 1960s, the SALT I, ABM and SALT II Treaties of the 1970s,
and the European Intermediate Nuclear Forces and the START I and II Treaties
of the 1980s. For a general assessment, see Alexander George, Philip Farley, and
Alexander Dallin, ed., *U.S.-Soviet Security Cooperation: Achievements, Failures,
Lessons* (New York: Oxford University Press, 1988).

34. Where disarmament aimed to improve security by reducing the numbers
and overall destructive potential of states to do damage to one another, arms control was conceived as a way to strengthen deterrence by reducing the likelihood
of unintentional nuclear use. In one of the most recent and well-developed arms
control proposals, arms control encompasses extensive disarmament, to a 'minimum deterrent' of several hundred warheads. Harold A. Feiveson, ed., *The Nu-

clear Turning Point: A Blueprint for Deep Cuts and De-altering of Nuclear Weapons (Washington, DC: Brookings, 1999).

35. Walter Millis and James Real, *The Abolition of War* (New York: Macmillan, 1963), p. 98.

36. Military organizations have a deep-seated interest in maintaining realms of operational autonomy, in larger rather than smaller budgets, and in configuring forces in order to win rather than simply deter wars. For a cogent explanation of these tendencies based on organization theory, see Barry Posen, *The Sources of Military Doctrine, France, Britain, and Germany between the World Wars* (Ithaca: Cornell University Press, 1984), pp. 41–80.

37. For rare treatments on this topic, see Peter Stein and Peter Feaver, *Assuring Control of Nuclear Weapons: The Evolution of Permissive Action Links* (Cambridge: Center for Science and International Affairs, Harvard University, 1987); and Peter Douglas Feaver, *Guarding the Guardians: Civilian Control of Nuclear Weapons in the United States* (Ithaca: Cornell University Press, 1992).

38. Scott D. Sagan, "The Perils of Proliferation: Organization Theory, Deterrence Theory, and the Spread of Nuclear Weapons," *International Security* 18, no. 4 (spring 1994), pp. 66–107; and Scott D. Sagan and Kenneth N. Waltz, *The Spread of Nuclear Weapons: A Debate* (New York: Norton, 1995).

39. Joseph Nye, "Nuclear Learning and U.S.- Soviet Security Regimes," *International Organization* 41, no. 3 (summer 1987), pp. 371–402 at 396.

40. Joseph Nye points out that learning has taken place concerning the destructiveness of nuclear weapons (radioactive fallout and electromagnetic pulse), escalatory potentials of command and control arrangements, proliferation, volatility of arms races, and the need for secure 'second strike' forces for stable deterrence. "Nuclear Learning and U.S.- Soviet Security Regimes," pp. 371–402.

41. A vehicle for nuclear learning has been natural scientists, who have been central players in the arms control 'epistemic community' composed of individuals sharing a consensus about causal relationships and a normative commitment, as well as privileged access to state decision-making processes. Emanuel Adler, "The Emergence of Cooperation: National Epistemic Communities and the International Evolution of the Idea of Nuclear Arms Control," *International Organization* 46, no. 1 (winter 1992). For a history of these interactions, see Matthew Evangelista, *Unarmed Forces: The Transnational Movement to End the Cold War* (Ithaca: Cornell University Press, 1999). For the restraining influence of international norms, see Nina Tannenwald, *The Nuclear Taboo: International Norms and Deterrence* (Cambridge: Cambridge University Press, 2006).

42. As Millis and Real observed forty years ago, arms control is "at best a stopgap solution" useful "to tide us over the next few perilous years," but "its potentialities are limited and it offers no foundation on which to build a viable world order." *The Abolition of War*, p. 98.

43. A particularly trenchant version of this insight, characterized as "declining cumulativity," is developed by van Evera, *The Causes of War*, pp. 105–16. Schell argues the problem of interstate aggression has declined greatly because of nuclear weapons and because "aroused national consciousness" has produced "increasingly strong, and increasingly successful, resistance to foreign domination," evidenced in Vietnam and Afghanistan. *Abolition*, pp. 145 and 146. Schell's recent treatment of unconquerablity emphasizes the spread on nonviolent resistance. *The*

Unconquerable World: Power, Nonviolence, and the Will of the People (New York: Henry Holt, 2003).

44. This expression was introduced and an earlier version of this argument is found in Deudney, "Nuclear Weapons and the Waning of the Real-State." Detailed analysis of small arms diffusion is found in Jeffrey Boutwell and Michael Klare, ed., *Light Weapons and Civil Conflict* (Lanham, MD: Rowman and Littlefield, 1999).

45. Franz Schurman, *The Logic of World Power* (New York: Pantheon, 1974); and Arthur Schlesinger, Jr., *The Imperial Presidency* (Boston: Houghton Mifflin, 1974), p. 11.

46. The concept of nuclear despotism is captured in the observation of Robert Osgood and Robert Tucker that nuclear weapons "give governments a power of tremendous devastation that is continually and instantly available, subject to a single decision, compressed into a moment, a decision that could be executed swiftly, irrevocably, and almost automatically without further political deliberation." Robert Osgood and Robert Tucker, *Force, Order, and Justice* (Baltimore: Johns Hopkins University Press, 1967), p. 14.

47. For trade-offs in nuclear command and control systems, see Bruce Blair, *Strategic Command and Control: Redefining the Nuclear Threat* (Washington, DC: Brookings, 1985); and Paul Bracken, *The Command and Control of Nuclear Forces* (New Haven: Yale University Press, 1983).

48. He also observes, "time is the great healer of mistakes, whether technical or human. The insistence on speed leaves insufficient time for double-checking; it denies opportunity for correction." Fred Charles Ikle, "Can Nuclear Deterrence Last Out the Century?" *Foreign Affairs*, 51, no. 2 (January 1973), pp. 267–285, at 271.

49. For analyses of nuclear mobilizations and accidents employing concepts of organizational theory and complex system management, see Charles Perrow, *Normal Accidents* (New York: Basic Books, 1984); Bruce Blair, *The Logic of Accidental Nuclear War* (Washington, DC: Brookings, 1993); and especially Scott D. Sagan, *The Limits of Safety: Organizations, Accidents, and Nuclear Weapons* (Princeton: Princeton University Press, 1993).

50. For discussions, see Alvin M. Weinberg, "Social Institutions and Nuclear Energy," *Science*, 177, no. 4043 (July 7, 1972), pp. 27–34; Gerald Garvey, *The City of the Second Sun* (Lexington, MA: Lexington Books, 1977); and Steven Mark Cohn, *Too Cheap to Meter: An Economic and Philosophical Analysis of the Nuclear Dream* (Albany: State University of New York Press, 1997).

51. The classic statement on the simultaneous hollowing and rescuing of democracy in the nuclear age is Josef Joffe, "Democracy and Deterrence: What Have They Done to Each Other?" in *Ideas and Ideals: Essays in Honor of Stanley Hoffmann*, ed. Linda Miller and Michael Joseph Smith (Boulder: Westview, 1993), pp. 108–26.

52. The basics of the proposal were developed by the nuclear physicist J. Robert Oppenheimer, refined into a policy report by Dean Acheson and Robert Lillienthal in the U.S. State Department, and presented by the financier Bernard Baruch. For a particularly good treatment, see Lenice N. Wu, *The Baruch Plan: U.S. Diplomacy Enters the Nuclear Age* (Washington, DC: Government Printing Office, 1972).

53. The assumption was that "if you don't try to develop atomic energy you can't control it," and "unless you know what the possibilities are, you will not be prepared to prevent their realization." J. Robert Oppenheimer, "International Control of Atomic Energy," in *Minutes to Midnight: The International Control of Atomic Energy,* ed. Eugene Rabinowitch (Chicago: Bulletin of the Atomic Scientists, 1959), pp. 56 and 59.

54. The expression 'recessed deterrence' was introduced in Deudney, "Nuclear Weapons and the Waning of the Real-State." For 'virtual arsenals,' see Michael J. Mazarr, "Virtual Nuclear Arsenals," *Survival* 37, no. 3 (autumn 1995), pp. 7–26; and Kenneth N. Waltz, "Thoughts about Virtual Nuclear Arsenals," *Washington Quarterly* 20, no. 3 (June 1997), pp. 153–61.

55. Schell's characterization of the essential realities of the nuclear era vividly conveys the contextual-materialist view of technology as nearly irreversible alterations in nature as it presents itself for human uses. "The world in which humans must live has been altered" by "twentieth century physics," which has revealed the "structure of matter." States are "powerless to return to its former Newtonian state" and are "simply obliged to adjust as best they could." *Abolition*, pp. 101 and 100.

56. Schell, *Abolition*, p. 135. For recent analyses of these links, see Richard L. Garwin and Georges Charpak, *Megawatts and Megatons: The Future of Nuclear Power and Nuclear Weapons* (Chicago: University of Chicago Press, 2003); and Paul Leventhal, Sharon Tanzer, and Steven Dolley, eds., *Nuclear Power and the Spread of Nuclear Weapons* (Washington, DC: Brassey's, 2002).

57. Schell, *Abolition*, pp. 115 and 110.

58. Schell, *Abolition*, pp. 122, 139, 122, and 161. Also see Jonathan Schell, *The Gift of Time: The Case for Abolishing Nuclear Weapons Now* (New York: Henry Holt, 1998).

59. The republican logic of nuclear concurrency appears in Jeremy Stone's observation that concentrating nuclear use authority in one individual "would seem to violate common sense" because "individuals are prone to failures of judgment in much less tense situations, and some kind of check and balance obviously would be preferable." Jeremy Stone, "Presidential First Use Is Unlawful," in *First Use of Nuclear Weapons: Under the Constitution, Who Decides?* ed. Peter Raven-Hansen (New York: Greenwood, 1987), p. 17.

60. Leonard Beaton, *The Reform of Power: A Proposal for an International Security System* (New York: Viking, 1972).

61. For an assessment of the unfavorable exchange ratios between terrorist attackers and defenders, see Richard Betts, "The Soft Underbelly of American Primacy: Tactical Advantages of Terror," *Political Science Quarterly* 117 (spring 2002), pp. 19–36. For overviews, see Richard A. Falkenrath, Robert D. Newman, and Bradley Thayer, *America's Achilles' Heel: Nuclear, Biological, and Chemical Terrorism and Covert Attack* (Cambridge: MIT Press, 1998); Walter Laquer, *The New Terrorism: Fanaticism and the Arms of Mass Destruction* (New York: Oxford University Press, 1999).

62. Paul Leventhal and Yonah Alexander eds., *Nuclear Terrorism: Defining the Threat* (London: Pergamon Brassey's, 1986); and Paul Leventhal and Yonah Alexander, *Preventing Nuclear Terrorism* (Lexington, MA: Lexington, 1987).

63. For a balanced assessment and critique of the Bush Doctrine, see Robert Jervis, *American Foreign Policy in a New Era* (New York: Routledge, 2005). For the limits of international law regarding terrorism and the impacts of the war of terrorism on state sovereignty and international law, see Richard Falk, *The Great Terror War* (New York: Olive Branch Press, 2003).

64. For a preliminary assessment of the threat to American civil liberties, see David Cole and James X. Dempsey, *Terrorism and the Constitution: Sacrificing Civil Liberties in the Name of National Security* (New York: The New Press, 2002).

65. For the dimensions of the problem, see Joseph Cirincione, *Deadly Arsenals: Tracking Weapons of Mass Destruction* (Washington, DC: Carnegie Endowment for International Peace, 2002). Of particular concern is the large arsenal and stockpiles of fissionable material from the Soviet Union, which has evoked a substantial U.S. aid program described in John M. Shields and William C. Potter, eds., *Dismantling the Cold War: U.S. and NIS Perspectives on the Nunn-Lugar Cooperative Threat Reduction Program* (Cambridge: MIT Press, 1997).

66. For the difficulties of controlling flows across borders, see Steven Flynn, *America the Vulnerable: How Our Government Is Failing to Protect us from Terrorism* (New York: HarperCollins, 2004).

67. For proposals along these lines, see Graham Allison, *Nuclear Terrorism: The Ultimate Preventable Catastrophe* (New York: Henry Holt, 2004); and Graham Allison and Andrei Kokoshin, "The New Containment: An Alliance against Nuclear Terrorism," *National Interest* 69 (fall 2002), pp. 35–43.

68. For the case for the abridgment of civil liberties, see Michael Ignatieff, *The Lesser Evil: Political Ethics in an Age of Terror* (Princeton: Princeton University Press, 2004); and Michelle Malkin, *In Defense of Internment: The Case for 'Racial Profiling' in World War II and the War on Terror* (Washington, DC: Regnery, 2004).

69. For discussions of this threat and arms control remedies, see Office of Technology Assessment, "Assessing the Risks," *Proliferation of Weapons of Mass Destruction* (Washington, DC: Government Printing Office, 1993), pp. 45–77; Susan Wright, ed., *Preventing a Biological Arms Race* (Cambridge: MIT Press, 1990); Joshua Lederberg, ed., *Biological Weapons: Limiting the Threat* (Cambridge: MIT Press, 1999); Jonathan B. Tucker, ed., *Toxic Terror: Assessing Terrorist Use of Chemical and Biological Weapons* (Cambridge: MIT Press, 2000); and Peter R. Lavoy, Scott D. Sagan, and James J. Wirtz, eds., *Planning the Unthinkable: How New Powers Will Use Nuclear, Biological, and Chemical Weapons* (Ithaca: Cornell University Press, 2000).

CONCLUSION

1. Orwell, *Nineteen Eighty-Four*, p. 34.

2. For important recent exceptions to this neglect, see James Robert Huntley, *Pax Democratica: A Strategy for the Twentieth Century* (New York: Palgrave, 1998); and Timothy Garton Ash, *Free World: America, Europe, and the Surprising Future of the West* (New York: Random House, 2004).

INDEX

Abernethy, David B., 355n2
absolutism, 53, 67–69, 116, 119
Acheson, Dean, 372n52
Acton, Lord, 151, 329n64
Adair, Douglass, 320n67
Adams, Henry, 216
Adams, John, 13, 142, 285n46
Adas, Michael, 309n30, 356n11
Adler, Emanuel, 355n79, 371n41
Adorno, Theodor W., 27, 289n1
Afghanistan, 255
Africa, 125, 218, 221
Agnew, John, 304n83
Ahrensdorf, Peter J., 289n5, 297n2
Alexander, James, 343n82
Alexander, Yonah, 373n62
Alighieri, Dante, 139, 323n9
Alker, Hayward, 296n48, 303n67
Allison, Graham, 374n67
Althusser, Louis, 314n15
Amsterdam, 123
anarchic state systems, 28, 44, 56
anarchy: alliances in, 58, 152; American
    union and, 164–69; axiality and, 44,
    225–26; balance and, 43, 49–50; divi-
    sion and, 42 78, 143, 147, 150, 158,
    180; European unions and, 154; first
    and second, 36; Hobbes and, 34, 38,
    73–75; idioms of, 8; insecurity from, 40,
    46; Kant and, 155–56; mixture and, 43–
    44; neorealism and, 77–78; North
    America as, 172–73; pre-state, 33; Real-
    ism and, 8; regimes and, 82; republics in,
    55–58; Rousseau and, 75, 153; state-of-
    nature and, 15, 18, 29, 33–34, 73–75;
    state-of-war, 34, 36, 74; state system,
    33, 76; varieties of, 33; violence interde-
    pendence and, 40–41; Wendt and, 84;
    world government and, 41, 273–76
anarchy-independence problematique, 28,
    41, 73
anarchy problematique, 8, 75, 77–78, 268
Anderson, M. S., 329n66
Anderson, Perry, 313n5, 317n35
Anderson, Thornton, 335n10

Angell, Norman, 204–5, 216, 352n41,
    353n44
Anthony, 111
Antwerp, 123
Appleby, Joyce, 298n21
Aquinas, Thomas, 94, 323n9
Archibugi, Daniele, 367n3
Arendt, Hannah, 293n29, 298n17
Aristotle, 18, 53, 62–63, 83, 85, 91–92,
    94–95, 97, 101–2, 107, 117, 286n51,
    293nn26–27, 297nn3–5,9, 306n4,
    307nn14–15, 308nn17,22, 309nn25,30,
    310n37, 312nn58–59, 317n31, 320n54,
    333n95
Armstrong, David, 319n51
Aron, Raymond, 368n7
Asia, 125, 144, 172, 200, 221
Ash, Timothy Garton, 374n2
Ashley, Richard, 299n31
Athenian democracy, 46; anti-tyranny and,
    46, 101–2; Aristotle on, 92, 101–2; As-
    sembly of, 102; courts in, 102; Liberal-
    ism of, 101–2; ostracism in, 102; Plato
    on, 92, 101–2; Thucydides on, 102–4;
    tragedy and, 103
Athens, 40, 99, 101–2
Augustus, 104, 111–12, 310n48
Aurelius, Marcus, 181
Australia, 184, 228–29
Avineri, Sholomo, 300n39

Bacevich, Andrew J., 348n116, 367n4
Bacon, Francis, 148, 196, 321n76,
    327n48, 349n8
Baechler, Jean, 326n45
Bailyn, Bernard, 298n20
balance of power: American union and,
    171–74; asymmetric balances, 49; bal-
    anced state system, 172; balancers, 142,
    147–50, 158; balancing, 55, 187; chan-
    neled balancing, 49; counterbalance,
    168; embedded balances, 49; Europe as
    'republic' and, 137, 142–47, 150–52; ex-
    ternal balancing, 56; Guicciardini on,
    130; interior balances, 49, 54, 56,